North American Regionalism

the
americas
in the
world

The Americas in the World

Jürgen Buchenau and Steven Hyland Jr., Series Editors

The Americas in the World series publishes cutting-edge scholarship about the Americas in global and transnational history, politics, society, and culture as well as about the impact of global and transnational actors and processes on the hemisphere. The series includes both works on specialized topics as well as broad syntheses. All titles aim at a wide audience.

Also available in the Americas in the World series:

The Dollar: How the US Dollar Became a Popular Currency in Argentina by Mariana Luzzi and Ariel Wilkis

North American Regionalism

Stagnation, Decline, or Renewal?

EDITED BY Eric Hershberg
AND Tom Long

UNIVERSITY OF NEW MEXICO PRESS

ALBUQUERQUE

ISBN 978-0-8263-6519-4 (cloth)
ISBN 978-0-8263-6520-0 (paper)
ISBN 978-0-8263-6521-7 (electronic)

Library of Congress Control Number: 2023941925

Founded in 1889, the University of New Mexico sits on the traditional
homelands of the Pueblo of Sandía. The original peoples of New
Mexico—Pueblo, Navajo, and Apache—since time immemorial have
deep connections to the land and have made significant contributions
to the broader community statewide. We honor the land itself and those
who remain stewards of this land throughout the generations and also
acknowledge our committed relationship to Indigenous peoples. We
gratefully recognize our history.

Cover photographs courtesy of the US Government and NASA
Designed by Isaac Morris
Composed in Albertan and Times

Contents

Acknowledgments

This book is the product of a community of scholars, far beyond those who have contributed chapters in the pages that follow. Over the last seven years, dozens of colleagues have joined us in dialogues and debates about the nature and future of North American regional cooperation and governance. Both the book and that broader community emerged under the auspices of American University (AU)'s Robert A. Pastor North American Research Initiative (NARI), established in 2016 as a joint effort of the Center for Latin American and Latino Studies (CLALS) and the School of International Service (SIS) to foster cutting-edge social science research focused on processes of North American integration. By supporting the production, exchange, and dissemination of scholarship devoted to North America and its potential trajectories, the NARI places AU at the forefront of a long-term research agenda that will inform future policy on North America.

NARI's origins go back to a commitment of several faculty at American University to establish a vehicle through which to honor the memory of our late colleague Bob Pastor. Drawing on Bob's spirit of advancing big ideas and instigating challenging debates, these colleagues decided to launch an effort that would create avenues for advancing intellectual and policy innovation around North America's potential future. That effort, all agreed, was sorely needed to fill a gap in scholarly production and networking. While a good number of young social scientists were carrying out research relevant to the themes that Bob had addressed in a succession of publications on North America, culminating in the *North American Idea*, there was virtually no institutional space to connect disparate voices. Nor was there a strong sense among young scholars of belonging to a community of "North Americanists." The notion that we might try to address this through an initiative at AU was the brainchild of Tom Long—Bob's last doctoral student—together with Eric Hershberg, Louis Goodman, and Jim Goldgeier, then dean of SIS, which had raised modest funds to make possible a continuation of Bob's intellectual and policy agendas.

To encourage facilitation of a productive network, we surveyed the pool of researchers who had been generating original research on diverse aspects of North America as a region. NARI endeavored to catalyze the emergence of a new generation of scholars, from various scholarly disciplines, and from Mexico, Canada, and the United States, devoted to the study of the region and its varied modes of insertion in the global system. Beginning in 2017, we convened subsets of participants in seminars and conference panels organized around particular issues. For the most part, the first NARI participants were early career scholars, including doctoral candidates, whose research encompassed a wide range of topics that shape regional dynamics, including migration, trade, finance and investment, energy, climate change, security, and political and social identities. These groups gathered in a series of closed workshops and public-facing events in Washington, Mexico City, and Ottawa, as well as conference venues in other locations and virtual seminars. As these collaborations developed, NARIstas were sometimes joined by veteran scholars and policy professionals from all three countries. Those encounters engendered conversations that resulted in clustering of interests around promising themes, numerous collaborative papers, and the consolidation of a loose network associated with the Pastor Initiative.

Besides the authors of chapters in the book, among the many scholars who took part in one or another of the meetings convened to advance the initiative's work, we especially thank Mark Aspinwall, Robert Blecker, Brian Bow, Alexandra Délano Alonso, Francesco Duina, Lauren Duquette-Rury, Malcolm Fairbrother, Gustavo Flores-Macías, Gaspare Genna, Leopoldo Gómez-Ramírez, Louis Goodman, Marcela López Vallejo, Gerardo Maldonado, Inu Manak, Claudia Maya, Clarisa Pérez-Armendáriz, and Christopher Wilson. Their insights have informed our selection of themes to emphasize, our understanding of North America's relevance to different currents of scholarship, and our conclusions regarding the potential impacts of steps that could plausibly be taken to foster a more dynamic North American region. In hosting NARI events, several institutions have joined AU in our effort to maximize the prospects of our efforts coming to influence the public arena. We are especially appreciative of the engagement of the Centro de Investigación y Docencia Económicas (CIDE), the University of Ottawa, the Mexican Cultural Institute, the Canadian Global Affairs Institute, and El Colegio de México.

Michael Millman at the University of New Mexico Press has provided strong support for the book, and we benefited from comments on the entire manuscript by Brian Bow and an anonymous reviewer. Alexandra Vranas and Christopher Kambhu were among the CLALS program coordinators who ably managed in person and, since 2020, virtual meetings of the network. Kyra Jones of the CLALS staff has deftly managed formatting as well as administrative details related to production of the final manuscript. Finally, we express our gratitude to the Pastor family, who have been champions of this initiative from the very beginning. By probing the limits and possibilities of North America as an idea and a region, we hope this book honors Bob's legacy.

Placing North America in a World of Regions

Eric Hershberg and Tom Long

AS NORTH American completes three decades since the 1994 inauguration of the North American Free Trade Agreement (NAFTA), the regional project the pact's archi-tects sought to catalyze finds itself buffeted by global events, threatened by political polarization, and overlooked by scholars. At the same time, the region approaches the milestone with a deeply integrated economy, burgeoning transnational connections, and an increasingly salient geopolitical rationale. On the one hand, the project of inte-grating the regional economy seems to have been bolstered—or at least saved—by an update of its core economic charter. However, instead of demonstrating cooperation, those negotiations were marred by threats and insults. The resulting US-Mexico-Canada Agreement (USMCA), in force since July 2020, stripped "North America" from the name of the region's founding pact. Nearly two decades ago, Andrew Hurrell (2006) dubbed North America "the region that dare not speak its name" (Hurrell 2006). With the advent of the USMCA and the twilight of the North American Free Trade Agreement (NAFTA), the label has proved prescient. North America is a region of contradictions; it is bound by myriad connections, but few institutions. Many ques-tion whether all this adds up to being a region at all (Clarkson 2008; Capling and Nossal 2009). Amid this constellation of challenges and opportunities, one might ask: What holds North America together?

Even economically focused regions like North America require a political project. But the idea of a cohesive North American region was never much loved by politicians, especially in the United States. In 2016, North America—and especially its central economic pact—emerged as the scapegoat for socioeconomic ills and nationalist angst during the campaign and presidency of Donald J. Trump. Trump's tariffs and border wall imperiled the ideal of a continental free market. The renegotiation of NAFTA, which had been in force since 1994, was forced on reluctant partners under the threat of a painful unilateral termination. The regional project survived, but it was damaged.

Just as that renegotiation was settled, a global pandemic erupted. COVID-19 cre-ated immediate challenges for North America, including nearly two years of highly restricted cross-border movement, accompanied by fast-tracked deportations under US public health regulations. Early US "vaccine nationalism" overshadowed epide-miological cooperation and the later, limited sharing of surplus doses. The economic response to the pandemic featured economic nationalism from the United States in the form of "buy American" provisions. That shock has been followed by the Russian invasion of Ukraine, which unleashed geopolitical tensions and deepened economic uncertainty.

These recent challenges hit a region that had already limped through two decades of obstacles and setbacks. After North America's inception in the early 1990s, it experienced an initial boom of regional trade. But trade and investment stagnated in 2001, buffeted by the head winds of thicker post-9/11 borders and rising competition from China. North America mostly had failed to strengthen or expand its regional institutions to advance a common agenda, defend regional interests, or spur new forms of cooperation. Faced with Trump and the pandemic, the old institutions—and the massive economic interests they helped create—faced existential threats.

Yet North America, as a region, matters. Tremendous volumes of trade and investment still crisscross the region. It survived securitized borders and Chinese competition—though not unscathed. It withstood Trump's bullying and the renegotiation of its founding pact, leading to a new regional agreement, effective since July 2020. In replacing NAFTA, the USMCA weakened some formal, trilateral elements but preserved and may turn out to have reinforced the region's core economic structures (Anderson 2020; Macdonald 2019), while introducing several innovations, for example, in digital trade. At least for the moment, the renegotiation seems to have defanged some of the US partisan opposition that circled NAFTA.

But there are caveats, starting with weak formal institutionalization and the imbalances caused by the geographic and gravitational centrality of the United States. The limited reach of North American institutions has left the region vulnerable to exogenous shocks and shifting political winds at the domestic level. The November 2021 restart of the North American Leaders' Summits after a long hiatus was welcome, but its sweeping pronouncements have been followed by minimal implementation. With few institutions and little attention from high places, there is no one to enunciate a clear "North American agenda" to the world or to consistently propose and implement shared solutions to shared problems.

It was precisely those shortcomings that led the prominent Canadian scholar Stephen Clarkson (2008) to ask whether North America was a region at all. In the wake of a charged renegotiation of North America's founding pact, Clarkson's question takes on new relevance. For three decades, "North America" was synonymous with the erstwhile North American Free Trade Agreement. NAFTA's disappearance suggests a need for a reconsideration not only of whether North America is a region, but also what sort of region it is. What are North America's contours? What, if anything, unites North American countries with one another and distinguishes them from the rest of the world? The geographical extension of regional forces into Central America and the Caribbean further blurs the constitution of what was long assumed to be a trilateral region. Given these uneven and expansive dynamics, there are good reasons to rethink the geography and membership of North America.

With those questions in mind, this volume aims to reconnect North America with International Relations' (IR) scholarship on regionalism. In the 1990s, North America was a central example of post–Cold War "new" regionalism. It seemed to offer an innovative model for linking developed and developing economies and incorporating (however tangentially) issues of labor and environment. The region often was included among the three main regional blocs, which were marked by the consolidation of the European project and the emergence of a Japan-centric Asian bloc (e.g., Hettne and Söderbaum 1998; Wyatt-Walter 1995, 84–88). However, given the absence of institution-building and political champions in the wake of NAFTA, North America has attracted little attention since then—even as the study of regionalism has boomed. Where does North America sit in what Amitav Acharya (2007) called the "emerging regional architecture of world politics"?

Bringing North America back into IR's "world of regions" offers benefits for rethinking how IR conceptualizes regions (Katzenstein 2005), and for how we understand North American dynamics. North America's experience can act as an antidote to several tendencies criticized by comparative and new regionalists: a fixation on formal institutions (Söderbaum 2015), a tendency to overvalue summitry and regionalist rhetoric (Malamud 2005), and teleological and Eurocentric expectations about regional development (Acharya 2016; Yukawa 2018). There is little doubt that North America's formal institutions remain few in number and limited in extent, as Diana Panke and Sören Stapel illustrate in this volume, but economic and societal integration and ad hoc cooperation outstrip the formal architecture (Bow and Anderson 2014). In contrast to the "declaratory regionalism" of South American counterparts (Jenne, Schenoni, and Urdinez 2017), North American leaders have tended to shun photo opportunities and avoid rhetorical enthusiasm. Finally, North America clearly did not develop as many advocates, inspired by the European Union (EU), had hoped (e.g., Pastor 2001; Aspinwall 2011, 167–69)—instead, it presents a case of high functional integration with minimal "spillover."

Despite its particularities, the North American experience suggests new forms and processes of regional cooperation and governance. In the dearth of formal organizations, long seen as the hallmark of a region, North America has developed myriad connections. Not unlike in Europe, economic integration remains extensive and complex, going well beyond traditional patterns of trade. Societies are similarly interwoven. A variety of state and non-state actors have developed diverse forms of regional governance to manage these dynamics. In practical terms, North America matters in terms of economic, social, and political geography to the states and populations of the northern Western Hemisphere. Although the region's low institutional density has limited its global salience, North America possesses a regional gravity greater than that generated by the United States alone. When analyzed across a gamut of issues, North American dynamics challenge the traditional dichotomy between state-led regionalism and non-state regionalization (Capling and Nossal 2009). Considering

North America as a region reveals processes and possibilities that differ from dominant paradigms and assumptions in the study of regionalism. This makes the region
more important, not less, as a case study.

This introductory chapter proceeds in four parts. First, we provide brief context
on North America as a region. Second, we address how North America relates to
different understandings of what constitutes a "region" in International Relations. This
volume's contributors were all asked to consider that question, instead of being given
a single starting point. Their responses inform how they studied regional dynamics,
and their debates shape the organization of this volume. Third, we build on those
conceptual debates to illustrate how consideration of North America suggests new
questions, puzzles, and explanations of regional dynamics that are important to the
broader field of regionalism studies. Fourth, we sketch out how recent developments
in the study of regionalism contribute to explaining North America, underscoring
possibilities for greater theoretical engagement between IR and area studies. Finally,
we provide an overview of this volume, describing the contributions and underscoring
the connections among them.

A Region's Rise, Fall, and Renewal?

From its beginnings, the project of North American region-building was simultaneously marked by ambivalence, crisis, and hope. Ambivalence was clear in the domestic
politics of the three signatories of the North American Free Trade Agreement. The
agreement was so divisive in Canadian and US politics that the countries' leaders
did not hold a summit to celebrate NAFTA's 1994 inauguration (Fairbrother 2019;
Cameron and Tomlin 2000). This ambivalence was echoed a quarter century later, when
Canadian prime minister Justin Trudeau skipped the USMCA ceremony, attended by
Trump and Mexican president Andrés Manuel López Obrador. In Canada, an earlier
free trade agreement with the United States had been controversial as well, marked
by concerns about transparency and sovereignty (Hart 1994). Only Mexican leadership was thoroughly enthusiastic at NAFTA's inception, but given their questionable
democratic credentials, they avoided an open domestic debate (Long 2015, 170–73;
Fairbrother 2019, 82–89). In addition, Mexican leaders were soon consumed by political and economic crisis, in the form of an insurgency in Chiapas, the assassination of
the leading presidential candidate, and a painful currency devaluation. These events
shook the foundations of the new region and renewed questions about the wisdom of
economic integration between two wealthy, advanced economies and one developing
country—then quite a novel feature of NAFTA (Pastor 2011, 55).

Despite these congenital concerns, the idea of North America also provoked a
fair amount of hope. Connections with the powerhouse US economy were promising
for the neighbors. NAFTA offered Mexico a road to development after a decade of

debt crisis, as well as a tool to "lock in" neoliberal reforms against pressures from populists and the left (Moreno-Brid, Nápoles, and Valdivia 2004, 1018). NAFTA's promise of seamless integration between the three economies also served as a catalyst for Canada's sluggish economy. For those reasons, the project's greatest supporters were often business leaders in Canada and the United States and technocratic elites in Mexico (Fairbrother 2019, 163). To its advocates, North America seemed a template for open regional economic integration in a globalizing world economy, a format for including new issues like labor and environmental protections in trade agreements, and perhaps a model for partnership with the new unipolar power. Some, like Robert Pastor (2001), held out hope for a "North American community" in which shared, long-term interests would triumph over short-term nationalism.

North America was also born of a changing geopolitical context. Though the emergence of NAFTA is most often considered in relation to the domestic politics of Canada, Mexico, and the United States, it was also a product of shifts in international politics—namely, the end of the Cold War, advances in European integration, and Japanese centrality in Asian manufacturing networks (Long 2015, 170). From its inception, North American leaders expressed concern about the region's place in a world of regions; for those leaders, North America was also an instrument to manage and shape global economic pressures and influence global economic rules. In addition to consolidating one region, North America's emergence reshaped other regions. In particular, NAFTA pulled Mexico northward and away from South America. Less noted is that it had a similar effect on Central American and Caribbean countries that were not party to NAFTA (Santa-Cruz 2019, 166–71). Concerned about their own access to the US market, Central American leaders pressured Washington for guaranteed market access, culminating in the regionwide trade agreement between the United States and Central America and the Dominican Republic, Dominican Republic–Central America Free Trade Agreement (CAFTA-DR). These forces dampened the always-shaky material impetus for Latin American cooperation, foreshadowing how China's rise would encourage divergent trajectories in the northern and southern tiers of Latin America (Covarrubias 2016; Malamud 2012, 172–73). Indeed, as Central America became ever more integrated with both the United States and Mexico—economically, demographically, and in the security domain—the region's "North Americanization" both challenged the trinational project and diminished tendencies toward Latin American integration.

While the decades following 1994 have been a mixed bag in many respects, it is hard to avoid the conclusion that North America's first years were also its best. Trade tripled from 1994 to 2001, and investment increased even faster: "the outline of a North America that was more than just a geographical expression was visible" (Pastor 2011, 5). Mexico became increasingly democratic, for the most part with its neighbors' support—though NAFTA was at best one cause among many (Cameron and Wise 2004; Calderón Martínez 2018). To a greater extent, NAFTA made real the old dream of industrialization. Mexico became a manufacturing exports powerhouse, including in sophisticated industrial sectors like automobiles and aerospace. However, Mexico industrialized as part of North American value chains instead of in pursuit of national economic autonomy; the results were often disappointing for growth, employment, and wages (Moreno-Brid, Santamaría, and Rivas Valdivia 2005; Blecker 2014). Some sectors of the Canadian economy became more dynamic (Trefler 2004), though over time Canada leaned more on oil and services exports and experienced similar pressures of deindustrialization as the US "rust belt."

As Malcolm Fairbrother (2019, 202) concludes, looking back at the NAFTA debate, claims of "both the advocacy and the opposition were overblown." What is clearer is that in NAFTA's wake, the three countries became increasingly interconnected—through tightly knit manufacturing chains, growing societal and cultural ties, legal and illicit markets, and even macroeconomic cycles. However, these deepening economic and social links spurred only piecemeal regional political responses (Genna and Mayer-Foulkes 2013; Bow and Anderson 2014). Ambivalence still reigned. Negative externalities often festered. In North America's largest country, the September 11, 2001, attacks produced a new, defensive focus on the borders; Middle Eastern conflicts diverted US attention, and nativist backlash undermined cooperative initiatives, especially around migration (Andreas and Biersteker 2003; Pastor 2011, 113–19). In a brief trilateral foray into security cooperation, the three countries sought to develop the Security and Prosperity Partnership (SPP) to reinvigorate regional cooperation and manage the post–September 11, 2001 "thickening" of the borders (see Toro, this volume). However, that project sparked political opposition and suffered from insufficient enthusiasm (Brodie 2016). The entry of China into the World Trade Organization shook the dynamics of world trade, weakening ties among the NAFTA countries, as Barbara Stallings explores in this volume. The second decade of North America was characterized by stagnation of the regional economic project, even as other forms of integration deepened—and in some cases, as noted, expanded to incorporate the northern countries of Central America.

For both the NAFTA signatories and the broader North American neighborhood, the economic integration trumpeted by corporate leaders and many economists (especially in Mexico) was accompanied by social ties of a sort largely ignored in studies of formal, state-led regionalism. Though US and Mexican politicians sold NAFTA as a mechanism to reduce migration, both documented and undocumented migration boomed during the same years that North America trade and investment grew fastest. A similar phenomenon arose with negotiation and implementation of CAFTA-DR. Indeed, in great numbers, Mexicans and Central Americans moved to the United States, including into the interior. And the population flow was more complex than is typically portrayed: by some estimates more than one million US citizens became residents in Mexico for business, retirement, or family ties (Masferrer, Hamilton, and Denier 2019). Deep exchanges also characterized US-Canadian social relations. Although it was smaller, tourism, educational exchange, and migration between Canada and Mexico also increased (Durazo Herrmann 2018); Canada remained an important destination for many Caribbean migrants. Social exchanges had economic ramifications, including massive flows of remittances. At the subnational level, political effects were complex and varied. These ranged from the influence of hometown associations and returnees on Mexican politics (Danielson 2017; Pérez-Armendáriz and Crow 2010) to forms of nativist backlash in both Canada and the United States (Bonikowski 2019; Mudde 2012). However, this "deep integration" was accompanied by limited formal governance and sporadic and uneven civil society engagement (Ayres and Macdonald 2006).

By 2010, the stagnation of the region's political project had given way to skepticism from all quarters. The Barack Obama and Stephen Harper governments showed little enthusiasm for North American projects, casting aside the limited cooperation of the George W. Bush years. The Felipe Calderón administration militarized the battle against crime, in direct cooperation with the United States (Ayres and Macdonald 2012). However, militarized interdiction did little to staunch the flow of drugs north, nothing to halt the flow of arms south, and worst of all exacerbated a wave of violence that consumed Mexico and spilled into El Salvador, Guatemala, and Honduras. Headlines about the violence further dampened political enthusiasm for visible cooperation in the region. If, as Gema Kloppe-Santamaría notes in chapter 6, security cooperation in broader North America—excluding Canada—took place under a shared, punitive paradigm, the failure of that approach fueled antagonisms that diminished appetites for broader cooperation.

In recent years, the challenges to North America—to its very character as a world region—have mounted and taken different forms in each of its three core countries. Reticence about integration has long been widespread, influencing domestic political dynamics in all three countries. Still, the November 2016 election of President Donald J. Trump was especially disruptive to the regional project. The visceral appeal of Trump's 2016 campaign to many sectors of the US population made plain the depth of anti-immigrant, anti-Mexico, and anti-internationalist sentiment in the US electorate. In addition to its racist currents, Trump's America First narrative was, by definition, antagonistic to multilateralism. Trump famously and repeatedly denounced NAFTA as the "worst trade deal ever." The campaign was followed by an administration in which tariffs and threats marked a contentious renegotiation of the region's founding economic pact. The deeper character of the region's asymmetrical interdependence came to the surface in hostile fashion (Long 2018; Ortega Ortiz 2019). Once in office, Trump delivered additional blows through restrictions on migration, tariffs on key goods, and frequent threats to terminate US adherence to North American institutions. If Mexico was particularly demonized, it bears recalling that the president routinely denigrated the leadership in Ottawa as well (Macdonald 2020).

In Mexico, the election of Andrés Manuel López Obrador in 2018 did not carry the same anti-US vitriol, but its effects have been similarly profound. Despite limited evidence of interest in international affairs or regional cooperation, López Obrador has shown a pragmatic streak in preserving economic relations with the United States while deflecting scrutiny of internal affairs (Rojas 2021). Long the most enthusiastic of the three North American governments, Mexico no longer seems likely to spur regional initiatives. There has been renewed distance from the United States even on matters prioritized by Washington, as suggested by López Obrador's hesitance to sanction Russia and his nonattendance at the US-hosted 2022 Summit of the Americas. Canada's approach of bilaterally managing relations with the United States—often its preference even in good times, as Asa McKercher notes in this volume—seems here to stay.

In the midst of these changes, Canada, Mexico, and the United States underwent a tense renegotiation of the region's founding economic pact. The North American project survived that process; however, in doing so, it became less "North American" than ever (Anderson 2020; Gantz 2020). In July 2020, the USMCA took force, superseding NAFTA. Even in the region's foundational document, each country refers to the agreement differently, putting its own name first. Such is the limited spirit of political cooperation in North America. In that environment, the 2020–2021 global pandemic and ensuing economic shock posed the greatest threat to international cooperation at least since September 11, 2001. The pandemic largely halted legal movement of people across borders in North America from early 2020 to the end of 2021. The continuation of trade represented something of a triumph for advocates of regional integration.

When the dust settled from the Trump shake-up, the newly negotiated USMCA had managed to preserve the core of the North American trading area, saved mostly by fears of backlash from corporate and agricultural lobbies (see Macdonald, this volume). The accord, often dubbed NAFTA 2.0, may have increased centripetal pressures for some industries, like auto manufacturing (see Morales, this volume). However, building North America hardly seemed to be the goal of the often-unfriendly renegotiation. Where a shared North American approach did grow, it appeared to be a sort of externality, as with the unannounced construction of a joint "Fortress North America" to exclude and criminalize politically unwanted migrants (see Castañeda et al., this volume). Neither those forms of policy coordination nor the new USMCA emerged from intentions to deepen or strengthen regional institutions; given that, their ambiguous effects on trilateral cooperation are hardly surprising. Clearly, high levels of interdependence and a host of shared challenges have not "spilled over" into the creation of more robust institutions. Counterintuitively, however, we argue that this is precisely why North America matters for the study of regionalism in IR.

North America and IR Approaches to Regionalism

The emergence of a novel "North America" coincided with renewed attention to regionalism in international economics (Wyatt-Walter 1995; de Melo and Panagariya 1993) and International Relations (Hurrell 1995; Katzenstein 1996; Hettne and Söderbaum 1998). In the early 1990s, North America's place in IR's study of regions and regionalism seemed clear. The first generation of work on North America was heavily shaped by liberal IR theories. This was fitting in several ways. First, North America has long been identified as an economic region, held together by trade. A focus on economics meant that liberalism's attention to absolute gains and reducing transaction costs seemed to offer considerable explanatory mileage. Second, the most visible rationales for North American regionalism emerged from liberal economic logics of harnessing comparative advantages (Fairbrother 2014). NAFTA had a liberal internationalist dimension, too, which linked the expansion of regional commerce to processes of democratization in Mexico and greater security at the regional level (Calderón Martínez 2018; Mayer-Foulkes and García-Barrios 2012). Third, the negotiation of NAFTA was an important case for liberal IR scholars interested in domestic preferences, interstate bargaining, and institutional formation (for example, Milner 1997). Seminal ideas from liberal IR, like interdependence, remain popular in discussions of North America (Bow 2010; Chabat 1997; Smith and Selee 2013). Meanwhile, other IR paradigms appeared to have less relevance. There was limited attention from realists (cf. Kupchan 1998), given the low place of security on the North American agenda. While constructivist theories of international organizations and regionalism gained traction generally (e.g., Barnett and Finnemore 2004), the absence in North America of evident regional identity or an international secretariat to exercise normative or bureaucratic agency limited attention.[1]

The region was less in sync with the theoretical currents that partially displaced liberalism after 2000, just as North America seemed to stagnate. For example, "new regionalism" sought to broaden the study of regions, moving beyond economics, geography, or organizations. But North America seemed stubbornly one-dimensional in its focus on trade and investment. In a survey of the literature, F. Duina (2016, 135) notes that "most scholarship on regionalism in North America focuses on NAFTA." North America was mentioned as an early case in B. Hettne and F. Söderbaum's seminal 1998 article on the "new regionalism approach," but generally followers of the approach dedicated less attention to North America than they did to other regions. In other realms of IR theory, North America received even less attention. One of the most influential IR studies of regional security, in 2003, observed that "most books on regional security omit a chapter on North America" (Buzan and Waever 2003, 268).

North America was *not* an example of post-hegemonic or post-neoliberal regionalism, given US centrality and its economic model. The literature on this phenomenon remained heavily South American in focus and prioritized political cooperation over economic integration (Sanahuja 2009; Serbín 2012). Though North America might have provided a useful counter-case, it unfortunately drew little attention in these debates (an exception, Morales 2017). Often, the implication seems to be that the problem is North America, not IR's dominant concepts of regions or theories of regionalism. Without the prominent supranational institutions or the rhetorical enthusiasm that attracted scholarly attention to other regional projects—such as the EU, Association of Southeast Asian Nations (ASEAN), or various South American efforts (Acharya 2014; Riggirozzi and Tussie 2012)—North America's place in the regional firmament dimmed further.

But if one starts more inductively with the North American experience, it points to flaws in IR's focus. Diplomatically driven regionalism may create a striking, but hollow, shell, with top-down regionalism, photo-opportunity summits, and formalized regional organizations overshadowing integration and implementation. North America offers a corrective to the twin fixation on formal organizations and rhetorical enthusiasm.

First, the study of regionalism has given pride of place to formal organizational structures; indeed, for some scholars, this is what distinguishes regionalism from cognate concepts like regionalization (Riggirozzi 2012; Fawn 2009). In an influential discussion of whether North America constitutes an international region, A. Capling and K. R. Nossal (2009, 148) agree that trends of regionalization are salient in North America but dismiss it as a case of regionalism. Their concern is institutional, and they argue that regionalism failed due to a lack of "state-led efforts to deepen regional-isation through the fostering of other formal mechanisms to support institutionalised cooperation and collective action." Clearly, North America has exhibited little expansion of creation of new regional institutional layers and competencies, as Panke and Stapel note in this volume.

Nonetheless, North America has highly integrated production networks (Wilson 2011), business-cycle convergence (Blecker 2014), substantial cross-national bureaucratic links, and noteworthy levels of migration-driven societal integration. One can hardly ignore profound effects wrought by drivers of regionalization that were in part unleashed—even if not contemplated—by NAFTA. As T. A. Börzel and T. Risse (2019) note, the prediction that economic interdependence and the emergence of supranational institutions move together seems true only in the European case. In stubborn contradiction to theoretical expectations, North America has not needed new institutions to maintain dynamic *regionalization*, with massive absolute and relative levels of trade and investment and multifaceted forms of social integration. Should it therefore be cast aside as a region or a form of regionalism? North American regionalism serves as a framework that shapes interdependence and interaction, even where it fails to present a unified face to the world.

Patterns of regional governance have responded to surging interactions, albeit in ways that are obscured by a focus on formal regional organizations. Instead, North America today exhibits diffuse governance, emanating from a variety of sources.

Governance emerges from coordination of civil-society actors (Kay 2011; Nolan García 2011), and mid-level bureaucrats and subnational officials in diverse issue areas (Aspinwall 2009; Kukucha 2020; López-Vallejo 2016). These inter-bureaucratic connections are a rooted regional practice, dating at least to informal cooperation described by R. O. Keohane and J. S. Nye (1977) in their classic work on complex interdependence. Private actors and subnational governments create regional governance structures to respond to other challenges, as Daniela Stevens describes in this volume regarding green energy.

Second, at times the study of regionalism has been swept up by leaders' rhetorical flourishes and the bright lights of major summits. European gatherings, the globe-spanning Asia Pacific Economic Cooperation (APEC) summit, the new Chinese-led Regional Comprehensive Economic Partnership (RCEP), and ASEAN meetings attract global media attention. There was little to put North America on the map, especially given IR's predisposition to executive branches of government. With only three leaders, the so-called Three Amigos summit (2005–2008, 2012, 2014, 2016, 2021–present) always lacked the wattage of those conclaves. Given friction between US president Obama and Canadian prime minister Stephen Harper, the North American Leaders' Summits grew sporadic before fading away entirely during Trump's combative term. Even in their heyday, North American summits did not produce many paeans to the region. The long-awaited return of North American summitry in November 2021 sought to overcome the pandemic's disruptions to travel and supply chains, while grappling with the expansion of migration at the US-Mexican border. If the meeting gave a breath of optimism to the beleaguered region, it also highlighted the increasingly assertive position of Mexico in asserting sovereign prerogatives and criticizing US protectionism and "buy American" provisions for infrastructure and green industries. Canada and Mexico share worries about lasting "America First" sentiment and economic policies, but they often direct those bilaterally toward Washington. Still, the one-day meeting, with limited bureaucratic buildup, suggests that top-down, executive branch initiatives are not the driving force of North American region-building. These trends continued with the next summit, which was pushed from November 2022 to the following January due to scheduling conflicts and amid escalating regional trade disputes.

The public and scholarly prominence of regional projects does not seem to reflect levels of regional integration or cooperation. In this respect, overlooked North America seems the inverse of recent iterations of high-profile regionalism in South America. During the first decade or so of this century, South American regional organizations added more features and expanded into new policy areas. Several regional organizations for a while enjoyed prominent political support—most notably Union of South American Nations (UNASUR) but also Mercosur, the Pacific Alliance, Alliance for the Peoples of Our America (ALBA), and the Community of Latin American and Caribbean States (CELAC). These attracted scholarly attention among Latin American observers of International Relations during the same years that the study of North America nearly disappeared. As noted, North American heads of state shied away from praising NAFTA (Bow and Santa-Cruz 2014). In part, this is because even smaller initiatives attracted intense criticism. North American summits were delayed and downplayed in response. However, regional outcomes also seemed inverted. In South America, much-touted UNASUR collapsed amid political divisions in 2019. In the end, the inter-presidential nature of South American organizations (Malamud 2015) and their reliance on "declaratory regionalism" (Jenne, Schenoni, and Urdinez 2017) allowed two decades of region-building to unravel in a matter of months. Unlike for NAFTA, no energetic, influential, and multifaceted coalition rose to UNASUR's defense. At the same juncture, North America's more limited, and decidedly less flashy, forms of regionalism muddled through four years of opposition from the president of its leading power.

North America, then, long has been an odd fit with different IR theories of regionalism. More surprisingly, that also applies to approaches like comparative regionalism that explicitly acknowledge variation in regional forms. A primary reason for this ambiguity, we suspect, is the role of the United States. The United States is North America's dominant force, but unlike a traditional regional power, it does not need to rely on its region to project its power internationally. The United States largely defines its international role more in global than regional terms. As a result, North America exhibits a defining, but ambiguous, asymmetry. While such dynamics differ from Europe—where Germany may be first among equals but is counterbalanced by several large states—it is worth noting that extreme asymmetry appears frequently in other regions. South Asia is asymmetric and Indo-centric. Russian-led initiatives in Central Asia and Southeast Europe take on hub-and-spokes dynamics under multilateral organizations, and South Africa is central to dynamics of southern African regional agreements through the pull of its market, capital, and clout or through small states' reactions to curtail its dominance (Libman and Obydenkova 2018; Alden and Schoeman 2015). Nor have these de facto "regional leaders" been uniformly committed to institutional projects. While China's initial expansion has had a strong regional focus, like the United States it sees itself increasingly as a global power. Understanding the dynamics of asymmetrical regions is an important task for comparative regionalism, and one to which North America should be central. It may be that such asymmetries militate against consistent governmental attention to regional projects from the hegemon—which has comparatively less at stake than the smaller partners (Womack 2016). Asymmetry also creates a gravitational pull in the region, however, meaning that these regions may be propitious sites for bottom-up construction of regions through diffuse governance, social integration, civil society transnationalism, and economic integration. Nonetheless, North America has often been consigned in the IR literature as little more than a free trade pact. We suggest all these factors make North America a particularly interesting example of regionalism—or at least of nearly any concept of regionalism that goes beyond formal regional organization.

North America: What Sort of Region?

The IR scholarship is rife with debates over how to know a "region" when we see it. Does a region need formal institutions? If not, how do we identify a region's boundaries? Must a region be capable of international action? As Söderbaum (2016, 22–23) notes, such questions have been prominent features of the study of (primarily European) regionalism since the late 1960s. Even within Europe, arguments over the concept of "region" have often implicitly referred to different sites, levels, and processes. But generally, contiguity, formal institutions, and economic interdependence were treated as the primary markers of a region during the Cold War.

When regionalism returned to center stage at the end of the Cold War, the debate over what made a region was shaped by the growing prominence of new theoretical perspectives, especially constructivism. In conceptual debates, the "region" was less frequently treated as a natural geographical entity, nor as synonymous with interdependence. As Hurrell (1995, 334) argued, "all regions are socially constructed and hence politically contested." Different social constructions and different political projects, then, will naturally envision different regions. Along those lines, many prominent scholars of "new" and comparative regionalism adopt a broad approach to conceptualizing the region, with two essential elements. First, following Hurrell, regions are understood as constructed, socially and politically, and not natural or objective. Second, regions are treated as an intermediate level of analysis, between the global and national, in which geographical proximity is necessary though not sufficient (Buzan and Waever 2003). The influential *Oxford Handbook on Comparative Regionalism* departs from the definition of "regions *as social constructions that make references to territorial location and to geographical or normative contiguity*" (Börzel and Risse 2016, 7, emphasis in original).

In North America, however, the boundaries of the region have rarely been queried. The most common indicators remain (weak) formal institutions and (stronger) trade interdependence. North America appeared to have been born as a three-country region produced by a discrete instance of economic institution-building under NAFTA. According to most accounts, "North America" was formed, essentially, by NAFTA (DePalma 2002; Thompson 2014). This account tends to emphasize separate national narratives until the late 1980s, which saw sudden momentum for a Canada-US trade agreement, followed by NAFTA (Pastor 2011, 42–56). Accounts with longer time-horizons note that this represented a change to informal understandings of "North America." By including Mexico, NAFTA expanded a previously bilateral North America, linked by economic factors, cultural affinities, and security community (Deutsch 1957; Santa-Cruz, this volume). These narratives of region-formation in North America should remind us how recent a construction the current, predominant understanding of "North America" really is. Still, for three decades, there was an apparent simplicity to North America: the assumption that it is three states, integrated by the market, under one principal institution. One might disagree about the depth of North American regionalism versus regionalization (Capling and Nossal 2009), but the geographical referent was usually assumed by scholars and policy makers alike.

However, when one begins to dig into the dynamics often understood to be at the heart of regions (and regionalism and regionalization), the apparent simplicity dissolves. Depending on whether one looks at trade, finance, migration, security, environment, infrastructure, identity, international relations, or patterns of governance, the region's contours expand, contract, or blur. For observers including Clarkson, North America's very cohesiveness as a region fades away (see also Santa-Cruz, this volume). Some of these expansive processes are usually linked to regionalization—largely non-state, transnational flows—the same feature that leads some to question whether North America is a site of regionalism at all (Capling and Nossal 2009). But this argument is premised on a narrow definition of regionalism as related to the state-led creation of regional organizations. Returning to *Oxford Handbook* concept of region, we suggest that these processes affect social and political constructions and are linked closely to geographical proximity.

Instead of assuming that the definition and boundaries of North America are self-evident, this volume returns to the question: "What is North America?" We have sought to foster conversation and debate around this question rather than imposing a single definition of the region. And indeed, the contributors to this volume have provided different answers to that fundamental query. All contributors are united in seeing regions, and region-building, as part of political projects and processes. No one insists on geographical essentialism. In other ways, though, important differences emerge. Some scholars in this volume point to the paucity of formal institutional development and the weakness of regional identities; they broadly concur with Clarkson and question North America's cohesiveness as a region. Others find consistent patterns of engagement and even governance involving state and non-state actors. Although these rarely culminate in formal organizations, they may produce regularized patterns of interaction and political projects developed with reference to geographical proximity.

In broad terms, the contributions draw on three different logics: a constructivist logic driven by social actors and identities, a new regionalist logic attentive to multifaceted connections, and a functional logic driven by formal institutions and economic forces. These lead to different geographies of North America, differing emphases on formal institutions versus informal processes, and attention to disparate groups of state, private-sector, and civil-society actors. Three of the contributors put this conceptual question front and center. We have organized this volume around the contributors' conceptual logics.

Volume Organization and Chapter Overviews

The volume's first set of chapters emphasizes the social construction of regions. In chapter 1, Arturo Santa-Cruz returns to fundamental concepts of region and order as they relate to occurrences of regionalism across the Western Hemisphere. In doing so, he denaturalizes the idea of the North American region and raises questions about its coherence. Santa-Cruz unpacks the social and political construction of regional order, stressing the role of a regional identity that makes the region distinct and cohesive in the eyes of the world. In this sense, he finds North America limited to the economic sphere in part due to US and Canadian preferences for a hub-and-spokes order. Adopting similar logics, Asa McKercher and María Celia Toro look at the construction of North America from the Canadian and Mexican vantage points, respectively. In chapter 2, McKercher looks historically at the meaning of North America for Canada, especially its largely bilateral connotation. Preferences for bilateralism have roots in geography and economic interests, but also in hierarchical ideas regarding US-Canadian commonality and Mexican otherness. Canadian elites have tended to construct North America as bilateral, holding to that understanding despite the creation of trilateral economic institutions. Their rationales were deeply embedded in the social, including long-standing tendencies to treat Mexico as an "other." In chapter 3, María Celia Toro directs our attention to the US-Mexican border, arguing that we can see regionalism's limitations quite clearly from this vantage point. Border governance emerges as a key test of region-building—or more often, as a point of friction that highlights different understandings of what the region is and should be. Grand designs for economic integration have often been arrested by competing calls to securitize borders or to open them to commerce—a recurring tension in the North American project that has often emerged from US domestic politics and security fears.

The second set of chapters draws more directly on ideas connected to the "new regionalism approach" (Hettne and Söderbaum 1998; Hettne 2005). This has some affinities with Santa-Cruz's conceptualization of the region as a social construction but applies a multi-actor lens that incorporates informal processes of region-building. In chapter 4, Laura Macdonald examines the effects of the Trump presidency on the region—a pivotal period that spurred the USMCA but also seemed to pose an existential threat to North America as it had been understood. As Macdonald notes, state-based, liberal, and functionalist theories of regionalism fare poorly as explanations for the emergence of Trump's threat to NAFTA. Nor can they explain why the threat subsided or the form of North America's reconstitution. A host of nongovernmental actors mobilized to shield North American regionalism from the whims of anti-regionalist state actors—almost the inverse of expectations of state-led regionalism. New regionalism's multi-actor approach sits at the heart of chapters on migration and insecurity. In chapter 5, Ernesto Castañeda, Michael Danielson, and Jayesh Rathod argue that another set of shared policy paradigms have produced a "Fortress North America" approach that pits Canada, Mexico, and the United States against (largely) Central American migrants—sometimes in complicity with the governments of those countries. High levels of regional policy coordination emerge without any notable institutionalization, though with direct and indirect pressure from the United States. Regimes of regional cooperation have emerged in ways that are "nationalistic and illiberal" and marked by hierarchies. Such practices extend North America beyond Canada, Mexico, and the United States—and incorporate parts of Central America on even more unequal terms. In chapter 6, Gema Kloppe-Santamaría shows how a common policy paradigm has characterized North American approaches to security—at times facilitating deep levels of regional cooperation. Kloppe-Santamaría sees a similar regional geography in issues of transnational security—though here Canada diverges from patterns of regional governance. State-led cooperation has emerged but in ways that are ad hoc, informal, and unequal. The consequence, she suggests, has been a misguided and failed security paradigm. The militarized and punitive paradigm that underpins this cooperation in Central America, Mexico, and the United States has produced more "regional bads" than regional public goods. In both chapters 5 and 6, we perceive how, when one decenters the process of region-making away from state leadership and formal institutions, North America's very geography shifts. In chapter 7, Daniela Stevens finds cooperation in places where IR theories of regionalism have rarely looked for it—through subnational and public-private initiatives to foment "energy regionalism." The role of multiple actors and heterogenous processes of region-making is also central to Stevens's account of cooperation in regional energy and transport infrastructure in North America. States play an important and catalyzing role in making energy regionalism work, she shows, but cooperation often centers on subnational governments and industry groups. Region-making here is concrete and bottom-up instead of rhetorical and executive-led. However, in the absence of consistent national and regional coordination, the success of those initiatives has been uneven.

The third section hews more closely to political economy's approach to regions, reinvigorating concepts of institutions and interdependence central to earlier studies of regional integration in the context of an increasingly multipolar world. In chapter 8, Isidro Morales suggests that centrifugal and centripetal forces drive, shape, and limit the development of regionalism. Morales sees these as competing regimes of mobility and confinement, connected to logics of economic gain and securitization. Morales shows how such forces—China, border thickening, and the proliferation of free trade agreements (FTAs) elsewhere—have different effects on certain sectors and geographical clusters of industry. These forces shape patterns of region-making in combination with narratives that politically construct regions and give them meaning. In chapter 9, Diana Panke and Sören Stapel, drawing on their dataset (Panke, Stapel, and Starkman 2020), focus on the competencies of formal regional organizations. By their metrics, North America has lacked the institutional dynamism of other regions—something they seek to explain. Their focus on formal regional organizations diverges somewhat from the attention to informal institutions and processes in much of the volume. That choice facilitates their cross-regional comparison of regional organizational competencies, and it underscores how limited formal institutionalization in North America has been. The comparison raises important questions about the region's formal institutional development, although as they note, the organizational focus omits many of North America's informal dynamics. Limited formal organizational development is not the only challenge for North America, however. In chapter 10, Barbara Stallings examines how the dramatic emergence of China has reshaped the economic underpinnings of North America, both in its post-NAFTA trilateral form and the broader regional environs. She sees North America as thin in construction and community, and further challenged by China's expanding role. China's entry into the WTO and its vertiginous growth created tremendous challenges for intraregional integration in North America, though these varied by country and industry.

As this brief conceptual comparison of the contributions suggest, North America as a region has been constructed in rather unexpected and even unintended ways. These have rarely left their mark in terms of new formal institutions or even changes to old institutions, with the notable exception of the USMCA. For some, three decades of North American regional dynamics will not have amounted to *regionalism*, at least when understood as "a primarily state-led process of building and sustaining formal regional institutions and organizations" (Börzel and Risse 2016, 7). However, we would argue that many of these processes have generated region-making by other means. North America, in our view, does exist—even if it does not fulfill the expectations of many advocates of regionalism. The result of North America's evolution has been an untidy array of social and political constructions with implications for regional governance across a broader North American geography.

Finally, in our conclusion to the volume, we return to the questions set out in this introduction—what can North America offer to the study of regionalism, and what can regionalist theories tell us about North America? We propose additional directions for this research agenda, especially looking at how North America may connect to theories of regionalism in IR. We assess the possibilities for North American cooperation going forward. The states and societies of the region must grapple with the implications of a global context in which the United States shares influence with China and other major powers, while also dealing with pressing challenges of development, migration, security, and climate change in the broader North American neighborhood.

Note

1. There are a handful of counterexamples, though they have tended to fall closer to IPE than IR (e.g., Castro-Rea 2016).

Bibliography

Acharya, A. 2007. "The Emerging Regional Architecture of World Politics." *World Politics* 59 (4): 629–52.

Acharya, A. 2000. *Constructing a Security Community in Southeast Asia: ASEAN and the Problem of Regional Order: ASEAN and the Problem of Regional Order.* Routledge.

"Regionalism beyond EU-Centrism." 2016. *The Oxford Handbook of Comparative Regionalism*, 109–30.

Alden, C., and M. Schoeman. 2015. "South Africa's Symbolic Hegemony in Africa." *International Politics* 52 (2): 239–54.

Anderson, G. 2020. *Freeing Trade in North America.* Kingston, ON: McGill–Queen's University Press.

Andreas, P., and T. J. Biersteker. 2003. *The Rebordering of North America: Integration and Exclusion in a New Security Context.* New York: Routledge.

Aspinwall, M. 2009. "NAFTA-ization: Regionalization and Domestic Political Adjustment in the North American Economic Area." *JCMS: Journal of Common Market Studies* 47 (1): 1–24.

Aspinwall, M. 2011. "Consequences of Regionalism." In *New Regionalism and the European Union: Dialogues, Comparisons and New Research Directions*, edited by Alex Warleigh Lack, Nick Robinson, and Ben Rosamond, 158–74. London: Routledge.

Ayres, J., and L. Macdonald. 2006. "Deep Integration and Shallow Governance: The Limits of Civil Society Engagement across North America." *Policy and Society* 25 (3): 23–42.

Ayres, J., and L. Macdonald. 2012. *North America in Question: Regional Integration in an Era of Economic Turbulence.* Toronto: University of Toronto Press. https://doi.org/10.3138/9781442690349.

Barnett, M. N., and M. Finnemore. 2004. *Rules for the World: International Organizations in Global Politics.* Ithaca, NY: Cornell University Press.

Beeson, M. 2020. "The Great ASEAN Rorschach Test." *The Pacific Review* 33 (3–4): 574–81.

Blecker, R. A. 2014. "The Mexican and US Economies after Twenty Years of NAFTA." *International Journal of Political Economy* 43, no. 2: 5–26.

Bonikowski, B. 2019. "Trump's Populism: The Mobilization of Nationalist Cleavages and the Future of US Democracy." In *When Democracy Trumps Populism: European and Latin America Lessons for the United States*, edited by K. Weyland and R. Madrid, 110–31. Cambridge: Cambridge University Press.

Börzel, T. A., and T. Risse. 2016. *The Oxford Handbook of Comparative Regionalism.* Oxford: Oxford University Press.

Börzel, T. A., and T. Risse. 2019. "Grand Theories of Integration and the Challenges of Comparative Regionalism." *Journal of European Public Policy* 26 (8): 1231–52.

Bow, B. 2010. *The Politics of Linkage: Power, Interdependence, and Ideas in Canada-US Relations.* Vancouver: University of British Columbia Press.

Bow, B., and G. Anderson. 2014. *Regional Governance in Post-NAFTA North America: Building without Architecture.* New York: Routledge.

Bow, B., and A. Santa-Cruz. 2014. "Polls, Parties, Politicization, and the Evolution of North American Regional Governance." In *Regional Governance in Post-NAFTA North America,* 188–216. New York: Routledge.

Brodie, J. 2016. "The Security and Prosperity Partnership: The Short History of a Strategic Bargain." In *Our North America: Social and Political Issues beyond NAFTA,* edited by J. Castro-Rea, 103–24. Abingdon, UK: Routledge.

Buzan, B., and O. Waever. 2003. *Regions and Powers: The Structure of International Security.* New York: Cambridge University Press.

Calderón Martínez, P. 2018. *NAFTA and Democracy in Mexico: A Successful Failure?* New York: Routledge.

Cameron, M. A., and B. W. Tomlin. 2000. *The Making of NAFTA: How the Deal Was Done.* Ithaca, NY: Cornell University Press.

Cameron, M. A, and C. Wise. 2004. "The Political Impact of NAFTA on Mexico: Reflections on the Political Economy of Democratization." *Canadian Journal of Political Science/Revue Canadienne de Science Politique* 37 (4): 301–23.

Capling, A., and K. R. Nossal. 2009. "The Contradictions of Regionalism in North America." *Review of International Studies* 35 (S1): 147–67.

Castro-Rea, J., ed. 2016. *Our North America: Social and Political Issues beyond NAFTA.* Abingdon, UK: Routledge.

Chabat, J. 1997. "Mexico's Foreign Policy after NAFTA: The Tools of Interdependence." In *Bridging the Border: Transforming Mexico-US Relations,* edited by Rodolfo O. De La Garza and Jesús Velasco, 33–47. Lanham, MD: Rowman & Littlefield.

Clarkson, S. 2008. *Does North America Exist?: Governing the Continent after NAFTA and 9/11.* University of Toronto Press.

Covarrubias, A. 2016. "Containing Brazil: Mexico's Response to the Rise of Brazil." *Bulletin of Latin American Research* 35 (1): 49–63.

Danielson, M. S. 2017. *Emigrants Get Political: Mexican Migrants Engage Their Home Towns.* Oxford: Oxford University Press.

de Melo, J., and A. Panagariya, eds. 1993. *The New Regionalism in Trade Policy.* Washington, DC: World Bank Publications.

DePalma, A. 2002. *Here: A Biography of the New American Continent.* New York: Harper Perennial.

Deutsch, K. W. 1957. *Political Community in the North Atlantic Area.* Princeton, NJ: Princeton University Press.

Duina, F. 2016. "North America and the Transatlantic Area." In *The Oxford Handbook of Comparative Regionalism,* edited by Tanja A. Börzel and Thomas Risse, 133–49. New York: Oxford University Press.

Durazo Herrmann, J. 2018. "Tan lejos y tan cerca. Las relaciones México-Canadá en perspectiva histórica." *Foro Internacional* 58 (2): 243–73.

Fairbrother, M. 2014. "Economists, Capitalists, and the Making of Globalization: North American Free Trade in Comparative-Historical Perspective." *American Journal of Sociology* 119 (5): 1324–79.

Fairbrother, M. 2019. *Free Traders: Elites, Democracy, and the Rise of Globalization in North America.* Oxford University Press.

Fawn, R. 2009. "'Regions' and Their Study: Wherefrom, What for and Whereto?" *Review of International Studies* 35: 5–34.

Gantz, D. A. 2020. "Important New Features in the USMCA." Mexico Center, Rice University's Baker Institute for Public Policy (May 5, 2020), 20–23.

Genna, G. M., and D. A. Mayer-Foulkes. 2013. *North American Integration: An Institutional Void in Migration, Security and Development.* New York: Routledge.

Hart, M. 1994. *Decision at Midnight: Inside the Canada-US Free-Trade Negotiations.* Vancouver: University of British Columbia Press.

Hettne, B. 2005. "Beyond the 'New' Regionalism." *New Political Economy* 10 (4): 543–71.

Hettne, B., and F. Söderbaum. 1998. "The New Regionalism Approach." *Politeia* 17 (3): 6–21.

Hurrell, Andrew. 1995. "Explaining the Resurgence of Regionalism in World Politics." *Review of International Studies* 21 (4): 331–58.

Hurrell, Andrew. 2006. "Hegemony in a Region That Dares Not Speak Its Name." *International Journal* 61 (3): 545–66.

Jenne, N., L. L. Schenoni, and F. Urdinez. 2017. "Of Words and Deeds: Latin American Declaratory Regionalism, 1994–2014." *Cambridge Review of International Affairs* 30 (23): 195–215.

Katzenstein, P. J. 1996. "Regionalism in Comparative Perspective." *Cooperation and Conflict* 31 (2): 123–59.

Katzenstein, P. J. 2005. *A World of Regions: Asia and Europe in the American Imperium.* Ithaca, NY: Cornell University Press.

Kay, T. 2011. *NAFTA and the Politics of Labor Transnationalism.* Cambridge: Cambridge University Press.

Keohane, R. O., and J. S. Nye. 1977. *Power and Interdependence: World Politics in Transition.* Boston: Little, Brown.

Kukucha, C. 2020. "Civil Society, Multilevel Governance, and International Trade in North America." In *The Multilevel Politics of Trade,* edited by Jörg Broschek and Patricia Goff, 158–84. Toronto: University of Toronto Press.

Kupchan, C. A. 1998. "After Pax Americana: Benign Power, Regional Integration, and the Sources of a Stable Multipolarity." *International Security* 23 (2): 40–79.

Libman, A., and A. V. Obydenkova. 2018. "Regional International Organizations as a Strategy of Autocracy: The Eurasian Economic Union and Russian Foreign Policy." *International Affairs* 94 (5): 1037–58.

Long, T. 2015. *Latin America Confronts the United States: Asymmetry and Influence.* Cambridge: Cambridge University Press.

Long, T. 2018. "La relación entre Estados Unidos y América Latina y el Caribe en la era Trump." *Revista Mexicana de Política Exterior* 114 (September–December): 157–75.

López-Vallejo, M. 2016. *Reconfiguring Global Climate Governance in North America: A Transregional Approach.* Abingdon, UK: Routledge.

Macdonald, L. 2019. "Upsetting the Apple Cart? Implications of the NAFTA Re-negotiations for Canada–US Relations." In *Canada–US Relations: Sovereignty or Shared Institutions*, edited by David Carment and Christopher Sands, 193–213. New York: Springer.

Macdonald, L. 2020. "Canada in the North America Region: Implications of the Trump Presidency." *Canadian Journal of Political Science* 53 (3): 1–16.

Malamud, A. 2005. "Mercosur Turns 15: Between Rising Rhetoric and Declining Achievement." *Cambridge Review of International Affairs* 18 (3): 421–36.

Malamud, A. 2012. "Moving Regions: Brazil's Global Emergence and the Redefinition of Latin American Borders." In *The Rise of Post-hegemonic Regionalism: The Case of Latin America*, edited by P. Riggirozzi and D. Tussie, 167–82. New York: Springer.

Malamud, A. 2015. "Interdependence, Leadership and Institutionalization: The Triple Deficit and Fading Prospects of Mercosur." In *Limits to Regional Integration*, edited by Sören Dosenrode, 163–78. Farnham, UK: Ashgate.

Masferrer, C., E. R. Hamilton, and N. Denier. 2019. "Immigrants in Their Parental Homeland: Half a Million US-Born Minors Settle throughout Mexico." *Demography* 56 (4): 1453–61.

Mayer-Foulkes, D., and R. García-Barrios. 2012. "Democracy and Development for Mexico." In *North American Integration: An Institutional Void in Migration, Security, and Development*, edited by Gaspare Genna and David Mayer-Foulkes, 78–93. New York: Routledge.

Milner, H. V. 1997. *Interests, Institutions, and Information: Domestic Politics and International Relations.* Princeton, NJ: Princeton University Press.

Morales, I. 2008. *Post-NAFTA North America: Reshaping the Economic and Political Governance of a Changing Region.* Basingstoke, UK: Palgrave MacMillan.

Morales, I. 2017. "The Renewal of US 'Free Trade' Diplomacy in the Americas: From NAFTA to a Deeper Agenda of 'Competitive Liberalization' for the Region." In *Post-hegemonic Regionalism in the Americas: Toward a Pacific–Atlantic Divide?*, edited by J. Briceno-Ruiz and I. Morales, 32–56. Abingdon, UK: Routledge.

Moreno-Brid, J. C., P. R. Nápoles, and J. C. Valdivia. 2004. "NAFTA and the Mexican Economy: A Look Back on a Ten-Year Relationship." *North Carolina Journal of International Law* 30 (4): 997.

Moreno-Brid, J. C., J. Santamaría, and J. C. Rivas Valdivia. 2005. "Industrialization and Economic Growth in Mexico after NAFTA: The Road Travelled." *Development and Change* 36 (6): 1095–1119.

Mudde, C. 2012. *The Relationship between Immigration and Nativism in Europe and North America.* Washington, DC: Migration Policy Institute.

Nolan García, K. A. 2011. "The Evolution of United States–Mexico Labor Cooperation (1994–2009): Achievements and Challenges." *Politics & Policy* 39 (1): 91–117.

Ortega Ortiz, R. Y. 2019. "Seguridad, migración y comercio en las relaciones México-Estados Unidos durante la presidencia de Donald Trump." *Foro Internacional* 59 (3–4): 733–62.

Panke, D. 2020. "Regional Cooperation through the Lenses of States: Why Do States Nurture Regional Integration?" *The Review of International Organizations* 15 (2): 475–504.

Panke, D., S. Stapel, and A. Starkmann. 2020. *Comparing Regional Organizations: Global Dynamics and Regional Particularities.* Bristol, UK: Bristol University Press.

Pastor, R. A. 2001. *Toward a North American Community: Lessons from the Old World for the New.* Washington, DC: Institute for International Economics.

Pastor, R. A. 2011. *The North American Idea: A Vision of a Continental Future.* Oxford: Oxford University Press.

Pérez-Armendáriz, C., and D. Crow. 2010. "Do Migrants Remit Democracy? International Migration, Political Beliefs, and Behavior in Mexico." *Comparative Political Studies* 43 (1): 119–48.

Riggirozzi, P. 2012. "Region, Regionness and Regionalism in Latin America: Toward a New Synthesis." *New Political Economy* 17 (4): 421–43.

Riggirozzi, P., and D. Tussie, eds. 2012. *The Rise of Post-hegemonic Regionalism: The Case of Latin America.* New York: Springer.

Rojas, R. 2021. "¿Amigos entrañables, vecinos distantes? Andrés Manuel López Obrador y Donald Trump." *Nueva Sociedad* 291 (January): 182–91.

Sanahuja, J. A. 2009. "Del regionalismo abierto al regionalismo pos-neoliberal: crisis y cambio en la integracion regional en America Latina." In *Anuario de la integracion regional en America Latina y el Caribe,* edited by L. M. Alfonso, L. Peña, and M. Vazquez. Buenos Aires: Coordinadora Regional de Investigaciones Económicas y Sociales.

Santa-Cruz, A. 2019. *US Hegemony and the Americas: Power and Economic Statecraft in International Relations.* Abingdon, UK: Routledge.

Shih, W. C. 2020. "Global Supply Chains in a Post-Pandemic World." *Harvard Business Review,* 2020. https://hbr.org/2020/09/global-supply-chains-in-a-post-pandemic-world.

Serbin, A. 2012. "El regionalismo 'post-Liberal' en America Latina y el Caribe: Nuevos temas, nuevos actores y nuevos desafios." In *Anuario de la integracion regional en America Latina y el Caribe,* edited by A. Serbin, L. Martinez, and H. Ramanzini Junior. Buenos Aires: Coordinadora Regional de Investigaciones Económicas y Sociales.

Smith, P. H., and A. D. Selee. 2013. *Mexico & the United States: The Politics of Partnership.* Boulder, CO: Lynne Rienner Publishers.

Söderbaum, F. 2015. *Rethinking Regionalism*. New York: Macmillan International Higher Education.

Söderbaum, F. 2016. "Old, New, and Comparative Regionalism." In *The Oxford Handbook of Comparative Regionalism*, edited by T. A. Börzel and T. Risse, 16–38. Oxford University Press.

Thompson, J. 2014. *Making North America: Trade, Security, and Integration*. Toronto: University of Toronto Press.

Trefler, D. 2004. "The Long and Short of the Canada-US Free Trade Agreement." *American Economic Review* 94 (4): 870–95.

Wilson, C. E. 2011. *Working Together: Economic Ties between the United States and Mexico*. Washington, DC: Woodrow Wilson International Center for Scholars.

Womack, B. 2016. *Asymmetry and International Relationships*. New York: Cambridge University Press.

Wyatt-Walter, A. 1995. "Regionalism, Globalization, and World Economic Order." In *Regionalism in World Politics: Regional Organization and International Order*, edited by L. Fawcett and A. Hurrell, 74–121. New York: Oxford University Press.

Yukawa, T. 2018. "European Integration through the Eyes of ASEAN: Rethinking Eurocentrism in Comparative Regionalism." *International Area Studies Review* 21 (4): 323–39.

PART I

Constructing a North American Region

CHAPTER ONE

An Embarrassment of Regions

North America and Regional Orders

Arturo Santa-Cruz

BOTH CRITICS and enthusiasts of the integration process that has taken place in the last three decades among Canada, the United States, and Mexico refer to the set of states as a continent.[1] "North America" has become a relevant political term. Nevertheless, the anchoring of political concepts on the division of land has been seriously questioned on epistemological grounds. As geographers Martin Lewis and Kären Wigen have pointed out in *The Myth of Continents*, even in the field of geology continental divisions are of minor utility. According to them, "If continents are simply irrelevant for physical geography, however, they can be positively pernicious when applied to human geography. Pigeonholing historical and cultural data into a continental framework fundamentally distorts basic spatial patterns, leading to misapprehensions of cultural and social differentiation" (Lewis and Wigen 1997, 36). For what Christopher Hemmer and Peter Katzenstein, following George Simmel, observed of borders applies to continents as well: they are "not a geographic fact that has sociological consequences, but a sociological fact that takes geographic form" (Hemmer and Katzenstein 2002, 587).

In any case, continental language in political science seems to have gone out of fashion. More common now is to refer to a set of closely interacting states as a "region"—a concept that it is not necessarily anchored in tectonic plates. But even here, North America's status is not always clear. More than a decade after the alleged founding treaty of the new regional compact, the North American Free Trade Agreement (NAFTA), had gone into effect, Robert Pastor asked: "Why then is North America not seen as a region?" (Pastor 2005, 202).

Things would change soon again, though. As Ann Capling and Kim Richard Nossal noted in 2009, "Students of regionalism almost reflexively include North America in their lists of regions in contemporary global politics" (Capling and Nossal 2009, 147). But is the new reflex a sound one? Since the beginning of the twenty-first century, there was indeed a flurry of articles on "regionalism" and "regionalization," often taking for granted the nature of their subject matter. It would seem that the recent emphasis on regionalism and regionalization has lost sight of the more fundamental discussion regarding the normative and social foundations of regions. In this chapter I embed the debate on regionalization and regionalism within the broader discussion on regional orders, and then contrast the case of the "new North America" (i.e., one composed by Canada, Mexico, and the United States [Clarkson 2008, 20]) with three widely acknowledged regional spaces in the Americas: the Western Hemisphere as a whole, Latin America, and Canada and the United States. I argue that politically constructed, normatively structured regional orders subsume both projects of regionalism and processes of regionalization, and that thinking of (the new) North America in light of regional orders reveals why calling it a region is not (yet?) warranted. Granted, as this volume's introduction notes, there might be different processes of region-making in North America. However, I would argue that what exists in this area nowadays is, fundamentally, "dual bilateralism": United States–Canada, United States–Mexico. The chapter's organization is straightforward: the first section is devoted to the analytical discussion, highlighting the importance of the broader concept of order and of two markers that might be useful to identify localized instantiations of it: "actorness" and "regionness"—two concepts that ultimately impinge on a sense of regional identity, or "we-ness." The following three sections deal with each of the aforementioned regions, respectively; the fifth section considers whether (the new) North America should be considered a region. I wrap up the argument in the concluding section.

On Regional Orders

The study of international political economy—irrespective of the level at which it is analyzed—presupposes the analytical distinction between politics and economics. In the literature on regional integration, such demarcation has been operationalized through the concepts of "regionalism" and "regionalization." Although it might mean different things to different scholars, there is a widely shared understanding of the former as a fundamentally state-led project of institution-building among a specific set of contiguous countries (Hurrell 1995, 334–38; Capling and Nossal 2009, 148). Regionalization, on the other, hand, while also being a term with multiple meanings, is usually understood as an informal process of increased integration, led by non-state actors in a defined group of neighboring states, usually on economic affairs (Hettne 2005, 545).

However, a clear-cut distinction between both concepts and their underlying basis might be problematic. Non-state-led processes can give rise to state projects, and vice versa; furthermore, as Etel Solingen has noted, "the market/politics distinction obscures the ways in which politics underlies regionalization and markets create conditions for the emergence and design of institutions" (Solingen and Malnight 2016). But more fundamentally for the topic at hand: What is the understanding of both terms' ("regionalism" and "regionalization") referent, that is, "region"? Regardless of the planned or spontaneous nature of the processes emphasized by each concept, do either "regionalism" or "regionalization" necessarily lead to the creation of meaningful *regions*? Processes of economic regionalization can be inert in political terms; analogously, exclusively formal regionalism might be irrelevant for the construction of important sociopolitical features, such as regional identities (Hettne and Söderbaum 2000, 462). On occasions, of course, both regionalism and regionalization might become catalysts of consequential regions (Katzenstein 2005).

The often-equivocal nature of statements in the literature about the relationship between "regionalism" and "regionalization," on the one hand, and "region," on the other, might have to do with the fact that the latter is a concept of manifold meanings. To attempt an answer to Pastor's (rhetorical?) question: because where some analysts see a region, others see none. Thus, whereas for some a region is a matter of transactional density (i.e., intensity of interactions), for others it is more a cultural or social affair. Nor is the salience of regions as a unit of analysis in International Relations (IR) a foregone conclusion (Hurrell 2005, 39).[2] For instance, the regional *problématique* does not figure in any of the arguably three most influential books in the discipline of the last eight decades: Hans Morgenthau's *Politics among Nations* (1948), Kenneth Waltz's *Theory of International Politics* (1979), and Alexander Wendt's *Social Theory of International Politics* (1999). However, regions have been a pervasive feature of international politics, at least since the 1950s.

The analytical case for the study of regions in International Relations rests not only on their peculiar features, but also on the way they change the interaction among the constitutive units of the overall system (as well as how they impact the interaction between them and non-state actors). As David Lake and Patrick Morgan have noted, regions are not simply the international system writ small, nor idiosyncratic grouping of states (Lake and Morgan 1997, 7). For it to make sense to compartmentalize the study of world politics, and add another level of analysis, regions should exhibit a distinctive dynamic (Hettne and Söderbaum 2000, 461; Buzan 2012, 22; Hurrell 2005, 40). Beyond the baseline definition of a region as consisting "of two or more member states in geographical proximity . . . characterized by regular interactions between them," for a region to be politically relevant in international politics it has to display some other distinguishing features, such as a "thicker" social fabric than that of the international system in general, a peculiar "diplomatic culture," or a characteristic institutional arrangement.[3] It is thus not just geographical proximity and the intensity of economic transactions that a region make, but also the distinctive manner in which the regional level processes global stimuli, thus affecting—at least as a sort of intervening variable—the course of the international system.[4]

But regions, like the state and the international system, do not simply exist or happen. They are politically and socially constructed—be it as continents, leagues, unions, or processes of regionalism or regionalization. Furthermore, regions are pregnant with history; they draw on the past in order to erect localized arrangements of worldwide power dynamics. And history, as well as current events and projects of future developments, are politically contested—a contestation that largely takes place through the identity-defining stories societies create. Regions are thus the result of social agents, but also of historical narratives and political border-drawing struggles (Pouliot 2012, 214–15).

Furthermore, regions require shared understandings if they are to endure. This may not be the only path to region-making, as this volume's editors note. Informal processes, or even more functional ones driven by political-economic factors, may shape regions as suggested by Laura Macdonald's and Isidro Morales's chapters, respectively. However, I would argue that, as politically constructed entities, regions need to deal first and foremost with a more fundamental matter: the socially pervasive problem of order. Order is essential for the creation and maintenance of regions—as it is of living organisms and of the physical world in general. At its simplest, order refers to a regular arrangement, which is to say that items belonging to such configuration stand in relationship to one another in accordance with some pattern (*Merriam-Webster*; Bull 1977, 3).

But in the social realm order acquires a more complex signification. For starters, as Adam Smith noted long ago, "social order is inherently a moral domain" (Smith 1759, in Hitlin 2014, 201). Social order is a moral domain because it refers to human values. That is, since human action is reflexive and goal-oriented, any social arrangement will be embedded in social standards. This of course does not mean that social orders are democratic, egalitarian, or just—most of them are not—but they do need to appear legitimate to their members if they are to endure (Bull 1977, 4; Rengger 2000, 1, 18). It is for this reason that, even from an analytical standpoint, social order is not only a descriptive concept the way, say, homeostasis or force might be; the concept of social orders is, as Raymond Aron noted, both descriptive and normative (as reported by Hoffmann 1966, 455–56).

Order has been a leitmotif in International Relations. Be it in the at times almost mechanical interpretation of the balance of power, in the purposeful coordination-oriented interpretation of institutions, or in the more sociological understanding of a society of states, the problem of order is pervasive in the discipline (Rengger 2000, 2; Paul 2012, 7, 12). What all interpretations of order in international politics share is the notion that, as Friedrich Kratochwil put it, "human action is 'rule-governed'" (Kratochwil 1978, 2). But it is not only a matter or rules. International order is a purposive, social endeavor; as Hedley Bull wrote, it is "a pattern of activity that sustains the elementary or primary goals of the society of states" (Bull 1977, 8). Moreover, systemic anarchy notwithstanding, international order also rests on legitimacy. No less a realist than Henry Kissinger has acknowledged as much; for him, "a consensus on the legitimacy of existing arrangements does not—now or in the past—foreclose competitions or confrontations, but it helps ensure that they will occur as adjustments within the existing order rather than as fundamental challenges to it" (Kissinger 2014, 9). Material capabilities are, of course, also an important element in the emergence and maintenance of a social order, but they do not "speak" by themselves—they have to be interpreted by the relevant actors (Wendt 1999, 96, 135, 371). Thus, for an international order to perdure, its members have to perceive it as "desirable, proper, appropriate within some socially constructed system of norms, values, beliefs, and definitions" (Suchman 1995, 574, in Reus-Smit 2017, 875).

Hence, to some extent, what goes for the international order goes for regional orders. To cite Kissinger again: "Regional orders involve the same principles applied to a defined geographic area" (Kissinger 2014, 9). But there is a caveat. As suggested before, a regional order is not simply the international order writ small. The above-mentioned features, such as the "diplomatic culture" or institutional arrangements, point not only to structural normative elements regional orders might share with the international one, but also to the idiosyncrasy of regional compacts, the distinctive manner in which they distill international incentives and in turn affect them. No order, no region.

The fundamental constructivist insight for the study of regionalism is that regional orders are localized normative and social constructs. Both elements (the normative and the social) are shot through and through by power relations and serve to delineate a sense of "we-ness"—and by extension also as a mechanism for the exclusion of others. It is by means of the dialectical relationship between the normative and social structures (with the former establishing region-specific values and the latter membership and internal hierarchy) that authority relationships are stabilized; frequently, due to the in-group relationship that might emerge, some sense of identity is created in the process (Reus-Smit 2017, 867, 869; Ayoob 1999, 249).

Regional identity, as identity in general, is of course a contested and elusive concept. Like the notion of "national interest"—so dear to IR theory—it is not a descriptive term, but one whose meaning has to be unveiled through the analysis of political processes (Kratochwil 1982, 3). Also, like national interest, identity is an unavoidable term in the practice and study of international relations—including its regional instantiations (Haglund 2009b, 345; Acharya 2012, 184).

Regional orders subsume both projects of regionalism and processes of regionalization but are more than their sum. Furthermore, regional orders need not be operationalized in terms of regionalism and regionalization, as there might not be a good analytical fit among them (cf. Whitaker 1954, 5). Regionalism and regionalization do not (necessarily) a region make; regional orders do. As noted, no order, no region. However, paraphrasing Martha Finnemore's question on international societies, "How do you recognize a regional order when you see one?" Well, we certainly cannot see a regional order, or more succinctly, a region, but we can elucidate it (Dunne 2008, 281). Two "markers" are particularly helpful in this endeavor: "actorness" and "regionness." The latter term refers to the internal workings of a region, its process of increased cohesiveness and distinctiveness. There are of course degrees of regionness—it is not a binary category (Hettne 2005, 548, 555–56; Hettne and Söderbaum 2000, 461). What gives a region cohesion is the enactment of its social and normative structure, a constant and evolving practice that in turn reinforces solidarity between its members (Pouliot 2012, 217, 220).

Actorness, on the other hand, refers to the capacity to relate to other actors, to play a role in the international arena; this capability depends on the recognition granted by others. Like regionness, actorness is not a fixed attribute, but an endowment that is continually negotiated through routine practice (Bretherton and Vogler 2006, 12; Hettne 2005, 555). In this sense, the "external" stands in a constitutive relation to the region—by being subject to others' recognition, the region is (partially) constituted by others, in a process analogous to the role interaction in the international system plays in the constitution of sovereign states.[5] Both internal and external dynamics interact in the making and unmaking of regions. As Michael Banks put it in a phrase anticipating by decades a famous constructivist tenet on anarchy, "Regions are what politicians and peoples want them to be" (Banks 1969, 338; Wendt 1992).

Standing for different facets of regional orders, actorness and regionness allow us to recognize/elucidate a region when we see/analyze one. Furthermore, and perhaps as important, both concepts allow us to compare the density of regional orders. Thus, for instance, as we will see in the next four sections, actorness and regionness—markers of regional orders—present themselves quite differently when we consider the Western Hemisphere as whole, Latin America, the "old" (bilateral) North America, and the "new" (trilateral) North America. Paying attention to these differences, even if cursorily, as done here for reasons of space, should shade some light on the issue of whether they have constituted regional orders, and how they might differ among themselves.

The Western Hemisphere

Soon after the first colony in the Americas gained its independence in 1776, a distinctive normative structure started to emerge in the hemisphere. Thomas Jefferson was the first to envision what came to be known as the "Western Hemisphere Idea." In 1808, Jefferson began to develop the notion that, as Arthur Whitaker summarized it, "the peoples of this Hemisphere stand in a special relationship to one another which sets them apart from the rest of the world" (Whitaker 1954, 1). When his successor James Monroe declared the 1823 doctrine that bears his name, Jefferson, in a private letter to the president, commented approvingly: "America, North, and South, has a set of interests distinct from those of Europe, and peculiarly her own. She should therefore have a system of her own, separate and apart from that of Europe" (in Gottmann 1951, 170).

But the US statesmen were not alone in this geopolitical design. The Monroe Doctrine was welcomed by most leaders in the emerging republics (Rojas 2009, 233; Gobat 2013, 1353). Liberator Simón Bolívar applauded it; Mexican president

Guadalupe Victoria referred to it as "President Monroe's memorable promise"; and in 1824 Colombia invoked the novel inter-American policy (Corrales and Feinberg 1999, 4; Victoria 1826, 299; Grandin 2012, 84). The hemispheric convergence rested in part in the common interest in keeping the European powers at bay, but also in the fact that the United States was seen as a model by the Spanish-American independence leaders (Rojas 2009, 232). For them, politically at least, the whole of the Americas was perceived as a unit (Rojas 2009, 33). By the fifth decade of the nineteenth century, the normative structure of the Americas, instantiated in the Western Hemisphere Idea, had taken form—a form, it should be noted, that required no legal institutionalization. As Whitaker noted, "the distinction between the idea and its various political expressions . . . should be constantly kept in mind" (Whitaker 1954, 5).

Interestingly, the interaction between the young republics of the hemisphere created a social structure in which the United States became hegemonic before it was a great power. The fact that it was regarded as a model by its southern neighbors for both its political and economic systems goes a long way in explaining the US position in the hemispheric social structure. Thus, when Pan Americanism emerged in the late nineteenth century, US leadership was a fact on the ground; the 1889–1890 International Conference of American States, centered mostly on economic affairs, was called by Washington (Carrillo 2018, 9).

By the early twentieth century the Western Hemisphere was recognized as a distinctive social order. Thus, for instance, the European powers sanctioned the Monroe Doctrine at Versailles (González 2010, 234). Internally, that is, within the hemisphere, the regional hegemon had a unique policy toward the other states of the "new world"; thus, for instance, they were excepted from the quota system Washington imposed in its 1921 immigration law—a special treatment that would last for decades (Pastor 1984, 38). Similarly, since the 1930s, the United States became more willing to accommodate its southern neighbors' urge to formally institutionalize their relationship. This mood only increased after World War II, during which there was close cooperation among the countries of the Americas; thus, Latin American countries pushed hard for the recognition, within the United Nations system, of regional organizations (Nye 1969, 720–721; Long 2020, 22). Notably, the American Declaration on the Rights and Duties of Man was passed before the United Nations' Universal Declaration of Human Rights (Sikkink 2019, 56).

Thus, the "separate system" Jefferson had envisioned for the Americas in the early nineteenth century would become formally institutionalized by the mid-twentieth century, with the promulgation of the Bogotá Charter and the establishment of the Organization of American States (OAS) in 1948. The hemispheric order embodied in the OAS founding document noted (in Article 5): "The solidarity of the American States and the high aims which are sought through it require the political organization of those States on the basis of the effective exercise of representative democracy," while also stating that "international order consists essentially of respect for the personality, sovereignty and independence of States." There was thus a manifest, productive tension in the social order of the Americas.

One instantiation of this tension is the legal realm. As suggested above, the emphasis on the nonintervention principle—one worked out by Latin American diplomats—would seem to be at odds with the imperative of representative government in the hemisphere. The complex interaction between these two tenets gave rise to the development of American (in the sense of Pan American, not US) law (Sikkink 1997, 719–20; Grandin 2012, 70; Kacowicz 2005, 44).

With periods of ups and downs, the hemispheric order would be substantially strengthened in the 1990s. There were three main reasons for this development: one was that in 1990 Canada joined the regional organization—upholding both the normative and social components of the regional compact, particularly regarding human and political rights (McKenna 1999); a second one was the economic agreement that came to be known as the "Washington Consensus" (one that, incidentally, definitely included Ottawa; Williamson 2000, 254; Anderson 2003, 95); hence, for instance, US president George H. W. Bush unveiled in 1990 the "Enterprise for the Americas Initiative: An Opportunity for Trade, Investment, and Growth." Significantly, though, the plan did not emanate from the United States. It was rather a response to a specific request made by Latin American leaders (Tulchin 1993, 60–61). This was followed up by the next US administration with the 1994 Summit of the Americas, in which the project for the (eventually failed) Free Trade Area of the Americas was launched.

The third reason for the strengthening of the hemispheric order in the 1990s was the consolidation of the democratic imperative that took place in those years (Domínguez 2007, 83–84; Santa-Cruz 2005). After several democracy-supporting measures taken during the decade, at the 2001 Quebec Summit of Heads of State of the Americas—at the request of some Latin American states—a "democracy clause" was adopted, and the Inter-American Democratic Charter was promulgated later that same year in Lima; the latter specified the criteria needed to collectively defend democratically elected regimes in the hemisphere. The hemispheric social order had thus been reinvigorated at the dawn of the twenty-first century.

The defense of human rights, democracy, and collective security systems at the regional level figure among the Western Hemisphere's more significant contributions to the international order. Those issues have pride of place in the Americas precisely because it was there that their launching to the international arena took place; this much is recognized by other international actors (Acharya 2018, 159–61, 184–85; IACHR 2013). As the previous account makes clear, the hemispheric order can be said to possess some degree of both actorness (i.e., capacity, based on others' recognition, to play a role in the international arena) as well as regionness (i.e., cohesiveness and distinctiveness). Interestingly, however, no meaningful sense of shared identity has emerged in the Western Hemisphere. The reason for this, in large part, has to do with the existence of an important fault line within the Americas—a topic I will delve into in the next section.

Latin America

Latin America has long been recognized as a region; in fact, its regionalism has been deemed the oldest in the world (Acharya 2016, 8). This is of course no mere idiosyncrasy or historical accident. It has to do with the construction of its regional order. As Edmundo O'Gorman noted, the "new world" was born with what he called a "Great Divide," a transplanted frontier that reproduced the cultural and political rivalries that existed in the "old world" (O'Gorman 1977, 5).

It is thus not difficult to see why, after independent states had emerged, Simón Bolivar (initially) summoned only "the formerly Spanish America" to the 1826 Panama Congress—not the English-speaking one (Dickins and Allen 1858, 901). It was not hard to surmise the criteria for membership in the Bolivarian project. As a Bolivian commentator put it some years later, the contributing factors to the proposed integrationist project included "the identity of origin, as they fought together for their freedom . . . the uniformity of language . . . the unity of religion . . . the similitude of customs . . . the type of government they have adopted" (Medinaceli 1862, 5; Brazil was not part of the plan).

Furthermore, the leaders summoned by Bolivar—and the convener himself—did not think of themselves and their peoples as "Latin Americans"—they identified themselves simply as "Americans" (for instance, Mexico's first name, as it appears in its 1813 Declaration of Independence, was *América Septentrional* ["Northern America"]; Gobat 2013, 1349). The "Latin American" construct would emerge a couple of decades later, mainly as a result of what were perceived as the imperialist aims of the United States—aims that at the time were being directed south of the transplanted frontier. It was indeed a Mexican newspaper, *El Siglo XIX*, probably the first one to suggest the term, writing about the "Latin race," in 1845; about a decade later, the concept "Latin America" was already used not only in Mexico, but in Central and South America as well—including Brazil, which was not originally included by it, as noted above. The adoption of the new identity had a clear political driver: the threat the United States (and other European powers) represented to the still maturing countries (Gobat 2013, 1351, 1346).

Interestingly, the estrangement from Washington, which, as noted in the previous section, had largely been seen as a model by the Spanish-American independence leaders, contributed to the creation of an "internal" dichotomy among the array of young countries: the division between (pro–United States) Liberals and (anti–United States) Conservatives. This ideological schism, one that would be reproduced in the countries of the region, always had the "Colossus of the North" as the implicit reference (O'Gorman 1977, 4).[6]

In any case, by the 1860s the former Spanish colonies in the hemisphere were recognized as an entity (i.e., as possessing actorness). Thus, in 1864 the *New York Tribune* reported a debate in Congress about Europe's designs over "what is called Latin

America" (*New York Tribune* 1864). The region had become a "subordinate system," one whose member states "share in some degree common ethnic, linguistic, cultural, social and historical bonds and whose sense of identity is sometimes increased by the actions and attitudes of states external to the system" (i.e., it possessed regionness [Cantori and Spiegel 1969, 362]). The relevant other, external to the system was, of course, the United States.

Thus, Latin American states went on to create an intricate normative and social structure, one in which the internal divide was always lurking, and the discreet rivalry between the two largest countries, Brazil and Mexico, has been a constant feature. As noted in the previous section, Latin American countries were instrumental in the development of what came to be known as American law. Their contribution, as suggested, was to a large extent for defensive reasons: an attempt to preserve their sovereignty (Kacowicz 2005, 44). In the economic sphere, Latin American states have also been active. They have persevered—without much success—in the creation of integrative mechanisms, such as the Special Latin American Coordinating Commission (later Latin American Economic System) (1964), the Central American Common Market (1960), and the Andean Pact (1969). Although, as noted, they have not been very effective in their integrative efforts, said organizations have served as vehicles for collective action (Bond 1978, 402). Latin American states have also made repeated attempts at creating more overtly political fronts, the latest of which is the (moribund) 2010 Community of Latin American and Caribbean States (CELAC). Evidently, the constant (if not very fruitful) determination of Latin American states to promote these mechanisms is because they resonate within each and every one of them; that is, there is a sense of shared identity that makes these strategies popular among the peoples of Latin America.

The Latin American regional order has, at least in some respects, some degree of cohesion (regionness) and identity (sense of "we-ness"); it is also recognized by others as an entity (actorness). It is thus not surprising that sometimes national leaders speak for the whole region, or that Latin America acts and is acknowledged by others as a bloc.[7]

Old North America

Two states usually do not suffice for a region. But in the case of Canada and the United States, as noted in the introduction and in Asa McKercher's chapter, both countries came to constitute what, at least until the early 1990s, was thought of as the North American continent, with its own regional order—and even a "special relationship" (Haglund 2009a). This North American regional identity was bilateral in nature. The understanding was even more relevant in the wider context of the hemispheric and the Latin American regional orders. The catalysts of regional integration were to some extent analogous to those in Latin America: customs, language, and religion. Frequent explanations for the congenial relationship between the "twins separated at birth" emphasizes cultural and historical commonalities; as Seymour Lipset put, it, the two countries "resemble each other more than either resembles any other nation" (Lipset 1990, 212).

But these factors are not sufficient to explain the amicable state of affairs that is associated with the two countries sharing the "longest undefended border." Things actually used to be quite different. As J. L. Granatstein and Norman Hillmer have pointed out, "North America's peaceful character, its penchant for arbitration over warfare, was largely a myth. There had been wars, rebellions, bloodshed, and strife aplenty as the relations between the two peoples sorted themselves out" (in Haglund 2004, 23). Still after confederation (in 1867), Washington often perceived Ottawa as a British imperial extension; in some sectors of Canada, on the other hand, it was considered "heresy" to regard their country as a North American one (Bernard-Meunier 2005, 704n3).

However, in a similar process to the one that took place in the southern neighbors of the United States—particularly Mexico—Washington's northern neighbor came to define its identity in relationship to it. As Canadian diplomat John Holmes put it, "the USA is and always has been an essential ingredient of being Canadian. It has formed us just as being an island formed Britain" (Holmes 1981, 107–8). As in the United States–Latin America relationship, the sentiment has not run both ways. As David Haglund wrote: "No American would seek to understand who he or she 'is' by conjuring up a Canadian 'other' to serve as a referent for his or her own sense of identity. Very few Canadians are immune from the psychological need to construct an American 'other'" (Haglund 2009a, 72). It seems that hierarchy has been an intrinsic component of old North America's social structure.

With the consolidation of both polities, by the early twentieth century the bilateral relationship had acquired a manifestly friendly character. For instance, the first book titled the *North American Idea* came out in 1917, preceding Robert Pastor's tome by nearly a century. Authored by Canadian journalist James A. Macdonald, the book states: "[the] North American idea is this: The right of a Free People to govern themselves," and argues that "it is in the United States and Canada, the two self-governing American nations of the Anglo-Saxon and Anglo-Celtic blood and background, that the North American idea has had its opportunity" (Macdonald 1917, 69, 72). Interestingly, the Canada–United States relationship was contrasted, in favorable terms, of course, to the one that existed among the European powers (a restating of the idea regarding the more pacific character of the New World: "These two American democracies, are, indeed, Europe's second chance"; Macdonald 1917, 72). Incidentally, the work was also explicit on why Mexico could not be part of North America: "Mexico, indeed, shares in the geography of North America, but not in its idea. . . . Mexico does not cherish the American standards of freedom" (Macdonald 1917, 70). The North American Idea was not just an isolated thought; Canadian prime minister Robert Borden supported it and even embraced it in his foreign policy (Page 1973, 37).

During the interwar period the practice, if not the "idea," of North America was widely adopted. In 1932 Secretary of State Henry Stimson spoke of the "common outlook, common tradition, common language and literature" upon which the bilateral relationship, "unique among the great peoples of the world," had been established (Shore 1998, 355). Along the same lines, four years later President Franklin D. Roosevelt remarked that "on both sides of the line we are so accustomed to an undefended boundary three thousand miles long that we are inclined perhaps to minimize its vast importance" (in Shore 1998, 355). The feeling was of course reciprocated north of the border. Shortly before the outbreak of World War II, Prime Minister Mackenzie King commented that his country's relations with its neighbor were so intimate that for some Canadians they were "not foreign relations at all" (in Shore 1998, 352). This was the normative structure the two countries had come to develop.

Canada–United States relations became closer during the Cold War—and it was during this period that the above-mentioned "special relationship" flourished. The 1958 North American Air Defense Command (NORAD; later North American Aerospace Defense Command) was perhaps the most emblematic sign of the intimate association between the neighbors—which, by their own understanding, constituted the North American region. However, as Holmes has noted, the security organization was in fact only the consequence of the tacit alliance already existing between the two countries (Holmes 1981, 52).[8] In the economic realm, as Robert Gilpin noted in the early 1970s, "The predominant fact on the North American continent has been the emergence . . . since the end of the Second World War of a highly interdependent continental economy" (Gilpin 1974, 852). In 1971, Canadian diplomat and politician Paul Martin Sr. (father of future prime minister Paul Martin) acknowledged not only the role played by its southern neighbor's economy on his country's well-being, but also the high regard in which he held the United States, when he said: "The fact that Canada has lived and prospered for more than a century . . . is evidence to all countries of the basic decency of the United States' foreign policy" (Martin 1971, 25). US president Ronald Reagan, for his part, noted in the 1980s that his country and Canada "share[d] a responsibility for the protection of the continent we peacefully share" (Skelton 1985). It was clear that the two countries had constructed a tight social structure.

However, up to the mid-1980s Canadians were rather reluctant to join their neighbor on anything resembling a political front or a supranational body. They preferred their close association to be based on the quotidian habits and practices on both sides of the border (Holmes 1981, 23, 106–7). They felt comfortable with the regionness they had constructed with their southern neighbor, but they did not want it to translate into actorness in the world stage. Furthermore, during that decade Ottawa remained outside the hemispheric-wide compact. As Holmes put it, "the Western Hemisphere was less real to us than the Northern, and we felt little in common with the Latin Americans" (Holmes 1981, 28).

Things changed radically in the Canadian front a few years later. First came

Ottawa's about-face on bilateral commerce matters, which culminated in the 1988 United States–Canada Free Trade Agreement; then, a couple of years later, as noted, in another major reversal, Canada joined the OAS; lastly, in 1992 it entered into an economic partnership with Mexico, through NAFTA. As we will see in the next section, though, old North America's social order did not change much after the addition of Mexico to the earlier bilateral trade arrangement. Albeit NAFTA gave birth to the new North America, it arguably still makes sense to talk about Canada and the United States as a region—one that, to this date, has kept a considerable degree of regionness and a low degree of actorness.[9]

New North America

What Stephen Clarkson has called "the new North America" is about three decades old. In 1990 Mexican president Carlos Salinas proposed to his US counterpart George H. W. Bush that their countries began negotiations leading to a trade agreement—an about-face on Mexican policy toward its northern neighbor no less significant than the Canadian one that had taken place a few years earlier. Ottawa, rather reluctantly, decided to join the talks, and after an agonizing legislative process in Washington (weeks before the agreement was voted on in Congress, it seemed doomed), NAFTA went into effect on January 1, 1994.

However, at least since the 1980s a process of "silent integration" between Mexico and the United States—mainly on economic affairs—had been transpiring. As noted in the previous section, the process of economic coupling between the Canadian and US economies had been going on at least since the end of World War II. Thus, what was really new in the "new North America" was the association between the "neighbors of the neighbor," that is, between Canada and Mexico. Their relationship had been cordial but distant; the year NAFTA went into effect actually marked only the fiftieth anniversary of the establishment of diplomatic relations between them (Santa-Cruz 2012). Cultural, diplomatic, and social links between the two countries were rather weak; in the economic sphere, for instance, in 1993 Mexico sent to Canada 3.01 percent of its total exports, whereas the Canadian share sent to Mexico was 0.44 percent in the same year (World Bank 2020).

With the economic agreement, the relationship between Ottawa and Mexico City grew—but not much, in relative terms. On trade matters the above-cited indicator on the Mexican side reached 3.12 percent in 2018, whereas on the Canadian side it went up to 1.41 percent (World Bank 2020). In security affairs, Canada became marginally interested in Mexico's *problématique* (Santa-Cruz 2020). The bilateral relationship, however, remains quite limited. In contrast, both Canada's and Mexico's connection with their common neighbor has grown considerably since NAFTA was enacted: for instance, bilateral trade in goods and services between the two northernmost countries increased by 201 percent; in the case of Mexico–US commerce, it has increased by 582 percent (USTR 2020a; USTR 2020b). And then of course there is the emergence of regional (i.e., trilateral) value chains, which have been the star of the integration process; they are particularly important in the aerospace, automotive, and electronics sectors. The Mexican-US agenda has also deepened in other areas, particularly security, but this is not a trilateral affair—and the same goes for Canada-US relations in this and other issue areas, as noted by Asa McKercher in his contribution to this volume. Light interdependence and institutionalization, as that evinced by this dyad, do not a meaningful region make.

There is hardly any regionness to talk of in the new North America. In the security arena, for instance, there is no sense of common threats (James and Hristoulas 2020, 68).[10] Taking a broad understanding of security, perhaps the exception has been public health; Pastor himself noted this area as a rare instance of coordination (Pastor 2011, 162). Trilateral cooperation during the 2009 H1N1 pandemic was intense and efficient. Right after the outbreak, the three countries perceived it as a common menace and acted through previously established, shared mechanisms. David Butler-Jones, the Canadian public health director, even spoke of a "North American way" of responding to public health problems developed by the three partners (in Santa-Cruz 2017, 179). Sadly, during the 2020 COVID-19 pandemic trilateral cooperation has been rather scarce (Davidow 2021). It would seem that, as Canadian diplomat Marie Bernard-Meunier put it, "what was possible to do as a trio and what was clearly in the interest of all three countries, we have done with NAFTA. . . . Of all the arguments that can be made in favour of North American integration, the only potentially compelling one is economic" (Bernard-Meunier 2005, 705, 710).

Likewise, new North America's actorness has been minimal. The three countries practically do not operate as a bloc of any kind in the international arena. Among the rare exceptions have been a few high-level trilateral diplomatic meetings to discuss potential common positions on topics such as human rights and public health in international fora; also, the three partners participated as a bloc in a meeting on security with the Central American Security System (Santa-Cruz 2020).

It is thus not surprising that a (new) North American identity has not emerged. For instance, between 2006 and 2016 the percentage of Mexicans who identify themselves as North Americans has averaged 7 percent (in contrast to 51 percent for the Latin American option); a similarly low level of identification with the supposed region happens in the other two countries (Maldonado et al. 2018, 42; Graves 2007, 123, 126). It could hardly be otherwise, given that the action among the three countries has by and large taken place in the economic realm. As the Mexican ambassador to Washington during the NAFTA negotiations later noted, "The fact is that we [Mexico and the United States] will be neighbors forever, we are partners for the moment, and we will never be friends. For them, we lack the stature to be treated as equals. That is the difference when they look to the north and they find the Canadians [to whom] they offer the respectful treatment friendship requires" (Montaño 2004, 71). As Celia Toro notes in her chapter, when managing the border between Mexico and the United States, the northern neighbor has historically expressed its distrust of the southern one, particularly since 9/11. The Trump administration's manifest lack of respect toward its southern neighbor certainly was unprecedented in its visibility, but it fit that longer pattern.

Thus, about three decades into the new North America we are still stuck in the "dual bilateralism" that has characterized the dynamics among the three partners: United States–Canada, United States–Mexico (Pastor 2011, 139, 150; Anderson 2020, 55). Some analysts have noted that NAFTA increased "localized instances of regionalism and regionalization" along both US borders—but that hardly qualifies as a three-country *region*, which is what the new North America is supposed to be (Duina 2016, 357). The hegemonic country has shown no interest in transcending this hub-and-spokes approach—and, incidentally neither has Canada, which has opted to preserve what is left of its "special relationship" with its neighbor (Capling and Nossal 2009, 164; Bow 2011, 4). As Laura Macdonald has noted, during the negotiations leading to the agreement that replaced NAFTA, the United States–Mexico–Canada Agreement (whose name elided any regional reference), some perceived that Ottawa was "throwing Mexico under the bus" (in Macdonald 2019, 159). Mexico, for its part, did show interest in deepening the trilateral scheme in the early 2000s, but it was rebuffed by its partners. Thus, the "reflex" (per Capling and Nossal) to include North America in the group of regions noted in the introduction does not seem to be a sound one. North America has not developed a truly regional order.

Conclusions

When in 2005 Pastor posed the question of why North America was not perceived as a region, he went on to put his query in context: "Why do people tend to consider the 'Americas' as a whole—the entire Western Hemisphere—more of a region than the three countries of North America?" (Pastor 2005, 202). The context did indeed provide a good deal for a possible answer: because the former possesses a regional order the latter lacks. This might sound counterintuitive, as North America is part of the Americas; however, it lacks the normative and social structure Britain's and Spain's former colonies started to build in the early nineteenth century. That is, regardless of whether the new North America, the one sprung by NAFTA, is seen as a project of regionalism or as a process of regionalization, as long as it is not endowed with a deeper regional order its status as a politically meaningful region will remain questionable.

As I argued above, the problem of order is pervasive in human affairs. That is why it has been present, sometimes more explicitly than others, in the IR literature. The "regional turn" in the field has also dealt with the constitutive role of order in this level of analysis. But the recent emphasis on regionalism and regionalization has, on occasion, substituted the more fundamental discussion regarding the normative and social foundations of regions with the more superficial dichotomy of state-led vs. social-led (i.e., political-led vs. economic-led) projects and/or processes of regional integration. Thus, the cardinal components that make a region politically meaningful often get lost. That is why keeping track of the normative and social structures that conform a regional order is useful for elucidating whether the intense interaction among a group of contiguous states qualifies as a region—in the political sense.

The construction—or not—of a regional order is a historically contingent process. Not all geographical clusters are born equal. Some develop into regions, and some do not. As the previous pages have illustrated, cultural, economic, political, and social factors evolved differently in each of the four areas covered. Resorting to the concepts of actorness and regionness as markers of regional orders, it was possible to show how they differed from one another. Thus, regarding actorness, it is clear that both the Western Hemisphere and Latin America stand ahead of the old and the new North America; in terms of regionness, Latin America and the old North America lay ahead, while the new North America would rank last and the Western Hemisphere somewhere in between. The cursory probe regarding the existence of regional orders in the four areas should shed some light on which instances could be rightfully considered a region. Based on this, I would resist the reflex to include the new North America in the list of politically relevant regions.

Notes

I would like to thank Eric Hershberg and Tom Long for their valuable comments on earlier versions of this chapter, as well as colleagues who offered feedback during virtual seminars held over the course of this project. Thanks are due as well to Christian Cabrera and Eduardo Sánchez for research assistance.

1. For example, Anthony De Palma, *Here: A Biography of the North American Continent* (2001); Stephen Clarkson, *Does North America Exist? Governing the Continent after 9/11* (2008); and Robert A. Pastor, *The North American Idea: A Vision of a Continental Future* (2011).
2. Previous studies on subordinate systems and spheres of influence are akin to the study of regions; cf. Cantori and Spiegel 1969, 362; Hast, 2014, 13.
3. Prys 2010, 485 for first quoted material; for importance of geographic proximity cf. Buzan 2012, 22. For the rest of quotations, Buzan 2010, 23; Hurrell 1998, 535; Katzenstein 2005, 6. See also Ayoob 1999, 248.
4. The analogy here is with one of the roles allegedly played by international regimes. Cf. Krasner 1983.
5. Cf. Wendt 1999, 182; Langenhove 2003. Although unlike the intercourse of "like units" in the modern state system, regions do not have an analytically

straightforward fit in the latter; Kissinger's famous remark—"Who do I call if I want to call Europe?"—is germane here.

6. Interestingly, Jefferson referred this way to his nation—before the United States became a country "of immense size or power" (*Merriam-Webster*); cf. Van Tassell 1997, 243.

7. Cf. UN News 2014, 2/7; FAO News 2020, 1/2; SRE 2020; R. Dominguez 2015, 19. This is not to suggest that the regional order has not been weakened during the last decade; cf. Legler and Santa-Cruz 2020.

8. For a similar argument regarding the institutionalization of US hegemony in the West after World War II, see Clark 2011, 143.

9. A recent instance of this is the US-Canada Joint Statement on Climate, which states that "the United States and Canada must and will play a leadership role internationally" on the matter. Cf. White House 2016.

10. There have been some trilateral meetings among the military brass, but that has not amounted to much in terms of a trilateral security agenda. Cf. Santa-Cruz 2020.

Bibliography

Acharya, A. 2012. "Ideas, Norms, and Regional Orders." In *International Relations Theory and Regional Transformation*, edited by T. V. Paul, 183–209. Cambridge: Cambridge University Press.

Acharya, A. 2016. "Advancing Global IR: Challenges, Contentions, and Contributions." *International Studies Review* 18 (1): 4–15.

Acharya, A. 2018. *Constructing Global Order: Agency and Change in World Politics*. Cambridge: Cambridge University Press.

Anderson, G. 2003. "The Compromise of Embedded Liberalism, American Trade Remedy Law, and Canadian Softwood Lumber: Can't We All Just Get Along?" *Canadian Foreign Policy Journal* 10 (2): 87–108.

Anderson, G. 2020. *Freeing Trade in North America*. Montreal: McGill–Queen's University Press.

Ayoob, M. 1999. "From Regional System to Regional Society: Exploring Key Variables in the Construction of Regional Order." *Australian Journal of International Affairs* 53 (3): 247–60.

Banks, M. 1969. "Systems Analysis and the Study of Regions." *International Studies Quarterly* 3 (4): 335–60.

Bernard-Meunier, M. 2005. "The 'Inevitability' of North American Integration?" *International Journal* 60 (3): 703–11.

Bond, R. D. 1978. "Regionalism in Latin America: Prospects for the Latin American Economic System (SELA)." *International Organization* 32 (2): 401–23.

Bow, B. 2011. *Getting Past the Bilateral-Trilateral Debate: A Pragmatic Functionalist*

Approach to North America. Calgary, AB: Canadian Defence & Foreign Affairs Institute.

Bretherton, C., and J. Vogler. 2006. *The European Union as a Global Actor*. London: Routledge.

Bull, H. 1977. *The Anarchical Society: A Study of Order in World Politics*. London: Palgrave Macmillan.

Buzan, B. 2010. "Culture and International Society." *International Affairs* 86 (1): 1–25.

Buzan, B. 2012. "How Regions Were Made, and the Legacies for World Politics: An English School Reconnaissance." In *International Relations Theory and Regional Transformation*, edited by T. V. Paul, 22–46. Cambridge: Cambridge University Press.

Cantori, L. J., and S. L. Spiegel. 1969. "International Regions: A Comparative Approach to Five Subordinate Systems." *International Studies Quarterly* 13 (4): 361–80.

Capling, A., and K. R. Nossal. 2009. "The Contradictions of Regionalism in North America." *Review of International Studies* 35 (S1): 147–67.

Carrillo, V. 2018. "México en la Unión de las Reúblicas Americanas: El panamericanismo y la política exterior mexicana, 1889–1942." PhD diss., El Colegio de México, Mexico.

Clark, I. 2011. *Hegemony in International Society*. Oxford: Oxford University Press.

Clarkson, S. 2008. *Does North America Exist? Governing the Continent after 9/11*. Toronto: University of Toronto Press.

Corrales, J., and R. E. Feinberg. 1999. "Regimes of Cooperation in the Western Hemisphere: Power, Interests, and Intellectual Traditions." *International Studies Quarterly* 43 (1): 1–36.

Davidow, J. 2021. "Preparándose para Joe." *Reforma*, January 6, 2021. https://busquedas.gruporeforma.com/reforma/Documento/Impresa.aspx?id=7542581.

De Palma, A. 2001. *Here: A Biography of the North American Continent*. Cambridge: Public Affairs.

Dickins, A., and J. C. Allen. 1858. *Documents, Legislative and Executive, of the Congress of the United States, from the First Session of the First Congress to the Second Session of the Thirty-Fifth Congress, Inclusive: Commencing March 4, 1789, and Ending March 3, 1859*. Vol. V. Washington, DC: Gales & Seaton.

Domínguez, J. 2007. "International Cooperation in Latin America: The Design of Regional Institutions by Slow Accretion." In *Crafting Cooperation, Regional International Institutions in Comparative Perspective*, edited by A. Acharya and A. Johnston, 83–128. Cambridge: Cambridge University Press.

Dominguez, R. 2015. *EU Foreign Policy towards Latin America*. Houndmills, UK: Palgrave Macmillan.

Duina, F. 2016. "North America and the Transatlantic Area." In *The Oxford Handbook of Comparative Regionalism*, edited by T. A. Börzel and T. Risse, 133–53. Oxford: Oxford University Press.

Dunne, T. 2008. The English School. In *The Oxford Handbook of International Relations*, edited by C. Reus-Smit and D. Snidal, 267–85. Oxford: Oxford University Press.

FAO News. 2020. "26 Latin American and Caribbean Countries Coordinate to Support the Regular Functioning of the Food System during the COVID-19 Crisis." April 3, 2020. http://www.fao.org/americas/noticias/ver/en/c/1269548/.

Gilpin, R. 1974. "Integration and Disintegration on the North American Continent." *International Organization* 28 (4): 851–74.

Gobat, M. 2013. "The Invention of Latin America: A Transnational History of Anti Imperialism, Democracy, and Race." *American Historical Review* 118 (5): 1345–75.

González, G. 2010. "Un siglo de política exterior mexicana (1910–2010). Del nacionalismo revolucionario a la intemperie global." In *México 2010, el juicio del siglo*, edited by M. A. Casar and G. González, 231–74. Mexico City: Taurus.

Gottman, J. 1951. "Geography and International Relations." *World Politics* 3 (2): 153–73.

Grandin, G. 2012. "The Liberal Traditions in the Americas: Rights, Sovereignty, and the Origins of Liberal Multilateralism." *American Historical Review* 117 (1): 68–91.

Graves, F. 2007. "North America: Mosaic, Community, or Fortress?" *Norteamérica* 2 (2): 105–29.

Haglund, D. G. 2004. "The Comparative 'Continentalization' of Security and Defence Policy in North America and Europe: Canadian Multilateralism in a Unipolar World?" *Journal of Canadian Studies* 38 (2): 9–28.

Haglund, D. G. 2009a. "The US-Canada Relationship: How 'Special' Is America's Oldest Unbroken Alliance?" In *America's "Special Relationships": Foreign and Domestic Aspects of the Politics of Alliance*, edited by J. Dumbrell and A. R. Schäfer, 60–75. New York: Routledge.

Haglund, D. G. 2009b. "And the Beat Goes On: 'Identity' and Canadian Foreign Policy." In *Canada Among Nations: 100 Years of Canadian Foreign Policy*, edited by R. Bothwell and J. Daudelin, 343–67. Montreal: McGill–Queen's University Press.

Hast, S. 2014. *Spheres of Influence in International Relations: History, Theory and Politics*. New York: Routledge.

Hemmer, C., and P. J. Katzenstein. 2002. "Why Is There No NATO in Asia? Collective Identity, Regionalism, and the Origins of Multilateralism." *International Organization* 56 (3): 575–607.

Hettne, B., and F. Söderbaum. 2000. "Theorising the Rise of Regionness." *New Political Economy* 5 (3): 457–72.

Hettne, B. 2005. "Beyond the 'New' Regionalism." *New Political Economy* 10 (4): 543–71.

Hitlin, S. 2014. "Social Psychological Ingredients for a Sociology of Morality." In *The Palgrave Handbook of Altruism, Morality, and Social Solidarity: Formulating a Field of Study*, edited by V. Jeffries, 195–217. New York: Palgrave Macmillan.

Hoffman, S. 1966. "Report of the Conference on Conditions of World Oder: June 12–19, 1965, Villa Serbelloni, Bellagio, Italy." *Daedalus* 95 (2): 455–78.

Holmes, J. W. 1981. *Life with Uncle: The Canadian-American Relationship.* Toronto: University of Toronto Press.

Hurrell, A. 1995. "Explaining the Resurgence of Regionalism in World Politics." *Review of International Studies* 21 (4): 331–58.

Hurrell, A. 1998. Security in Latin America. *International Affairs* 74 (3): 529–46.

Hurrell, A. 2005. "The Regional Dimension in International Relations Theory." In *Global Politics of Regionalism: Theory and Practice,* edited by M. Farrell, B. Hettne, and L. V. Langenhove, 38–53. London: Pluto Press.

IACHR. 2013. *United Nations Organization,* March 21, 2013. https://www.oas.org/en/iachr/activities/un.asp.

James, P., and A. Hristoulas. 2020. "North America: The Peaceful Region." In *The Rise of Regions: Conflict and Cooperation,* edited by J. Kugler and R. Tammen, 55–76. London: Rowman and Littlefield.

Kacowicz, A. M. 2005. *The Impact of Norms in International Society: The Latin American Experience, 1881–2001.* Notre Dame, IN: University of Notre Dame Press.

Katzenstein, P. J. 2005. *A World of Regions: Asia and Europe in the American Imperium.* Ithaca, NY: Cornell University Press.

Kissinger, H. 2014. *World Order: Reflections on the Character of Nations and the Course of History.* London: Allen Lane.

Krasner, S. D. 1983. "Structural Causes and Regime Consequences: Regimes as Intervening Variables." In *International Regimes,* edited by S. D. Krasner, 1–22. Ithaca, NY: Cornell University Press.

Kratochwil, F. 1978. *International Order and Foreign Policy.* Boulder, CO: Westview Press.

Kratochwil, F. 1982. "On the Notion of 'Interest' in International Relations." *International Organization* 36 (1): 1–30.

Lake, D. A., and P. M. Morgan. 1997. *Regional Orders: Building Security in a New World.* University Park: Pennsylvania State University Press.

Langenhove, L. V. 2003. "Theorising Regionhood." UNU/CRIS e-working papers W2003/1.

Legler, T., and A. Santa-Cruz. 2020. *Two Decades of Hemispheric Order Upheaval in the Americas.* Mexico City: Instituto Matías Romero.

Lewis, M. W., and K. E. Wigen. 1997. *The Myth of Continents: A Critique of Metageography.* Berkeley: University of California Press.

Lipset, S. M. 1990. *The Values and Institutions of the United States and Canada.* New York: Canadian American Committee.

Long, T. 2020. "Historical Antecedents and Post-World War II Regionalism in the Americas." *World Politics* 72 (2): 214–53.

Macdonald, J. A. 1917. *The North American Idea.* New York: Fleming H. Revell Company.

Macdonald, L. 2019. "Stronger Together? Canada-Mexico Relations and the NAFTA Renegotiations." *Canadian Foreign Policy Journal* 26 (2): 152–66.

Maldonado, G., K. Marín, G. González, and J. Schiavon. 2018. *Los mexicanos ante los retos del mundo: Opinión pública, líderes y política exterior*. Mexico City: CIDE.

Martin, P. 1971. "The American Impact on Canada." In *The Star-Spangled Beaver: 24 Canadians Look South*, edited by J. Redekop, 25–35. Toronto: Peter Martin Associates Limited.

McKenna, P. 1999. "Canada, the United States, and the Organization of American States." *The American Review of Canadian Studies* 29 (3): 473–93.

Medinaceli, B. 1862. *Proyecto de confederación de las repúblicas latino-americanas, ó sèa, Sistema de paz perpétua en el Nuevo Mundo*. Sucre, BO: Tipografía de Pedro España.

Merriam-Webster. https://www.merriam-webster.com/.

Montaño, J. 2004. *Misión en Washington 1993–1995. De la aprobación del TLCAN al préstamo de rescate*. Mexico City: Planeta.

Morgenthau, H. 1948. *Politics among Nations: The Struggle for Power and Peace*. New York: McGraw-Hill.

New York Tribune. 1864. "XXXVIIIth Congress—First Session." *New York Tribune*, January 8, 1864.

Nye, J. S. 1969. "United States Policy toward Regional Organization." *International Organization* 23 (3): 719–40.

O'Gorman, E. 1977. "La gran dicotomía americana: Angloamérica e Iberoamérica." *Vuelta* (September): 4–7.

Page, D. M. 1973. "Canada as the Exponent of North American Idealism." *American Review of Canadian Studies* 3 (2): 30–46.

Pastor, R. A. 1984. "U.S. Immigration Policy and Latin America: In Search of the 'Special Relationship.'" *Latin American Research Review* 19 (3): 35–56.

Pastor, R. A. 2005. "North America and the Americas: Integration among Unequal Partners." In *Global Politics of Regionalism: Theory and Practice*, edited by M. Farrell, B. Hettne, and L. V. Langenhove, 202–21. London: Pluto Press.

Pastor, R. A. 2011. *The North American Idea: A Vision of a Continental Future*. Oxford: Oxford University Press.

Paul, T. V. 2012. "Regional Transformation in International Relations." In *International Relations Theory and Regional Transformation*, edited by T. V. Paul, 3–21. Cambridge: Cambridge University Press.

Pouliot, V. 2012. "Regional Security Practices and Russian-Atlantic Relations." In *International Relations Theory and Regional Transformation*, edited by T. V. Paul, 210–30. Cambridge: Cambridge University Press.

Prys, M. 2010. "Hegemony, Domination, Detachment: Differences in Regional Powerhood." *International Studies Review* 12 (4): 479–504.

Rengger, N. J. 2000. *International Relations, Political Theory and the Problem of Order*. New York: Routledge.

Reus-Smit, C. 2017. "Cultural Diversity and International Order." *International Organization* 71 (4): 851–85.

Rojas, R. 2009. *Las repúblicas de aire: Utopía y desencanto en la revolución de Hispanoamérica.* Mexico City: Taurus.

Santa-Cruz, A. 2005. *International Elections Monitoring, Sovereignty, and the Western Hemisphere Idea: The Emergence of an International Norm.* New York: Routledge.

Santa-Cruz, A. 2012. *Mexico-United States Relations: The Semantics of Sovereignty.* New York: Routledge.

Santa-Cruz, A. 2017. "Integración regional con signos vitales: La cooperación en salud pública en América del Norte." In *Integración en América del Norte (1994–2016),* edited by M. Tawil, I. Aguilar Barajas, N. A. Fuentes Flores, J. A. Le Clercq, S. Núñez García, and L. Ruano Gómez, 169–86. Mexico City: Colegio de México.

Santa-Cruz, A. 2020. "¿Volver al futuro? La renegociación del TLCAN y la relación en materia de seguridad en la relación México-Estados Unidos." In *La reestructuración de Norteamérica a través del libre comercio: del TLCAN al TMEC,* edited by O. Contreras, G. Vega, and C. Ruiz, 465–79. Mexico City: El Colegio de México.

Shore, S. M. 1998. "No Fences Make Good Neighbors: The Development of the Canadian-US Security Community, 1871–1940." In *Security Communities,* edited by E. Adler and M. Barnett, 333–67. Cambridge: Cambridge University Press.

Sikkink, K. 1997. "Reconceptualizing Sovereignty in the Americas: Historical Precursors and Current Practices." *Houston Journal of International Law* 19 (3): 705–29.

Sikkink, K. 2019. *Evidence for Hope: Making Human Rights Work in the 21st Century.* Princeton, NJ: Princeton University Press.

Skelton, G. 1985. "Reagan, Mulroney at 'Shamrock Summit': U.S., Canada Agree to Fight Acid Rain." *Los Angeles Times,* March 18, 1985. https://www.latimes.com/archives/laxpm-1985-03-18-mn-22399-story.html.

Solingen, E., and J. Malnight. 2016. "Globalization, Domestic Politics, and Regionalism." In *The Oxford Handbook of Comparative Regionalism,* edited by T. A. Börzel and T. Risse, 64–86. Oxford: Oxford University Press.

SRE. 2020. "Joint Statement of the Special Video Conference of China and Latin American and Caribbean Countries' Foreign Ministers on COVID-19."

Suchman, M. 1995. "Managing Legitimacy: Strategic and Institutional Approaches." *Academy of Management Review* 30 (3): 571–610.

Tulchin, J. 1993. "La iniciativa para las Américas: ¿Gesto vacío, astuta maniobra estratégica, o notable giro en las relaciones hemisféricas?" In *América Latina y la iniciativa para las Américas,* edited by F. Rojas, 53–80. Santiago, CL: FLACSO.

UN News. 2014. "Leaders from Latin America, Caribbean Region Urge Action to Erase Inequality, Spur Development." September 24, 2014. https://news.un.org/en/story/2014/09/478492.

USTR. 2020a. "Canada: U.S.-Canada Trade Facts. Office of the United States Trade Representative." https://ustr.gov/countries-regions/americas/canada.

USTR. 2020b. "Mexico: U.S.-Mexico Trade Facts. Office of the United States Trade Representative." https://ustr.gov/countries-regions/americas/mexico.

Van Tassell, D. H. 1997. "Operational Code Evolution: How Central America Came to Be 'Our Backyard' in U.S. Culture." In *Culture & Foreign Policy*, ed. V. M. Hudson, 231–61. Boulder, CO: Lynne Rienner Publishers.

Victoria, G. 1986 [1826]. *Guadalupe Victoria: Correspondencia diplomática*. Mexico City: SRE.

Waltz, K. 1979. *Theory of International Politics*. New York: McGraw-Hill.

Wendt, A. 1992. "Anarchy Is what States Make of It: The Social Construction of Power Politics." *International Organization* 46 (2): 391–425.

Wendt, A. 1999. *Social Theory of International Politics*. Cambridge: Cambridge University Press.

Whitaker, A. P. 1954. *The Western Hemisphere Idea: Its Rise and Decline*. Ithaca, NY: Cornell University Press.

White House. 2016. "US–Canada Joint Statement on Climate, Energy, and Arctic Leadership."

Williamson, J. 2000. "What Should the World Bank Think about the Washington Consensus?" *World Bank Research Observer* 15 (2): 251–64.

World Bank. 2020. "Trade Balance, Exports and Imports by Country [World Integrated Trade Solution]." https://wits.worldbank.org/.

CHAPTER TWO

Ménage à Deux

Canada and the Limits of the North American Idea

Asa McKercher

IN HIS 2011 manifesto *The North American Idea*, Robert Pastor laid out a forward-thinking agenda to link Canada, Mexico, and the United States together in a close North American community. Amid growing regionalism in other areas of the world and a slate of transnational issues requiring attention, he contended that it made sense for the three North American countries to work together to better harness their continent's resources. In the decade that followed, Pastor's idea of trilateralism encountered considerable opposition. While much attention has focused on the nativist and protectionist attitudes embodied in Trumpism in the United States, trilateralism faced an uphill battle even in Canada, where many policy and opinion makers looked warily upon further integration among the three North American countries. Canadian skepticism has centered upon Mexico, long viewed—despite brief periods of support for trilateralism—as a distraction from the all-important relationship with the United States. Unsurprisingly, then, amid the Trump-induced renegotiation of the North American Free Trade Agreement (NAFTA), there were calls, most prominently from former prime minister Stephen Harper (Panetta 2017), for Ottawa to cut Mexico City loose and conclude a bilateral deal with Washington.

This Canadian preference for bilateralism is not new. Rather, it is deeply engrained in Canadian attitudes about North America as a region. A century before Pastor, Canadian journalist James A. Macdonald authored his own study of *The North American Idea*. Unlike Pastor, Macdonald's conception of North America ended at the Rio Grande, a viewpoint that was hardly unique among Canadians nor one that has dissipated. If one understands a region as a political and social construct, it becomes clear that Canadians have often constructed North America in a narrower and often bilateral sense. Examinations of Canadian policy toward North America or of the state of North American regionalism must acknowledge the socially constructed nature of the very idea of region—ably explored by the editors in their introduction and by Arturo Santa-Cruz in the previous chapter—and the resulting limits on Canadian thinking about what constitutes "North America." Indeed, as Santa-Cruz notes, "regions, like the state and the international system, do not simply exist or happen. They are socially constructed." For many Canadian officials, the North American region was defined in terms that excluded Mexico—let alone the countries of Central America.

Examining Canadian foreign policy makers' ideas about North America over the past century, this paper historicizes current debates about the future of North America, showing that Canadians have consistently rejected efforts to create a trilateral approach to continental affairs. This attitude—reflected in the policies of Liberal and Conservative governments alike—stems from a long-standing consensus rooted in cultural attitudes that have purposefully defined "North America" as consisting of Canada and the United States, with Mexico as an "other"—poor, fractious, and non-white (Castro-Rea 2012, 1). This narrow understanding of the North American region has overlapped with a sense in Ottawa that wider contacts with Mexico City through a trilateral framework might undermine a perceived special relationship (Haglund 2009) with Washington. Taken together, anxiety over Mexico's reception among US officials and Canadian limitations in defining the North American region have not only stymied the development of a trilateral relationship, but also they have limited the growth of Mexican-Canadian ties, leaving an "unfinished agenda" (Rozental and Bugailiskis 2012). Despite some brief moments of trilateralism, Canadians have preferred dealing with the United States and Mexico à deux just as they have conceptualized a North America limited in scope.

Roots of Bilateralism

Speaking at Vanderbilt University's undergraduate convocation in 1917, Canadian journalist James A. Macdonald addressed "the North American Idea," his phrase defining the unique relationship between Canada and the United States. From the daily interchange between Canadians and Americans to the avoidance of coercive diplomacy by either Ottawa or Washington—the early 1900s had witnessed several bilateral agreements over resource sharing—Macdonald contrasted this situation and the unguarded border with the bloody conflict in Europe. Between Canada and the United States, he proclaimed, lay "more than five thousand miles of war's neglected opportunity!" (Macdonald 1917, 69). In his remarks, Macdonald was clear to exclude Mexico. What he saw as the "civilized internationalism of the North American continent" stretched "from the Mexican border to the North Pole" (Macdonald 1917, 70), and although Mexico shared "in the geography of North America," it differed too much culturally and politically from Canada and the United States. The North American idea, Macdonald affirmed, was rooted in Canadians and Americans' "Anglo-Saxon and Anglo-Celtic blood and background" (Macdonald 1917, 189), which were absent in Mexicans, who, as a result, lacked "standards of freedom" (Macdonald 1917, 72) that formed the bedrock of Canada-US relations. Macdonald's definition of North

America rested on the pseudoscientific racism of the era, which categorized countries and continents—including "Latin America" (Tenorio Trillo 2017)—according to cultural identity. Here, this culturally defined idea of North America as a region consisting of two members of the so-called Anglosphere of English-speaking nations (Vucetic 2011)—omitting French Canadians and other minorities in both countries—clearly and purposefully excluded Mexico.

Macdonald's conception of the North American region was widely accepted in Canada, at least among the Anglophone elite. For instance, in their 1938 overview of Canadian foreign policy, Robert A. MacKay and Benjamin Rogers—two future stars of the postwar Canadian foreign service—saw Canada as "a North American country" but confined their vision of North America to Canada and the United States (MacKay and Rogers 1938, 5). Similarly, a decade later, Vincent Massey, formerly Canadian ambassador in Washington and high commissioner in London, explained in *Foreign Affairs* that Canada had little interest in involving itself in Latin American affairs, in part due to geographical distance, and in part because of the "striking cultural differences between the nations of North and South America" (Massey 1948, 694). And Massey's conception of North America excluded Mexico, which, evidently for cultural reasons, was part of a different region. If Anglophone Canadians felt little affection for Mexico, among French Canadians the situation was markedly different, with Quebecois nationalists in particular finding common cause and cultural ties with Mexicans (Demers 2014). But in official circles in Ottawa, the preference to confine North America to the United States and Canada was strong: "The United States is the only American nation with which we must take joint action" (Massey 1948, 696), Massey explained, adding elsewhere that Ottawa's priority lay in cultivating good relations with Washington by building on the fact that no other country enjoyed "such close and friendly contacts with the United States as we do" (Massey 1947). As Massey was emphasizing, Canada had a special relationship with the United States.

This special relationship was the product of the Second World War. The conflict accelerated Canadian-American interdependence in economic and military spheres, cementing intergovernmental ties. As officials characterized it, this trend was "an historically inevitable development" that came about "more quickly, with less of a bargaining or of a bullying spirit involved in the negotiations, and with greater and more mutual satisfaction in the results" (American and Far Eastern Division 1942) than might otherwise have been the case absent the pressure of war and "the personal friendship" of Prime Minister William Lyon Mackenzie King and President Franklin Delano Roosevelt. Close cooperation continued into peacetime, helped by a booming continental economy but also the dawning Cold War.

Reaching out to Mexico

Against the background of deepening Canadian-American relations, Canada took the step of establishing diplomatic relations with Mexico, doing so in 1944 amid a wartime expansion of contacts with Latin American countries. Canada's objective was to find new markets outside of Nazi-occupied Europe, and Mexico loomed large. The country, wrote Hugh Keenleyside, the first Canadian ambassador in Mexico City, was "the most important potential market in America—apart from the United States" (Canadian Embassy, Mexico City 1945). However, he recognized that among Canadians, including in government circles, the tendency was "to think of Mexico as 'being in the US sphere' and consequently not worth very much Canadian effort." In short, to Canadian officials, Mexico's geographic proximity was a blessing and a curse.

Keenleyside's observation about the limits of Canadian interest was correct, and over the next decade and a half—the so-called golden years of Canada's postwar internationalism—Ottawa paid little attention to Mexico or Latin America. Amid Cold War crises and upheavals wrought by the formal decolonization of Europe's empires, Canadian attention lay elsewhere. The sole exception was a five-week trade mission through the region undertaken in 1953 by Trade and Commerce Minister C. D. Howe. Mexico was the final stop on Howe's tour, the nature of which encapsulated the extent of Canadian interest. The contrast between the economic focus on Latin America and the broader base of Canada-US relations was stark; where Canadians saw themselves as sharing a region with the United States, Mexico and Latin America fell well outside that. The 1950s saw the further drawing together of Canada and the United States, from continental defense efforts to the formation of a joint cabinet committee to manage the massive levels of bilateral trade and investment. This close cooperation created anxiety among some Canadians. In 1955, for instance, senior diplomats worried about the bogey of "continentalism" (Léger 1955), with a "continental approach" to economic matters tying Canada too closely to its southern neighbor and undermining the broader international effort to liberalize trade (Department of External Affairs 1955). Here, continentalism was used in its historic sense, referring purely to Canadian integration with the United States. Mexico's exclusion from this well-established, circumscribed sense of the continent clearly showcased the limited nature of Canadian understandings of their region. Fears of continentalism had, for instance, led Canadian voters to reject a free trade agreement with the United States in the 1911 federal election. Similarly, in 1948, Prime Minister King had rejected a draft customs union negotiated between Canadian and US diplomats. As he told his successor, Louis St. Laurent, "while it might be sound economically," the agreement "would be fatal politically" (King 1948).

Early Trilateralism

While in Canada continentalism centered on relations with the United States, in Washington a different continental notion emerged when, in mid-1955, State Department officials considered the efficacy of arranging for Canadian prime minister Louis St. Laurent and US president Dwight Eisenhower to travel to Mexico City to meet Mexican president Adolfo Ruiz Cortines and discuss "problems of continental interest" (Dulles 1955). Passing on the recommendation to Eisenhower, Secretary of State John Foster Dulles noted that the meeting could serve as a trial effort toward "establishing some sort of a three-nation board" and arranging periodic trilateral meetings of the heads of government. When the idea was eventually raised with Canadian officials, they delayed responding for several months, eventually voicing considerable skepticism. As Arnold Heeney, Canada's Washington ambassador, explained to Dulles, Ottawa resented an effort "to equate the relations between the United States and Canada and the United States and Mexico" (Canadian Embassy, Washington 1956a). Canadians, he added, "were naturally somewhat jealous of the especially intimate association" with the US government. In the view of Canadian officials, expanded ties with Mexico risked the special relationship.

These doubts aside, St. Laurent eventually agreed to meet his US and Mexican counterparts on the grounds of not wishing to offend Eisenhower. Still, the Canadians had little time for "the rather artificial framework of North American continental affairs" (Pearson 1956) and ensured that the summit at White Sulfur Springs, Georgia, consisted of two overlapping bilateral meetings, with a brief trilateral tour d'horizon. During the trilateral session, Eisenhower made a pitch for "the moral support of Canada and Mexico" (Canadian Embassy, Washington 1956b) and stated that he "would like to see the North American continent [act] as a unit in its intellectual and moral approach to world problems." Confronted with this bold approach, St. Laurent demurred, and there was no follow-up action on the US president's idea of building a more expansive North American region.

Still, the White Sulfur Springs summit was an important milestone in Canada-Mexico relations, marking the first meeting of a Canadian prime minister and Mexican president. This development was not lost on observers. Asked by a reporter why Canadian prime ministers had not shown more interest in Mexico to that point, Canada's spokesperson explained, in a comment revealing of both Canadians' preoccupation with the United States and their conception of Mexico's value, "It's a long way off, and en route to Mexico there's Florida and other places to spend the winter" (White House 1956). Offering a different explanation, Canadian foreign minister Lester Pearson put the matter more succinctly: when asked what Canada and Mexico had in common, he quipped, "the USA" (Ford 1982). Canada's foremost statesperson, a man synonymous with Canadian postwar internationalism, had little time for Mexico. Interestingly, while official Ottawa showed little enthusiasm for Eisenhower's continental push, the Canadian press took the opposite view. The trilateral approach was "a good thing, worth repeating at regular intervals" (Vancouver *Daily Province* 1956), a welcome example of "continental diplomacy" (Halifax *Chronicle-Herald* 1956), and an important corrective to the three countries' tendency to act "as though they were on different planets" (*Edmonton Journal* 1956). Whatever the merits of the case for a trilateral continentalism, Canadian authorities prioritized their special relationship with Washington.

Sleeping with an Elephant

Then came a shock in 1957: Canada's Liberal government, in power since 1935, was ousted by John Diefenbaker's Progressive Conservatives. A fierce nationalist, Diefenbaker decried the Liberals' longtime approach to the United States, one, he contended, that had transformed Canada into "a virtual forty-ninth economic state in the American union" (Newman 1956). To reverse this trend, the Tories sought to expand Canada's economic horizons beyond the United States. Latin America featured prominently in this strategy, a result of which was the first official visit by a Mexican president to Canada (1959) and the first visit by a Canadian prime minister to Mexico (1960). These trips were important milestones in that bilateral relationship, and Diefenbaker relished his voyage, during which he recognized that Mexico was one of three "North American neighbours" (Beaulne 1960). But these exchanges saw no movement toward any trilateral activity, and bilateral ties remained largely economic. "Canadians," Diefenbaker recognized, "seldom look beyond the United States" (Diefenbaker 1960). Moreover, as he complained, Americans had a tendency "to treat Canada like Mexico" (Macmillan 1957), a comment indicating indignation that US officials might put Canadians on the same plane as Latin Americans, but also a sense—one he shared with successive generations of Canadian foreign policy makers—of Ottawa's unique ties with Washington.

The notion of a special Canada-US relationship took a battering over the following decade, amid differences over the economic embargo of Cuba and the Vietnam War, the saga of Ottawa's acceptance of nuclear weapons, and rising Canadian economic nationalism. While US and Canadian officials proved to be "tolerant allies" (Donaghy 2002), unwilling to upend the bilateral status quo, the tensions caused some concerns about the state of play. In 1967, for instance, A. E. Ritchie, a senior Canadian diplomat overseeing relations with Lyndon Johnson's administration, congratulated Saul Rae on the latter's appointment as ambassador to Mexico. "It should be a pleasant and interesting posting," Ritchie wrote, "particularly while a Texan President is in the White House and is taking special interest in Mexico (certainly more than in Canada)" (Ritchie 1967). One sees here the same sense of jealously that a later generation of Canadian officials felt when President George W. Bush paid his first foreign visit to

Mexico, not Canada. Importantly, there was little official interest in cultivating relations with Mexico in order to offset US power. With Lester Pearson as prime minister from 1963 to 1968—and despite the upheaval of the sixties—Canada remained wedded to the special relationship.

Sparring between Washington and Ottawa continued throughout the Pierre Trudeau era (1968–1984), as Canadian nationalists sought to reassert sovereignty over Canada's culture, economy, and natural resources. The United States was the target of these efforts, and Trudeau famously summed up the zeitgeist in remarks to the Washington Press Club: "Living next to you is in some ways like sleeping with an elephant. No matter how friendly and even-tempered is the beast, if I can call it that, one is affected by every twitch and grunt" (Granatstein and Bothwell 1990, 51). Canadian concerns over the grasping nature of US influence in their country raised bilateral tensions, as did the Trudeau's government's outreach to communist Cuba and China, its cuts to military spending, and—under domestic pressure—its implementation of protectionist economic and cultural measures. Complaining of that "son of a bitch Trudeau," President Richard Nixon recognized that "Canada has its own right to its destiny and no Canadian politician could survive without that ideology," but added, "we have to look out for our own interests" (Nixon 1971). Clearly the Canada-US special relationship was under strain. Nixon himself announced its end during a speech to a joint session of the Canadian Parliament in 1972 (Nixon 1972).

As for Mexico, it figured prominently in Trudeau's efforts to reach out to the Global South, and Canada hosted visits by Mexican presidents Luis Echeverría (1973) and López Portillo (1980), while Trudeau paid state visits to Mexico in 1976 and 1982. Moreover, modeled on similar bodies formed by Canada with the United States and Japan, in 1971, Ottawa and Mexico City created a joint ministerial committee on economic issues, which met in 1973, 1977, and 1981. These meetings of ministers and senior officials were an important sign of increasing bilateral economic activity. And it was the tendency to view Mexico through an economic lens that typified Canadians' views of their southernmost North American neighbor. During his 1976 visit to Mexico City, Trudeau recognized that "Canada and Mexico occupy the same continent" (Trudeau 1976) and were separated "by the world's most advanced economy." Even though they shared the "experience of dealing at close quarters, and in many significant spheres of endeavour, with that economy," the ideas of a common approach to dealing with the United States or of a trilateral framework to balance US power were beyond Trudeau's government. A suggestion along these lines came from Jack Pickersgill, a longtime civil servant, member of Parliament (MP), and Liberal Party insider, who in 1973 wrote to Canadian foreign minister Mitchell Sharp to recount a recent visit to Mexico. Describing it as "a North American country oriented to the rest of this continent and not southward" (Pickersgill 1973), he outlined the common cause of Canadians and Mexicans in resisting US cultural and economic influence. To this end, Pickersgill urged nurturing economic ties with Mexico as well as finding "a common political interest, so little developed, to consult each other on relations with the United States and to support each other in Washington." While foresighted, Pickersgill's suggestion found little purchase in official Ottawa, where, despite the Trudeau-era tensions with Washington, faith remained in the special relationship.

A North American Accord?

The Canadian preference for the North American status quo was made evident during Ronald Reagan's presidency. In November 1979, the conservative icon launched his campaign for the Republican nomination for presidential candidate by calling for a "North American accord" (Reagan 1979). Committing to convening a meeting with Canadian and Mexican officials to "sit in on high level planning sessions with us, as partners, mutually concerned about the future of our Continent," Reagan stated—in comments that, three decades later, few US conservatives would dare to voice—a goal of ensuring the continent-wide movement of people and commerce. "Within the borders of this North American continent," he proclaimed, "are the food, resources, technology and developed territory which, properly managed, could dramatically improve the quality of life of all its inhabitants." A bold idea, it was, as Canadian diplomats found when they inquired about it, "vague and still in conceptual form" (Canadian Consulate, New York 1979). Following talks with Reagan campaign officials, the Canadian embassy in Washington concluded that it was simply "an effective campaign ploy" tapping into the "widespread positive American attitude towards Canada" (Canadian Embassy, Washington 1979).

Campaign politics aside, Reagan evidently felt strongly about the accord. Soon after his election win he told one Canadian journalist of the need to draw North America "more closely together" (Reagan 1980), for amid a coming decade filled with challenges, "close cooperation among the United States, Canada, and Mexico can result in a lasting contribution to world peace." Weeks later, Alexander Haig, Reagan's nominee for secretary of state, affirmed at his Senate confirmation hearing that the president-elect's "first priority" was the improvement of relations with Mexico and Canada (Canadian Embassy, Washington 1981a). For the Republican administration, there was some sense of a regional agglomeration wherein the three North American countries could cooperate together.

With the North American accord outliving the election campaign, Canadian officials sought to dissuade the incoming administration from pursuing the notion of an expanded regional concept. It was clear that Reagan was keen on emphasizing US dealings with Canada and Mexico, but in the view of the Canadian embassy in Washington, "trilateralism as such is not [a] desirable goal" (Canadian Embassy, Washington 1981b). Instead, the embassy advised using the momentum around improving North American relations for Canada's own purposes, to "perhaps try to sustain symbolism a trois while milking mechanism a deux." Thankfully for the Canadians Mexico's government also showed little enthusiasm for the accord, and in a phone call with the new US president, Prime Minister Trudeau told Reagan simply that Canada welcomed his interest in improving bilateral ties with both of its North American neighbors (MacGuigan 1981). The idea of North American integration was out of step with the nationalist zeitgeist in Canada, and, as in the past, trilateralism seemingly threatened Canadian access in Washington. Meeting with Haig shortly after Reagan's inauguration, Canadian foreign minister Mark MacGuigan stressed the "special relationship which exists between Canada and the USA" (Department of External Affairs 1981a). When Reagan and Trudeau met for the first time during the former's visit to Ottawa in March 1981, the prime minister admitted that tripartite meetings with the Mexican president "might be useful to discuss 'North America and the world'" (Department of External Affairs, 1981b), and the president assured his Canadian counterpart that he had no interest in a "form of common market." This conversation was the last time these two leaders discussed Reagan's accord, which was subsumed by mutual recrimination between Ottawa and Washington on a host of issues. The Reagan-Trudeau period was ill-timed for new region-building initiatives.

Toward NAFTA

Just over a decade later, Mexico, Canada, and the United States agreed to the North American Free Trade Agreement. NAFTA was the product of unique circum-stances. First, came the 1988 Canada-US Free Trade Agreement (CUSFTA), the result of Brian Mulroney's efforts to improve the post-Trudeau state of Canada-US relations. As he had promised shortly after his election win in 1984, "Good relations, super relations, with the US will be the cornerstone of our foreign policy" (Urquhart 1984). Seeking to preserve if not expand Canadian access to its most important market made economic sense, particularly with rising protectionism in Congress. Despite more than two decades of nationalist concern with reliance on the Americans, Canadian trade with the United States remained entrenched: in 1971, the United States accounted for 67 percent of Canadian exports and 70 percent of imports; in 1984, as Trudeau left office, the numbers had grown to 76 percent of exports and 71 percent of imports (Hart 2002, 282, 365). Given this tangible marker of the importance of the United States to Canada, the preference for a bilateral trade agreement—and wider prioritizing of the bilateral relationship—is hardly a surprise. The idea of a free trade deal itself had gained prominence in a 1984 report published by the Trudeau-appointed Royal Commission on the Economic Union and Development Prospects for Canada.

While it made economic sense, CUSFTA sparked considerable nationalist opposition in Canada, leading to a bruising election on the issue in 1988. The Mulroney
government's victory—in parliamentary seats, but not the popular vote—came two
weeks after Reagan's vice president, George H. W. Bush, won his own electoral contest. Mulroney and Bush established an easy rapport, and after less than a year in
office, the president called his Canadian counterpart to sound him out on an informal
get-together with the Mexican president to discuss mutual economic issues. Mindful
of Mulroney's domestic situation, Bush was careful to note that he "did not want to
give the impression of pushing Canada into some sort of North American trading
block" (Bush 1989). For his part, Mulroney welcomed the idea, admitting that "Canada
is guilty of neglecting its southern neighbors, instead focusing all of its attention on
Europe and the Pacific." This was no offhand comment: under Mulroney's government,
Canada entered the Organization of American States, a sign that he was committed to
engaging Latin America, Mexico included. For all the nationalist cant about Mulroney
as a "Yankee Doodle Dandy" (McDonald 1995), his conception of Canada's place in
the world was expansive.

But what of North America? Mulroney's warm words for Bush's proposal masked
Canadian concerns over a potential US-Mexico trade agreement, Washington and
Mexico City's initial goal. In Ottawa, officials worried that this pact would undermine
the benefits of CUSFTA—such as Canada's attractiveness to foreign investment—and
mean that the US would establish a "hub and spoke" (Burney 2005, 158–59) approach
to economic relations with its neighbors. Overall, Canadian policy was defensive in
nature, meant to preserve special economic ties with the United States rather than
expand market access with Mexico, at least as a primary goal (Cameron and Tomlin
2000, 63–68). In his memoirs, Mulroney recounted that he raised these concerns with
Bush, pressing him to allow Canada to join the negotiations and telling him, "We are
not going to be on the periphery of anybody's economic activity" (Mulroney 2007,
730–31). In the record of the actual telephone exchange, the prime minister was less
strident: "I would be very grateful if we could be at the table from the start," he asked.
"We won't delay things or get in the way" (Bush 1990a). As Mulroney explained, "If
Canada were left out," his government "could get whipsawed domestically." The United
States and Mexico agreed to permit Canada to join in trade talks, and the resulting
negotiations were tough, with the Canadian side, as Bush complained at one point,
coming "on like a ton of bricks" (Bush 1990b). Once a deal was struck, Mulroney called
to congratulate his US counterpart. Praising the agreement, Canada's prime minister
indicated that although his country was "not a big player with Mexico . . . we hope to
be" (Bush 1992). Still, his focus remained on the bilateral relationship with the United
States, and he mused that because of NAFTA "the US and Canada will be better
served in the year 2000 and beyond and will be better positioned in the world."

A Reluctant Trinity

At its core, NAFTA was an economic pact, but to some observers (Weintraub 1994) it seemed to herald—for good or ill—a move toward deeper trilateral integration. However, there were practical limits to a more wide-ranging agenda predicated on an expansive view of the North American region. While Canadian officials gave grudging recognition to the need for regional economic links, there was little impetus toward formalizing trilateral political or cultural links. In Ottawa region-building had its limits. Upon becoming Canadian foreign minister in 1996, Lloyd Axworthy found that within Canada's Department of Foreign Affairs and International Trade there existed no focus on North America beyond economic matters (Axworthy 2004, 109–10). Although he made some efforts to encourage greater attention to non-trade issues among the foreign policy bureaucracy, he observed that the roadblock remained the fact that many Canadians "still nurture illusions about our so-called special relationship" (Axworthy 2004, 106) with the United States. The 1990s did see expanded Canada-Mexico trade and investment and the development of closer civil society relations, and there were even calls for closer bilateral cooperation on international security challenges (Klepak 1996). Momentum toward a trilateral arrangement extending beyond economic matters was lacking. In his 2001 book on North America, Anthony DePalma rightly referred to Mexico, Canada, and the United States as "a reluctant trinity" (DePalma 2001). The previous year, Vicente Fox, the new Mexican president, had proposed closer North American integration along the lines of the European Union. After meeting Fox, Prime Minister Jean Chrétien rejected the idea. "We have the United States," he stated, "which is enormous, and two countries that are much smaller on either side. [I don't think] we can apply European rules" (Scoffield 2000). For Chrétien, there was little interest in either a common front with Mexico to temper US power or a wider region-building effort.

At the same time, the Canada-US relationship remained foremost for Ottawa. Following George W. Bush's announcement that his first foreign trip as president would be to Mexico—a natural destination for the Texan—Canadian authorities scrambled to organize an early meeting between Chrétien and Bush, scoring a White House visit eleven days before the presidential trip to Mexico. "The government pays a lot of attention to Canada," a US spokesperson assured Canadians worried that their country was losing its privileged place in Washington. "Mexico is not supplanting Canada as our newest best friend" (Brown 2001). In terms of special ties, the dawn of the new millennium saw several proposals for Canada and the United States to pursue efforts aimed at "Easing an 'Obsolete' Border" (*Ottawa Citizen* 2001a). Proponents of the idea included Mulroney (*Ottawa Citizen* 2001b), but also the new US ambassador in Ottawa, Paul Cellucci, who spent summer 2001 floating a trial balloon for a so-called Canada-US Partnership (CUSP) that would see bilateral integration along the lines of a customs union (Cellucci 2007, 78–79; Stewart 2017, 91).

Security Trumps Trade

Then came the September 11, 2001, attacks. CUSP disappeared, and the subsequent thickening of the border, as well as the Bush administration's "security trumps trade" mindset, prompted a panicked flurry of Canadian efforts to ensure the flow of commerce across an increasingly guarded frontier. The preliminary result was the 2001 Smart Border Accord, a security arrangement between Ottawa and Washington. Although Mexico later reached its own bilateral accord with the United States, Canada's willingness to deal alone with the United States signified Canadians' primary interest. A 2002 House of Commons report put the matter succinctly: "realism requires acknowledging the primacy of the Canada-United States relationship for Canadian purposes" (House of Commons 2002, 19). However, MPs added that Canada "must not neglect the counterbalancing potential of our still limited partnership with Mexico" (House of Commons 2002, 21). Nor were they alone in outlining the need for Canada to counterbalance US power. After all, the post-9/11 nature of US foreign policy—brash, unilateral, and militaristic—created a sense that Mexico and Canada had a common interest in closer cooperation. Axworthy saw "a strong and inclusive partnership" between Ottawa and Mexico City as "the key to advancing a progressive agenda in North America" (Axworthy 2004, 122). And, in a symbolic move, in 2005 Paul Martin's short-lived government issued its *International Policy Statement* labeling Mexico a "partner" and calling for more engagement with that country "bilaterally and trilaterally, to ensure that the North American Partnership is truly continental in character" (Department of Foreign Affairs and International Trade 2005). To this end, in 2004 both countries had agreed to the Canada-Mexico Partnership, which promised to expand bilateral relations beyond trade and investment. This initiative was woefully technocratic, with little citizen engagement, a limitation on most efforts toward North American integration. People-to-people contacts between Canadians and Mexicans pale in comparison to the extent and range of civil society links between Canadians and Americans, from trade associations and sports leagues, to academic groups and labor unions. Warm feelings for Mexico aside, the United States remained, as the Martin government's strategy document put it, the "bedrock" of the "continental partnership," "built upon more than two centuries of close economic, security and personal ties."

The Canada-US special relationship was hardly smooth in the immediate years following the 9/11 attacks. Ottawa's failure, first, to join the US-led "coalition of the willing" into the Iraqi quagmire and, second, to take part in the Ballistic Missile Defense boondoggle caused anger in Washington, as did government officials' comments about President Bush's mental limitations. Still, Canada sent troops to Afghanistan and assisted US security agencies in the wider War on Terror. Mexico, in contrast, used its temporary seat on the United Nations (UN) Security Council to frustrate US efforts against Iraq in the lead-up to the war in 2003, and it pulled out of the Inter-American

Treaty of Reciprocal Assistance, or Rio Treaty, the Western Hemisphere's collective security pact. Such was the perilous state of US-Mexican relations that some Canadian Cabinet ministers pondered bringing Mexico into the North American Aerospace Defense Command (Graham 2016, 313) as a means of ameliorating the situation. Doing so would risk the special Canada-US relationship, however, and so it was a nonstarter. Other tensions between Mexico and the United States over drug smuggling and immigration threatened Canada, which feared Washington's imposition of blanket border controls. "Increasingly," recalled Bill Graham, Canadian foreign minister from 2002 to 2004, "border issues came to mean the US-Mexico border," with Canada "sideswiped" as a result (Graham 2016, 155). Nor did this tendency end with the Bush administration. In 2009, Janet Napolitano, Barack Obama's Homeland Security secretary, and, importantly, the former governor of Arizona, counseled about the "need to be sensitive to . . . the very real feelings among southern border states and in Mexico that if things are being done on the Mexican border, they should also be done on the Canadian border (Ibbitson 2009)." Such talk, equating Canada with Mexico, offended Canadians' amour propre and threatened their sense of a special relationship with the United States.

Napolitano's worrying comments came just as Canadian-Mexican relations reached a low point, with the decision of Stephen Harper's Conservative government to impose visas on travelers from Mexico, a blow to notions of freedom of movement throughout the continent. Furthermore, under Harper, Canada backed away from several trilateral initiatives that had been implemented to promote continental integration. The major development in this regard had been the 2005 Security and Prosperity Partnership (SPP), the culmination of several earlier efforts to promote economic competitiveness and rationalization alongside security initiatives directed at terrorism and transnational criminal networks. The SPP suffered from being narrowly focused and technocratic in the extreme, and although the conspiracy-minded feared that it heralded a North American Union, with little citizen engagement and a limited mandate, the prospects for integration were slim (Ayres and Macdonald 2006; Golob 2008). Commenting on the impenetrable bureaucratic nature of the SPP and similar initiatives, one US embassy officer wryly suggested a new program, "North American Strategy for Advancing Legal Dialogue on Regulatory Integration Policies," or NASALDRIP (Stewart 2017, 77).

Three Amigos?

Whatever its economic value, the SPP had been agreed to at a meeting in Waco, Texas, which inaugurated the North American Leaders' Summits (NALS). Popularly known as the Three Amigos summits, the NALS marked an experiment in trilateral diplomacy. It was a brief one: in 2010, Harper canceled the NALS that Canada was due to host. Amid frosty Canada-Mexico relations thanks to the visa requirement, the Three Amigos did not convene for the remainder of Harper's premiership, and in 2014 Mexican president Enrique Peña Nieto canceled a visit to Canada. The Canadian prime minister's preference was to focus on the United States—it is no surprise that amid the NAFTA renegotiation in 2017, Harper recommended ignoring the Mexicans in favor of a bilateral US-Canada deal. As prime minister, he sought to distance Canada from Mexico, abandoning the trilateral SPP in favor of the 2011 Beyond the Border Initiative, a bilateral arrangement with Washington to harmonize certain customs, law enforcement, and security procedures. While one might be quick to condemn Harper's move away from trilateralism, it was in line with decades of Canadian thinking and policy, a reminder of the relatively new nature of Canada's dealings with Mexico, particularly through a trilateral framework.

The situation changed again under Prime Minister Justin Trudeau. Shortly after his election win in 2015, he proclaimed "I want to say this to this country's friends around the world: Many of you have worried that Canada has lost its compassionate and constructive voice in the world over the past 10 years. Well, I have a simple message for you on behalf of 35 million Canadians. We're back" (Murphy 2015). As part of this commitment, his government sought to rekindle a trilateral approach to North American affairs. In June 2016, Trudeau hosted Peña Nieto and Obama for a revived NALS, and that December Canada lifted the Mexican visa requirement. By then, Donald Trump had been elected to the presidency on a slate of tearing up NAFTA and closing the US border with Mexico. Some figures within the Canadian government indicated a willingness to abandon Mexico to its fate in Trump's Washington. "We love our Mexican friends," remarked one unnamed source (Ljunggren 2017), "but our national interests come first and the friendship comes second." A trade department officer added, "Mexico is in a terrible, terrible position. We are not." Several prominent Canadians jumped to Mexico's defense (Carmichael 2017; Robertson 2017), including Michael Kergin, a former Canadian ambassador to the United States. "He's certainly got Mexico in his sights," Kergin stated with regard to President Trump, before emphasizing that NAFTA was "a three-way agreement. What hits Mexico will inevitably have an impact on us" (Freeman 2017).

Evidently sharing this judgment, the Trudeau government committed to working with Mexico. "NAFTA," asserted Canadian foreign minister Chrystia Freeland, "is a three-country agreement" (Fife 2017). This decision to move ahead with the Mexicans was in line with Trudeau's support for trilateralism. "We're friends, we've been very friendly for a long time" (CBC News 2017), Freeland explained during a meeting with Mexico's economy minister in advance of the first round of trade talks in Washington, adding, "we have been building for some time a very strong relationship with Mexico." Given this warm rhetoric, the Canadians received a rude shock a year later, in August 2018, when Washington and Mexico City concluded their own bilateral deal (Dale 2018). The Canadians put aside their considerable anger (Wherry 2019, 148), and the trilateral United States–Mexico–Canada–Agreement (USMCA) was soon struck, its name, avoiding "North America" and "Free Trade," a nod to Trump's pathologies.

Conclusions

What the USMCA renegotiation appears to show is that despite Mexico's conclusion of an initial bilateral deal—as Canada had done with the 2001 Smart Border Accord and the 2011 Beyond the Border Initiative—the reality of continental relations will outlive the rhetoric of Trumpism. Still, the protectionism embodied in Trump—found, too, within elements of the Democratic Party—appears to be with us for some time to come. In this light, it is sensible for Canada and Mexico to work more closely together to advance bilateral and regional initiatives. The upside of the USMCA process may, then, be closer Canadian-Mexican cooperation (Macdonald 2020). But taking this path will mean that Mexicans and Canadians will have to overcome their preference for viewing one another—in María Teresa Gutiérrez-Haces's evocative phrase—as *Los vecinos del vecino* ("the neighbors of the neighbor"; Gutiérrez-Haces 2015).

For Canadians, pursuing this goal will mean tempering the tendency to jealously guard the special relationship with the United States (which shows little sign of dissipating given the close intergovernmental ties that exist and the continued flow of trade, investment, and people). It will also mean adopting a more expansive view of the North American region and jettisoning deeply entrenched attitudes that exclude Mexico. It is worth pointing out that Chrystia Freeland's affirmations of Canadian-Mexican friendship came exactly a century after James A. Macdonald advanced his notion of the North American Idea, an idea—in a trilateral context—whose time may have come.

Bibliography

American and Far Eastern Division. 1942. Report on Canadian Representation with the United States of America, March 31, 1942, Library and Archives Canada, RG 25, file 1415–40.

Axworthy, L. 2004. *Navigating a New World: Canada's Global Future.* Toronto: Knopf.

Ayres, J., and L. Macdonald. 2006. "Deep Integration and Shallow Governance: The Limits of Civil Society Engagement across North America." *Policy and Society* 25 (3): 23–42.

Beaulne, Y. 1960. Memorandum of Conversation between the Prime Minister and the Mexican Foreign Minister, April 22, 1960, in Mexico, Library and Archives Canada, RG 25, file 11563–19–40.

Brown, D. 2001. "And the Winner Is . . . Chretien, First to Visit Bush." *Washington Post*, February 4, 2001.

Burney, D. H. 2005. *Getting It Done: A Memoir*. Montreal: McGill–Queen's University Press.

Bush, G. H. W. 1989. Telephone Conversation with Prime Minister Brian Mulroney of Canada, October 3, 1989, George H. W. Bush Library, Memoranda of Conversations and Telephone Conversations. https://bush41library.tamu.edu/archives/memcons-telcons.

Bush, G. H. W. 1990a. Memorandum of Telephone Conversation with Brian Mulroney, Prime Minister of Canada, September 10, 1990, George H. W. Bush Library, Memoranda of Conversations and Telephone Conversations. https://bush41library.tamu.edu/archives/memcons-telcons.

Bush, G H. W. 1990b. Memorandum of Conversation with President Salinas, September 30, 1990, George H. W. Bush Library, Memoranda of Conversations and Telephone Conversations. https://bush41library.tamu.edu/archives/memcons-telcons.

Bush, G. H. W. 1992. Memorandum of Telephone Conversation with Prime Minister Mulroney of Canada, August 12, 1992, George H.W. Bush Library, Memoranda of Conversations and Telephone Conversations. https://bush41library.tamu.edu/archives/memcons-telcons.

Cameron, M., and B. Tomlin. 2000. *The Making of NAFTA: How the Deal Was Done*. Ithaca, NY: Cornell University Press.

Canadian Consulate, New York City. 1979. Telex 2306, November 19, 1979, Library and Archives Canada, RG 25, file 20-USA-19.

Canadian Embassy, Mexico City. 1945. Despatch 449, December 22, 1945, Library and Archives Canada, RG 25, file 5682–40.

Canadian Embassy, Washington, DC. 1956a. Telex 207, February 3, 1956, Library and Archives Canada, RG 25, file 50329–40.

Canadian Embassy, Washington, DC. 1956b. Telex 601, March 29, 1956, Library and Archives Canada, RG 25, file 50329–40.

Canadian Embassy, Washington, DC. 1979. Telex 6650, December 19, 1979, Library and Archives Canada, RG 25, file 20-USA-19.

Canadian Embassy, Washington, DC. 1981a. Telex 143, January 12, 1981, Library and Archives Canada, RG 25, file 20–1-2-USA.

Canadian Embassy, Washington, DC. 1981b. Telex 254, January 16, 1981, Library and Archives Canada, RG 25, file 20–1-2-USA.

Carmichael, K. 2017. "Canada Shouldn't Throw Mexico Under the Bus to Placate Donald Trump." *Canadian Business*, February 6, 2017.

Castro-Rea, J. 2012. "Introduction." In *Our North America: Social and Political Issues beyond NAFTA*, edited by J. Castro-Rea, 1–24. Farnham, UK: Ashgate.

CBC News. 2017. "Chrystia Freeland meets with Mexico's Economy Minister," August 15, 2017. https://www.cbc.ca/player/play/1025305667814.

Cellucci, P. 2007. *Unquiet Diplomacy*. Toronto: Key Porter.

Dale, D. 2018. "Trump Tries to Put Squeeze on Canada as US and Mexico Make NAFTA Breakthrough." *Toronto Star*, August 15, 2018.

Demers, M. 2014. *Connected Struggles: Catholics, Nationalists, and Transnational Relations between Mexico and Quebec, 1917–1925*. Montreal: McGill–Queen's University Press.

DePalma, A. 2001. *Here: A Biography of the New American Continent*. New York: Public Affairs.

Department of External Affairs. 1955. Brief for Ministers, "Vote on the 'Continental Approach,'" September 14, 1955, Library and Archives Canada, RG 20, file 7–1385.

Department of External Affairs. 1981a. Outgoing Telex PGN-0023, February 2, 1981, Library and Archives Canada, RG 25, file 20–1-2-USA.

Department of External Affairs. 1981b. Outgoing Telex EGL-0057, March 11, 1981, Library and Archives Canada, RG 25, file 20–1-2-USA.

Department of Foreign Affairs and International Trade. 2005. *International Policy Statement: A Role of Pride and Influence in the World—Overview*.

Diefenbaker, J. G. 1960. Memorandum to Howard Green, April 24, 1960, Library and Archives Canada, RG 25, file 12426–40.

Donaghy, G. 2002. *Tolerant Allies: Canada and the United States, 1963–1968*. Montreal: McGill–Queen's University Press.

Dulles, J. F. 1955. Memorandum to the President, August 15, 1955, D. D. Eisenhower Library, J. F. Dulles Papers, White House Memoranda Series, box 3, folder WH Correspondence—General 1955 (2).

Edmonton Journal. 1956. "Neighborhood Meeting." March 19, 1956.

Fife, R. 2017. "Canada Won't Abandon Mexico in NAFTA Talks, Freeland Says." *Globe and Mail*, February 22, 2017.

Ford, R. A. D. 1982. Memorandum to de Montigny Marchand, June 10, 1982, Library and Archives Canada, MG 31 E73, vol. 2, file Correspondence, External Affairs.

Freeman, A. 2017. "Trump Has Aimed His NAFTA Criticism at Mexico but Canada Is Now Worried." *Washington Post*, January 19, 2017.

Golob, S. R. 2008. "The Return of the Quiet Canadian: Canada's Approach to Regional Integration after 9/11." In *An Independent Foreign Policy for Canada? Challenges and Choices for the Future*, edited by Brian Bow and Patrick Lennox, 83–99. Toronto: University of Toronto Press.

Graham, B. 2016. *The Call of the World: A Political Memoir*. Vancouver, BC: UBC Press.

Granatstein, J. L., and R. Bothwell. 1990. *Pirouette: Pierre Trudeau and Canadian Foreign Policy*. Toronto: University of Toronto Press.

Gutiérrez-Haces, M. T. 2015. *Los vecinos del vecino: La continentalización de México Canadá en América del Norte*. Mexico City: Universidad Nacional Autónoma de México.

Haglund, D. 2009. "The US-Canada Relationship: How 'Special' Is America's Longest Unbroken Alliance?" In *America's "Special Relationships": Foreign and Domestic Aspects of the Politics of Alliance*, edited by J. Dumbrell and A. Schäfer, 60–75. Routledge, 2009.

Halifax *Chronicle-Herald*. 1956. "Now for Action!" March 30, 1956.

Hart, M. 2002. *A Trading Nation: Canadian Trade Policy from Colonialism to Globalization*. Vancouver: University of British Columbia Press, 2002.

House of Commons. 2002. Standing Committee on Foreign Affairs and International Trade Report: *Partners in North America: Advancing Canada's Relations with the United States and Mexico*.

Ibbitson, J. 2009. "Obama's Message: Glory Days of Open Border Are Gone." *Globe and Mail*, March 26, 2009.

King, W. L. M. 1948. Diary Entry, March 25, 1948, Library and Archives Canada, William Lyon Mackenzie King Diary. https://library-archives.canada.ca/eng/collection/research-help/politics-government-law/pages/diaries-william-lyon-mackenzie-king.aspx.

Klepak, H. 1996. *Natural Allies? Canadian and Mexican Responses on International Security*. Ottawa, ON: Carleton University Press.

Léger, J. 1955. Memorandum to Lester B. Pearson, September 23, 1955, Library and Archives Canada, RG 25, file 50316–2-40.

Ljunggren, D. 2017. "Canada to Mexico on NAFTA: You Might Be on Your Own." *Reuters*, January 24, 2017.

Macdonald, J. A. 1917. *The North American Idea*. Toronto: McClelland, Goodchild & Stewart.

Macdonald, L. 2020. "Stronger Together? Canada-Mexico Relations and the NAFTA Re-negotiations." *Canadian Foreign Policy Journal* 26 (2): 152–66.

MacGuigan, M. 1981. Memorandum to the Prime Minister, "Telephone Call from President Reagan," January 21, 1981, Library and Archives Canada, RG 25, file 20–1-2-USA.

MacKay, R. A., and E. B. Rogers. 1938. *Canada Looks Abroad*. Toronto: Oxford University Press.

Macmillan, H. 1957. Note to Lord Home, June 30, 1957, The National Archives of the United Kingdom, PREM 11/2133.

McDonald, M. 1995. *Yankee Doodle Dandy: Brian Mulroney and the American Agenda*. Toronto: Stoddart.

Massey, V. 1947. "Should Canada Join the Pan-American Union?" *Maclean's Magazine*, August 15, 1947.

Massey, V. 1948. "Canada and the Inter-American System." *Foreign Affairs* 26.

Mulroney, B. 2007. *Memoirs.* Toronto: McClelland & Stewart.

Murphy, J. 2015. "Canada to End Airstrikes in Syria and Iraq, New Prime Minister Trudeau Says." *The Guardian,* October 21, 2015.

Newman, P. C. 1956. "Who Really Owns Canada?" *Maclean's,* June 9, 1956.

Nixon, R. M. 1971. Richard M. Nixon Tapes, December 11, 1971, Rmn_734, Richard M. Nixon Library.

Nixon, R. M. 1972. "Address to a Joint Meeting of the Canadian Parliament," April 14, 1972. The American Presidency Project. https://www.presidency.ucsb.edu/node/254646.

Ottawa Citizen. 2001a. "The Case for Easing an 'Obsolete' Border." August 4, 2001.

Ottawa Citizen. 2001b. "Mulroney Calls for Canada-US Customs Union." June 19, 2001.

Panetta, A. 2017. "Harper to Trudeau: Canada Is 'Napping on NAFTA.'" *Maclean's,* October 17, 2017. https://www.macleans.ca/politics/harper-to-trudeau-canada-is-napping-on-nafta/.

Pearson, L. B. 1956. Memorandum to Louis St. Laurent, January 25, 1956, Library and Archives Canada, RG 25, file 50329–40.

Pickersgill, J. W. 1973. Letter to Mitchell Sharp and Attached Memorandum, "A Superficial View of Mexican-Canadian Relations," March 26, 1973, Library and Archives Canada, RG 25, file 20-CDA-9-AMRICA LAT.

Reagan, R. 1979. Transcript, Official Announcement, November 13, 1979, Library and Archives Canada, RG 25, file 20-USA-19.

Reagan, R. 1980. Letter to John D. Harbron, December 29, 1980, Library and Archives Canada, MG 31 D224, vol. 9, file 28.

Ritche, A. E. 1967. Note to Saul Rae, May 18, 1967, Library and Archives Canada, MG 31 E44, vol. 5, file Diary File, May 1967.

Robertson, C. 2017. "Canada and Mexico Must Stand Together amid Trade Threats." *Globe and Mail,* January 16, 2017.

Rozental, A., and A. Bugailiskis. 2012. *Canada among Nations 2011–2012: Canada and Mexico's Unfinished Agenda.* Montreal: McGill–Queen's University Press.

Scoffield, H. 2000. "Chrétien Rejects Mexico's Vision." *Globe and Mail,* August 23, 2000.

Stewart, J. 2017. *Strangers with Memories: The United States and Canada from Free Trade to Baghdad.* Montreal: McGill–Queen's University Press.

Tenorio Trillo, M. 2017. *Latin America: The Allure and Power of an Idea.* Chicago: University of Chicago Press.

Trudeau, P. E. 1976. "Mexico-Canada Association Harmonious and Effective." Canada, Department of External Affairs, *Statements & Speeches* no. 76/9, January 23, 1976.

Urquhart, J. 1984. "An Outspoken US Friend in Ottawa." *Wall Street Journal,* September 24, 1984.

Vancouver *Daily Province*. 1956. "They Should 'Do It Again.'" March 29, 1956.

Vucetic, S. 2011. *The Anglosphere: A Genealogy of a Racialized Identity in International Relations*. Palo Alto, CA: Stanford University Press.

Weintraub, S. 1994. *NAFTA: What Comes Next?* Westport, CT: Praeger.

Wherry, A. 2019. *Promise and Peril: Justin Trudeau in Power*. Toronto: HarperCollins.

White House. 1956. Press Conference Transcript, March 16, 1956, D. D. Eisenhower Library, James Hagerty Papers, box 14, folder U.S.-Mexico-Canada Conference—Press Conference.

CHAPTER THREE

The Two US-Mexico Borders and the Limits of the North American Project

María Celia Toro

REGIONS ARE shaped not only by interdependences, institutions, and identities, but also by the relative power of regional actors. As a result, the political construction of regions is largely a matter of establishing regions' limits: which countries belong and which are left out. Regions are also identified by how countries that belong to them consider themselves part of a common project. These elements—power asymmetries, limits, and common projects—are often starkly expressed where countries meet as shared borders. And yet the literature on regions has not focused on the coordination of border policies as an important indicator of the existence of a regional compound.

To understand how the North American project has been constructed and contested—and by whom—this chapter focuses on the US-Mexican border as a site of both intense connection and of friction. In a well-established region, border management should result from international negotiations between the region's members. But in North America, no trilateral negotiation of a border governance regime has taken place. Instead, the United States has predominated in the creation of two borders—an economic and a security border—along the US-Mexico divide. This duality and the lack of progress in regional border governance has stifled the North American project.

Over the last three decades, US-led border governance policies have defined the North American project by establishing a US-Mexico border, and, in turn, a region centered on the interests of big business and oriented toward export enclave production. The North American region has been shaped not only by a small set of economic actors, but also by reactionary US domestic politics.

In the 1990s, the North American Free Trade Agreement (NAFTA) launched a sizable reorganization of manufacturing in the three North American countries, which called for faster methods to move the increasing flow of goods across borders. By the end of the decade, North America had become the world's most powerful international economic bloc. This economic integration project did not include, however, a trilateral agreement regarding the movement of people across the region. This weakness, which Mexico tried unsuccessfully to remediate since NAFTA's inception, limited the benefits of market liberalization for Mexico and created an unresolved tension between the two countries, namely, a systematic crossing of Mexican workers without documents into the United States to find better-paying jobs.

The United States response to the terrorist strikes of September 11, 2001, represented an unexpected shift in US priorities and policies. "Homeland security" became the paramount concern. Under the guise of preventing another attack, the United States declared war on Afghanistan in 2001 and invaded Iraq in 2003. Bolstering homeland security included a heightened opposition to "open borders" and enhanced surveillance of anything and everyone entering the United States by land, air, and sea. President George W. Bush called for a major overhaul of border transit and management to guarantee border safety. These deep changes would inevitably affect millions of Mexican migrants and the normal functioning of trade under NAFTA.

After September 2001 the United States, and perhaps even Canada, lost interest in advancing the North American vision, but not in maintaining the trilateral free trade agreement and the regional alliance for production. Although the US clearly conditioned the continuation of free trade to a "partnership for security," it refused to negotiate a North American "security perimeter" in the months following 9/11. Instead of opting for a regional framework, the United States signed, in December 2001, the Canadian proposal of a "smart border" agreement and, in March 2002, a less ambitious version of it with Mexico. In practice, however, life at the two US land borders would unfold in quite different ways over the next two decades, leaving Mexico in a precarious position in North America.

Trade and investments between the three North American countries continued, but at a lower rate of growth (see Morales, and Stallings, this volume). In an effort to keep the North American idea alive and boost trade-led economic growth, Canada and, in particular, Mexico advanced in 2005 the idea of a Security and Prosperity Partnership of North America (SPP), which the United States was willing to sign, but not to nurture. After limited progress, the SPP was terminated in 2009; it would be the last, albeit unsuccessful, major trilateral endeavor up to 2017, when—at the request of President Donald Trump—the renegotiation of NAFTA began. The two junior partners promptly joined forces and paid the costs of transforming NAFTA into the United States–Mexico–Canada Agreement (USMCA),[1] which entered into force in July 2020 (Macdonald, this volume).

Neither the primacy of security over trade nor Canada's lukewarm interest were insurmountable obstacles for the continuation of the North American vision. In fact, successful regions often have their origin in security interests and concerns. The unraveling of the North American fabric began instead, I would argue, at the US-Mexican border. September 11 magnified the voices of the many groups that had stressed, for decades, the perils of an "open" or "porous" border to the south. They were joined by constituencies who had opposed NAFTA on economic grounds since the beginning, anticipating a massive loss of jobs in the United States. Legal and undocumented migration, slowly but surely, produced a nationalist and nativist reaction in the United States. The terrorist attacks conferred greater legitimacy on nativist calls for "sealing the border" with Mexico to impede the unauthorized transit of people (including a possible terrorist) and block the smuggling of drugs—another US-Mexico burgeoning market as of the 1970s. The incapacity of the United States and Mexico to effectively regulate the regional markets for cheap labor and drugs would prove fatal for the North American project. After 2001, maintaining open borders, in particular with Mexico, became politically unacceptable in the United States, enhancing the political space that Donald Trump would take advantage of in 2016.

After 9/11, the US policy paradigm assumed that the country's challenge was to prevent the entry of terrorists, drug smugglers, undocumented workers, or falsely documented visitors *at the border*, while protecting the North American production and export platform. As a result, the United States established, in practice, two borders with Mexico: one, open as an avenue for trade—as in an enclave economy; the other, closed by means of extending the US wall along different sections of the common frontier and of financing an extraordinary buildup of security personnel and surveillance technologies—to deter a variety of threats. These dueling borders imposed high costs both in the United States and Mexico. By dampening the benefits and increasing the costs of trading across borders for Canada, Mexico, and the United States, all while leaving festering political problems unaddressed, North America's border governance undermined support for the creation of a safe and prosperous North American community.

Over the last two decades, the persistent exodus of Guatemalans, Hondurans, and Salvadorans traversing Mexico to reach the United States has become an additional challenge. More recently, migration through Mexico from even further afield, including Cuba, Haiti, and Venezuela, has generated intense political debates within the United States. The response of the US, Canada, and Mexico to these changing regional dynamics will shape the future of the North American region. A trilaterally negotiated and managed response to organize and accommodate people fleeing from poverty, violence, and climate change that opens a road for inclusion could trigger a renewal of the North American project. The political construction of North America, however, points in the opposite direction, toward the consolidation of a "secure border" with Mexico and the sealing of the Mexican border with Guatemala, which will stand in the way of advancing the consolidation of a tripartite North America, by excluding Mexico, magnifying identity concerns, and tearing apart the transnational social and family links that the North American project has forged.

US Border Policies before NAFTA

Border policies have been the most important US instrument to regulate the international (mostly regional) markets for labor and drugs. These policies have an internal and an external dimension: "closing the border" and "exporting" interdiction. Emphasis on one or the other dimension has shifted over time, although they frequently intersect. Suppressing the production and exportation of drugs from third countries (through so-called source country control programs) has been the preferred US strategy to prevent drugs from reaching their consumers. Fortification of the border and expulsion of migrants has been the dominant approach to deter Mexicans and, more recently, Central Americans from entering the United States without proper documentation (Castañeda et al., this volume). The intensification of police activity at specific border points, organized as major law enforcement campaigns or "special operations," has also been part of the law enforcement repertoire to stop illicit drugs and unauthorized migrants before they enter US territory. These twin programs, the domestic—focused on the border—and the international, have changed the organization of undocumented migration and of drug smuggling without effectively stemming the flow of either drugs or migrants into the United States, and yet they have always been extremely popular among US legislators, interested bureaucracies, and public opinion.

US concern about the security of its southwestern border has a long history. Only a few years after the US government unilaterally put an end to the Bracero Program in 1964, the border with Mexico and unauthorized migration were considered "unmanageable." This bilateral guest-worker agreement, which began in 1942, allowed US employers, for twenty-two years, to legally hire Mexican workers. During that time, 4.5 million contracts for temporary workers were signed (Andreas 2000, 33), for 2 million Mexicans who were hired by US farmers and ranchers, while many others began crossing the border without documents, also in search of employment (Rosenblum 2011, 9). The cancellation of the program and the imposition of country quotas, mandated by the Immigration and Naturalization Act of 1965—as D. S. Massey has cogently argued—did not stop the hiring of an abundant low-skilled Mexican workforce; it only transformed it into undocumented workers: "the flows quickly reestablished themselves under undocumented auspices" (Massey 2021, 34).

Unauthorized migration became a major issue in the bilateral agenda during the 1980s. The need to reduce this type of migration gained political salience in California, Texas, and Arizona in those years, and became a prominent issue at the federal level in the 1990s and quite a contentious one in the twenty-first century.

As had happened in the past, important changes in US immigration laws to address the problem of undocumented migrants, such as the Immigration Reform and Control Act of 1986 (IRCA), were accompanied by a considerable buildup in law enforcement budgets and personnel. Funds for the Border Patrol more than tripled during that decade, from approximately $83 million in 1980 to around $261 million in 1990, while the almost 3,000 Border Patrol agents in 1980 grew to about 5,000, ten years later (Dunn 1996, 180–81). This spending and stricter border enforcement did not deter migrants from attempting to cross anyway: in 1986, the Border Patrol reported "the largest annual number of apprehensions—1,693,000" (Alden and Roberts 2011, 2–3).[2] As the number of apprehensions increased as a result of tougher enforcement, the narrative of "an invasion of illegal aliens" took hold in the United States, despite the fact that Mexican migration in those years was mostly circular, and consequently the undocumented population living in the United States grew only slightly (from 0.3 million in 1965 to 3.2 million in 1986 and to 3.5 million in 1990) (Massey 2021, 43). From 1965 to 1985, the vast majority of workers entering the US without documents went back and forth between Mexico and the United States, to the same destination and type of employment—mostly in agriculture (Massey 2021, 35–36).

As for drugs, the border was declared "out of control" toward the end of the 1960s, as Mexican smugglers became the most important suppliers of marijuana and heroin for an expanding number of American drug users. Calls for "closing the border" to keep drug smugglers out have since become part of US political discourse (Craig 1980; Reuter 1988). Major eradication programs to counter illicit cultivation in Mexico were launched with US assistance in the 1970s. Although occasionally effective in the short run, in the end eradication and border interdiction policies only led to a reorganization of the illegal drug market, under shrewder hands, which Mexico has been unable to tame ever since.

In 1982, President Ronald Reagan defined drug trafficking as a threat to US national security and officially declared a "war on drugs" (especially focused on cocaine), expanding President Richard Nixon's 1969 policy focus against marijuana and heroin. From the beginning, these US policies affected bilateral relations. The two US presidents organized special operations at the US-Mexican border in 1969 and in 1985, curtailing cross-border trade and transit.

In the early 1980s, the US successfully disrupted, in Florida, the well-established Andean-Caribbean-US trafficking route, bringing about major changes in the drug trade: Latin American traffickers inundated the US market with the white powder, enticed by the rise in prices (in Miami, cocaine reached an all-time high of $55,000 a kilo) (Reuter 1988, 3), and established a new smuggling corridor through Mexico. After reaching this peak, prices began to fall and have remained basically stable, but still very high when compared to production and transportation costs in Mexico and other Latin American countries. Confronted with both wealthy and powerful "drug lords," and the fury of the United States, the Mexican government reorganized its drug programs. By the end of the eighties, the antidrug law enforcement budget in Mexico represented almost 70 percent of the attorney general's office total budget. Seeking the impossible—namely, closing the gap between the price of drugs in Mexico and in the United States—the Mexican government embarked in an over-criminalization strategy that would end up severely weakening Mexico's criminal justice system (see

Kloppe-Santamaría, this volume). However, prohibition and ever more stringent law enforcement in Mexico have not reduced the drug market in the United States—the largest in the world—or in Mexico (basically an export market). Instead, they have fueled corruption and violence, which, in conjunction with the high prices of drugs in the American market, maintained by stricter border controls, have kept the illegal business thriving, resulting in devastating consequences for both Mexico and the United States.

NAFTA Years

President Carlos Salinas (1988–1994) envisioned a North American project for Mexico. He considered NAFTA a means to fully integrate the Mexican economy into world markets and to advance more quickly up the development ladder by "exporting goods rather than people." Bordering the United States was perceived, contrary to long-standing tradition, as a great, and until then, largely wasted opportunity.

In the United States, NAFTA was part of the US global trade strategy and was considered an economic bargain that would benefit selected American industries, in particular those, such as the automotive industry, that could shift assembly lines to Mexico to reduce costs. Equally important, the trade agreement was meant to curtail the flow of undocumented immigrants by boosting economic growth and job creation in Mexico (Pastor 2001). This vital US interest, however, was not left exclusively in the hands of the market, as a "visible hand"—accelerating the fortification of the border— would accompany the trade liberalization strategy.

Many feared that opening borders to trade would facilitate drug smuggling, as traffickers could easily conceal their merchandise among an increasing legitimate cargo. As a result of these concerns, in the 1990s, the policy of opening borders to trade while closing them to unauthorized migrants, drug smugglers (Andreas 1996), and terrorists—later known as the policy of "smart borders"—became entrenched.

The NAFTA economic boom and the gap between wages in Mexico and in the United States kept fueling migration. According to the Pew Hispanic Center, the number of Mexicans migrating to the United States reached its peak in 2000, when approximately 700,000 headed north, compared to 300,000 in 1991 (Passel, D'Vera, and Gonzalez-Barrera 2012, figure 1.3).

To appease anti-immigrant sentiment, particularly in border states, the Clinton administration supported several major law enforcement operations in the mid-1990s—such as "Hold the Line," "Gatekeeper," and "Safeguard," to name just a few—to stop migrants and drug traffickers.[3] From 1992 to 2000, the Border Patrol budget tripled, surpassing $1 billion annually, while the number of agents more than doubled.

Consequently, the number of instances in which foreigners, most of them Mexican, were apprehended at the border grew from close to a million in 1994 to more than a

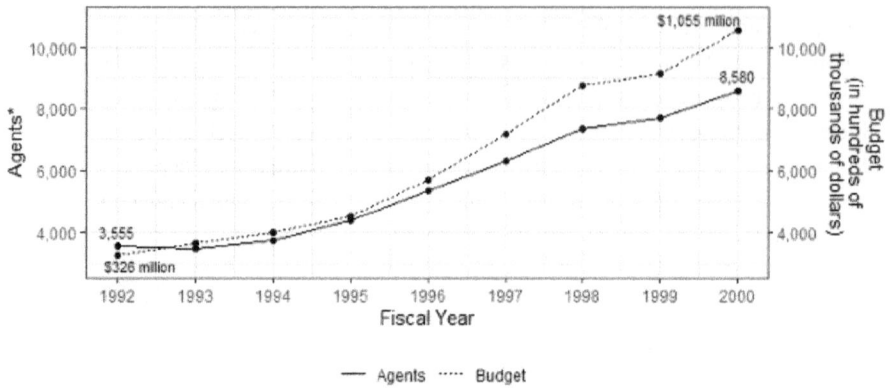

Figure 3.1. US Customs and Border Patrol Budget and Number of Agents (1992–2000).

million and a half in 2000, coming close to the largest number of apprehensions ever (in 1986). In that same period, generally considered *the glory days* for NAFTA, migrants were apprehended and returned to their home countries more than one and a half million times every year (Toro 2017, 229).

The construction of fences in high-traffic segments of the dividing line was conspicuous in the 1990s, as was investment in surveillance technologies—camera systems, surveillance towers, drones, ground sensors, etc. Between 1994 and 1996, the governments of California, Arizona, and New Mexico contributed to the financing of walls along different sections of the border. Nativist groups, calling for the construction of an "impenetrable border" between Tijuana and San Diego, were particularly vocal (Dunn 1996, 66–67).

In the 1990s, border walls were announced as a way to reduce drug smuggling, although the aim of also deterring undocumented migration was clear. Immigration and Naturalization Service (INS) officials recognized that, while unauthorized entry into the US would not be prevented, those attempting to cross the border would be forced into more remote and dangerous areas, which made them more vulnerable to smugglers, apprehension, or death; this may have contributed to the death of more than 1,600 men, women, and children in the desert between 1993 and 1997 (Eschbach et al. 1999, 430). In 2000, INS was reporting that, on average, one migrant died each day (not all of them Mexicans) (as cited in Flynn 2002). Furthermore, intensified border enforcement led to considerably higher fees paid to coyotes or *polleros* in Mexico.

Except for the large US-Mexican labor market, the NAFTA strategy for "managing interdependence," and the commerce and investment boom, received special attention by the three trading partners and was a harbinger of things to come. In 2000, people legally crossed the US-Canada and the US-Mexico borders 500 million times. Intraregional exports, as a percentage of total exports, went from around 30 percent in 1982 to 56 percent in 2001. By 2000, US "exports to its neighbors were 350 percent greater than exports to Japan and China and 75 percent greater than exports to the EU." The annual flow of US direct investment to Mexico grew from $1.3 billion in 1992 to $15 billion in 2001 (Pastor 2004, 126–27).

Border infrastructure had to be expanded and modernized to expedite new trade flows between Mexico and the United States, which more than tripled between 1993 and 2000 (Vega and Campos 2020, 131–35), reaching nearly half a million dollars of cross-border trade every minute (US Census Bureau 2021). In addition, border infrastructure had to be updated to allow for a more intense crossing of people; for example, in 2000, the number of US-Mexican border crossings (including pedestrians, as well as occupants in personal and commercial vehicles) attained a record figure of 144 million, a 47 percent increase from the 97.5 million registered in 1995 (Wilson and Lee 2013, 68).

Important investments were made to speed trade flows, in particular to build new ports of entry. Between 1994 and 2000, at least five new international bridges and their corresponding ports of entry began operating in Texas alone (Texas Department of Transportation 2015).[4] Their construction, and other related expenses, such as road improvement—with an approximate cost of $188 million—were mostly funded by the federal and, in the case of the Camino Real Bridge, by the local government as well (Texas Department of Transportation, 2015). Additionally, through the Transportation Equity Act for the 21st Century (TEA-21), enacted in June 1998, the US Congress allowed funding for a total of $140 million per year between 1999 and 2003 for infrastructure projects along the northern and southwestern borders (US General Accounting Office 1999, 33). By 2002, there were fifty ports of entry, ten of which had been constructed between 1994 and 2002 (Andreas 2003, 6).

For all these efforts, bottlenecks at the US-Mexican border persisted. The US response to the terrorist attacks of September 11, 2001, would only magnify and complicate the shortcomings of a border policy that was poorly conceived to handle the economic integration that NAFTA entailed, let alone the unprecedented US security concerns that were ushered in after that dramatic event. It was within this pre-9/11 border management regime, whose aim was to keep out "unwanted" goods and people while facilitating trade flows (often referred to as the policy of searching for the needle in the haystack), that the US government tried to accommodate its new homeland security border policies. This "smart borders" approach, in the end unsustainable, eventually led to the creation of "two borders"—one with a focus on security, and the other with the imperative of streamlining cross-border commercial transit. The decision dealt a serious blow to the North American vision of a prosperous region that could compete with other emerging economic blocs, which would have called for a trilaterally negotiated border management regime, or else, as the Hart-Rudman

Commission proposed in 1998 (Alden 2009, 33), for border policies that relied on intelligence and selective targeting as "the most effective way to keep the terrorists out of the United States." But neither the North American approach nor the selective targeting proposal prospered, as an exacerbated fear of terrorism post 9/11would soon transform the politics of border control. The establishment of two borders, an economic border and a security border, was a cumbersome solution that would only undermine support for the North American project in the United States.

After 9/11: The Economic Border

On the tragic morning of September 11, 2001, in a televised message that appeared alongside the image of the World Trade Center collapsing in New York, one could read: "The border with Mexico is closed." Indeed, the three North American countries closed their borders, almost simultaneously, to prevent the crossing of a terrorist into the United States. Commercial traffic between the two countries came to a standstill. The immediate US response was a careful inspection of all border crossings—which would become a fundamental part of the US global strategy against terrorism—followed by draconian measures against Arab and Muslim immigrants. As Norman Neureiter put it, the job of the Department of Homeland Security (DHS), created in 2003 to confront the new threat, was "to build walls around America to keep us safe from anything—disease, nuclear, radioactive or humans—that might cross our borders" (as cited in Alden 2009, 23). Over the next decade, DHS would virtually transform everything pertaining to goods and people (documented and undocumented) entering US territory.

There were many proposals at the time to create a security perimeter that would reduce the checking time of flows at the border to facilitate intraregional trade, none of which was seriously considered. Different ideas were advanced about what a security perimeter would entail. Shortly after 9/11, in November 2001, President Vicente Fox called for a "North American Security Policy" to coordinate border policies and increase information sharing on immigration and customs between the three trading partners (as cited in Serrano 2003, 65n2). The Mexican government was obviously worried about either confronting a "Fortress America" or being left outside a possible US-Canada security perimeter, which was another proposal. Robert Pastor suggested "the creation of a North American Customs and Immigration Force to be used on the perimeter of North America where illegal goods and drugs are most likely to enter" (as cited in Noble, 2005, 475–76). To reconcile the fact that security borders had "suddenly become more sensitive," with the need to keep the economic borders open, Gary Hufbauer and Gustavo Vega proposed the creation of a "Common Frontier," where Canada and Mexico would integrate their own intelligence and surveillance systems with the Department of Homeland Security (Hufbauer and Vega 2003, 133 and 145).

The deliberation over a security perimeter was eventually abandoned, and the idea of a North American agreement on security was pushed to the side. Another effort to agree on a trilateral framework to address US security concerns without affecting the partnership for production was the Security and Prosperity Partnership (SPP), of particular interest to Mexico, although originally a 2003 Canadian proposal of the Council of Chief Executives. Signed by Canada, Mexico, and the United States in 2005, it already distinguished between the security agenda and the economic one. While it did not last long, it offered many proposals to improve regulatory cooperation and border infrastructure, thus enhancing the economic border in ways favorable to big business.

The United States chose homeland security instead. The dominance of a national security dimension in US border policies was costly to both Canada and Mexico. Trapped by the United States' heightened concern for the protection of its homeland, these two neighbors found themselves in an extremely vulnerable position and had little choice but to accommodate the superpower's understandable, though often exaggerated, demands. In the end, Canada quickly signed the US-Canada Smart Border Declaration, in December 2001, which Mexico emulated, albeit with far less resources, signing in March 2002 the US-Mexico Border Partnership Action Plan. A smart border, it was argued, would be "one that better secures our borders while also speeding the free flow of people and commerce" (as cited in Meyers 2003, 23), by sorting out legitimate from illegitimate entries. Thus, customs, border, and immigration policies drastically changed to become a first line of defense against terrorists.

Bilateral trade was hit fast and hard. For Mexican officials, coping with the disruption of border traffic became an imperative, as 70 percent of Mexican exports to the United States cross the US-Mexico border by land. Foreign trade represented slightly more than 60 percent of Mexico's GDP; 80 percent of its exports were shipped north; and 40 percent of these were intra-firm trade (i.e., composed of US goods that are imported by Mexico in the first place to be incorporated into products that are then exported back to the United States). Understandably, keeping the border open was a priority for Mexico and US businessmen, who successfully negotiated with their respective governments to protect cross-border production chains from traffic jams at US border ports of entry. The Mexican government was ready to harmonize its customs policies with the US, train new personnel, adapt advanced surveillance technology, and cooperate in the expansion and adaptation of border infrastructure.

There was a limit, however, to what the new Customs and Border Protection (CBP) agency could accomplish at the border without seriously affecting the legal transit of goods and people. On both sides, customs and border-crossing procedures were restructured to establish "fast lanes" for certified cargo and "trusted travelers," instead of trying to sort goods and people into those that were allowed and those that were not. Checking and preclearance, away from the physical border, became the preferred government-business strategy to avoid the traffic congestion at points of entry, in particular to facilitate the transit of goods for firms, such as car manufacturers, that have to cross between the two countries various times before their final products are ready for sale. The Secure Electronic Network for Travelers Rapid Inspection (SENTRI) was expanded in order to develop "an inspection process that expedites the legal entry of low-risk border crossers in non-commercial vehicles . . . while maintaining the security and integrity of the United States border" (US Department of Justice, Office of the Inspector General 2000). The first SENTRI lane was established in 1995, in the Otay Mesa port of entry. Participants in the SENTRI program can, after meeting several requirements and undergoing a background check, enjoy limited inspection in specific lanes (US Department of Homeland Security, Office of Immigration Statistics 2019). At least two other SENTRI lanes were opened before 2001, one in El Paso, in 1999, and another in San Ysidro, in 2000. By 2008, the SENTRI program had been expanded to nine lanes in nine ports of entry along the southwestern border (Secretaría de Relaciones Exteriores 2008, 91). The following years saw considerable growth, and the number of SENTRI lanes increased to seventeen, distributed among twelve ports of entry (Lee and Wilson 2013, 71).

Big firms were able to cover the additional costs of guaranteeing safe cargos, as required by the Customs–Trade Partnership against Terrorism (C–TPAT), but small and medium-sized firms did not have the capacity or the means to adjust to the new regulations. In 2002, the Mexican government offered tax reductions to export firms to facilitate their adaptation to the new security requirements. By March 2006, 638 Mexican firms had been certified, but 461 could not get the export certificate. By 2012, 10,291 companies were certified under C–TPAT, including only slightly more than 1,000 Mexican manufacturers and 900 carriers (Lee and Wilson 2013, 72). As of September 2016, C–TPAT had 11,490 members worldwide: US-based importers and exporters represented 41 percent; foreign manufacturers accounted for 14 percent; highway carriers allowed to cross the US-Mexico border totaled 8 percent; and Mexican long-haul highway carriers that do not cross the border represented only 3 percent (US Government Accountability Office 2017, 8).

In short, the United States and Mexico were able to keep a NAFTA corridor open that disproportionally benefited the large companies engaged in the global value chains business, reinforcing an export-led enclave economy in Mexico (i.e., one particularly driven by foreign investment, that does not necessarily foster domestic development). In order to find the needle, the new economic border made the haystack smaller (Bersin 2020, 189). The public-private cooperation was extraordinary. The aftermath of 9/11 certainly affected US-Mexican trade, but once the dust settled, the effects were less than those of the 2008 US economic recession.

A similar approach was adopted to reopen the border for trade during the COVID-19 pandemic, which led to the second major closure of the border in the twenty-first century, this time on public health grounds. While the border remained open for "essential activities" and "essential workers," it was closed, of course, as of March 2020 and until November 2021, for everything and everybody else. US-Mexican trade declined from approximately $612 billion in 2019 to $534 billion in 2020. Three months into the pandemic and after the necessary border adjustments, however, bilateral trade began to pick up until fully recuperating its pre-pandemic level. In fact, in 2021, bilateral trade reached $661 billion, the highest figure in many years (US Census Bureau 2021).

After 9/11: The Security Border

Things looked quite different, however, on the "security" front in the aftermath of September 2001. The pressure on US politicians to "seal the border" with Mexico was enormous. Relying on its traditional practices, the US government stationed more Border Patrol officers along the border, doubling their numbers, between 2001 and 2013, to reach a peak of 18,600, multiplying the agency's budget more than three times (see figure 3.2), and building more fences—which by 2011 covered close to 700 miles (Alden and Roberts 2011, 1), that is, more than a third of the 2,000-mile common border and longer than the 600-mile border between Mexico and Guatemala. According to DHS, in 2011 approximately 900 miles of the US-Mexican frontier were under strict surveillance (as cited in Alden and Roberts 2011, 3).

The new border security measures forced a violent reorganization of drug traffickers in Mexico and, above all, affected migrants. Immigration (documented and undocumented) and drug smuggling were seen in a new light after 9/11. Identifying and scrutinizing unauthorized immigrants was considered protection against the surreptitious entrance of terrorists; and if organized crime (in particular drug traffickers) could fund or smuggle terrorists into the United States, it, too, had to be stopped. Consequently, law enforcement at and beyond the border became an important part of US homeland security activities and institutions.

The enforcement of migration laws changed drastically, as DHS took over jurisdiction of migration issues, and undocumented migrants were considered a threat to national and internal security (Tutasig 2014). Funding for the Customs and Border Protection agency grew at a staggering rate, from nearly $5.9 billion in fiscal year 2003 (Department of Homeland Security 2005, 13) to $15 billion in 2021 (US Congressional Research Service 2021, 6).

The decision to drastically escalate enforcement at the border occurred just when undocumented migration to the United States began to decline. In 2010, Mexican migration to the United States reached a historically low figure of 140,000 (Passel, D'Vera, and González-Barrera 2012, fig. 1). The number of those apprehended and returned also diminished. Total apprehensions (not only of Mexicans) dropped sharply after 2000, to fewer than 450,000 in 2010—"the lowest number since 1972" (Alden and Roberts 2011, 2–3)— precisely during the years when Border Patrol agents doubled in number.

Yet, after September 11, the US government embarked on a more systematic deportation (or removal) of immigrants, affecting Mexicans in particular. Unlike "returns" or "voluntary" departures, removals have more serious consequences, as individuals that are

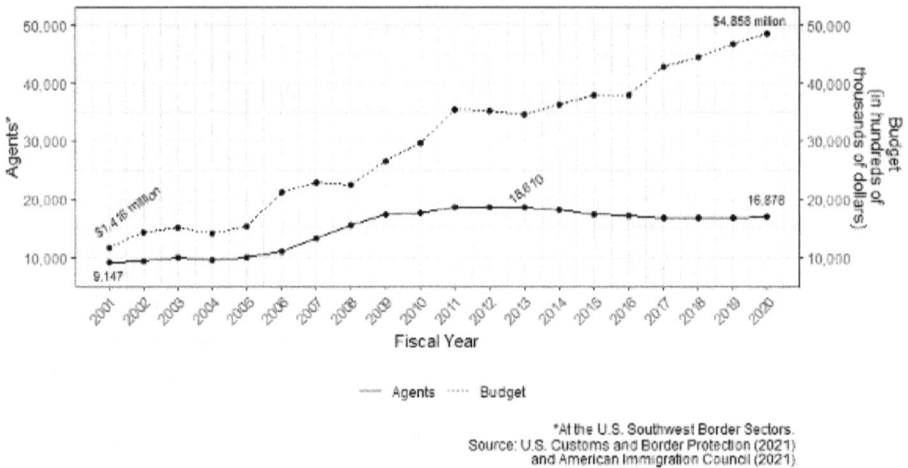

Figure 3.2. US Customs and Border Patrol Budget and Number of Agents (2001–2020).

detained on administrative or criminal charges, and "removed" from the country can be permanently banned from reentering the United States or severely restricted from doing so in the future (many have to wait between ten and twenty years before applying for a visa). Removals of unauthorized migrants from different countries increased considerably after 2005, although they declined slightly in 2018 under the Trump administration to around 328,000; in 2013 more than 435,000 immigrants were removed, compared to 165,000 in 2002 (US Department of Homeland Security, Office of Immigration Statistics 2019). According to A. Goodman, in 2016 "three out of every four expulsions from the United States" were "formal deportations" or removals (Goodman 2020, 167).

The harassment of Mexican migrants dealt a major blow to the transnational social fabric knitted by the dynamic integration of labor and manufacturing markets across borders and to the possibilities of fully integrating these migrants into American society. Those forces that, as Andrew Seele has stressed, have built bridges across the fences and transformed the social and cultural landscape both in the United States and in Mexico (Seele 2018) are now under attack by large segments of American society. Of special concern for the North American community was the criminalization of immigrants to facilitate their deportation, as misdemeanors were reclassified as felonies when committed by undocumented migrants (*The Economist* 2014; Flynn 2002). Equally disturbing was the detention and removal of "criminal aliens" living in the interior of the United States, often for more than a decade, some with children born in the United States.

Subtracting the large number of Mexicans returned and removed from the decreasing number of migrants heading north, in 2012 the Pew Hispanic Center reported that the net migration from Mexico was down to zero and that since 2010, "the return flow to Mexico probably exceeded the inflow from Mexico," a trend that may have continued until the second year of the Trump administration. Today, most Mexicans in the United States are either documented or on temporary work visas, and less than half of the estimated 10.5 million undocumented migrants living in the United Sates are Mexican. The number of H2A and H2B visas increased during the Trump years, and President Joseph Biden has announced the expansion of these and other temporary worker visas for Mexicans and Central Americans.

The end of Mexican mass migration to the United States and its important implications for the North American region have been overlooked by recent changes in the organization of Central American migration flows arriving at the Mexican-US border and Donald Trump's rhetoric depicting this transformation as an assault on the US southern frontier. The organization of migration coming from Guatemala, Honduras, and El Salvador into "caravans," the outflow of families and unaccompanied minors, and the large number of people from these three countries claiming asylum, can be attributed not only to the decline in living standards, climate change, and the increase in violence affecting those countries, but also to US immigration policies and their traditional emphasis on border control. Starting in 2020, increasing numbers of Cubans, Haitians, and Venezuelans were also arriving to the Mexican border with Guatemala, with the intention of reaching the US border, hoping to make an asylum claim or to cross undocumented.

The COVID-19 pandemic completely modified human mobility. The adoption of Title 42 in March 2020 to counter it "had the counterproductive effect of significantly increasing the number of arrests at the border" (American Immigration Council 2022, 7). This provision, which tried to limit the spread of the virus by allowing for the immediate expulsions of migrants and of asylum seekers arriving at the US border, led many, in particular single adults, to try to cross the border various times without risking penalties for repeated crossing. According to the American Immigration Council, more than 1.8 million expulsions were carried out under Title 42 between March 2020 and May 2022, yet half of all single adults from Mexico, Guatemala, Honduras, and El Salvador who were expelled had been apprehended shortly before. While the increase in the number of people reaching the US-Mexico border as of April 2020 may be less than the number of "encounters" suggests, apprehensions have swelled to levels not seen in the last two decades.

At least since the beginning of this century, the United States has successfully exported its policies of closing the border to Mexico and other countries in the region. Having transitioned from being primarily a source of emigration to a migration corridor, Mexico has been struggling to fend off Central American emigrants at its southern border. It does so in order to prevent the organization of transit across its territory by criminal organizations, as well as to attend to United States requests for cooperation. Between fiscal years 2002 and 2017, Mexico deported close to 1.9 million people from Guatemala, El Salvador, and Honduras, while the United States deported 1.1 million (Flores, Bustamante, and López 2019). In the end, this has resulted in two permanent filters—one on the Mexico-Guatemala border, and one on the US-Mexico border—rather than leading to a trilateral negotiation of a North American security perimeter, where responsibility for the management of the external and internal borders of North America (which could include Central American countries) is shared by the members of the North American community.

The post-9/11 changes in the region resulted in part from a watershed decline of Mexican unauthorized migration to the United States. Mexican migration has dwindled for a variety of reasons: economic (in particular, the 2008 financial crisis), demographic, and fear of dying in the desert or falling prey to organized crime. Both coyotes and migrants have become easy targets for criminal groups in Mexico who have turned to extortion and kidnapping of migrants for ransom, human trafficking, or forced recruitment for illegal activities. To escape from harassment and deportation in the United States, or to reunite with family members who have been removed, might also explain why many Mexicans are returning or deciding not to travel.

Still, I believe the most robust hypothesis for the decline in the flow of Mexican undocumented migration is Massey's, who claims that it simply reflects the end of circular or temporary migration—characteristic of the second half of the twentieth century. This has been perhaps the most conspicuous and documentable result of a more effective "control of the border," and one of the most consequential for the weakening of the North American regional project. The "militarization" of the border has resulted in many migrants avoiding their frequent trips to bring money and visit family in Mexico (and eventually retire in their home country), as these journeys became both expensive and risky. Unable to pay the costs of crossing into the US—in 2010 a coyote could charge up to $2,700 (Massey 2021, 40), and in 2022 the price surpassed $5,000—and afraid of being detained or deported at the border or within US territory, migrants opted to postpone their visits to Mexico and stayed for ever longer periods in the United States. The end result was an increase in the stock of migrants living undocumented in that country. From 1988 to 2008, the years when the Border Patrol budget and personnel showed an astonishing increase, "the undocumented population [in the US] grew from 2 million to 12 million" (Massey 2021, 32).

Similar arguments can be made for drug trafficking, which has become a second order of concern on the list of threats to US national security. In general, drug seizures by the Border Patrol, "the primary drug-interdicting organization along the Southwest border," have been decreasing over the last years (US Customs and Border Protection 2018), in particular of cocaine and marijuana, though less so of heroin and fentanyl, which have increased. Although it is practically impossible to accurately assess the volume of drugs illegally entering the United States, there is, indeed, scant evidence to affirm that policing the border or supporting antidrug policies in other countries significantly reduces drug smuggling. Rather, the contraband of marijuana, cocaine, heroin, methamphetamines, and, lately, fentanyl increases or decreases in response to price differentials between Mexico and the United States, and to changes in US demand; and its organization responds to antidrug law enforcement.

The unprecedented inspections at US ports of entry and stricter surveillance of the border at large, may well have affected drug traffickers, because the complete overhaul of border procedures and personnel probably disrupted, at least temporarily, their long-established bilateral networks. Some of the drug traffickers reoriented their business to the Mexican market—a small one, by any account—and, most consequentially, diversified into other lucrative criminal activities. To be sure, the change in the number and type of crimes in Mexico (kidnapping, human trafficking, and extortion), evident as of the beginning of this century, coupled with the pernicious impacts of decades of over-criminalization of the Mexican drug market, has turned into a serious domestic security problem and a major political challenge. The impact on Mexico's image abroad, especially in the United States, has been appalling. The tremendous costs of the "war on drugs" in Mexico (criminality, impunity, violence, and corruption) and the vicious circle of tightening border enforcement, conducive to an ever more reckless reorganization of unauthorized crossings of people and of drug smuggling, that in turn triggers larger budgets and personnel to guarantee "border security," points in the direction of fragmentation rather than to the consolidation of a North American compound.

The US Option for Two Borders and Its Consequences for the North American Region

It is difficult to know how much tougher law enforcement at the border has actually deterred undocumented migrants and drug smugglers—their declared goals before 9/11—or prevented the entry of a terrorist post-9/11. However, it does not seem to matter. As different academics have pointed out, it is striking how little effort and funding goes into actually assessing the effectiveness of border policies, which, today, are mostly oriented toward preventing irregular migration and the arrival of Central American citizens asking for asylum at the US-Mexican border. Indeed, it is hard to find a constituency interested in examining the impact of increased surveillance at the border on the contraband of drugs and the irregular transit of people; and although deterrence has been extremely costly for other countries in the region as well, studies that address the effects of US border policies inside and beyond US borders are also few. As Edward Alden and Bryan Roberts (2011, 7–8) point out, the US government has "no real understanding of how much border control improves when the number of Border Patrol agents, sensors, or miles of fencing increases." There is simply no consensus on what accounts for variations in the flows, and it is far from clear that border policies per se can account for them.

The various reasons for the decline over the last decade in unauthorized migration and drug smuggling are not the focus of public debate nor of official discourse, which opens the door to unsubstantiated claims that the shrinking of clandestine transnational markets results from more sophisticated surveillance and ever larger numbers of Border Patrol officials. Worse still, the lack of interest in understanding how such large, illegal international drug and labor markets developed may also account for the ease with which facts are ignored and foreigners are blamed for violating the law. In fact, considering the evidence presented above, Americans should be less worried today about the integrity of their southern border than in the past. However, they are not.

Disregarding a variety of proposals—to agree on concerted trilateral efforts to manage the region's internal and external borders, to identify common security risks, and to jointly address regional migration and refuge—the United States has opted for border policies geared toward appeasing the anxieties of the US Congress and the public at large regarding a "security problem" at the border, which has never been explained or documented, yet is always exaggerated for political gain. Indeed, spending on border security—a popular, though not necessarily sound, policy—seems to be more about US domestic politics than about imminent external threats. What prevails, then, is the well-known mantra: the only way of dealing effectively with an "unwanted" labor force or with dangerous substances is to close the border and "seriously enforce" antidrug and immigration laws. In the end, these calls for stronger surveillance rest on the manipulation of fear, only made easier after September 11, and have become an important element in internal political struggles, which of course indicate that not all Americans support current border policies and draconian proposals to address legitimate concerns for unauthorized migration.

This political game became a dangerous one in 2016, when Donald Trump, the Republican presidential candidate, was able to arouse the passions of a large number of American voters with his promise to "build that wall" along the entire US-Mexico border—"the loudest audience chant at his rallies" (Danner 2016, 73). Explaining the resonance of Trump's xenophobic discourse is an old and carefully instilled idea of an unprotected southwestern border that can be easily trespassed by hordes of "illegals," most of them Mexicans and, more recently, Central Americans from the so-called Northern Triangle (Guatemala, Honduras, and El Salvador).

The fencing and manning of the US-Mexico border—intensified after 9/11—has, by and large, become incompatible with the creation of a North American community—in particular, after Trump, who, as Laura Macdonald put it, created "perhaps the most serious crisis the North American region has faced" (Macdonald 2020, 2). I fully subscribe to her statement when it comes to Mexico. Trump not only threatened to cancel NAFTA but also depicted the US southern border as an imminent danger to public and national security, and declared a "national emergency" in response to the arrival of refugees at the US-Mexican border in 2019. The relative absence of a North America regional identity has facilitated visions, overwhelmingly in the United States, that depict the border and neighboring countries to the south as threats, and Mexicans (and Central Americans) living in the United States as a challenge to American identity. Focusing on the border "line" to deter these "threats" accounts for the existence of a "security border" starkly at odds with more harmonious ideals of a North American community.

On the other hand, the "economic border" has been strongly lobbied for by the business communities in the three North American countries (the American Chamber of Commerce, in particular), who pushed hard for the quick reopening of the border after 9/11, the renegotiation of NAFTA into USMCA, and the designation of global and regional value chains as "essential economic activities" during the pandemic. However, while business interests have focused on the challenges of border management, they generally have shown little interest in promoting broader visions of North America as a cohesive region. Instead, the border governance system, as Tony Payan has argued, is a site of negotiations for different interests and actors, where "economic actors [have] reaffirmed their view of the border as a strategic resource" (Payan 2020, 41), not a space for region-building.

Advancing toward a North American community would have required different drug and migration policies, ones that would not have relied on the criminalization of the participants in these regional labor and drug markets, and on the fortification of the border. The US-led border governance regime canceled the possibilities of reducing the number of undocumented migrants living in the United States and of integrating part of the Mexican labor force into US society; it has also been a big obstacle for Mexico to become a partner for security and not a security problem that "can spill over" into the United States. Above all, relaunching the North American project calls for a better understanding of the costs and consequences for the organization of these regional markets of trying to contain them at the common border.

Much can be learned by analyzing regions from the perspective of how borders are defined and organized. In North America the border governance system has been designed by the United States, largely in response to US domestic constituencies that demand border security, in particular after September 11, 2001, and an open border to trade and investment. At its southern border, the United States has privileged the opening of a trade corridor heavily weighted in favor of big business, as in an enclave economy, and has relied on "sealing the border" and "exporting interdiction" to stem unauthorized migration and the contraband of drugs, thus transferring the costs of regulating these illegal markets to Mexico, one of its North American partners, and other countries. The failure to effectively govern the regional flows of unauthorized migrants and refugees will stand in the way of building a prosperous and secure North American region and community. Until that changes, the political project of region-building will be stalled.

Though many dynamics of interdependence suggest the inclusion of Central America in the North American region (perhaps by extending the benefits of free trade to Central American countries and incorporating them into climate change mitigation programs), the political construction of the North American project remains limited by inequalities that manifest in border management. Here, we see how US power and politics exclude not just Central America, but also much of the Mexican population, from full membership in the North American region.

The North American project, now severely weakened, reminds us that regions are political endeavors, always difficult to advance, forged by states and societies that have a common vision. President Biden may find a better a way to regulate the regional markets for labor and for drugs, which today include Central America. He has reversed many of Donald Trump's policies, among others, the enlargement of the wall, the massive deportation of unauthorized migrants, and their large-scale confinement in detention centers, as well as the separation of families. Nevertheless, courts repeatedly blocked his attempts to cancel the Migrant Protection Protocols of the Trump era, better known as the "Remain in Mexico" program that sends thousands of asylum seekers, mostly from Central American countries, to wait on the Mexican side of the border for their court proceedings. His administration continued enforcement of Title 42 into May 2023 and is still fighting to preserve the Deferred Action for Childhood Arrivals (DACA) that temporarily protects undocumented young adults from deportation. And yet Trump's nativist rhetoric will resound in the ears of many Americans for some time. In the short run, the interest in changing the governance of the US-Mexican border will be scant. This peculiar border, which unites and separates these two neighbors, is likely to remain the longest, busiest, and most patrolled border in the world.

Notes

I would like to thank Diego del Moral and Daniela Hall for their valuable research assistance, as well as Eric Hershberg and Tom Long for their helpful comments. Luicy Pedroza also offered relevant remarks.

1. Tratado México–Estados Unidos–Canadá, TMEC, in Spanish, and Accord Canada–États Unis–Mexique, ACEUM, in French.
2. The number of apprehensions is not the same as the number of migrants crossing, as a migrant can be apprehended various times.
3. For an analysis of the many "operations" (at least ten) implemented along the US-Mexican border before 2000, see Andreas (2000).
4. Pharr-Reynosa International Bridge of the Rise (1995), Bridge of the Americas (1998), Camino Real International Bridge (1999), Veterans International Bridge at Los Tomates (1999), and World Trade Bridge (2000).

Bibliography

Alden, E. 2009. *The Closing of the American Border: Terrorism, Immigration, and Security Since 9/11*. New York: Harper Perennial.

Alden, E., and B. Roberts. 2011. "Are US Borders Secure? Why We Don't Know, and How to Find Out." *Foreign Affairs* 90, no. 4 (July/August): 19–26.

American Immigration Council. 2021. "The Cost of Immigration Enforcement and

Border Security." January 20, 2021. https://www.americanimmigrationcouncil.org/research/the-cost-of-immigration-enforcement-and-border-security.

American Immigration Council. 2022. "A Guide to Title 42. Expulsions at the Border." May 25, 2022. https://www.americanimmigrationcouncil.org/research/guide-title-42-Expulsions-border#:~:text=Title%2042%20not%20only%20applies,and%20ask%20for%20humanitarian%20protection.

Andreas, P. 1996. "US-Mexico: Open Markets, Closed Border." *Foreign Policy* 103 (Summer): 51–69.

Andreas, P. 2000. *Border Games: Policing the US-Mexico Divide*. New York: Cornell University Press.

Andreas, P. 2003. "A Tale of Two Borders. The U.S.-Canada and U.S.-Mexico Lines after 9-11." In *The Rebordering of North America: Integration and Exclusion in a New Security Context*, edited by P. Andreas and T. J. Biersteker, 1–23. New York: Routledge.

Bersin, Alan D. 2020. "Lines and Flows 2: The Beginning and End of Borders in North America." In *North American Borders in Comparative Perspective*, edited by G. Correa-Cabrera and V. Konrad, 180–203. Tucson: University of Arizona Press.

Craig, R. B. 1980. "Operation Intercept: The International Politics of Pressure." *The Review of Politics* 42 (4): 556–80.

Danner, M. 2016. "The Magic of Donald Trump." *The New York Review of Books*, May 26, 2016, 73.

Dunn, T. J. 1996. *The Militarization of the US-Mexico Border, 1978–1992*. Austin: University of Texas.

The Economist. 2014. "America's Deportation Machine: The Great Expulsion," February 7, 2014. https://www.economist.com/briefing/2014/02/07/the-great-expulsion.

Eschbach, K., J. Hagan, N. Rodriguez, R. Hernandez-León, and S. Bailey. 1999. "Death at the Border." *International Migration Review* 33 (2): 430–54.

Flores, A., L. Noe-Bustamante, and M. H. Lopez. 2019. "Migrant Apprehensions and Deportations Increase in Mexico, but Remain Below Recent Highs." FacTank. News in the Numbers. Pew Research Center. June 12, 2019. https://pewrsr.ch/2F3L2Eo.

Flynn, M. 2002. "US Anti-Migration Efforts Move South." Americas Program. July 3, 2002. https://www.americas.org/1612/.

Goodman, A. 2020. *The Deportation Machine: America's Long History of Expelling Immigrants*. Princeton, NJ: Princeton University Press.

Hufbauer, G. C., and G. Vega. 2003. "Whither NAFTA: A Common Frontier?" In *The Rebordering of North America: Integration and Exclusion in a New Security* Context, edited by P. Andreas and T. J. Biersteker, 128–52. New York: Routledge.

Lee, E., and C. E. Wilson. 2013. "The State of Trade, Competitiveness and Economic Wellbeing in the US-Mexico Border Region." In *The State of the Border Report: A Comprehensive Analysis of the US-Mexico Border*, edited by E. Lee and C. E. Wilson, 60–87. Washington, DC: Mexico Institute, Woodrow Wilson International Center.

Massey, D. S. 2021. "What Were the Paradoxical Consequences of Militarizing the

Border with Mexico?" In *The Trump Paradox: Migration, Trade, and Racial Politics in US-Mexico Integration*, edited by R. Hinojosa-Ojeda and E. Telles, 32–46. Oakland: University of California Press.

Meyers, D. W. 2003. "Does 'Smarter' Lead to Safer? An Assessment of the US Border Accords with Canada and Mexico (Insight No. 2)." Migration Policy Institute. June 23, 2003. https://www.migrationpolicy.org/research/does-smarter-lead-safer-assessment-border-accords-canada-and-mexico.

Nau, H. 1984–1985. "Where Reagonomics Works." *Foreign Policy* 57 (Winter): 14–37.

Noble, J. 2005. "Fortress America or Fortress North America." *Law and Business Review of the Americas* 11 (3): 461–526.

Passel, J., C. D'Vera, and A. González-Barrera. 2012. "Net Migration from Mexico Falls to Zero—and Perhaps Less." Pew Hispanic Center. April 23, 2012. http://www.pewhispanic.org/2012/04/23/net-migration-from-mexico-falls-to-zero-and-perhaps-less/.

Pastor, R. A. 2001. *Toward a North American Community: Lessons from the Old World for the New.* Washington, DC: Institute for International Economics.

Pastor, R. A. 2004. North America's Second Decade. *Foreign Affairs* 83, no. 1 (January/February): 124–35.

Payan, T. 2020. "Actors, Strategic Fields, and Game Rules: Examining Governance at the US-Mexico Border in the Twenty-First Century." In *North American Borders in Comparative Perspective*, edited by G. Correa-Cabrera and V. Konrad, 39–71. Tucson: University of Arizona Press.

Reuter, P. 1988. *Can the Borders Be Sealed?* Santa Monica, CA: RAND Corporation.

Rosenblum, M. R. 2011. *Obstacles and Opportunities for Regional Cooperation: The U.S.-Mexico Case.* Washington, DC: Migration Policy Institute.

Seele, A. 2018. *Vanishing Frontiers. The Forces Driving Mexico and the United States Together.* New York: Public Affairs.

Serrano, M. 2003. "Bordering on the Impossible. U.S.-Mexico Security Relations after 9-11." In *The Rebordering of North America: Integration and Exclusion in a new Security Context*, edited by P. Andreas and T. J. Biersteker, 46–67. New York: Routledge.

Texas Department of Transportation. 2015. "Texas-Mexico International Bridges and Border Crossings: Existing and Proposed 2015." https://ftp.dot.state.tx.us/pub/txdot-info/iro/international-bridges.pdf.

Toro, M. C. 2017. "Vicisitudes del acercamiento mexicano a Estados Unidos." In *Integración en América del Norte (1994–2016): Reflexiones desde el PIERAN*, edited by M. Tawil Kuri, I. Aguilar Barajas, N. A. Fuentes Flores, J. A. Le Clercq, S. Núñez García, and L. Ruano Gómez, 221–41. Mexico City: El Colegio de México-PIERAN.

Tutasig, A. 2014. "Immigration: A National Security Threat?" Committee on US Latin American Relations. September 8, 2014. https://cuslar.org/2014/09/08/immigration-a-national-secuirty-threat/.

Secretaría de Relaciones Exteriores. 2008. "Segundo Informe de Labores." https://sre. gob.mx/images/stories/doctransparencia/infolab/2infolab.pdf.

US Census Bureau. 2021. "Trade in Goods with Mexico." https://www.census.gov/ foreign-trade/balance/c2010.html.

US Congressional Research Service. 2021. "Comparing DHS Component Funding, FY 2021: In Brief (Publication No. R46630)." January 4, 2021. https://fas.org/sgp/ crs/homesec/R46630.pdf.

US Customs and Border Protection. 2014. "U.S. Border Patrol: Enacted Border Patrol Program Budget by Fiscal Year [1990–2013]." https://www.hsdl. org/?abstract&did=756939.

US Customs and Border Protection. 2018. "Border Patrol Overview." http://www.cbp. gov/border-security/along-us-borders/overview.

US Customs and Border Protection. 2020a. "US Border Patrol Fiscal Year Staffing Statistics (FY 1992–FY 2019)." https://www.cbp.gov/document/stats/ us-border-patrol-fiscal-year-staffing-statistics-fy-1992-fy-2019.

US Customs and Border Protection. 2020b. "Southwest Border Migration FY 2020." https://www.cbp.gov/newsroom/stats/sw-border-migration-fy2020.

US Customs and Border Protection. 2021. "U.S. Border Patrol Fiscal Year Staffing Statistics (FY 1992–FY 2020)." https://www.cbp.gov/document/stats/ us-border-patrol-fiscal-year-staffing-statistics-fy-1992-fy-2020.

US Department of Homeland Security, Office of Immigration Statistics. 2019. "Yearbook of Immigration Statistics 2018." https://www.dhs.gov/immigration-statistics/ yearbook/2019.

US Department of Justice, Office of the Inspector General. 2000. "Inspection of the Secure Electronic Network for Travelers' Rapid Inspection." https://oig.justice. gov/reports/INS/e0019/bckgnd.htm.

US General Accounting Office. 1999. "US-Mexico Border: Issues and Challenges Confronting the United States and Mexico (Publication No. GAO/NSIAD-99–190)." June 1999. https://www.gao.gov/assets/nsiad-99-190.pdf.

US Government Accountability Office. 2017. "Supply Chain Security. Providing Guidance and Resolving Data Problems Could Improve Management of the Customs-Trade Partnership against Terrorism Program (Publication No. GAO-17-84)." February 2017. https://www.gao.gov/assets/gao-17-84.pdf.

Vega Cánovas, G., and E. Campos Ortiz. 2020. "El Tratado de Libre Comercio de América del Norte a sus veinte años: balance y perspectivas." In *Los acuerdos comerciales regionales y el TLCAN*, edited by M. C. Toro, 131–70. Mexico City: El Colegio de México-PROMEC.

PART II

New Regionalism and North America

CHAPTER FOUR

"I Was All Set to Terminate"

New Regionalism Theory, the Trump Presidency, and North American Integration

Laura Macdonald

ON APRIL 22, 2017, the 100th day of his presidency, Donald Trump reportedly had decided to announce that he planned to withdraw the United States from the North American Free Trade Agreement (NAFTA), the keystone of the modern North American region. He told reporters from the *Washington Post*: "I was all set to terminate. . . . I looked forward to terminating. I was going to do it" (Parker et al. 2017). This decision would have fulfilled his campaign promise to tear up the agreement, which he called "one of the worst deals ever signed." Trump did follow up on many of his populist threats related to trade, such as pulling out of the Trans-Pacific Partnership (TPP) agreement, launching a trade war with China, and engaging in protectionist actions on aluminum and steel imports.

What led to Trump's decision to push ahead with renegotiating NAFTA rather than withdrawing? Trump said that he backed down on his threat because of phone calls with the leaders of Canada and Mexico, as well as conversations with advisors. It seems, however, that by the time he spoke with Canadian prime minister Justin Trudeau and Mexican president Enrique Peña Nieto, he had already decided to continue with renegotiating the deal, partly because of opposition to withdrawal from some members of his cabinet, including Commerce Secretary Wilbur Ross and Agriculture Secretary Sonny Perdue. Perdue brought with him to his meeting with Trump a map of the United States, showing the areas that would be negatively affected by closing the door on NAFTA, including manufacturing and agricultural trade losses that would hit many areas of the country that were seen as "Trump country." And the Trump administration also received pressure from businesses across the country who lobbied effectively through the US Chamber of Commerce to forestall a decision to sign an order to withdraw (Parker et al. 2017). The eventual result was the signing of the United States–Mexico–Canada Agreement (USMCA).

What does this episode, as well as the content of the USMCA and more recent events like the impact of the COVID-19 pandemic, tell us about how we should think about the nature and future of North America? On the one hand, the uncertainty caused by Trump's threat to withdraw displays the fragility as well as the asymmetry of the region, given the capacity of the United States, which represents by far the biggest market among the three countries, to convincingly threaten to jump ship with little thought for its partners. Both of the weaker countries' economies would likely be devastated by the collapse of the agreement, while the US leader had the luxury of contemplating withdrawal and could leverage that comfort level to demand a stronger deal for the United States. On the other hand, even the wildly unpredictable populist Trump did bow to pressure from US domestic interests that would be negatively affected by such a decision, reflecting the importance of regional supply chains and the political implications of trade disruption. Even if the formal trade agreement just barely managed to stagger through the Trump presidency, the impact of the COVID-19 pandemic, as well as the rise of China and US-China trade tensions, may signify an intensification of informal forms of regional integration in the future.

These events suggest the need for a serious rethinking of theoretical explanations of regional formation and transformation in the North American context. As discussed in the introduction to this volume by Eric Hershberg and Tom Long, North America has received little attention in the dominant approaches to regional integration. In the next section of this chapter, I review competing theories of regionalism in the light of recent events in North America. I argue that dominant theories such as functionalism, neo-functionalism, and liberal intergovernmentalism, which were devised largely to analyze the European case, are inadequate for understanding the complexities of recent events in North America. I also argue that the dominant theoretical framework in the economics literature, based on neoclassical theories of trade, provides little insight into the real-world politics of regional integration. Instead, I argue that the new regionalism approach, which emerged in order to explain processes emerging in non-European sites beginning in the 1980s, provides greater conceptual tools to explain these phenomena. New regionalism theorists often share social constructivists' emphasis on the role of ideas and subjective perceptions in the construction of regions. These elements are brought out in the first section of this volume, particularly in chapter 2 by Arturo Santa-Cruz. My approach, drawing on new regionalism theory, however, argues that such identities are in part an outcome of the economic processes that he says define the North American region. As we see in the anecdote at the beginning of this chapter regarding President Trump's decision to renegotiate NAFTA rather than ripping it up, the informal processes of regionalization, including the construction of regional value chains, generate new understandings of identity and interest that have acquired considerable strength over time. After this theoretical discussion, I show how the new regionalism approach helps illuminate some recent events and processes in the region: Trump's protectionist policies; the nature and mixed content of the USMCA; the impact of the COVID-19 pandemic, the role of regional supply chains, and the regional connections established by civil-society actors. New regionalism theory may also help us understand the problems of "building

North America back better," given the inequities, asymmetries, and injustices that have accumulated over time, following the path dependency established with the original NAFTA agreement.

Theoretical Approaches to North American Integration

As suggested in the introduction to this volume, theoretical discussion of North American regionalism has been relatively limited. This lack of theoretical evaluation may relate to the often-polemical nature of the discussion that surrounds the NAFTA, in which academic exchanges have been limited by assumptions that the agreement is in general either obviously good or obviously bad, with little need for debate or deeper investigation. The deep controversies surrounding NAFTA meant leaders were reluctant to praise or even refer to the region, limiting the possibility for the construction of elite-driven identity construction as one could argue occurred in the European Union. These polarized responses to North American integration reflect the lack of agreement about the economic, social, and environmental impacts of free trade agreements, for which NAFTA is often taken as the prime example. Business elites, liberals, and economists tend to portray free trade as an unadulterated good, which will bring jobs, prosperity, investment and growth, unions, environmentalists, and social movements. In contrast, critics on both left and right of the political spectrum often view it as a clear threat to national identity, policy autonomy, levels of social and economic equality, democracy, and environmental sustainability.[1] When contrasted with the vast amount of money that has been poured into the field of European studies, North American studies is seriously unloved and underfunded, with few institutions, journals, or funding sources devoted to this analysis.[2] In any case, theoretical assumptions are often taken for granted or implicit in academic analysis of the region, rather than clearly identified. As a result, analysts differ on what constitutes a "region" or "regionalization," and whether or not this process is expanding, static, or contracting. Moreover, approaches initially developed in Europe were often imported into North America, without adequate consideration of differences in context or of the alternative theoretical approaches developed in other parts of the world, as if the European Union were the only game in town when it comes to regional integration. The result has been an excessive focus on the institutional and formal dimensions of regionalism, with inadequate attention to the informal, non-state, and noninstitutional dynamics at work.[3]

The dominant theoretical approach to regional integration in the European Union, which has been exported to other parts of the world, has been neo-functionalism. This theory emerged in response to critiques of the earlier functionalist approach which was developed by founders and promoters of the European Community, such as David Mitrany (1966). Functionalists had argued for the construction of transnational institutions designed to address specific technical issues. They believed that progress in one such area, like the production of coal and steel, would "spill over" into other areas where cooperation would benefit all parties involved. The result would be the gradual construction of new supranational technical institutions that would replace nation-states (O'Brien 1995, 696). Functionalist theory was criticized, however, for its tendency to see regional integration as an essentially automatic and technocratic process, with little attention to political realities.

In response, theorists like Ernst Haas (1958) incorporated insights from liberal pluralist theory in the development of neo-functionalism, which was somewhat clearer about the political processes involved in promoting integration. In contrast with classical realists, who saw nation-states as the main actors in the international system, neo-functionalists emphasized the role of a diverse array of elite actors, including interest groups, functionaries, parties, and international organizations. These actors engaged in bargaining processes to advance the general welfare and the provision of public goods. A process of political learning would occur as both elites and citizens gradually transfer attachment to these supranational institutions. This process becomes self-reinforcing and automatic through the operations of various feedback mechanisms, including "spillover," in which actors recognize the need for supranational institutions and rules to be extended in response to the unintended consequences of earlier forms of cooperation. Although the path toward higher levels of regional integration is not necessarily completely smooth, the dominant assumption is that this is bound to be the direction of change over time (Hooghe and Marks 2019, 1114–15).

Haas defined political regional integration as "the process whereby political actors in several distinct national settings are persuaded to shift their loyalties, expectations and political activities to a new center, whose institutions possess or demand juris-diction over pre-existing national states. The end result is a new political community, superimposed over the pre-existing ones" (1958, 16, cited in Dosenrode 2015, 3). The criterion for evaluating whether or not a region exists, and whether regional integration is progressing, is therefore the shift of aspects of authority and legitimacy previously attributed to the nation-state toward a supranational institution or organization. The main example of this process, and the one on which the theory is modeled, is the European Union. The theory suffered, however, from its failure to account for set-backs and the often fitful and sporadic nature of progress in the process of integration in Europe, and more generally was criticized for its deterministic and technocratic character (Moravscik 1993, 476).

In response to these critiques, Andrew Moravcsik (1993) proposed what would become another influential theoretical approach to understanding regional integra-tion, which he called "liberal intergovernmentalism." He summarizes three essential elements of this approach: "the assumption of rational state behaviour; a liberal theory of national preference formation; and an intergovernmentalist analysis of interstate negotiation" (1993, 480). He argues that states make the decision to move toward or away from higher levels of regional integration as a result of a rational cost-benefit analysis, which is informed by domestic political processes in which different societal groups (mostly firms) compete for influence, form national and transnational coalitions, and promote new policy interests in line with those interests and coalitions. The liberal part of the theory rests on the idea that national interests are not predetermined by objective factors as realists normally suggest but are determined through a pluralist process of domestic political conflict and bargaining among stakeholders. Once a state's interests and preferences are decided, it then engages in a process of interstate strategic interaction (1983, 481). Both neo-functionalists and liberal intergovernmentalists assume that economic interests are the prime driving factor in actors' decision-making processes, as higher levels of economic integration give rise to pressures toward cooperation to solve common problems (Moravscik 1983, 485). Like neo-functionalists, liberal intergovernmentalists identify regionalism as consisting of the development of higher levels of institutionalization to facilitate cooperation.

Despite the fact that both neo-functionalism and liberal intergovernmentalism assume that the forces driving integration are primarily economic (although national security motivations are also sometimes mentioned), they pay little attention to the details of the economic processes at work that create the pressures that result in integration. Both theories are compatible, however, with the dominant approach to integration within the field of economics, which is based on neoclassical assumptions about rational actor behavior and the benefits to firms and countries of higher levels of trade and integration. These benefits derive from processes of specialization, economies of scale, and the diversion of resources into countries' comparative advantages.[4] One prominent example of a trade theorist who applied these ideas to regional integration was Hungarian economist Béla Balassa. Drawing upon the work of Jacob Viner and others, Balassa discussed the economic benefits associated with higher degrees of regional integration. In contrast with the political approaches discussed above, in this approach regional integration is defined in terms of economic policies (i.e., the process of elimination of discrimination in trade relations between a group of states). Balassa (1961) famously distinguished between various stages of integration, beginning with a free trade area, and progressing through a customs union, common market, and ultimately economic union. This is an evolutionary dynamic, and it involves not just elimination of tariffs but gradually higher levels of coordination of economic, monetary, and fiscal policy, which eventually will be managed by supranational institutions.

Not surprisingly, the work of economists is largely silent on the political dynamics that might result in such outcomes.[5] However, neoclassical trade theory assumes that while free trade results in a net gain in general economic welfare, there are both winners and losers associated with such processes. Winners may be consumers, who will pay lower prices for their goods, or owners and workers in firms that maintain a comparative advantage and are internationally competitive, while losers may be located in declining industries. Moreover, the political problem is intensified by the fact that the beneficiaries of free trade tend to be diffuse (and the benefits relatively shallow), while those who suffer the costs tend to be concentrated in a few sectors, and the costs may be quite intense (such as those suffered by workers in rust-belt industries who lose jobs that are relocated to sites with lower wages). The danger this poses, from this neoclassical perspective, is that powerful interest groups representing a small but vocal minority may be able to hijack the political process through lobbying or political mobilization and prevent the state from adopting pro–free trade policies that are assumed to benefit the majority of the population. To avoid this outcome, regional elites often adopt trade policy decision-making processes that are nontransparent and closed to participation from unions or other actors who may not agree with the idea that the benefits from free trade will "trickle down" to the rest of the population. Neoclassical trade theorists generally fail to engage seriously with the common failure of states to address issues of distribution and the potentially toxic political fallout from such failure, as has been seen in recent years in the United States and elsewhere. They also tend to assume that corporations' behavior is virtually synonymous with the common good, while constituencies opposed to free trade and deeper integration are representing special interests.

All these approaches to regional integration have been challenged in recent years by the emergence of the so-called new regionalism(s) approach (NRA), which provides a less parsimonious and less prescriptive approach to understanding the dynamics behind regional integration, as well as the potential negative impacts of this process (which the liberal approaches described above tend to minimize). The NRA differs from these approaches in both its definition of regional integration and its theoretical framework for explaining the phenomenon. The word "new" in the name signifies that this strand of theorization emerged later than the approaches discussed above. While some of its early proponents were based in Europe, this approach responded to the different character that later regional integration processes throughout the world took on beginning in the late 1980s, compared with the process followed in Europe.

The "new" also indicates, however, that the theorists advocating this approach self-consciously distance themselves from several elements of the "older" approaches: specifically the rationalist ontology, and the institutionalist, statist, and Eurocentric biases. NRA theorists lean instead toward constructivist understandings of regionalism and region. Nevertheless, the incorporation of insights from international political economy mean that NRA theory integrates consideration of material factors and the existence of multiple actors and processes at work in a region. In this respect, NRA differs from a Wendtian version of constructivism, which leads to an emphasis on a unified sense of regional identity, as discussed by Arturo Santa-Cruz in this volume. Björn Hettne, one of the founders of the NRA approach, insists, for example, on the existence of multiple political actors and contestation, rather than a coherent identity:

Today, researchers acknowledge the fact that there are no "natural" regions: definitions of a "region" vary according to the particular problem or question under investigation. Moreover, it is widely accepted that it is how political actors perceive and interpret the idea of a region and notions of "regionness" that is critical: all regions are socially constructed and hence politically contested. (2005, 544)

Frederik Söderbaum distinguishes between "regionalism" and "regionalization," which permits the inclusion of diverse processes that might not fit into more parsimonious definitions of regionalism:

"Regionalism" represents the policy and project, whereby state and non-state actors cooperate and coordinate strategy within a particular region or as a type of world order. It is usually associated with a formal program, and often leads to institution building. "Regionalisation" refers to the process of cooperation, integration, cohesion and identity creating a regional space (issue-specific or general). (2009, 479)

In this approach, then, institutions "often" form part of regionalism, but they are not synonymous with it, and regionalism is embedded in broader political, economic, cultural, and other processes of regionalization which shape it. Non-state actors (not limited to firms) may, moreover, play equally important roles as states in these processes. Elsewhere, Söderbaum differentiates between "formal" and "informal" processes of regionalism and argues that the regional interstate organizations found in more formal forms, are "a second-order phenomenon," while the primary causal significance is attributed to the broader processes that "underlie regionalisation in a particular geographical space" (2011, 54). Regions are also, because of their socially constructed character, heterogenous, and their spatial boundaries are blurred (2011, 54). As a result, this approach sidelines the idea that regions need to possess a clear, cohesive identity, as suggested in Santa-Cruz's chapter.

Given its shifting and historically contingent nature, regionalism is shaped by the contextual processes in which it emerges. While the "old" regionalism was a product of the Cold War and embedded liberalism, the "new regionalism" is both a product of, and a reaction against, aspects of globalization. In contrast with the liberal approaches described above, globalization is understood as inherently uneven in its impacts, and the spread of capitalist relations need not be understood as inherently positive or efficiency-producing. In parts of the Global South in particular, regionalization may be primarily driven by a desire of vulnerable states to insulate themselves from the harsh liberalizing impacts of the global economy, not as a path to greater liberalization (Shaw, Grant, and Cornelissen 2011, 10). In other cases, however, regional development may emerge as much as a result of corporate strategies as of state directives and may facilitate the development of regional supply chains (Shaw, Grant, and Cornelissen 2011, 16). In contrast with the liberal approaches that adopt either technocratic or pluralist understandings of the political process, in the NRA, the politics of regional integration are often deeply contested, as a result of the uneven and often exploitative impact of processes of regional integration that benefit state and corporate elites over the interests of common citizens and noncorporate civil-society actors.

Overall, I argue, several aspects of the NRA provide a more satisfactory understanding of North American integration processes than the Eurocentric and rationalist approaches laid out above. In the next section I lay out the ways in which the NRA helps illuminate critical elements of recent developments in the North American region, including the rise of populist, nationalist policies under US president Donald Trump, the renegotiation of NAFTA, the role played by regional value chains, and the impact of the pandemic.

North America beyond NAFTA?

What do these theoretical perspectives tell us about the events that have played out in the North American region over the last few years, in particular the rise of Trump and the near-death experience of the NAFTA? At one level, these events confirm once again the failure of the North American region to live up to the ideals of neo-functionalism or even liberal intergovernmentalism. Nevertheless, I argue, drawing upon the insights of NRA, that North America goes beyond NAFTA, and that the region that exists cannot be explained by rationalist, teleological, or Eurocentric proposals.

Much of the commentary on the politics of the North American region has been shaped explicitly or implicitly by the neo-functionalist approach, modeled on the European Union (EU). For supporters of deeper integration in the North American continent, the weaknesses of the institutional structure of the North American region have limited its capacity to achieve higher levels of cooperation. Robert Pastor, for example, chided North American leaders (except for Mexico's first democratically elected president, Vicente Fox), for failing to learn from the experience of "the longest-running, most successful regional trading scheme, the European Union" (2001, 2). Pastor therefore recommended the construction of new institutions (a North American Commission, a North American Parliamentary Group, a Permanent North American Court on Trade and Investment, and regular meetings of cabinet ministers) to bind the three countries of the region together and help them to tackle their common problems (2001, 100–103).

Pastor's book was published in August 2001, just before the September 11 attacks that seemed to doom even further this optimistic liberal perspective. The temporary closing of the two US land borders terrified both the Canadian and Mexican governments as well as business elites in all three countries about the potential for anti-terrorism measures to derail movement toward continental integration. The Security and Prosperity Partnership of North America (SPP) was eventually launched in 2005 by the leaders of the three countries as a way of pushing forward "deep integration" while addressing the security concerns of the US government. In this version, however, integration was pursued without creating new trinational institutions. The SPP took the form of trinational committees directed by the executive branches of the three countries, which would report annually to a North American Leaders' Summit convened by the three heads of state. The SPP failed to achieve much progress, however, and eventually was eliminated in 2009 after the election of Democratic president Barack Obama (Ayres and Macdonald 2012). The cancellation of the SPP is a good example of the weakness of neo-functionalist accounts that assume the smooth and seamless process of ever-deeper political integration over time.

The 2016 election of Donald Trump and his coming to power in 2017 seemed to pose an even more perilous threat to the liberal vision of the region promoted by pro-integration forces, as well as the interpretation of dominant theories of regionalism. Trump's erratic, bombastic, and often apparently irrational policy style contrasts vividly with the calm, rational, and technocratic style of decision-making expected in functionalist, neo-functionalist, and liberal intergovernmentalist approaches. This does not mean, however, that Trump's style was entirely lacking in logic or social foundations. His invocation of the dangers of free trade policies to American workers and the American nation did not emerge out of the blue but reflected many of the concerns and rhetorical flourishes of NAFTA opponents dating back to Ross Perot and Pat Buchanan. Unions and other left-wing opponents of NAFTA had raised similar concerns, but without the xenophobic elements so common in the right-wing critics' discourses. Senior US trade negotiator Robert Lighthizer similarly warned of the "dark side" of free trade and globalization in a 2020 *Foreign Affairs* article:

> Between 2000 and 2016, the United States lost nearly five million manufacturing jobs. Median household income stagnated. And in places prosperity left behind, the fabric of society frayed. Since the mid-1990s, the United States has faced an epidemic of what the economists Anne Case and Angus Deaton have termed "deaths of despair." They have found that among white middle-aged adults who lack a college education—a demographic that has borne much of the brunt of outsourcing—deaths from cirrhosis of the liver increased by 50 percent between 1999 and 2013, suicides increased by 78 percent, and drug and alcohol overdoses increased by 323 percent. From 2014 to 2017, the increase in deaths of despair led to the first decrease in life expectancy in the United States over a three-year period since the 1918 flu pandemic.
>
> Trade has not been the sole cause of the recent loss of manufacturing jobs or of the attendant societal distress. Automation, productivity gains, foreign currency manipulation, and the financial crisis of 2008 have played

key roles, as well. But it cannot be denied that the outsourcing of jobs from high- to low-wage places has devastated communities in the American Rust Belt and elsewhere. (Lighthizer 2020)

While the USMCA, negotiated by Lighthizer and his Canadian and Mexican counterparts, contained some elements of traditional US trade policy based on promoting the position of US-based high-tech corporations and cultural industries, it also contained elements of traditional economic nationalism designed to protect US jobs and to counter the rise of China.

As a result of these diverse intellectual and political influences on the agreement, analysts differ on the actual impact the USMCA will have on political and economic relations in North America. Many commentators called the new deal essentially "NAFTA 2.0"—representing a modestly updated version of the original NAFTA (Long 2019). Greg Anderson argues that despite Trump's intentions to cancel or at least substantially alter NAFTA, the pressure to get a deal done quickly militated against many fundamental changes from the NAFTA template, resulting in an agreement that largely rescued the status quo, rather than introducing radical new elements.

Nevertheless, argues Anderson, "first and foremost, the USMCA represents a significant decline in the already tenuous nature of trilateralism" (2020, 159). He argues that the negotiating process often seemed to be on two different tracks (US-Canadian and US-Mexican), as a result of the Trump administration's obsession with some aspects of the US-Mexico relationship. The final text "significantly downgrades the notion of North America as a trilateral economic zone" based on "tenuous, but real, trilateralism" in three respects (Anderson 2020, 159–60).

First, the agreement requires that to qualify as made in North America under the rules of origin, 40 percent of cars and 45 percent of trucks must be manufactured by workers who earn at least sixteen dollars per hour, a condition that cannot be met in the foreseeable future in Mexican plants. Certainly, this provision favors the United States (and Canada). Secondly, the provisions in NAFTA's chapter 19 that permitted Canada and Mexico to challenge US trade remedy actions were dropped for relations between the United States and Canada, but maintained for the United States and Mexico. Chapter 19 created binational dispute resolution panels to challenge the use of antidumping or countervailing duties by one party against another member state. The United States pushed hard throughout the talks for the elimination of these provisions altogether, which the Trump team saw as an unacceptable limitation on US sovereignty, but for Canada, this was a nonnegotiable requirement for any new agreement, and it refused to back down. Canada's main motivation in seeking the NAFTA agreement in the 1980s was to provide an institutional mechanism to limit the capacity of the United States to engage in what it saw as arbitrary trade remedy actions. Mexico, in contrast, apparently viewed this aspect of the NAFTA as expendable and didn't insist on its inclusion (Gantz 2019, 4–5). As a result, the two countries are treated differently in the final text (chapter 31 of the USMCA). Finally, the investor state dispute settlement mechanism (ISDS) enshrined in chapter 11 of NAFTA will be dropped for disputes involving the United and Canada, while the United States and Mexico agreed to maintain this mechanism in a few key sectors.

Overall, the USMCA does represent a modest intensification of the already acute dominance of the United States in the North American region. It is clear that Mexico got the worst deal since both the previous administration of Enrique Peña Nieto and the incoming one of Andrés Manuel López Obrador were desperate to get a deal at almost any cost. Canada had greater structural power to withstand US pressure and push for its own priority, the maintenance of the state-to-state dispute resolution mechanisms (see Macdonald 2020c). This does not imply, however, that the regionness of North America has necessarily declined, since only liberal theories of regionalism expect that regionalization is inevitably accompanied by stronger institutionalization and greater equality among the members. NRA theories, which draw on critical international political economy theory, view asymmetry and political dominance of a hegemon as a fundamental and inescapable element of the new regionalisms that emerged in the 1980s. In this respect, this approach responds to many of the concerns raised consistently by Canadian and Mexican authors about the dominance of the United States in the operations of the North American region.[6] This does not mean, however, that the non-hegemonic states within a region completely lack agency, as we see both in Canada's insistence on maintaining a state-to-state dispute settlement mechanism, and Mexico's strategic decision to fight this battle.

In fact, in some respects the provisions of USMCA may result in an increase in (asymmetrical) regionness. For example, section 32:10 provides that any one of the three signatories must provide the other signatories advance notice of any intent to negotiate a free trade deal with a "non-market country" (read China) and transparency on the results. Trump stated after the deal was reached that the USMCA "will bring all three Great Nations closer together in competition with the rest of the world" (BBC 2018). In other words, Trump and his chief trade negotiator Lighthizer saw the USMCA as part of an attempt to strengthen North American ties (on US terms) to counter the perceived growing threat from China (these threats are discussed in the chapters in this volume by Stallings and Morales). At the same time, the provisions in the USMCA on labor rights and the separate side deals between the United States and Mexico and between Canada and Mexico on labor reform in Mexico may have a positive long-run impact on wages and working conditions in Mexico, something that may counteract some of the asymmetries of the region.[7] The NRA's emphasis on the impact of global economic and geopolitical conditions on the construction of regions is of relevance here, in contrast with the European theories reviewed above, which focus on factors internal to the region.

Another important insight we can draw from the NRA to interpret recent dynamics in North America is its focus on informal economic processes of regionalization, including the construction of regional and global value chains. This is an aspect of regionalization that is largely overlooked by dominant liberal theories, which are based on neoclassical economic assumptions. As argued by Richard Baldwin and Javier Lopez-Gonzalez, while there is much discussion of global value chains, it is really more accurate to speak of regional value chains, dominated by what they call Factory Europe, Factory Asia, and Factory North America. Of these, Factory North America displays the "most intensive supply-chain networks" (Baldwin and Lopez-Gonzalez 2015, 1696). These regional blocs are not internally homogenous, but are structured in a hub-and-spoke pattern around the regional leader (the United States in the case of Factory North America) (Baldwin and Lopez-Gonzalez 2015, 1718). An analysis of the regional dynamics encouraged by value chains thus accentuates the asymmetries built into regional economic blocs, in contrast with liberal theories of regional integration that emphasize dynamics promoting internal homogeneity and attenuation of asymmetries between members of the region.

As discussed above, Trump's decision to move ahead with the NAFTA renegotiations rather than scrapping the deal reflected in part the probable political and economic fallout within the United States of cancellation. The importance of regional value chains was also illustrated vividly after 9/11 when some US-based auto plants had to shut down because of the temporary closing of the US land borders (Reinsch et al. 2019). Excessive focus on the institutional dimensions of regionalism (or lack thereof, in the case of North America) has led to an inadequate understanding and evaluation of the importance of the regional value chains that have emerged in the North American region. As argued by Gustavo Vega Cánovas and Francisco Campos Ortiz (2021, 155), these value chains, particularly in the automotive sector, are the most tangible result of the NAFTA agreement:

> Over the past 25 years, vast regional production chains have been created in North America. The United States, Mexico and Canada are, respectively, the third, fourth, and sixth largest exporters of the automotive industry worldwide. In the United States, 40% of the automobiles in the market are imported, mainly from Mexico, Canada, Japan, and South Korea. In turn, Mexico has become the largest export market for auto parts to the United States, almost tripling the value of the second largest exporter to the Mexican market, Canada.

The impact of the new rules of origin (ROOs) and other aspects of the USMCA on regional value chains is unclear. For example, under these ROOs auto manufacturers need to certify that 75 percent of their steel and aluminum comes from the United States, Canada, or Mexico in order to qualify for duty-free status under the USMCA, a substantial increase from 62.5 percent in NAFTA. These represent the most stringent rules in any trade agreement (Reinsch et al. 2019, 19). The goal of the new rules on the part of the United States was to encourage more firms to produce their goods and create more jobs in the United States (and possibly Canada), but this could drive up costs and prices of finished goods. Companies might choose to respond by ignoring these requirements and paying the 2.5 percent United States Most Favored Nation tariff as set by the World Trade Organization, and could decide instead to move more of their production to Mexico to take advantage of the still much lower labor costs there (Reinsch et al. 2019, 21). The introduction of a sixteen-year "sunset clause" in USMCA also contributes to the complexity and risk associated with firms' decision-making (Forde 2020). Overall, the new rules seem likely to result in the Big Three automakers locating more of their production processes in North America and capturing more of the local market, at a cost of a less competitive position in non–North American markets, thus intensifying the shift toward regionalization (Reinsch et al. 2019, 36).

While the overall impact of the USMCA on levels of regionalization is unclear and likely mixed, the additional impact of the COVID-19 pandemic may tip the balance in the direction of higher levels of regional production. The pandemic resulted in the closing of land borders within North America to all but essential travelers, and disrupted supply chains around the world. Many firms may be considering a "nearshoring" strategy, moving supply chains closer to home to help mitigate the impact of future global supply chain shocks. According to a survey of Canadian firms by the Global Commerce Centre, more than one-third of respondents said that the disruptions caused by COVID-19 in supply chains led them to source more inputs from local suppliers. Respondents did not differentiate between the impacts on their production when sourcing inputs from Canada or the United States, reflecting the already high level of integration of North American supply chains (Conference Board of Canada 2020, 4–5). An October 2022 survey from the Shanghai branch of the US Chamber of Commerce showed that more than sixty US companies had decided to cut their investments in China in 2022, more than twice as many as in 2021. Mexico has benefited from these decisions as a result of its proximity to the United States and low labor costs: its manufacturing sector grew at a rate of 5 percent in 2022 (Bove 2022). These shifting dynamics associated with the construction of regional value chains are largely overlooked by mainstream theories.

New regionalism approaches also highlight other informal processes that are ignored or under-theorized in more conventional approaches. Many of these processes, including the environment, migration, energy markets, etc., are examined in other chapters in this volume. Another important theme that NRA illuminates is the role non-state actors may play in shaping regional spaces. While traditional theories focus almost exclusively on the role of state or corporate actors, Timothy M. Shaw, J. Andrew Grant, and Scarlett Cornelissen argue in an overview of theories of new regionalism that from this perspective, civil-society actors are a significant factor, even sometimes a catalyst, of processes of regionalization (2011, 16). Alex Warleigh-Lack

(2006, 753) similarly argues that the new regionalism is "shaped voluntarily by actors from the bottom-up rather than imposed by foreign powers or cultivated by actors at the new centre."

In North America, the launch of the NAFTA negotiations in the 1990s ignited the coalescence of transnational activism opposed to the agreement as a whole or aspects of it, including labor unions, environmentalists, women, faith-based organizations, and human rights activists. These activists opposed the neoliberal tenets and corporate strategies underlying the agreement and engaged in diverse processes of transnational political activism that challenged the trajectory of North American integration for over a decade. While they failed to defeat the agreement, they did succeed in placing nontraditional trade issues such as labor rights and environmental issues on the agenda, including in the creation of the labor and environmental side accords.

In general, there was a decline in cross-border activism after NAFTA, but significant civil society cooperation still occurred in some areas. The side agreements also created some opportunities for transnational cooperation among labor and environmentalist activists on the North American scale, who were able to publicize violations and push for higher standards in both areas (Macdonald 2020b; Gabriel and Macdonald 2021). Additionally, the cross-border networks established during the fight against NAFTA carried over into campaigns against other neoliberal trade agreements, including the Free Trade Area of the Americas (FTAA) proposal launched by President Bill Clinton in 1994. After the FTAA proposal was defeated, there was a dispersal of civil-society activity and a tendency toward more localized activism rather than centralized national coalitions or coordination among civil societies in the three countries. Anti-NAFTA discourses associated with the civil-society actors on the political right also undoubtedly influenced the right-wing populist discourses of Trump and his supporters. These right-wing actors did not establish strong transnational linkages, but there were forms of cross-border influence and political learning occurring, particularly between Canada and the United States. With the introduction of new labor provisions in USMCA, increased cooperation is occurring between labor unions and civil society activists in the three countries. Both the Biden and Trudeau governments are also providing significant support to promote labor rights in Mexico, through the backing of civil-society actors.

Overall, the North American region continues to be shaped by transnational activism and cross-border influences in a wide range of areas including Indigenous and feminist struggles, campaigns against anti-Black racism, cooperation among environmentalists, and many other themes. Even if these forms of cooperation are not institutionalized, and include influences from outside of the region, they represent an important dimension of regionalism overlooked in more traditional theories.

Conclusion

Regions are often messy, complicated, and slippery phenomena. Their boundaries are shifting, and they overlap with other forms of territorial governance. As argued by Wendy Larner and William Walters (2002, 391), the "legacy of earlier theoretical formulations is impeding the analysis of the 'new regionalism.'" Older theoretical approaches, often based on the European experience, fail to capture much of what is interesting and important in contemporary manifestations of regionalism around the world. New regionalism approaches began to appear on the scene in the 1980s; as they developed, they were partly inspired by the emergence of NAFTA, which seemed to give rise to a new type of region. Theorists within this approach challenged earlier approaches like functionalism, neo-functionalism, and liberal intergovernmentalism, as well as neoclassical trade theories. They highlighted various dimensions of regionalism such as the role of global economic and political forces in the birth, life, and decline of regions; took issue with the state-centric and Eurocentric character of earlier approaches; and emphasized instead more informal dimensions of regionalism as well as the hierarchical and asymmetrical character of regions. The work of these theorists is less teleological, since regions are seen as having no clear end point, and capable of stagnation or decline.

As argued in this chapter, events over the last few years help confirm the usefulness of the NRA. The unpredictable and erratic character of the Trump presidency helps to question the rationalist assumptions of earlier approaches, and the NRA is better equipped to explain such factors as the role of regional value chains, the impact of the COVID-19 pandemic, and the role of non-state actors. The NRA might also help account for other important dimensions of regionalism in North America that I have not addressed here, such as the mutable character of membership and borders. This theoretical approach suggests that countries that are not part of the NAFTA, such as the Central American states, particularly the Northern Triangle states, can in some respects be considered part of North America, not just geographically, but through the informal connections created through migration, value chains, the flow of weapons and money, and transnational actors like the *maras* (gangs). The *Mara Salvatrucha* (MS-13) in fact originated among Salvadoran immigrants in Los Angeles, and spread in Central America when youth were deported back to El Salvador. The emphasis of the NRA on external changes in the global political economy on the region can also help us understand the ways in which the rise of China could reenforce rather than undermine North American regionalism, as suggested by Barbara Stallings in this volume. Growing Western rivalry with China and the way in which the pandemic has exposed the fragility of far-flung value chains may result in greater nearshoring of investment by US-based multinationals and financial interests in coming years, and increased interregional rivalry. Given its post-positivist theoretical assumptions, an NRA approach does not seek to predict the future of the region, but it can yield important insights into understanding evolving power relations in an unpredictable global order.

Notes

1. See, for example, MacArthur 2001 vs. Hufbauer and Schott 2005, two analyses of NAFTA which are worlds apart in their views of the nature of the trade agreement and its impacts.

2. There is only one journal devoted to the study of the region, *Norteamérica*, and a couple of research institutions: for example, the Centro de Investigaciones sobre América del Norte (CISAN) at the Universidad Nacional Autónoma de México (UNAM) (where *Norteamérica* is based). There is a larger number of academic programs that allow students to specialize in the study of North America, including Carleton University, McGill University, and Wilfrid Laurier University in Canada; Brown University, Dartmouth College, Harvard, Stanford, University of California, Berkeley, University of North Carolina at Chapel Hill, University of Texas at El Paso, and Yale University in the United States; and UNAM, Colegio de México, Tecnológico de Monterrey, and Universidad de Guadalajara in Mexico. There is no dedicated funding source available for North American studies. The only funding source I am aware of dedicated to North American studies was the Programa Interinstitucional de Estudios sobre la Región de América del Norte (PIERAN), based at El Colegio de México, which provided small grants to trinational teams of researchers between 1994 and 2016.

3. Some notable exceptions include: Ayres and Macdonald 2012; Bow 2015; Castro-Rea 2013; Duina 2006; and Morales 2008.

4. Malcolm Fairbrother (2020, 4) argues provocatively that although politicians are often seen as obeying the precepts of liberal economics when adopting policies that promote globalization, they actually subscribe to a form of "folk economics" that owes more to mercantilism and the lived experiences of businesspeople than to true economic science.

5. See the work of heterodox economist Dani Rodrik for an exception to this claim. Rodrik (2018) argues that contemporary trade agreements, which go well beyond at-the-border trade rules to cover a wide array of domestic rules and regulations, are driven by the rent-seeking behavior of politically well-connected special interests and multinational corporations.

6. See, for example, the work of Canadian Stephen Clarkson (2008) and Mexican María Teresa Gutiérrez Haces (2015).

7. See DiCaro and Macdonald 2021, DiCaro and Macdonald 2022, and CISAN 2022 for a discussion of the labor mechanisms contained in the USMCA and its annexes, and progress as of mid-2022 for improving labor rights in Mexico.

Bibliography

Anderson, G. 2020. *Freeing Trade in North America*. Montreal: McGill–Queen's University Press.

Ayres, J., and L. Macdonald. 2012. "Democratic Deficits and the Role of Civil Society in North America: The SPP and Beyond." In *North America in Question: Regional Integration in an Era of Economic Turbulence*, edited by Jeffrey Ayres and Laura Macdonald, 334–60. Toronto: University of Toronto Press.

Bow, Brian. 2015. "Legitimacy, Politicization and Regional Integration in North America." In *The Legitimacy of Regional Integration in Europe and the Americas*, edited by Achim Hurrelmann and Steffen Schneider, 33–56. New York: Palgrave Macmillan.

Balassa, Béla. 1961. *The Theory of Economic Integration*. London: George Allen & Unwin Ltd.

Baldwin, R., and J. Lopez-Gonzalez. 2015. "Supply-Chain Trade: A Portrait of Global Patterns and Several Testable Hypotheses." *The World Economy* 38 (11): 1682–1721.

Bove, T. 2022. "Years of Global Supply Chain Chaos Could Mean a Nearshoring Jackpot for the Americas in 2023. *Fortune*. December 23, 2022. Accessed December 30, 2022. https://fortune.com/2022/12/23/supply-chain-chaos-leading-to-2023-nearshoring-boom-latin-america/.

Castro-Rea, J. 2012. *Our North America: Social and Political Relations beyond NAFTA*. Farnham, UK: Ashgate.

CILAS. 2022. "3 Años de la reforma laboral 2019 y del capítulo 23 del T-MEC: Balance y Perspectivas." Accessed June 17, 2022. http://cilas.mx/documento-completo-balance-a-3-anos-de-la-reforma-laboral-2019-y-del-capitulo-23-laboral-del-t-mec-2/.

Clarkson, S. 2008. *Does North America Exist? Governing the Continent after NAFTA and 9/11*. Toronto: University of Toronto Press.

Conference Board of Canada. 2020. "Bringing Them Home: Reshoring Supply Chains is Not a Panacea." Issue Briefing, October 20, 2020. Accessed February 28, 2021. https://www.conferenceboard.ca/e-library/abstract.aspx?did=10827.

Del Real, J. A., and S. Sullivan, 2016. "Trump: TPP Trade Deal 'Pushed by Special Interests who Want to Rape Our Country.'" *Washington Post*, June 28, 2016. Accessed February 28, 2021. https://www.washingtonpost.com/news/post-politics/wp/2016/06/28/trump-tpp-trade-deal-pushed-by-special-interests-who-want-to-rape-our-country/.

DiCaro, A., and L. Macdonald. "Union Win at Mexican Auto Plant Brings New Hope for Labour Rights." *Hill Times*, June 9, 2022. Accessed June 17, 2022. https://www.hilltimes.com/2022/06/09/union-win-at-mexican-auto-plant-brings-new-hope-for-labour-rights/366309.

DiCaro, A., and L. Macdonald, "CUSMA's Labour Mechanisms: A Testing Ground for Protecting North American Workers." *CCPA Monitor Magazine*, July 19, 2021.

Accessed on June 17, 2022. https://monitormag.ca/articles/cusmas-labour-mecha-nisms-a-testing-ground-for-protecting-north-american-workers.

Dosenrode, S. 2015. "On Regional Integration." In *Limits to Regional Integration*, edited by S. Dosenrode, 1–16. Farnham, UK: Ashgate.

Duina, F. 2006. *The Social Construction of Free Trade: The EU, NAFTA and Mercosur.* Princeton, NJ: Princeton University Press.

Fairbrother, M. 2020. *Fair Traders: Elites, Democracy, and the Rise of Globalization.* Oxford: Oxford University Press.

Gabriel, C., and L. Macdonald. 2021. "New Architectures for Migration Governance: NAFTA and Transnational Activism around Migrants' Rights." *Third World Quarterly* 42 (1): 68–85.

Gantz, D. A. 2019. "The United States-Mexico-Canada Agreement: Settlement of Disputes." Rice University's Baker Institute report, May 2, 2019. Accessed on May 10, 2021. https://scholarship.rice.edu/bitstream/handle/1911/107947/bi-report-050219-mex-usmca-3.pdf. .

Gutiérrez-Haces, M. T. 2015. *Los Vecinos del Vecino: La continentalización de México y Canadá en América del Norte.* Mexico City: Universidad Nacional Autónoma de México and ARIEL.

Haas, E. B. 1958. *The Uniting of Europe: Political, Social and Economic Forces, 1950–1957.* Stanford, CA: Stanford University Press.

Hernández, L. 2021. "¿Cómo impactará a México la nueva política de Biden 'Buy American'?" *El Financiero*, January 19, 2021. Accessed February 28, 2021. https://www.elfinanciero.com.mx/economia/buy-american-luz-y-sombra-para-mexico.

Hettne, B. 2005. "Beyond the New Regionalism." *New Political Economy* 10 (4): 543–71.

Hooghe, L., and G. Marks. 2019. "Grand Theories of European Integration in the Twenty First Century." *Journal of European Public Policy* 26 (8): 1113–33.

Hufbauer, G. C., and J. J. Schott. 2005. *NAFTA Revisited: Achievements and Challenges.* Washington, DC: Institute for International Economics.

Inglehart, R. F., N. Nevitte, and M. Basáñez. 1996. *The North American Trajectory: Cultural, Economic, and Political Ties among the United States, Canada, and Mexico.* New York: Aldine de Gruyter.

Larner, W., and W. Walters. 2002. "The Political Rationality of 'New Regionalism': Toward a Genealogy of the Region." *Theory and Society* 31: 392–432.

Lighthizer, R. E. 2020. "How to Make Trade Work for Workers." *Foreign Affairs* 99 (4): 78–84, 86–92.

Long, H. 2019. "The USMCA Is Finally Done. Here's What Is in It." *Washington Post*, December 10, 2019.

MacArthur, J. R. 2001. *The Selling of "Free Trade": NAFTA, Washington, and the Subversion of American Democracy.* Berkeley: University of California Press.

Macdonald, L. 2020a. "Canada in the North American Region: Implications of Trump and the NAFTA Re-negotiations." *Canadian Journal of Political Science* 53 (3): 505–20.

Macdonald, L. 2020b. "Le militantisme de la société civile transnationale nord améric-aine avant et après l'ALENA." In *L'Amérique du Nord: Une histoire des identités et des solidarités*, edited by Catherine Vézina and Maurice Demers, 123–42. Quebec City: Presses de l'Université Laval.

Macdonald, L. 2020c. "Stronger Together? Canada-Mexico Relations and the NAFTA Re-negotiations." *Canadian Foreign Policy Journal* 26 (2): 152–66.

Mitrany, D. 1966. *A Working Peace System*. Chicago: Quadrangle Books.

Morales, I. 2008. *Post-NAFTA North America: Reshaping the Economic and Political Governance of a Changing Region*. London: Palgrave Macmillan.

Moravscik, A. 1983. "Preferences and Power in the European Community: A Liberal Intergovernmentalist Approach." *Journal of Common Market Studies* 31 (4): 473–524.

O'Brien, R. 1995. "North American Integration and International Relations Theory." *Canadian Journal of Political Science / Revue canadienne de science politique* 28 (4): 693–724.

Parker, A., P. Rucker, D. Paletta, and K. DeYoung. 2017. "'I Was All Set to Terminate'": Inside Trump's Sudden Shift on NAFTA." *Washington Post*, April 27, 2017.

Reinsch, W. A., J. Caporal, M. Waddoups, and N. Tekarli. 2019. *The Impact of Rules of Origin on Supply Chains: USMCA's Auto Rules as a Case Study*. Washington, DC: Center for Strategic and International Studies.

Rodrik, D. 2018. "What Do Trade Agreements Really Do?" *Journal of Economic Perspectives* 32 (2): 73–90.

Schmitter, P. 1970. "A Revised Theory of Regional Integration." *International Organization* 24 (4): 836–68.

Shaw, T. M., J. A. Grant, and S. Cornelissen. 2011. "Introduction and Overview: The Study of New Regionalism(s) at the Start of the Second Decade of the Twenty-First Century." In *The Ashgate Research Companion to Regionalisms*, edited by T. M. Shaw, J. A. Grant, and S. Cornelissen, 330. Farnham, UK: Ashgate, 330.

Söderbaum, F. 2009. "Comparative Regional Integration and Regionalism." In *The SAGE Handbook of Comparative Politics*, edited by T. Landman and N. Robinson, 477–96. London: Sage.

Vega Cánovas, G., and F. Campos Ortiz. 2021. "The United States-Mexico-Canada Agreement (USMCA): Challenges and Opportunities in the Global Environment of the Coronavirus." In *Implementing the USMCA: A Test for North America*, 148–76. Mexico City: Senado de la República, Centro de Investigación Gilberto Bosques.

Warleigh-Lack, A. 2006. "Toward a Conceptual Framework for Regionalisation: Bridging 'New Regionalism' and 'Integration Theory.'" *Review of International Political Economy* 13 (5): 750–71.

CHAPTER FIVE

Fortress North America

Theorizing a Regional Approach to Migration Management

Ernesto Castañeda, Michael Danielson, and Jayesh Rathod

Introduction: North America as an immigration system

IN NORTH America and elsewhere, the institutionalization of openness to trade and financial flows in bilateral, regional, and international agreements contrasts with the limits on people's free movement (Dadush 2017; Castañeda and Shemesh 2020). Despite NAFTA and the USMCA, the absence of comprehensive migration discussions within the North American agenda, and the near-absence of regional institutions to manage migration, is noteworthy (see Toro, this volume). This contrasts with the inclusion of substantial immigration agreements as part of Mercosur and the Schengen Area in Europe. This regional variation seems puzzling when considering that the free movement of people could be seen as a public good (Dadush 2017, 119). More regional and international cooperation on migration could produce total economic gains and help ameliorate short-term distributional effects both for immigrant-sending countries subsidizing labor reproduction and for the immigrant-receiving countries, where short-term social expenditures for local governments may increase earlier than the eventual fiscal benefits for federal governments. However, one does not need to be a specialist in migration or international politics to know that the free movement of people across borders is not viewed as a positive by most states and a significant share of public opinion.

At the time NAFTA was negotiated, the principal source of irregular migration to the United States consisted of Mexican laborers, and some architects of the agreement posited that it would boost the Mexican economy and diminish migration. Because migration was considered a controversial topic, however, no regional migration regime was introduced, beyond provisions facilitating the temporary entry of business visitors and investors. Formal regional institutions defined North America as trilateral in scope and economic in nature. However, while those formal institutions remain largely unchanged, the dynamics of migration suggest there is a broader North American regional system of quite a different sort. Over the past decade, migration through the US-Mexico border consisted of increasing shares of Salvadorans, Guatemalans, and Hondurans.[1] While there has been no North American equivalent of the Schengen in terms of free movement of people within member states, we argue that there are common goals, which the United States, Canada, and Mexico pursue through indirect forms of regional cooperation. Nevertheless, rather than being a regionalist project, this cooperation has been nationalistic and illiberal. The North American migration system that has emerged is fundamentally restrictionist, both externally and internally (Camacho-Beltrán 2019). Furthermore, the goals are hegemonically defined by the United States.

The tensions over migration in North America are emblematic of an enduring paradox of political liberalism dating to the European Enlightenment: the ostensible internal openness of liberal states is often built upon the explicit exclusion of external others—immigrants, particularly those of color (Castañeda 2019) and internal minorities—women, minors, and enslaved peoples and their descendants. W. E. B. Du Bois ([1915] 2014) wrote about the democracy paradox, in which the expansion of civil and social rights within Europe was coupled with European colonialism. David FitzGerald and David Cook-Martín (2014) write about how the most liberal and democratic countries—like the United States—were the first to establish racist and eugenicist immigration policies. Such illiberal practices often contradicted proclaimed liberal norms. Therefore, it would be naïve to assume that all regional coordination and collaboration must be guided by human rights and liberal principles or encoded in formal international agreements. Despite likely interpretive biases among liberal internationalist and functionalist scholars who focus on regionalism, there is no fundamental reason to think that regional cooperation and collaboration need be "liberal" either externally or internally. States within a region do not meet as equals, as the hegemonic dynamics in North America clearly show (see Toro, this volume).

When possible, states prefer to let Central Americans migrate to another country in the region. A useful analogy for our argument can be provided by how immigrant destinations within the United States have changed in the last decades. Sociologist Ivan Light argued (2006) that Los Angeles, an old Mexican-immigrant destination, started enforcing policies and undergoing dynamics that reduced immigration (housing and warehouse ordinances made housing more expensive and house-sharing more difficult) and "deflected" much of these immigrant flows to "new destinations" within the United States (Massey 2008; Marrow 2011). In the same ways, the increasing number of immigrants, refugees, and asylum seekers rejected by the United States may find themselves settling in Canada or Mexico. Like squeezing a balloon, the application of pressure in one area directs the air to other areas.

This chapter seeks to identify both consistency and variations among the North American states limiting the arrival of asylum seekers and immigrants, principally but not exclusively those from Northern Central America (NCA). NCA includes Guatemala, El Salvador, and Honduras, and is analogous to the term "Northern

Triangle," which is often used by US Defense and Homeland Security officials to talk about national security. We argue that, considered together, Canadian, Mexican, and US asylum policies constitute a limited, but identifiable, regional migration system. On the most basic level, an examination of how the United States, Mexico, and Canada have responded to Central American migration allows for a rich description that uncovers the unique historical, geopolitical, sociological, and legal factors that shape migration policy in each country. As described more fully in section 3 below, this examination yields interesting similarities, including shared responses to key historical moments and similar narratives about the "worthiness" (or lack thereof) of Central American migrants. This contrasts with other times, including during the 1980s, when the countries' posture toward Central American refugees and migrants diverged.

Beyond these noteworthy similarities and differences, the topic of Central American migration invites a deeper analysis of how the countries' migration policies have created an interdependent system through a blend of explicit cooperation, domestic policy dynamics, and the underlying demographic, social, and geographic structures that tie the countries and peoples of North America together. Our analysis suggests that, on the whole, the policies of the three countries are designed to limit access to migrants and asylum seekers, and in particular, to discourage strongly overland migration and asylum requests at the border. In this regard, all three countries have, in practice, embraced the broader global trend of the externalization of border controls (see FitzGerald 2019). Our term for the region's interdependent approach to migration management is "Fortress North America," in the same way that the emergence of continental exclusion policies has led to the moniker "Fortress Europe." The North American system is less intentionally constructed as a supranational, regional system than the European system, and as with other aspects of regionalism addressed in this book, it is institutionally thin. Insofar as it exists as a cooperative system, coordination has been more ad hoc in nature, has fluctuated depending on the particular administration in office, and has been powerfully shaped by US hegemony, Mexico's relative dependency, and Canada's subtle use of its geographic position. Most often, immigration authorities in the three countries work to keep Central American and other migrants away from North America. To understand the dynamics that underlie this system, we draw upon theories of migration policy diffusion and interdependence. These bodies of theory, which we expand and refine for the North American context, help explain both shared exclusionary approaches as well as country-specific variations.

Theoretical Background: Competitive and Cooperative Interdependence in Migration Systems

We frame our analysis of the emergence of Fortress North America with attention to the interplay between competitive and cooperative dynamics of the countries' largely restrictionist migration policy goals, which themselves have been influenced, to varying degrees, by internal political considerations, structural factors, and explicit and implicit racial bias. Scholars are increasingly analyzing the role of policy in shaping migration dynamics (e.g., de Haas et al. 2019; FitzGerald 2019; FitzGerald and Cook-Martín 2014; Zolberg 2008). Although Jagdish Bhagwati (2003) argued that borders are "beyond control," Hein de Haas and colleagues (2019, 887) find that restrictive immigration policies do have a small negative impact on immigration rates. However, consistent with research on the effects of US border enforcement policy (e.g., Massey et al. 2008; Cornelius 2005), they find that the effectiveness of immigration restrictions is undermined by immigrants' actions and that the policies' unintended consequences make their effect on net migration "ambiguous" (de Haas et al. 2019, 907).

What is unambiguous is that countries view immigration—particularly irregular migration—as a "problem" that they need to control (Benton-Cohen 2018). As Daniel Ghezelbash argues, contemporary states essentially have the same goal: to keep "unwanted irregular migrants and asylum seekers away from their territories" (2018b). The prerogative of exclusion is the key driver of migration governance at the domestic, regional, and global levels. We find that to a large degree Mexico, the United States, and even Canada each share this goal. They also share some constraints, including their domestic immigration laws and obligations under international law, including those set out in the 1951 Refugee Convention and the 1967 Protocol.

There are variations across the three countries regarding which classes of noncitizens are "unwanted." At the very least, it seems that the constraints imposed by international and domestic law, and the shared norms that undergird these laws, are being tested given the current global context, where nationalism and enhanced border controls are becoming the norm undergirding idealized mono-ethnic nation-states (Castañeda 2020).

There are two principal mechanisms through which international and domestic laws constrain states from keeping "undesirables" from immigrating or seeking asylum: legal constraints and liberal normative expectations. Legally, governments that seek to curtail irregular migration and limit access to asylum can be constrained domestically by courts and legislation, even if they are not concerned with international image and legitimacy. Empirical analyses of migration and asylum policy also show how states "circumvent normative constraints" by shifting "the level at which policy is elaborated and implemented," often to the supranational level (Guiraudon and Lahav 2000, 164; see also FitzGerald 2019, 49). Domestic implementation and interpretations of international law vary and might also explain different policy outcomes. Nonetheless, diffusion theory suggests that similar policy outcomes may be linked to a common cause, especially insofar as ad hoc regional policy coordination emerges in response to a perceived crisis (Geddes 2021).

States may deepen their interdependence around migration policy through explicit cooperation toward a common goal or an implicit competition where two or more states seek to achieve the same migration-related goal. Ghezelbash suggests that competitive pressures among neighboring states to deter unwanted migrants will cause a "race to the bottom" toward more restrictive deterrence policies. Echoing Ghezelbash (2014, 2018a), Thomas Gammeltoft-Hansen and colleagues discuss the recent emergence of "cooperative deterrence" policies (Gammeltoft-Hansen and Hathaway 2015), and a broader "deterrence paradigm" (Gammeltoft-Hansen and Tan 2017). Gammeltoft-Hansen and James Hathaway (2015) characterize the refugee policies of wealthy states as duplicitous in that they seek to deter would-be refugees from reaching their territory without formally rejecting or withdrawing from their international treaty obligations under the Refugee Convention. However, these policies are also likely to run afoul of international and domestic law, and courts may constrain states' most restrictionist impulses.

A counterargument suggests that some elected officials may respond to a neighbor's restrictionist policies with a more pro-immigrant approach because this fits with the state's identity, say, as being hospitable to those in need. The state also may wish to distinguish itself from a neighboring state. However, in the current context, migrant-friendly rhetoric is often paired with fundamentally restrictive approaches (Vollmer 2016). Such a humanitarian and welcoming image is valued by Canada, though its protected geographic location, buffered by both the United States and Mexico, make it easier to perform humanitarianism while making it very difficult for irregular migrants to reach its territory. Mexico, in its 2011 migration reform and the rhetoric of several recent presidents, has sought to distinguish itself from the United States as being welcoming to migrants and as acting in compliance with international law and norms; however, in practice, the country has become a "vertical frontier for the United States" (FitzGerald 2019, 1240). Conversely, geopolitical objectives and domestic political imperatives may drive policies that truly are more welcoming, as was often the case during the Cold War.

To square the sometimes contradictory goals of maintaining commitments to international and domestic laws while keeping "undesirable" immigrants and asylum seekers out, states have engaged in the politics of *non-entré*—that is, sidestepping their treaty obligations and the duty of non-refoulement by not allowing asylum seekers to reach their territories in the first place (Gammeltoft-Hansen and Hathaway 2015, 241). They argue that states care about and are constrained by refugee law today principally insofar as they retain a symbolic commitment to its core principles. They care about this in part because this projection of support is important to ensure that developing countries—which house the lion's share of refugees—continue to respect refugee law

(Gammeltoft-Hansen and Hathaway 2015, 240). This informal compact between developed and developing states may be unraveling.

Gammeltoft-Hansen and Hathaway identify a typology of seven categories of *non-entré* policy: 1) diplomatic; 2) direct financial incentives; 3) equipment, machinery, and training; 4) deployment of immigration authorities to work in destination or transit countries directly; 5) enforcement operations in origin or transit countries; 6) direct migration control role in origin or transit countries; and 7) enforcement by international organizations, such as the European Union (EU) migration agency Frontex. These types are not mutually exclusive, and states typically employ them in some combination.

Gammeltoft-Hansen and his colleagues outline solid legal arguments to challenge the propriety of the "deterrence paradigm." Notwithstanding, they argue that these policies and practices are proliferating and becoming the dominant ones to handle refugees, limiting the role of international law. What might be more critical is the extent to which international laws are interpreted, institutionalized, and implemented in each state. Whereas norms and laws have been defined and advanced at the global level—including the Refugee Convention and Protocol, the Global Compact on Migration, and the Global Compact on Refugees—states often act individually and collectively in regional contexts to enact migration governance.

North American states attempt to limit Central American asylum seekers and migrants from traveling through and settling in their respective countries. The construct "Fortress North America" suggests that each country prioritizes the first goal articulated by Ghezelbash: to limit and select its immigrants. For all three, today, this generally means limiting the overland entry of Central American migrants. Despite rhetorical differences and seeming tensions on this issue, all three countries' actual practices are consistent with this goal. We further argue that a combination of interrelated factors explains variations in how each state seeks to achieve this goal and how this, in turn, shapes their cooperation to do so. These factors include: 1) the internal relationship among the three North American states, and the use of migration policy as a tool for cooperation (e.g., bilateral agreements), for negotiation/coercion, and for drawing competitive contrasts; 2) the global image each country seeks to project regarding its humanitarian commitments and adherence to international law, and the variations in these commitments across administrations; 3) structural economic, social, and geographic determinants of migration flows, including the presence of established migration pathways or networks; and 4) racist conceptions and pressure from restrictionist and nativist groups. It is necessary to analyze simultaneously these interdependent policy contexts—all of which support a broader goal of limiting overland asylum seekers and migrants from Central America and other countries.

Central American Migration to North America: Modern History and Present-Day Dynamics

The countries of Northern Central America (NCA) have suffered from endemic violence and social exclusion, persistent problems that have intensified over the past decade. The well-founded belief among the populations is that their political elites lack the will and capacity to ensure minimal security and well-being, helping generate extraordinary pressures to emigrate. The resulting waves of irregular movement of migrants and asylum seekers have been framed as a crisis by the US and Mexican governments, and the countries' principal immigration policy goal has been to deter the unregulated influx. At the same time, Canada has been geographically buffered from the irregular flow of Central American migrants by Mexico and the United States. This has made it much easier for Canada to reconcile the potentially competing goals of projecting a humanitarian image and complying with international law while keeping unwanted irregular migrants and asylum seekers away. This section analyzes these contemporary migration dynamics, associated crisis narratives, and domestic and regional policy responses within a broader historical context.

United States: A Legacy of Exclusion and Legal Liminality

Immigration processes in the United States have become longer, more expensive, and arduous for applicants since September 11, 2001, with policy rhetoric focused on deterrence and self-deportation, depending on the administration in power. A long history of exclusion (Castañeda 2019) and deportation (Kanstroom 2012; Golash-Boza 2015) has created a whole ecosystem around detaining, jailing, and deporting immigrants that Adam Goodman (2020) calls "the deportation machine."

The US immigration system has consistently shown skepticism toward Central American migrants and asylum seekers, resulting in exclusionary practices tempered by the occasional provision of legal status, typically non-permanent in nature. In the 1980s, the United States played a significant role in various Central American conflicts, positioning the region as a battleground in the Cold War. As the conflicts exacted a horrific humanitarian toll, particularly in Guatemala and El Salvador, tens of thousands of migrants fled northward, seeking protection in the form of asylum. Given the United States' geopolitical objectives and the narrative it had propagated regarding the conflicts in Central America, US leadership refused to recognize the migrants as political refugees. Instead, State Department officials referred to these individuals as "economic" migrants, unworthy of permanent protection. The political rhetoric reverberated in the asylum adjudication process, with near-systematic denials of Central American asylum claims except for Nicaragua (Coutin 2003; Wasem 2020, 252). As an illustration, at the start of fiscal year 1996, there were 63,000 new asylum cases and 137,000 pending cases from El Salvador; but only 157 were approved (US

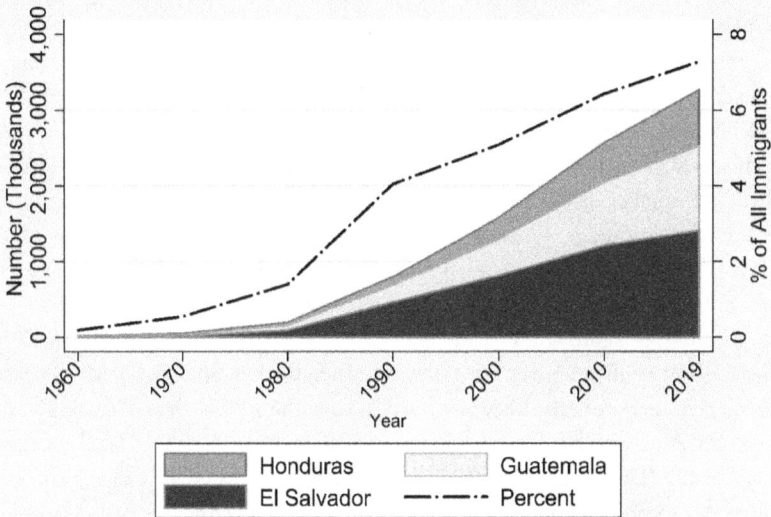

Source: Migration Policy Institute (MPI) Data Hub. Analysis by author.

Figure 5.1. Northern Central American Immigrants in the US. Numbers and Percent of All Immigrants, 1960 through 2019.

Immigration and Naturalization Service 1997, 90).[2] Faith-based groups and others ultimately filed suit against the US government in *American Baptist Churches v. Thornburgh*, resulting in a settlement agreement that permitted many of these migrants the opportunity to reapply for asylum.

Notwithstanding this practice of exclusion, the US government has employed temporary immigration statuses to provide a measure of stability for Central Americans in the United States. In 1999, the US government designated Hondurans and Nicaraguans as eligible for Temporary Protected Status (TPS). Two years later, the US government designated El Salvadorans for TPS. Each of these designations was premised on natural catastrophes that prohibited the safe return of migrants residing in the United States. The designations remain in effect today, as litigation has resuscitated many of these TPS designations despite repeated efforts by the Trump administration to terminate them. Such temporary statuses permit the US government to save face vis-à-vis the international community and relevant domestic stakeholders while denying migrants a lasting status that might ultimately lead to US citizenship. This practice complements the theory advanced by Gammeltoft-Hansen and Hathaway; by funneling displaced people from northern Central America into a liminal status (Menjívar 2006), the United States can nominally comply with domestic and international law and loosely adhere to the principle of nonrefoulement, while effectively sidestepping the Refugee Convention. This allows the United States to avoid the complex endeavor of refugee adjudication that flows from its international legal obligations by giving these refugees a liminal status instead that renders some of them deportable in the future.

While the United States sought to exclude and limit the integration of Central Americans displaced by civil war and natural disasters, these efforts have largely failed to limit the number of Central Americans traveling and settling in the country. The number of Salvadoran-, Guatemalan-, and Honduran-born migrants living in the United States has grown consistently since the 1980s, as has the percentage of immigrants to the United States born in these countries, which includes green-card holders and refugees (see figure 5.1). Demographically, though, Northern Central Americans still make up a small minority of the foreign-born in the United States, suggesting that recurring narratives of crisis may be driven by something other than demographics.

Central American migrants also have been saddled with racialized labels of criminality and vice (Dudley 2020). In the 1990s, narratives regarding the dangerousness of Central American gangs buoyed efforts to expand grounds for deportation based on criminal conduct and mandatory detention during pending immigration proceedings for persons with even relatively minor criminal records. Although the US government has acknowledged the pervasiveness of gang violence in Central America, it has deployed various legal arguments to deny asylum protection to those escaping this violence. Echoing arguments made in the 1980s, some within the government have argued that today's Central American migrants are economic migrants seeking better opportunities. Others have argued, despite evidence to the contrary, that the situation is one of "generalized violence"—not of targeted persecution—and that asylum is, therefore, an inappropriate remedy. Adjudicators have used the peculiarities of asylum law—including the requirement that persecution be motivated by specific reasons—in concluding that many claims do not comply technically with narrow legal requirements. A seminal example is how past attorneys general, the Board of Immigration Appeals, and some immigration judges have interpreted the criteria for "particular social group" under the Immigration and Nationality Act.

The downward trend in asylum acceptance rates from 2015 to 2020 reflected, in part, a shift in the treatment of asylum claims as a result of policy changes during the Trump administration, including the June 2018 opinion issued by Attorney General Jeff Sessions to reverse US policy on asylum claims based on domestic violence or victimization by gangs. To tie the hands of adjudicators and limit the availability of relief, Sessions issued a binding decision in *Matter of A-B-*, undoing a precedent that allowed survivors of domestic violence a pathway to receive asylum. More broadly, *Matter of A-B-* signaled skepticism about asylum claims premised on acts of "private violence." On the enforcement side, the Trump administration deployed a host of tactics designed to disincentivize asylum seeking, especially for those from Central

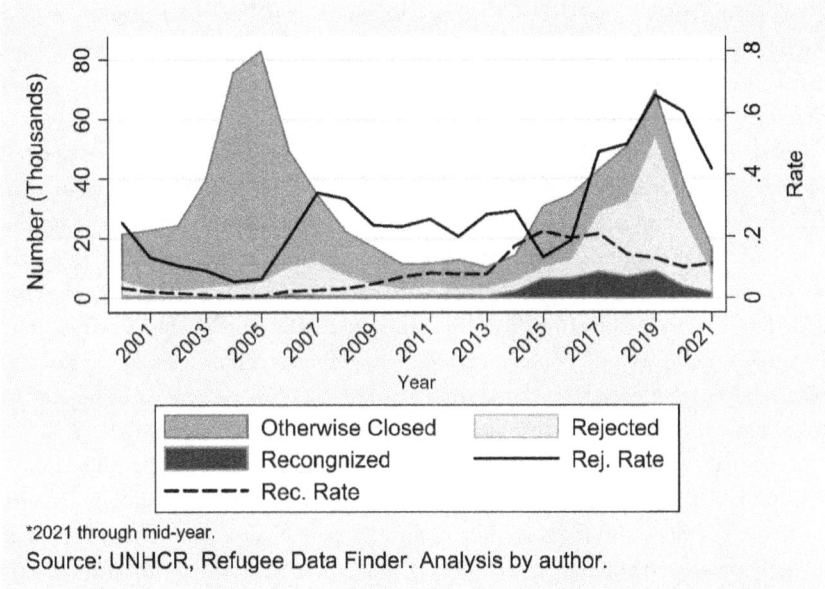

*2021 through mid-year.
Source: UNHCR, Refugee Data Finder. Analysis by author.

Figure 5.2. NCA Asylum Claims in the US. Recognition, Rejection, and Attrition (2000–2021).

America. During the COVID-19 pandemic, the United States invoked a little-known provision in Title 42 of the US Code and closed the land borders due to public health concerns. The pandemic enabled even stricter migration-related controls, preventing asylum seekers and other humanitarian migrants from entering the United States and having access to immigration relief. By the end of Trump's term, his administration had made it basically impossible to seek asylum at the border. It deployed tactics including family detention, family separation, the expanded use of detention generally, the "Remain in Mexico" policy (officially known as the Migrant Protection Protocols, or MPP), and the creation of long waits at ports of entry along the border through a practice known as metering. The Biden administration has rolled back some of these policies—including via the rescission of *Matter of A-B-*[3] and the declaration of a formal end to the metering policy (Department of Justice 2021). Attempts to cease the invocation of Title 42 and to roll back MPP have been blocked by the courts, and arguably were halfhearted to begin with.[4]

The recognition of asylum claims from these Central American countries declined drastically from more than 9,000 in 2019 to 3,900 in 2020 and 1,870 in the first half of 2021 due to the COVID-19 pandemic and the effective shutting down of new asylum cases through Title 42 expulsions and other measures. Even still, considering this decline in recent historical context shows that the recognition of asylum claims from these countries has been extremely rare, and the low 2020 number was still higher than at any point before 2014 (UNHCR 2021, author analysis). Figure 5.2 graphs the total number of asylum decisions (left axis), including recognitions, rejections, and claims that were otherwise closed, as well as recognized and rejected claims as a share of total closed cases (right axis).

An upward trend in the number and rate of denials began in 2015 and accelerated thereafter, with the number of rejections jumping to more than 20,000 from more than 6,000 from 2016 to 2017. This trend continued with the number of rejections of asylum claims from these countries peaking at almost 46,000 in 2019, before falling to 23,000 in 2020 and 7,000 in the first half of 2021 largely because of federal responses to the COVID-19 pandemic. During this period, the rate of rejections as a share of decisions also grew steadily to peak at 66 percent in 2019 before declining sharply in 2020 and 2021. The recognition rate declined from a 2015 peak of 21 percent to 10 percent in 2020 before increasing slightly to 11 percent in the first half of 2021.

Criminalization of immigrants and the militarization of the border are also inhibiting transit from Mexico into the United States. Though more visible in Trump's discourse and disregard for governing norms, the phenomena are not new: President Bill Clinton started building border fencing and increased agents deployed at the border. George W. Bush continued this trend, and Barack Obama implemented border enforcement with more effect than any of his predecessors. The common thread was exclusion, and the consistent message to Central Americans has been: "don't come." The Biden administration has indicated some fundamental changes to its posture toward Central American migration flows, including policy reversals on safe third country agreements, delayed attempts to end the Remain in Mexico/MPP program, and provision of substantial funds to humanitarian and development assistance efforts in Central America. The Biden administration is also seeking to implement wider reforms to the asylum system. Among them is the "Asylum Officer Rule," which could provide a more hospitable and less adversarial process for asylum seekers by moving initial adjudication of claims for those subjected to expedited removal proceedings from immigration court to Department of Homeland Security (DHS) asylum officers. However, this reform—which is being challenged in court by attorneys general from a group of conservative states—is coupled with reforms to expedite immigration court decisions that will make it difficult for asylum seekers to secure representation and may end up sacrificing justice in the name of expediency (CGRS 2022b). Thus, despite attempts to roll back of some of the Trump administration's most restrictive policies and other reforms, both official rhetoric and policy confirmed that the primary goal of limiting Central American immigration and provision of asylum remained unchanged.

The bigger picture that this analysis of asylum cases necessarily omits is that many migrants and asylum seekers never reach US territory in the first place. The United States has worked with the Mexican government to limit the arrival and presence of Central American migrants through externalized border controls and programs such as Remain in Mexico/MPP; it has extended this cooperation to include interdiction practices within Central America itself.

Mexico: Transit and Destination Country for Central American Refugees

Mexico plays a key, if ironic, role in the North American migration regime. Mexico is at once instrumental in establishing Fortress North America, while at the same time its citizens are excluded from the greater regional free movement allowed to Canadian and US citizens. Clearly, being part of a single commercial region does not confer de facto equality; instead, an internal hierarchy is defined by US interests. This power disparity—especially between the United States and Mexico, but also between Mexico and some Central American countries—leads to a dynamic of policy extortion and coercive negotiation. As a result, Mexico occupies a role as the vertical border buffer between the United States and Central America. Most explicitly, the Trump administration used the NAFTA renegotiation to ensure Mexico's already crucial role as a buffer state that deported more migrants to Central America than the United States. According to official figures, 635,761 Central Americans were deported and returned by Mexican immigration authorities between 2015 and 2019 (Gandini et al. 2020, 31). Mexico has "una política migratoria de puertas cerradas hacia el sur y de puertas abiertas hacia el norte [a policy of closed doors toward the South, and one of open doors toward the North]" (Gandini et al. 2020, 121).

Mexico has played a unique and varied role with respect to Central American refugees, serving as a transit country for migrants traveling to the United States and Canada while also absorbing some Central Americans for whom Mexico became a destination country. Mexico passed a new immigration law in 2011 intended to make Mexico more hospitable to immigrants and asylum seekers. The law was framed as a way to show how Mexico—a country that complained about the treatment of its nationals in the United States—treated immigrants in a generous and humanitarian fashion. Nonetheless, the letter and spirit of the law have not been closely observed, including in relation to Central American arrivals. It is more suggestive of country branding and competition to project an aura of being pro-immigrant and pro-refugee. Nevertheless, the extent to which this law did not fundamentally improve the treatment of migrants shows how cooperative deterrence pushed by the United States shaped how the law was implemented in practice. In reality, Mexico reacted in many ways to deflect migration: 1) Mexico dramatically increased its patrolling of its southern border with Guatemala; 2) Mexico increased its number of deportations of the foreign-born; and 3) Mexican immigration agents do not present readily to refugees the option to apply for asylum in Mexico. In an example of national deflection of immigrants over a Fortress North America policing role, Mexican local and federal authorities facilitated the passage of caravans through the country to get them closer to the US border for the United States to process them until the Mexican government agreed (under pressure from Trump to close the border to trade) to the Remain in Mexico/MPP program (Gandini et al. 2020, 93).

In what seemed like a course correction, during its first months in office, the Andrés Manuel López Obrador administration instituted a humanitarian visa policy that let migrants stay in Mexico legally and safely. The numbers of applicants quickly became overwhelming, however, while the policy produced an unintended consequence of making travel to the US border much cheaper. As a consequence, the program was scaled down and then neglected, leaving intact the core exclusionist feature of the North American migration regime.

A Connected History

Mexico and Central America share a long and complex history, with common Indigenous foundations, the experience of colonization, integration after independence from Spain, and, ultimately, the creation of independent states. For purposes of the present inquiry, the civil wars and conflicts in Central America throughout the 1980s and 1990s serve as a useful starting point in understanding Mexico's posture toward Central American migrants. Those conflicts generated many political refugees, prompting a series of formal responses from the Mexican government.

The influx of Central American migrants into Mexico during this time encouraged the Mexican government to form the Commission for Refugee Assistance in 1980. In 1981, over 80,000 Guatemalans fleeing genocide arrived in Chiapas, Mexico. In that year alone, Mexico granted protection to 46,000 Guatemalans escaping the country's civil war, establishing refugee camps in the south, and later allowing them to settle in the country. Many of these people eventually became Mexican citizens (Stein 2015). Although the Mexican government was at first unprepared for the number of people seeking refuge in the country, the government ultimately built health clinics, roads, and refugee camps to assist the arriving migrants. Despite these efforts to support the migrants, repatriation was a key component of the Mexican strategy, even as early as the 1980s. In 1987, an agreement was made between Mexico, Guatemala, and the United Nations High Commissioner for Refugees (UNHCR) to create "basic conditions and human rights standards for repatriated refugees" (Ogren 2007, 208). According to Cassandra Ogren, "by 2001, over 75 per cent of Guatemalan refugees had repatriated voluntarily . . . while the 23,000 who decided to remain in Mexico were granted the right to naturalize" (2007, 208).[5] Salvadoran refugees arrived in Mexico in even larger numbers during this period, hitting 140,000 in 1981 and remaining at around 120,000 until rapidly declining in 1989 (UNHCR, author calculations).

Once the conflicts ended, the state institutions were weak and unable to repair the social fabric. In turn, as noted above in the US context, Central American nationals heading northward were commonly labeled as economic migrants (Menjívar 2000). This framing has persisted through the present. Nevertheless, as French journalist

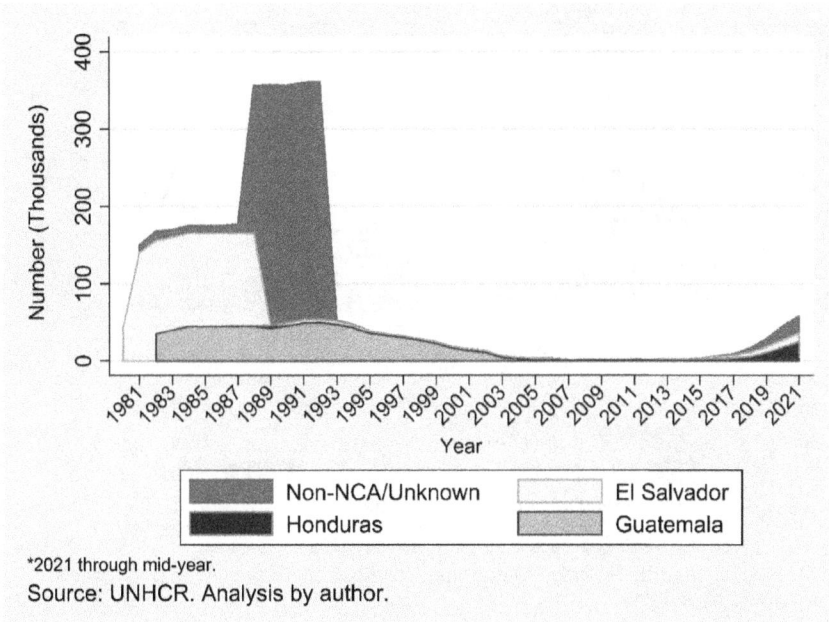

*2021 through mid-year.
Source: UNHCR. Analysis by author.

Figure 5.3. Refugees in Mexico, 1980–2021.

Emmanuelle Stein explains, many migrants entering Mexico "flee general insecurity produced by violent **non-state** actors (VNSA) and the civil war, rather than **direct threat or persecution from the government** of their home country. Moreover, Central America is not considered a conflict zone according to the definition of International Humanitarian Law" (Stein 2015, emphasis in original), but this does not mean that they are not suffering from lack of security provision by the state and that they are not targeted as individuals or families through, for example, gang recruitment (Dudley 2020). Because cartels and other VNSA are committing the violence, in many cases, Mexico did not recognize these individuals as political refugees. Indeed, it was not until 2011 that Mexico passed the Law on Refugees and Complementary Protection, which offered, on paper, protection for asylum seekers who are being persecuted by non-state actors (Stein 2015).

In recent years, Mexico has faced significant scrutiny for its treatment of Central American migrants. A centerpiece of Mexican migration policy is the Southern Border Strategy, announced in 2014. The Southern Border Strategy was designed to increase security and the detention of migrants attempting to enter Mexico's southern border. It came immediately in the wake of the "surge" of unaccompanied minors that created a political problem for the Obama administration, which in turn leaned on Mexico to interrupt people before they could get to the US border. The Fortress's walls were

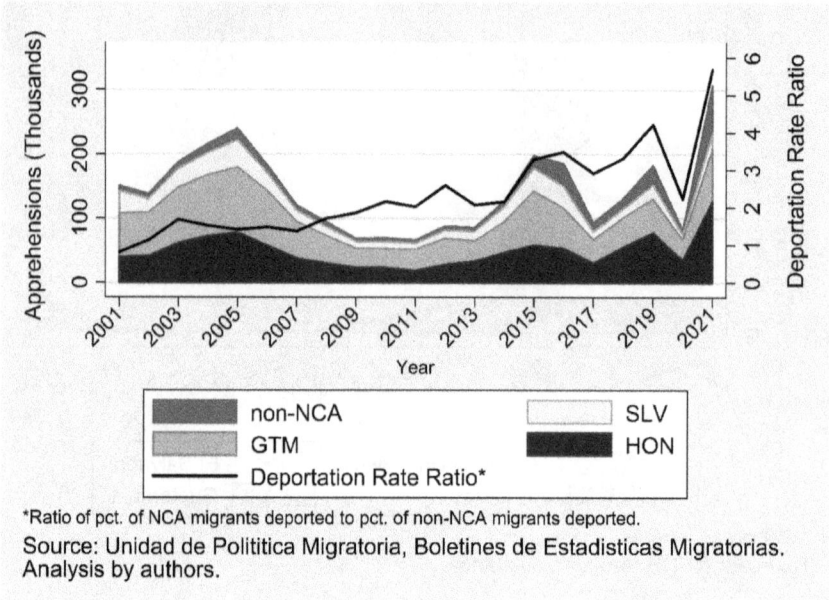

*Ratio of pct. of NCA migrants deported to pct. of non-NCA migrants deported.
Source: Unidad de Polititica Migratoria, Boletines de Estadisticas Migratorias.
Analysis by authors.

Figure 5.4. Apprehensions and Deportations by Mexico. NCA Migrants More Likely to Be Apprehended and Deported.

pushed outward to Mexico's border with Guatemala, and, when that did not work, additional barriers were erected within Mexico itself.

After the strategy was introduced, in a one-year period, apprehensions of migrants increased by 79 percent, from 97,245 (July 2013–June 2014) to 174,159 (July 2014–June 2015). The increase over two years (July 2014–June 2016) was 85 percent (Isacson et al. 2017). Between 2013 and 2016, over 520,000 people from Central America's "Northern Triangle" were arrested by Mexican authorities, and 517,249 of those people were deported (Villasenor and Coria 2017).

While these increases are striking, examining available data over the past two decades shows how Mexico has had a relatively consistent role as the first line of enforcement for Fortress North America, with the exception being the period of the great recession centered in the United States and before the violence crisis of the 2010s. Figure 5.4 plots the total number of migrants apprehended by Mexican migration authorities and examines the varying treatment of migrants from Northern Central America compared to others (Unidad de Política Migratoria, author analysis). The number of apprehensions (left axis) is consistently dominated by migrants from the subregion, especially Guatemala and Honduras, while others make up a small but growing share. Until 2019, virtually all migrants from Northern Central America

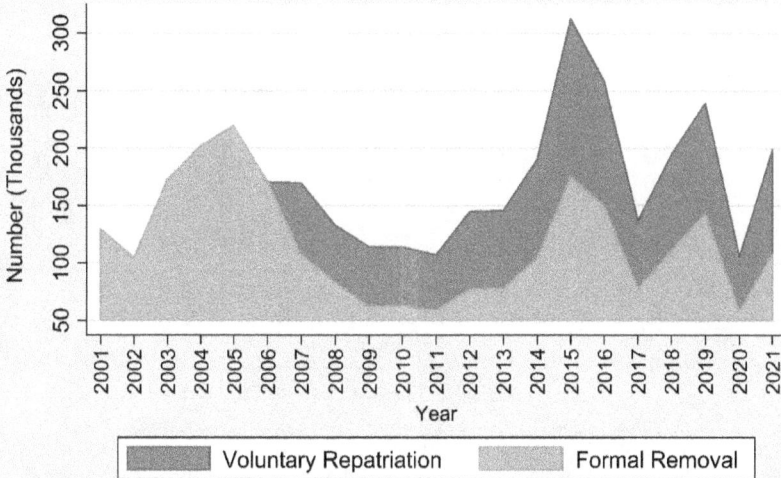

Source: Unidad de Polititica Migratoria, Boletines de Estadisticas Migratorias. Analysis by authors.

Figure 5.5. Deportations of NCA Migrants. Formal Removals and "Voluntary" Repatriations.

apprehended were removed to their countries of origin, and they consistently have been more likely to be deported than migrants from other countries (right axis).

These data understate the extent to which Mexico's Southern Border Strategy and its long-standing deportation practices have been centered on removing Central Americans from its territory. This is because in 2006 and 2007, the governments of Mexico, El Salvador, Guatemala, Honduras, and Nicaragua signed an updated Memorandum of Understanding to ensure "the dignified, ordered, speedy, and safe repatriation of Central American nationals traveling overland" (Unidad de Politica Migratoria).[6] Figure 5.5 shows the total number of deportations, including formal removals (*devueltos*) and "voluntary" repatriations of NCA migrants by Mexican authorities.[7] Figure 5.6 compares total deportations ("voluntary" and formal) from Mexico and the United States over the past two decades and offers a clear picture of the extent to which Mexico has become the primary and arguably most effective barrier to keep migrants and would-be asylum seekers from reaching the United States.

Those NCA migrants who do enter Mexican territory face roadblocks to advancing an asylum claim in Mexico. Axel García, a former volunteer with UNHCR Mexico and officer for the Commission for Refugee Assistance, explained in 2008 how the legal system for refugees in Mexico was "not in accordance with the international law of refugees and ha[d] no provision for courts dealing specifically with

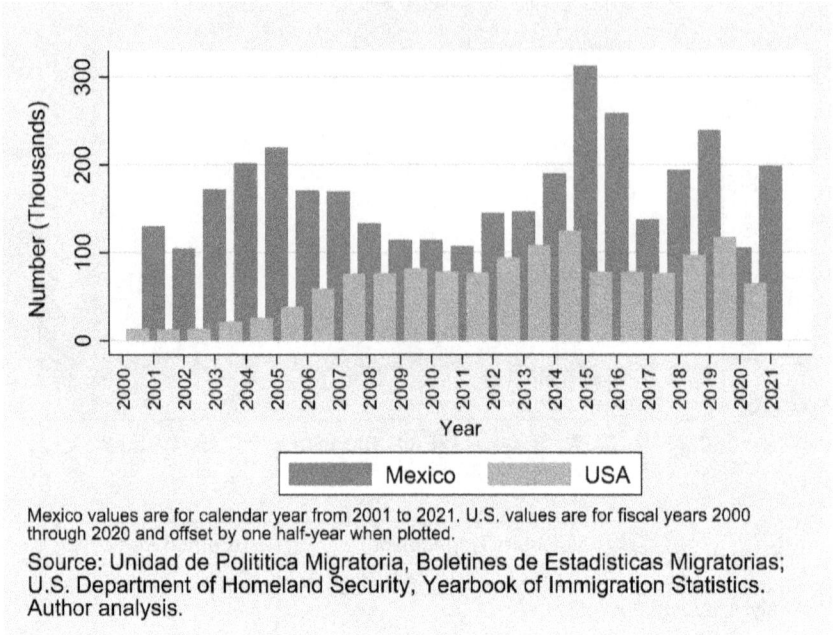

Mexico values are for calendar year from 2001 to 2021. U.S. values are for fiscal years 2000 through 2020 and offset by one half-year when plotted.
Source: Unidad de Polititica Migratoria, Boletines de Estadisticas Migratorias; U.S. Department of Homeland Security, Yearbook of Immigration Statistics. Author analysis.

Figure 5.6. Mexico Deports More NCA Migrants Than the US.

migration or refugee issues" (2008). More recent accounts confirm significant deficiencies in Mexico's asylum system. Esmeralda Lopez and Melissa Hastings (2016, 1119) explain that "many migrants are not informed of their right to asylum when they enter detention centers." In fact, in 2013, 68 percent of the people held within Mexico's largest detention center were not aware of their right to asylum (Lopez and Hastings 2016, 1119–20). Minors and other vulnerable persons are especially likely victims of these due process deficiencies: of the unaccompanied children and adolescents who arrived in Mexico between 2013 and 2016, only 1.1 percent applied for asylum, and of those, a mere 230 (.4 percent) successfully obtained refugee or asylum status (Villasenor and Coria 2017). Would-be asylum seekers are often not reliably informed about their right to claim asylum (Amnesty International 2018; Gandini et al. 2020). In some cases, state actors affirmatively discourage or block potentially qualifying immigrants from applying for asylum. Furthermore, Article 33 of Mexico's constitution allows the executive branch to force any alien to leave Mexico without any trial or hearing (Ogren 2007, 216).

Mexico has a very short "asylum clock," requiring claims to be filed within one month of entering the country. Recently acceptance rates have increased, but lingering critiques include long delays in adjudication, an agency that is very under-resourced given the number of people seeking protection in Mexico, and the lack of sufficient

personnel to process claims. Finally, many asylum seekers and migrants are apprehended in Mexico when trying to reach the United States and may choose to accept
"voluntary return" to their home country in hopes of making another attempt to cross.
So, Mexico operates as a border wall in many ways, making it more difficult for immigrants coming from outside of Mexico to make it to the United States or Canada by
land (Varela 2019).

Canada: Humanitarian Image with Cycles of Restrictive Asylum Policies

The Canadian experience with Central American immigration differs significantly
from that of both the United States and Mexico, in that far fewer Central American
migrants have sought to enter or seek refugee protection in Canada. Geography has
been a key determinant for these lower numbers. Nevertheless, statistically speaking,
Canada has awarded refugee protection to a larger *proportion* of Central American
applicants (García 2006b, 119). Although Canada is often perceived as being more
welcoming to refugees, the country has alternated between open and more restrictive approaches from the 1980s to the present and has embraced some of the same
tropes about the danger of irregular migration from the Northern Triangle. Moreover,
while touting its refugee resettlement program, Canada has deployed various strategies to limit the ability of overland migrants to seek and obtain refugee protection
at the Canadian border. Furthermore, according to FitzGerald's analysis (2019, 59),
a Canadian visa policy change in 2009 by the Conservative government of Stephen
Harper was "openly motivated" by "the goal of reducing the number of Mexicans
applying for asylum."

Before 1970, "there was virtually no history of Latin American migration to Canada"
(Simmons 1993, 283). Laws passed in Canada during the 1960s and 1970s eliminated
restrictions on immigration, facilitating arrivals from Latin America, Africa, Asia, and
the Middle East. The Canadian Immigration Act of 1976 established a framework for
immigration and refugee protection (García 2006b, 120–21). In the 1970s, Canada
began to offer protection to a significant number of Chileans fleeing the Pinochet
regime, marking one of the first significant inflows of Latin American migrants to
Canada.

After the outbreak of civil war in 1979, Salvadoran refugees began arriving in
Canada. In 1979, Canada received only 108 Salvadoran migrants, but that number
grew substantially in the years to follow, reaching 4,290 in 1990 (Simmons 1993,
294). Guatemalans and Nicaraguans likewise migrated to Canada in the 1980s, but
in smaller numbers. Between 1982 and 1987, Canada admitted nearly 16,000 refugees
from Central America, the majority from El Salvador (García 2006a). It is estimated
that there were over 56,000 refugees or displaced persons in Canada in 1987 from El
Salvador, Guatemala, and Nicaragua (Lacroix 2004, 147). The Canadian government

even instructed its consulates in the United States to issue visas to Central Americans facing deportation. Moreover, asylum grant rates for Central Americans during this time were substantially higher in Canada than in the United States (García 2006a). Canada's refugee policy "was an important way to distinguish Canada culturally and politically from the United States" (García 2006b, 130). Canada received the 1986 Nansen Medal from UNHCR for its efforts to protect refugees, including Central Americans (Lacroix 2004, 147).

Canada's welcoming posture toward Central American migrants was linked to the country's distinct policy position on the conflicts in Central America and, according to FitzGerald, also was "a means of promoting its international brand as a beacon of humanitarianism" (FitzGerald 2019, 127). The Canadian Parliament had issued a report in 1982, recommending that Canada focus on Central American foreign policy and adopt policies "independent in tone and substance from the policies of the United States" (García 2006b, 125). Unlike the United States, which viewed the conflicts through a strategic Cold War lens, Canada viewed the conflicts as home-grown and rooted in economic and political inequality. Instead of providing military aid, Canada offered funds to UNHCR, the Red Cross, and other organizations to support various forms of humanitarian assistance (García 2006a). Despite its distinct approach, Canada avoided direct critiques of the US position on Central America, and the United States never penalized Canada for adopting divergent asylum policies (García 2006b, 126–27).

The arrival of these large numbers of Central American migrants ultimately led to a backlash against Canada's more permissive migration policy. In 1986, after the passage of the Immigration Reform and Control Act in the United States—which regularized immigrants and sought to constrict employment opportunities for unauthorized migrants and strengthen enforcement efforts into the future—large numbers of Central Americans sought protection in Canada (Simmons 1993, 201). Between December 2006 and February 2007, nearly 10,000 refugees—mostly Central Americans—entered Canada (García 2006a). The arrival of these migrants contributed to hyped-up narratives of refugees flooding the borders (Lacroix 2004, 150). Parliament was recalled to address the situation, and in 1987 new laws were passed (Bills C-55 and C-84) to tighten the refugee determination process. Faith-based organizations and other nonprofits vigorously advocated to decrease these laws' restrictive aspects (García 2006a). Nevertheless, the policies did result in a substantial reduction in the number of Central American border entrants in Canada (García 2006b, 132).

Another restrictive immigration measure, Bill C-86, was approved in 1993. The law further streamlined hearings and tightened eligibility criteria for asylum and included a provision relating to applicants who had passed through a safe country. In all of the 1990s, only 6,906 asylum applicants were filed in Canada by El Salvadoran applicants, and 4,357 applications by Guatemalan nationals (UNHCR 2001). Nevertheless, Canada continued to enjoy a global reputation for relatively permissive refugee policies, and the overall number of refugees and immigrants steadily rose throughout the decade. However, public polling revealed concern about the country's immigration and multicultural policies (García 2006b, 152–53).

After the 9/11 attacks, in December 2002, Canada and the United States formalized a bilateral safe third country agreement after almost a decade of negotiations (García 2006b, 140–42), which enabled the Canadian government to return to the United States thousands of asylum seekers at Canadian land borders who had transited through the United States en route to Canada. In the year of implementation, refugee claims dropped from a prior five-year average of 35,095 to just under 21,000 (Grant and Rehaag 2016, 226). In the years that followed and through the present, the agreement has imposed a significant limitation on Central American and other asylum seekers who have traveled northward after passing through the United States. Any would-be asylum seeker who wishes to avoid the harsh effects of the agreement must arrive at an airport or a seaport—typically requiring a visa, which can be challenging to obtain.

In 2012, Canada clamped down on asylum seekers once again, with the enactment of new federal legislation that resulted in a 49 percent decline in asylum claims that year (Reynolds and Hyndman 2015, 41). The law, among other things, gave the government greater flexibility to select Designated Countries of Origin (DCOs), which are states presumed to be relatively safe. Mexico was designated as a safe country of origin in 2013, sharply reducing the number of asylum claims (FitzGerald 2019, 59). Additionally, the 2012 law called for the capture of biometrics for a larger swath of arriving immigrants, including temporary immigrants. With the dismantling of asylum protections in the United States during the Trump administration—particularly for Central American migrants—many advocates in Canada encouraged the government to withdraw from the safe third country agreement. A lawsuit by refugee advocates made its way through the federal courts in Canada, designed to compel the government to withdraw from the agreement. A federal judge initially struck down the agreement, finding that it infringed on the Canadian Charter of Rights and Freedoms. However, in April 2021 the Federal Court of Appeal overturned the lower court's decision and upheld the agreement as constitutional. Notably, one of the plaintiffs in this lawsuit was a Salvadoran woman who experienced severe domestic violence in her country of origin.

There are loopholes in the safe third country agreement wherein those who arrive at a country between official ports of entry are eligible to apply for asylum—which became especially relevant in 2017 when many Haitians, among others, arrived in Canada, and particularly to the French-speaking province of Quebec, in anticipation of the end of TPS protection in the United States. This caused the number of asylum claims to spike and renewed calls by advocates in Canada to stop recognizing the United States as a safe country (see FitzGerald 219, 129).

Overall, the Canadian refugee protection approach has privileged the refugee resettlement program, whereby refugees are identified overseas and selected for resettlement in Canada. By contrast, consistent with the logic of "Fortress North America," the Canadian government has sought to discourage the spontaneous arrival of asylum seekers at Canadian borders. Over the years, the media have referred to the latter as "bogus refugees" or "queue jumpers" (Reynolds and Hyndman 2015, 42–44). Even the Canadian government has implicitly endorsed this rhetoric, suggesting that those who arrive at the border are diverting government resources from more worthy refugees (Jackson and Bauder 2013, 364). In recent decades, refugees arriving by boat have generated especially virulent public reactions. These include the arrival of the *Amelie*, a boat carrying 173 Sikh refugees in 1987, and the arrival in 1999 of boats carrying nearly 600 Chinese refugees (Jackson and Bauder 2013, 364).

The resettled refugees, however, tend to come from a relatively small number of countries, suggesting that this favored approach is not accessible to many (Reynolds and Hyndman 2015, 42–44). Moreover, Canada has explicitly embraced the trend toward externalization of border controls with its Multiple Borders Strategy. This initiative began in 2003 seeking to "push the border out" and undertake screening of putative immigrants far from the actual Canadian border, including the migrant's country of origin. The core objective of this strategy is to prevent unwanted arrivals at Canadian borders. Consistent with this approach, the strategy embraces using the term "irregular migrant" to describe these unwanted arrivals, even if they are asylum seekers (Reynolds and Hyndman 2015, 45).

Although Canada presents itself as a beacon of humanitarian protection—and by some metrics, its refugee and immigration policies are relatively generous—domestically, migration policy has been a frequent site of contestation. Indeed, as Marie Lacroix (2004, 147) observed, "refugee policy in Canada is one of the most controversial and debated political and social issues." Canada has at specific junctures welcomed Central American migrants, particularly during the 1980s, but since then it has instituted reforms to its asylum and refugee system that effectively inhibit many Central American migrants from advancing asylum claims. The politics of externalization of border control (and the corollary preference for resettled refugees), along with the safe third country agreement, make it extremely difficult for northbound Central Americans to find protection in Canada.

Canada's unique relationship with the United States also plays out in its refugee policies. While the countries are inextricably intertwined economically and socially, Canada has sought to distinguish itself from the United States on certain matters of social policy. While laudable from a humanitarian standpoint, Canada has nevertheless acquiesced to US pressure to securitize aspects of its migration policy. The Canadian government has also capitulated to domestic political pressure and has imposed various restrictions on migration and refugee processes (see McKercher, this volume).

The MPP as Example of the North American Immigration System

Recent developments in North American migration policy perfectly encapsulate the arguments advanced here. In 2018 and early 2019, the Trump administration framed Central American migration—including the imminent arrival of migrant caravans (see Gandini et al. 2020)—as a crisis requiring a more aggressive response. Among the responses was the promulgation of the Migrant Protection Protocols in January 2019, colloquially known as the "Remain in Mexico" policy. Under this protocol, the US government returned certain foreign nationals to Mexico while their immigration proceedings were pending.

Despite the significant burden placed on Mexican authorities, the Mexican government acquiesced to the practice. When similar ideas were floated in 2018, some predicted that the Mexican government—particularly one led by López Obrador—would more strongly contest the practice. Instead, the Mexican government reiterated its commitment to humanitarian protection, and suggested that returned individuals would be given an opportunity to seek protection in Mexico, should they qualify. This response allowed the Mexican government to embrace a rhetorically distinct approach from the United States while submitting itself to the United States' externalized enforcement policy.

The MPP showed Mexico playing an active, visible role in Fortress North America. The end of the program was not brought about by Mexico's refusal to keep cooperating or by having de facto refugee camps in its northern border cities, nor even by Trump's electoral loss. Indeed, the fate of MPP remains to be seen, as lawsuits brought by conservative state attorneys general have produced temporary orders requiring the Biden administration to administer the program "in good faith"—something that it has done while expanding coverage of the program to asylum seekers from the entire Western Hemisphere.

The statutory basis for the Migrant Protection Protocols technically applies to migrants entering via the northern border (from Canada), though the program as announced focuses exclusively on the southern border. The US and Canadian governments have discussed possible revisions to the US-Canada Safe Third Country Agreement to close the "loophole" that allows persons who evaded inspection (i.e., did not present themselves at a port of entry) to seek asylum in Canada, even if they already attempted to do so in the United States. For example, media statements show that Canadian border security minister Bill Blair signaled a move in this direction, given the large numbers of asylum seekers who had recently arrived from the United States. At the same time, Canadian immigration minister Ahmed Hussen proposed eliminating the policy that limited asylum seekers' rights from countries deemed to be "safe." These simultaneous developments perfectly encapsulate Canadian migration policy and Fortress North America's dual nature: the entrenchment of rigid and externalized border controls, with occasional concessions to stakeholders and a commitment to supporting "regular" migration.

Migration Systems within Regional Projects: North America and Europe

While North America is explicitly an economic region since NAFTA and the renegotiated USMCA, these constitutive accords intentionally avoided addressing immigration in a holistic way, including only scattered provisions for specific professions. Nonetheless, the United States, Mexico, and Canada have created a system meant to deflect Central Americans and other immigrants of color from impoverished backgrounds. Despite these efforts, the large percentage of El Salvadorans, Guatemalans, and Hondurans going to the USMCA region is indicative of both the dire conditions in these countries and the profound economic, social, political, and historical ties across the larger region (see Giorguli-Saucedo et al. 2016). Thus, in the migration domain, Northern Central America is, undeniably, a defining feature of North American dynamics. Many proposed agreements have pointed to this direction,[8] and they reflect the porousness of the Central American and North American borders to goods, capital, drugs, organized crime, and people (see Kloppe-Santamaría, this volume). Securitarian agreements, the war on drugs, and the criminalization of gangs extend from Canada to Colombia. Relations within the North American region are unequal in terms of power and economic might, but they show mutual dependence and close relationships; this is clearest for labor supply and demand. As Mexican immigration to the United States reached net zero after the financial crisis of 2007, Central Americans increasingly supplement the main labor force, allowing the growth in construction and service industries in large American cities, including the Washington, DC, metropolitan area.

We have argued that North America is a regional system in terms of contemporary immigration dynamics, and that these regional dynamics include Guatemala, El Salvador, and Honduras. It is a region in which people from these Central American countries increasingly live. However, even if some have been economically and socially integrated for decades, the recurring cycles of politically motivated "crisis" show that newly arriving Central American adults are not welcomed at all, or at best are not welcome as equals—and their governments are complicit in this exclusion through the policing of political borders.

The apparent contrast in terms of regional integration is the European Union (EU). In particular, the Schengen Area, which guarantees the free movement of goods and people throughout the area, successfully decouples border policing from local and national political administration and elections (Castañeda and Shemesh 2020). In contrast, North America still aims to restrict the movement of people, however unsuccessfully and at a high human cost. Nevertheless, the externalization of borders to Mexico and, more recently, through the cooperation of Guatemalan, Salvadoran, and Honduran armed forces is parallel to what the European Union has been doing to extra-regional economic migrants and asylum seekers (Vollmer 2016). The European Union has active buffers in Southern Europe, the Mediterranean, Turkey, and Libya.

For example, the many deals that encourage Turkey to act as a refugee holder show the parallels between the North American and European migration systems, especially regarding their regional exclusionary goals. Turkey has used its geographic position and the EU's interest in reducing migration from Syria and the Middle East as leverage to gain aid and tacit political support for President Recep Erdogan's autocratic regime. This is echoed in the negotiations and exchanges (wielding both carrots and sticks) used in recent years to persuade emigrant-sending Central American countries to accept safe third country agreements and, in the case of Guatemala, to physically enforce the bottleneck at the border to block the flow of people north. The effect is similar: to push the border further south.

Notes

We thank editors Tom Long and Eric Hershberg, as well as Dennis Stinchcomb, for editorial help. We also thank Claudia Masferrer, Alexandra Délano, Clarisa Pérez-Almendáriz, Celia Toro, Rodolfo Casillas, Francisco Alba, and the rest of the participants in the North American Research Initiative (NARI) meetings at the Colegio de Mexico in 2018.

1. In fiscal year 2019, more than two-thirds of apprehended migrants were from Northern Central America. However, the past two years have seen increasing shares of Mexican migrants as well as migrants from elsewhere in the Western Hemisphere and beyond. In April 2022 alone, for example, more than 20,000 Ukrainians were processed at the Southwest land border, almost all in San Diego.

2. This number of approvals represents only 3 percent of cases adjudicated by the Asylum Officer Corps, compared to a 22 percent approval rate for all nationalities. It is revelatory that only 2,600 Salvadoran refugees or asylees were granted legal permanent residency, compared to almost 17,000 Nicaraguans and more than 121,000 Cubans (INS 1997, 95).

3. However, as of this writing, the administration had still not issued regulations clarifying the circumstances under which someone should be considered a member of a particular social group, as ordered by the president in a February 2021 executive order (see CGRS 2022a).

4. While the administration suspended and terminated MPP shortly after coming to office, after a federal district court in Texas ordered DHS to "enforce and implement MPP in good faith" the program was reinstated in December 2021 and expanded to cover nationals from all countries in the Western Hemisphere.

5. Note that refugees in Chiapas did not obtain a right to legal status until 1998, which was partly due to the Zaptista uprising (Lopez and Hastings 2016, 1113).

6. Translated from Spanish by the authors.

7. Notably, the United States long used a similar policy to control its southern border,

where the vast majority of Mexican deportations were "voluntary returns," without a formal deportation order. The value of this practice to the US government was found in the speed with which migrants apprehended by the Border Patrol could be deported. However, its utility as a deterrent to unauthorized migration is questionable. Indeed, the system "worked" for many years because immigrants were more than happy to be returned to Northern Mexico to be able to quickly make another attempt.

8. CAFTA-DR, the Puebla Process of 1996 (see Kron 2013; FitzGerald 2019), Merida Initiative/CARSI (Insight Crime 2011), 2014's Programa Frontera Sur, Andrés Manuel López Obrador (AMLO)'s southern development proposal.

Bibliography

Asylum Access. 2014. "Mexico," *Asylum Access.*

Benton-Cohen, K. 2018. *Inventing the Immigration Problem: The Dillingham Commission and Its Legacy.* Cambridge, MA: Harvard University Press.

Bhagwati, J. 2003. "Borders Beyond Control." *Foreign Affairs* 82 (1): 98–104.

Camacho-Beltrán, E. 2019. "Legitimate Exclusion of Would-Be Immigrants: A View from Global Ethics and the Ethics of International Relations." *Social Sciences* 8 (8): 238. https://doi.org/10.3390/socsci8080238.

Castañeda, E. 2019. "Building Walls: Boundary Making between Mexicans and Americans." Lanham, MD: Lexington Books.

Castañeda, E. 2020. "Introduction to 'Reshaping the World: Rethinking Borders.'" *Social Sciences* 9 (11): 214. https://doi.org/10.3390/socsci9110214.

Castañeda, E, and A. Shemesh. 2020. "Overselling Globalization: The Misleading Conflation of Economic Globalization and Immigration, and the Subsequent Backlash." *Social Sciences* 9 (5): 61. https://doi.org/10.3390/socsci9050061.

Center for Gender and Refugee Studies (CGRS). 2022a. "Deadly Inertia: Needless Delay of 'Particular Social Group' Regulations Puts Asylum Seekers at Risk." U.C. Hastings, Center for Gender and Refugee Studies, February 10, 2022. Accessed May 31, 2022. http://cgrs.uchastings.edu.

Center for Gender and Refugee Studies (CGRS). 2022b. "New Asylum Rule Sacrifices Justice in the Name of Speed." U.C. Hastings, Center for Gender and Refugee Studies, March 24, 2022. Accessed June 1, 2022. http://cgrs.uchastings.edu.

Center for Migration Studies (CMS), and Cristosal. 2017. "The Central American Humanitarian Crisis and US Policy Responses." *CMS-Cristosal report*, June. New York and San Salvador: CMS and Cristosal. http://cmsny.org/publications/cms-cristosal-report.

Coutin, S. B. 2003. *Legalizing Moves: Salvadoran Immigrants' Struggle for US Residency.* Ann Arbor: University of Michigan Press.

De Haas, H., M. Czaika, M-L. Flahaux, E. Mahendra, K. Natter, S. Vezzoli, and M. Villares Varela. 2019. "International Migration: Trends, Determinants, and Policy Effects." *Population and Development Review* 45 (4): 885–922.

Department of Justice. 2021. 28 I&N Dec. 307 (A.G. 2021), Matter of A-B-, Respondent, Decided by Attorney General, June 16, 2021. US Department of Justice Office of the Attorney General. Accessed May 31, 2022. https://www.justice.gov/eoir/page/file/1404796/download.

Dadush, U. 2017. "Regional Public Goods: The Case of Migration." In *21st Century Cooperation: Regional Public Goods, Global Governance, and Sustainable Development*, edited by A. Estevadeordal and L. W. Goodman, 119–36. New York: Routledge.

Du Bois, W. E. B. (1915) 2014. *The World and Africa and Color and Democracy*. Oxford: Oxford University Press.

Dudley, S. S. 2020. *MS-13: The Making of America's Most Notorious Gang*. New York: Hanover Square Press.

FitzGerald, D. 2019. *Refugee beyond Reach: How Rich Democracies Repel Asylum Seekers*. New York: Oxford University Press.

FitzGerald, D., and R. Arar. 2018. "The Sociology of Refugee Migration." *Annual Review of Sociology* 44: 387–406.

FitzGerald, D., and D. Cook-Martín. 2014. *Culling the Masses*. Cambridge, MA: Harvard University Press.

Gandini, L., A. Fernández de la Reguera, and J. Narváez Gutiérrez. 2020. *Caravanas*. Mexico City, Mexico: UNAM.

Gammeltoft-Hansen, T., and J. C. Hathaway. 2015. "*Non-Refoulement* in a World of Cooperative Deterrence." *Columbia Journal of Transnational Law* 53: 235–84.

Gammeltoft-Hansen, T., and N. F. Tan. 2017. "The End of the Deterrence Paradigm? Future Directions for Global Refugee Policy." *Journal of Migration and Human Security* 5 (1): 28–56.

García, A. 2008. "International Refugee Law in Mexico." *Forced Migration Review* 31 (October). https://www.fmreview.org/sites/fmr/files/FMRdownloads/en/climat-echange/garcia.pdf.

García, M. C. 2006a. "Canada: A Northern Refuge for Central American Migrants." Migration Policy Institute Migration Information Source.

García, M. C. 2006b. *Seeking Refuge: Central American Migration to Mexico, the United States, and Canada*. Berkeley: University of California Press.

Geddes, A. 2021. *Governing Migration Beyond the State: Europe, North America, South America, and Southeast Asia in a Global Context*. New York: Oxford University Press.

Ghezelbash, D. 2014. "Forces of Diffusion: What Drives the Transfer of Immigration Policy and Law Across Jurisdictions?" *International Journal of Migration and Border Studies* 1 (2): 139–53.

Ghezelbash, D. 2018a. *Refuge Lost: Asylum Law in an Interdependent World*. Cambridge: Cambridge University Press.

Ghezelbash, D. 2018b. "Refuge Lost." *Asylum Insight: Facts & Analysis.* Accessed January 4, 2023. https://www.asyluminsight.com/c-dan-ghezelbash.

Giorguli-Saucedo, S. E., V. M. García-Guerrero, and C. Masferrer. "A Migration System in the Making: Demographic Dynamics and Migration Policies in North America and the Northern Triangle of Central-America." Policy paper, Center for Demographic, Urban and Environmental Studies. Mexico City: El Colegio de México. https://cedua.colmex.mx/proyecto/a-migration-system-in-the-making/home.

Golash-Boza, T. 2015. *Deported: Immigrant Policing, Disposable Labor and Global Capitalism.* New York: New York University Press.

Goodman, A. *The Deportation Machine: America's Long History of Expelling Immigrants.* Princeton, NJ: Princeton University Press.

Grant, A., and S. Rehaag. 2016. "Unappealing: An Assessment of the Limits on Appeal Rights in Canada's New Refugee Determination System." *University of British Columbia Law Review* 49 (2016): 203–74.

Guiraudon, V., and G. Lahav. 2000. "A Reappraisal of the State Sovereignty Debate: The Case of Migration Control." *Comparative Political Studies* 33, no. 2 (March): 163–95.

Insight Crime. 2011. Central America Regional Security Initiative (CARSI). Accessed April 11, 2021. https://insightcrime.org/uncategorized/central-america-regional-security-initiative/.

Isacson, A., M. Meyer, and H. Smith. 2017. "Mexico's Southern Border Security, Central American Migrants, and US Policy." *WOLA Advocacy for Human Rights in the Americas.* https://www.wola.org/wp-content/uploads/2017/06/WOLA_Mexicos-Southern-Border-2017-1.pdf.

Jackson, S., and H. Bauder. 2013. "Neither Temporary, Nor Permanent: The Precarious Employment Experiences of Refugee Claimants in Canada." *Journal of Refugee Studies* 27 (3): 360–81.

Jones, R. C. 2014. "The Decline of International Migration as an Economic Force in Rural Areas: A Mexican Case Study." *International Migration Review* 48 (3): 728–61. doi:10.1111/imre.12085.

Kanstroom, D. 2012. *Aftermath: Deportation Law and the New American Diaspora.* New York: Oxford University Press.

Labrador, R., and D. Renwick 2018. "Central America's Turbulent Northern Triangle." *Council on Foreign Relations,* January 18, 2018. https://www.cfr.org/backgrounder/central-americas-turbulent-northern-triangle.

Lacroix, M. 2004. "Canadian Refugee Policy and the Social Construction of the Refugee Claimant Subjectivity." *Journal of Refugee Studies* 17: 147–66.

Light, I. H. 2006. *Deflecting Immigration: Networks, Markets, and Regulation in Los Angeles.* New York: Russell Sage Foundation.

Lopez, E., and M. Hastings. 2016. "Overlooked and Unprotected: Central American

Indigenous Migrants Women in Mexico." *New York University Journal of International Law and Politics* 48 (4): 1105–24.

Marrow, H. 2011. *New Destination Dreaming: Immigration, Race, and Legal Status in the Rural American South.* Stanford, CA: Stanford University Press.

Massey, D., J. Arango, H. Kouaouci, A. Pellegrino, and J. E. Taylor. 1998. *Worlds in Motion: Understanding International Migration at the End of the Millennium.* Oxford: Oxford University Press.

Massey, D. 2008. *New Faces in New Places: The Changing Geography of American Immigration.* New York: Russell Sage Foundation.

Massey, D., J. Durand, and N. Malone. 2002. *Beyond Smoke and Mirrors: Mexican Immigration in an Era of Economic Integration.* New York: Russell Sage Foundation.

Menjívar, C. 2000. *Fragmented Ties: Salvadoran Immigrant Networks in America.* Berkeley: University of California Press.

Menjívar, C. 2006. "Liminal Legality: Salvadoran and Guatemalan Immigrants' Lives in the United States." *American Journal of Sociology* 111 (4): 999–1037. https://doi.org/10.1086/499509.

Musalo, K., and E. Lee. 2017. "Seeking a Rational Approach to a Regional Refugee Crisis: Lessons from the Summer 2014 Surge of Central American Women and Children at the US-Mexico Border." *Journal on Migration and Human Security* 5 (2017): 137–79.

Ogren, C. 2007. "Migration and Human Rights on the Mexico-Guatemala Border." *International Migration* 45 (4): 203–43.

Passel, J., D. Cohn, and A. Gonzalez-Barrera. 2012. "Net Migration from Mexico Falls to Zero—and Perhaps Less." Pew Hispanic Center. Washington, DC: Pew Research Center.

Reynolds, J., and J. Hyndman. 2015. "A Turn in Canadian Refugee Policy and Practice." *Seton Hall Journal of Diplomacy and International Relations* (Spring/Summer): 41–55.

Simmons, A. 1993. "Latin American Migration to Canada: New Linkages in the Hemispheric Migration and Refugee Flow System." *International Journal* 48 (2): 282–309.

Stein, E. 2015. "Mexico Refugee Policy: A Traditional Asylum Sanctuary Turning into a Hostile Land, New Wave of Migrants from Central America in Mexico." *Classe Internationale,* October 10, 2015. https://classe-internationale.com/2015/10/10/mexico-refugee-policy-a-traditional-asylum-sanctuary-turning-into-a-hostile-land-new-wave-of-migrants-from-central-america-in-mexico/.

Stephen, L. 2017. "Cross-Border Gender Violence and Indigenous Women Refugees from Guatemala." *CIDOB Magazine D'afers Internacionals* 117: 29–50.

Unidad de Politica Migratoria. Various years. *Boletines Estadísticos: Extranjeros Presentados y Devueltos.* Accessed March 18, 2021. http://www.politicamigratoria.gob.mx/es/PoliticaMigratoria/Boletines_Estadisticos.

United Nations High Commissioner for Refugees (UNHCR). 2001. *Asylum Applications in Industrialized Countries: 1980–1999.*

United Nations High Commissioner for Refugees (UNHCR). 2015. *Protection and Solutions Strategy for the Northern Triangle of Central America 2016–2018.*

United Nations High Commissioner for Refugees (UNHCR). 2021. "Population Figures: UNHCR Data on Displacement." Accessed March 18, 2021. https://www.unhcr.org/refugee-statistics/download/?url=E1ZxP4.

US Immigration and Naturalization Service (INS). 1997. *Statistical Yearbook of the Immigration and Naturalization Service, 1996.* Washington, DC: US Government Printing Office. Accessed March 18, 2021. https://www.dhs.gov/immigration-statistics/yearbook.

Varela, A. 2019. "México, de 'frontera vertical' a 'país tapón.' Migrantes, deportados, retornados, desplazados internos y solicitantes de asilo en México." *Iberoforum, Revista de Ciencias Sociales de la Universidad Iberoamericana* 14 (27): 49–76.

Villasenor, A., and E. Coria. 2017. "Protection Gaps in Mexico." *Forced Migration Review* 56: 6–8.

Vollmer, B. 2016. "New Narratives from the EU External Border—Humane Refoulement?" *Geopolitics* 21 (3): 717–41. doi:10.1080/14650045.2016.1154843.

Wasem, R. 2020. "More Than a Wall: The Rise and Fall of US Asylum and Refugee Policy." *Journal on Migration and Human Security* 8(3): 246–65.

Zolberg, A. 2008. *A Nation by Design: Immigration Policy in the Fashioning of America.* Cambridge, MA: Russell Sage Foundation Books at Harvard University Press.

CHAPTER SIX

When Cooperation is Not Enough

North America's Security Paradigm and the Failure to Protect Citizens' Security

Gema Kloppe-Santamaría

THIS CHAPTER examines North America's security paradigm and its detrimental consequences for citizens' security and well-being. It does so by focusing on the domestic and regional security initiatives promoted by the governments of the United States, Mexico, and the governments in the Northern Triangle of Central America (NTCA)—El Salvador, Honduras, and Guatemala. I define North America's security paradigm as the concurring and mutually reinforcing implementation of punitive, militarized, and state-centered security responses to crime on behalf of the countries of this region. This paradigm stands in sharp contrast to other security approaches—such as the citizen security and human security paradigms—that prioritize the protection of human life and the promotion of integral policies aimed at tackling the institutional and social determinants of criminal violence (Gasper 2005; Kloppe-Santamaría and Abello-Colak 2019). As can be expected, each of these paradigms and their corresponding security policies rely on different metrics to judge their failure or success. North American government officials tend to measure the success of punitive approaches in terms of drug seizures, number of gang members or kingpins apprehended, migrant detentions, and the dismantling or weakening of criminal organizations (US-CBP 2021; Felbab-Brown 2014). In contrast, actors that promote interventions based on the citizen and human security paradigms use metrics such as the impact of such interventions on levels of homicide, overall victimization, perceptions of crime, and levels of interpersonal trust (Berk-Seligson et al. 2014). Even if the latter metrics are sometimes incorporated by North American security officials, the emphasis is distinctively on securing the borders and stopping the illicit flows that compromise them.

Although the North American region traditionally encompasses Canada, Mexico, and the United States, this chapter excludes Canada and includes the countries of the NTCA. Before explaining the empirical basis for this reimagining of the North American region, it is worth clarifying the concept of region that informs my work. Building on the theoretical framework put forward by the new regionalism approach (NRA) discussed by Laura Macdonald in this book, I understand regions as social and historical constructs that are neither fixed nor "natural" but are instead dependent on informal and political processes. As argued by Björn Hettne, what is defined as a region depends on "the particular problem or question under investigation" (Hettne 2005, 544, quoted in Macdonald, this volume). Hence, a region can be analyzed with respect to a policy problem, the coincidence of policies, and their shared effects among a given number of countries. When it comes to dominant security policies and their impact, I argue that the boundaries and membership of the North American region need to be reconsidered in order to reflect the concurring and reinforcing punitive policies adopted by Mexico, the United States, and the countries of the NTCA.

Why exclude Canada and include instead the countries of the NTCA? First, while Canada has turned increasingly toward punitive antidrug policies, Mexico and the United States share a longer and more pervasive history of repressive drug-control strategies, a history that is very much connected to the "mutual securitization" of drug enforcement characterizing the bilateral relation (Teague 2019b; Odeh 2013). Secondly, Canada's lower levels of incarceration, its focus on harm-reduction strategies, and its greater emphasis on preventive and community forms of policing shed light on a security approach that differs significantly from the North American paradigm examined here (Cheatham and Maizland 2020).

On the other hand, citizens from the NTCA represent, together with Mexican nationals, the largest share of US undocumented immigrants and are also the main target of US aggressive deportation policies. These deportation policies have heightened the transnational dimension of gangs and organized criminal groups (OCGs) and have also intensified the need to implement regional and coordinated security responses between these countries (Brick et al. 2011; Santamaría 2016). Furthermore, the countries of the NTCA are, together with Mexico and Colombia, the most important recipients of US-sponsored security initiatives and programs in the Latin American region (Meyer and Martin 2021). Centered for the most part on repressive and militarized approaches, these programs and the domestic responses they generate are a key component of the North American security paradigm. In short, given these countries' migration and deportation patterns and their shared emphasis on militarized and repressive approaches, the dynamics of violence and insecurity between Mexico, the United States, and the NTCA are deeply intertwined, as are the failed responses articulated by these countries.

When examining North America's security failures, most authors have pointed to the misalignments and asymmetries characterizing US-Mexico security cooperation (Toro 1999; Bow 2012; Benítez Manaut 2012; Serrano 2019). According to these interpretations, Mexico's weaker position within the bilateral relation has pushed it to follow US priorities and mandates, often with detrimental consequences. Examples include the US government's reluctance to recognize arms trafficking as a key factor fueling criminal organizations in Mexico as well as the United States' traditional emphasis on tackling the drug problem by curtailing the supply of drugs abroad instead of addressing drug consumption at home (Serrano 2019, 212–14). Adding to these misalignments, scholars have referred to key irritants in the bilateral relation, which include US unilateralism and US one-way and top-down scrutiny over Mexico's levels of corruption, impunity, and human rights violations, both of which provoke nationalist and defensive attitudes on behalf of Mexican political elites (Bow 2012, 81; Hristoulas 2012, 165).

While recognizing the importance of these factors in limiting North America's security cooperation and its capacity to enhance citizens' security and well-being, this chapter argues that, by and large, the failure of governments in the United States and Mexico to effectively address the challenges posed by transnational security threats is driven by the inherent shortcomings of a North American security paradigm centered on punitive and repressive responses. More so, I argue that the countries of the NTCA are an integral part of the North American security paradigm. Informed by domestic factors and propelled by US-supported initiatives, governments in the NTCA have actively promoted *mano dura* (heavy-handed or iron-first) responses to gangs and militarized counter-narcotic strategies (Cruz 2011). These policies have resulted in higher levels of criminal violence and have pushed thousands of people to migrate north, thus adding to the cycle of deportations and insecurity impacting Central American citizens.

The limitations associated with North America's security paradigm explain why, even at moments in which these countries have aligned their interests and cooperated fully against the threats posed by criminal organizations, violence and drug-related deaths have remained high. Mexico's recent surge in levels of lethal violence, for instance, began precisely during the years wherein cooperation with the United States, via the Mérida Initiative, was at its height (i.e., 2008–2010). Similarly, in the NTCA, homicide rates reached unprecedented levels in the late 2000s and early 2010s at a time when these countries were closely collaborating with the United States through the Central America Regional Security Initiative (CARSI) (Santamaría 2016, 262). As these examples indicate, regional cooperation and shared patterns of regional governance did not produce what might be considered "regional public goods." To the contrary, recent historical evidence suggests security cooperation alone does not guarantee more effective protection of citizens' physical integrity. Instead, building a safer North American region requires moving away from the current security paradigm and advancing toward an alternative that places the protection of human life as its main goal.

The chapter is divided into three main sections. The first describes the general context of insecurity and violence impacting the safety and well-being of the population of these countries. This section discusses homicides and other high-impact crimes produced by OCG and gangs, but also highlights other forms of harm, including state-sanctioned killings and deaths produced by drug abuse. The second section provides an overview of the security paradigm that characterizes domestic responses to crime in the United States, Mexico, and the NTCA, paying particular attention to the use of massive incarceration and militarized strategies to counter criminal groups, as well as the detrimental effects these strategies have had on human rights and citizens' security. The third section examines North America's main bilateral and regional security cooperation efforts over the last decades, with special emphasis on the Mérida Initiative and CARSI. This section further reflects on how these cooperation efforts both reflect and contribute to reinforcing the domestic factors driving North America's security paradigm.

Taken together, these three sections identify the existence of common challenges among the United States, Mexico, and the NTCA as well as the ways in which punitive responses—promoted at the domestic and regional levels—have helped reinforce the dynamics of insecurity and violence characterizing this region. In the conclusion I stress the importance that transitioning from a punitive and state-centered approach toward an integral and human-centered paradigm would have for the future of North American integration.

The Current (In)Security Crisis

In 2008, only a year after President Felipe Calderón (2006–2012) launched a militarized strategy to counteract drug trafficking organizations (DTOs), Mexico experienced a significant surge in levels of lethal violence. Homicide rates continued to increase the following years and have remained high over the last decade, reversing a downward trend that had begun during the mid-1940s (Piccato 2013). With more than 35,000 homicides reported each year, the number of people murdered in the country reached record levels during 2018 and 2019 (INEGI 2020). Despite the initial effects of the COVID-19 pandemic and the lockdowns in slowing down criminal activities in Mexico and neighboring countries, homicides reached a new high in 2020 (International Crisis Group 2020; Reuters 2020).

In the NTCA homicides have also been on the rise since the early 2000s and in the wake of these countries' decision to implement mano dura policies to tackle gang-related violence. Whereas in Guatemala homicide rates have oscillated between 24 and 45 homicides per 100,000 inhabitants, in El Salvador and Honduras they surpassed the region's historic threshold, particularly during the first half of the 2010s (UNODC 2021). In Honduras, there were 83.8 homicides per 100,000 inhabitants reported in 2011 (equivalent to 7,104 deaths), and in El Salvador the homicide rate for the year 2015 was 105.2 per 100,000 inhabitants (equivalent to more than 6,000 killings during that year) (UNODC 2021).

Although homicides have shown a downward trend since 2015 in the countries of the NTCA, other high-impact crimes have remained at epidemic levels (Beltrán

2017). Extortions, in particular, have been on the rise and have increasingly become a key source of income for *maras*. Through the use of violence and intimidation, these gangs tax ordinary people—from small-business owners to taxi drivers—and establish territorial control over entire neighborhoods (Global Initiative 2019). In Mexico, high-impact crimes such as kidnappings, extortions, and forced disappearances have experienced a surge over the last years, together with expressive forms of violence such as hangings, mutilations, and mass killings (Justice in Mexico 2020).

Despite the centrality of drug-related activities on Mexico's current levels of insecurity and violence, several scholars have pointed at the diversification of OCGs beyond drug trafficking, and at the state's responsibility in the production of violence, as equally important drivers (Trejo and Ley 2020). Mexican OCGs are now involved in human trafficking, fuel theft, and kidnappings—activities that are at times undertaken with the involvement of Mexico's law enforcement officials. The justice apparatus is part of the problem: in 2018 alone, 93 percent of crimes were neither reported nor investigated (INEGI 2019; Beittel 2020, 32). In terms of abuse of force, a government survey carried out in the year 2016 revealed that more than 80 percent of people detained by the armed forces were subject to intimidation or torture (Tucker 2020). In the NTCA, extortions involve the direct participation of corrupt officials and members of law enforcement who benefit from the profits of this criminal activity and add to the impunity surrounding this crime (Global Initiative 2019, 14). Scholars and human rights organizations have documented cases of torture, police abuse, and extrajudicial killings perpetrated by police and military, who continue to reproduce the abusive and biased practices from these countries' authoritarian past (Cruz 2011). In March 2022, for instance, Salvadoran president Nayib Bukele (2019–present) declared a "war on gangs" in the country that resulted in the arrest of 38,000 people in less than three months. These arrests were carried out violently, without due process, and singled out young men from marginalized areas who were accused of being gang members without a proper investigation (Phillips 2022).

Police abuse in the United States is also widespread, particularly in regard to racial and ethnic minorities and the urban poor (Patten 2016; Alexander 2012). Although the racialized dimensions of policing are not new to a country with a long history of racial segregation and violence, repressive and militarized forms of policing in the United States are closely connected to the war on drugs (Bobo and Thompson 2006, 451). These crime-control strategies are bipartisan in origin, with political elites from both parties supporting since the 1970s the adoption of more punitive drug policies, including the intensification of mandatory-minimum requirements and the use of mass incarceration to fight the war on drugs (Lassiter 2015, 127, 138).

In all these countries, perceptions of crime, together with a deep sense of distrust in state authorities, have added to the proliferation of vigilante groups and self-help forms of justice, which often contribute to deepen levels of violence and insecurity. In Mexico, self-defense forces that pledged to protect communities against predatory activities have themselves been linked to criminal organizations (Le Cour Grandmaison 2016). Additionally, lynchings have become a prevalent feature of Mexico's context of insecurity, and their incidence has also increased, alongside social cleansings, in several localities of Guatemala (Kloppe-Santamaría 2020; Núñez 2018, 131–51). Similar to Mexican self-defense forces, these expressions of vigilante justice do little to shield people from harm and instead add to the climate of insecurity and violence experienced by thousands of citizens across the country. In the United States, support for militias and vigilante forms of justice became seemingly more acute under the Trump presidency, but they are part of an "American tradition" (Obert 2020). Directed against suspected criminals, undocumented migrants, and informed by racial prejudice, US expressions of vigilantism add to a climate of polarization and insecurity that is undermining of the rule of law.

In addition to these expressions of violence and insecurity, drug consumption and drug abuse have produced high levels of harm on citizens' physical and mental health. Opioid overdose accounted for close to 80 percent of drug-related deaths in the United States in 2016, with opioid-related deaths adding to a historic decline on US life expectancy in the last years (Haskins 2019). Today, Mexico is considered the main source of heroin and methamphetamines in the United States. The Mexican criminal market was further fueled with the arrival of fentanyl, a powerful synthetic opioid that began to be trafficked by Mexico's OCGs including the Sinaloa Cartel and the Cartel Jalisco Nueva Generación (CJNG) around 2013 (Felbab-Brown et al. 2020). Although most overdose deaths have been reported in the United States, recent studies suggest that drug abuse related to opioids is on the rise in Mexico, and that a targeted public health response focused on high-risk groups should be implemented in order to prevent an opioid-use epidemic similar to that experienced by the United States (Goodman-Meza et al. 2019).

As these examples make clear, DTOs and gangs are not the only factor impacting the security and well-being of citizens in Mexico, the United States, and the NTCA. And yet most security cooperation efforts have prioritized the control and dismantling of these criminal groups under the premise that their eventual neutralization will stop the flow of drugs coming into the United States and reduce the levels of violence, crime, and corruption impacting Mexican, US, and Central American citizens.

North America's Security Paradigm: Its Domestic Dimension

As stated in the introduction, North America's security paradigm consists in the concurring and mutually reinforcing implementation of punitive, militarized, and state-centered security responses to crime on behalf of the governments of this region. At the domestic level, the United States and Mexico have since the 1970s privileged punitive and repressive responses to tackle the consumption, cultivation, production, and trafficking of drugs. Similarly, over the last twenty years, the countries of the NTCA have responded to the presence and spread of transnational criminal gangs through the implementation of mano dura policies.

With their emphasis on punitive responses, the United States, Mexico, and the countries of the NTCA have all emphasized the use of mass incarceration as a preferable tool of crime control. In the United States, incarceration rates have experienced a dramatic surge over the last fifty years. Between 1980 and 2000, for instance, there was a 300 percent increase in the number of individuals incarcerated in the country (Patten 2016, 86). Crime levels have decreased steadily since the 1990s, and yet this country continues to have the largest incarcerated population in the world (Robertson 2019). This contrast suggests that incarceration is not driven by crime per se, but by perceptions of crime, racial prejudice, as well as by the potential electoral benefits of tough-on-crime approaches (Alexander 2012). Incarceration has profound but uneven consequences. According to some estimates, Black men lose 3.09 years of life expectancy due to imprisonment; for Latino men the loss in life expectancy is 1.06 years and for white men 0.50 (Schrader 2019, 2).

The increase in US incarceration levels is directly connected to this country's war on drugs, which from the beginning of the 1970s, has promoted tough-on-crime policies, the prosecution of low-level users and dealers, and mass arrests. Whereas in 1980 there were 41,000 individuals incarcerated due to drug offenses, by the end of 2010 this number exceeded 500,000 people (Odeh 2013, 202–3). Further illustrating the weight of the war on drugs, by 2011 more than half of federal inmates in the United States were imprisoned in connection to drug crimes (Odeh 2013, 199). Mass incarceration has had a particularly pernicious impact on Black, Latino, young, and urban poor men who are, as a result of these policies, overrepresented in the US criminal justice system (Provine 2011, 46; Schrader 2019, 2; Alexander 2012). In the year 2000, for instance, three-fourths of all drug offenders in US state prisons were African Americans and Latinos despite the fact that whites represented the vast majority of illegal drug users and dealers (Lassiter 2015, 127).

In Mexico, incarceration rates have increased 175 percent since 1972, also in connection to punitive responses to crime as well as the outlawing of drug-related activities, from consumption and possession to the cultivation, production, and trafficking of drugs. According to 2016 data, 43 percent of people in Mexico's federal prisons are held under drug-related charges (Chaparro Hernández and Pérez Correa 2017, 74–75). Similar to the United States, the vast majority of inmates are young men with limited education and employment opportunities and who occupy the lower echelons of criminal structures (Pérez Correa and Azaola 2012). Although prison population rates had been on the rise since the last decades of the twentieth century and the beginning of the 2000s, this tendency accelerated under the administration of President Felipe Calderón (2006–2012), who decisively stepped up Mexico's war on drugs. From 156 inmates per 100,000 inhabitants in 2000, by 2012 this rate had reached the figure of 203 inmates per 100,000 inhabitants (World Prison Brief Data, n.d.), exacerbating the problems of corruption, violence, and overcrowding characterizing Mexico's prison system (Bergman 2014).

In the fragile democracies of the NTCA, anti-narcotic and anti-gang policies have also prioritized mass incarceration and zero tolerance approaches since the beginning of the 2000s. Such approaches have increased the police's discretionary use of force and the criminalization of young males from marginalized areas (Cruz 2011). In all three countries, prison population rates have steadily increased since 2000. In Guatemala the number of inmates per 100,000 inhabitants went from 62 to 140 between 2000 and 2018; in Honduras it increased from 184 to 229; and in El Salvador the prison population rate skyrocketed from 132 to 617 inmates during the same period (World Prison Brief Data, n.d.). In addition to saturating penitentiary systems that were already pierced by problems of corruption and the presence of criminal networks, a focus on massive imprisonment has increased these gangs' cohesiveness, organizational capacity, and predilection toward violence, as well as their recourse to predatory crimes such as extortions (Wolf 2017). More so, these policies have escalated human rights violations and the extrajudicial killing of criminalized youth in ways that are reminiscent of the levels of brutality experienced by these countries during their civil wars (Cruz 2011).

At the domestic level, North America's security paradigm has added to the policing and criminalization of ethnic and racial minorities and economically marginalized populations.

In the United States, drug-policing strategies have created incentives for the police to intervene in poor and Black neighborhoods through stop-and-frisk tactics that have resulted in the disproportionate harassment and arrest of the poor and of people of color (Cooper 2015; Patten 2016, 94). While having little to no effect in reducing street-level drug activities, these practices have heightened Black communities' perception of the police as a repressive and biased institution (Bobo and Thompson 2006, 451–58).

In Mexico, drug-policing strategies have consistently targeted poor and marginalized communities. Whereas during the 1970s Mexican authorities utilized the war on drugs in order to target peasants and political opponents (Teague 2019a), in the present-day context militarized antidrug policies have made journalists, human rights activists, Central American migrants, and the urban poor more susceptible to violence and coercion on behalf of state and criminal actors. During Enrique Peña Nieto's administration (2012–2018), 161 human rights defenders were murdered in the country (Hinojosa and Meyer 2020). According to the Committee to Protect Journalists, in the year 2019, Mexico became the world's most dangerous country for journalists due to the violent practices of criminal organizations and public officials' involvement in the drug business (Lakhani et al. 2020).

Notwithstanding the alternation of power between different political parties at the federal level, security responses in Mexico have continued to emphasize repression during the last decade. This is so despite the fact that both presidents Enrique Peña

Nieto (2012–2018) and Andrés Manuel López Obrador (2018–present) pledged to promote prevention and harm reduction strategies and move away from militarized policies. López Obrador, for instance, promised to abandon Mexico's war on drugs and to demilitarize the country's security policies by placing greater emphasis on the professionalization of the police and the socioeconomic roots of insecurity. He further promised to prioritize the protection of victims, the legalization of certain drugs, and the provision of amnesty to eligible criminals. Just as his predecessor, however, López Obrador has continued to promote the participation of the military in public security operations and to privilege the arrest and extradition of top criminal leaders (Serrano 2019). López Obrador's newly created National Guard sheds light on his approach to security issues. The National Guard, an institution that was supposed to operate under civilian control, is instead dominated by a military ethos as reflected by the fact that most of its members belong to the military and that, as of August 2020, 80 percent lacked training and certification as police officers (Meyer 2020).

In the NTCA, mano dura policies and repressive forms of policing have also contributed to the criminalization of youth living in poor and marginalized areas. Since their implementation in the early 2000s, these policies have facilitated police's discretionary faculties to carry out massive arrests against young males suspected of belonging to gangs (Ungar 2009). Similar to Mexico, these policies have been replicated by different administrations, regardless of their party affiliation or political ideology. Saliently, in El Salvador, the governments of presidents Mauricio Funes (2009–2014) and Salvador Sánchez Cerén (2014–2019) from the leftist party Farabundo Martí National Liberation Front (FMNL) reproduced and even stepped up the repressive anti-gang strategies promoted by previous right-wing and conservative governments. With the exception of a short-lived truce among gangs partially supported by Funes, repressive policies under these governments increased, with gangs being classified as terrorist groups in 2015 and being subjected to even harsher forms of punishment (Cruz and Durán-Martínez 2016). Although journalists and experts suspected the existence of a new gang truce in El Salvador enabled by the Bukele administration, a "state of exception" decree implemented by this government in 2022 to "wipe out" gangs made it clear that mano dura continues to be the dominant approach to tackle crime in the NTCA (Phillips 2022). A potential exception to the rule might be Honduran leftist president Xiomara Castro (2022–present), who has proposed concrete policies to move away from militarized and iron-fist polices by focusing instead on community forms of policing and investment in mental health issues (Asmann and Robbin 2022).

Following the 9/11 terrorist attacks, US anti-gang and counter-narcotics strate-gies have been accompanied by this country's increasing securitization of migration (Hristoulas 2012, 168–69; see Toro, this volume). Characterized by harsher border con-trols, massive deportations, and the criminalization of Mexican and Central American migrants within US territory, this securitized approach to migration has furthered the policing of communities of color in the United States. It has also amplified the dangers faced by undocumented migrants who, forced to travel through more remote territories, have become even more exposed to criminal gangs operating in Mexico and along the US-Mexico border. More so, the steady and significant increase in US deportations of Mexican and Central American nationals since the year 2000—including individuals with criminal records—has added to the territorial dispersion of transnational gangs across Mexico and the NTCA (Santamaría 2016, 263). Although Mexico has repeatedly critiqued harsher US migration policies, in practice it has been a strategic partner of the United States in its efforts to contain Central American migrants through more severe deportation policies and the further militarization of the country's southern border (Castañeda et al., this volume).

In Mexico and the NTCA, militarized and repressive strategies have amplified state actors' discretionary use of force, enabled the further penetration of state institutions by criminal actors, and provoked an upsurge in human rights violations (Flores Macías 2018; Cruz 2011). Reflecting this reality, some of the most visible violent events in recent years have involved police and military personnel acting in conjunction with powerful OCGs. An illustrative example includes the massacre of nineteen undocumented migrants—sixteen from Guatemala—in Camargo, a small community in the Mexican state of Tamaulipas in January 2021. In the year 2010, in this same state, seventy-two migrants were massacred by the criminal organization of Los Zetas. In the case of the Camargo massacre, eight of the twelve state police officers implicated in this atrocity were members of a special unit armed and trained by the United States (Lindsay-Poland 2021).

Reinforcing North America's Security Paradigm: Bilateral and Regional Efforts

North America's security paradigm has been carried out at the domestic level by each of these countries but has also been fostered transnationally via binational and regional security cooperation efforts and the implementation of US-funded programs in Mexico and Central America. The United States' decision to expand its antidrug policies beyond its national borders has served to expand militarized operations, eradication campaigns, and security strategies centered on the capture, extradition, and neutralization of top criminal leaders south of the Río Bravo. Far from being a top-down imposition, however, the promotion of punitive responses by Mexico and the countries of the NTCA reflect these countries' proclivity to advance state-centered, short-term, and repressive security responses. In Central America, the legacies of civil war and a recent past punctuated by human rights violations have further deepened these security responses' harmful effects on democracy and the rule of law (Cruz 2011). In Mexico, these policies have contributed to reproduce the abusive practices of this country's recent authoritarian past (Pérez Ricart 2020).

Launched in 2007 by the US and Mexican governments, the Mérida Initiative remains the most ambitious bilateral cooperation effort on matters of security to date. The initiative broke new ground in terms of the levels of coordination, bilateral trust, and alignment of interests between these countries. Saliently, the initiative advanced an understanding of security as a shared responsibility. Whereas Mexico recognized, at least in principle, the need to address its problems of corruption, the United States pledged to tackle the US demand of drugs and the illicit trafficking of weapons as two factors that had a direct impact on the escalation of criminal violence (Olson 2017; Congressional Research Service 2020).

Cooperation on matters of security between these two countries is certainly not new. During the 1970s, for instance, the United States and Mexico increased their collaboration on anti-narcotics strategies. After unilaterally shutting down the border through Operation Intercept (1969), the US government began to promote more collaborative efforts to eradicate the cultivation of drugs, chiefly opium and marijuana, in Mexican territory (Teague 2019b). Some of these efforts were institutionalized through the implementation of Operations Canador (1970–1975), Trizo (1975–1976), and Condor (1977–1987). These bilateral operations expanded the presence of agents from the Drug Enforcement Administration (DEA) in Mexico, with the explicit goal of training Mexican police officers and gathering information that could facilitate the apprehension of major drug traffickers (Toro 1999; Pérez Ricart 2020).

Although Operation Condor stands as the most ambitious of these antidrug efforts, these campaigns shared the goal of countering the supply of drugs in the US through the use of herbicides in Mexico and the neutralization of major Mexican drug traffickers (Cedillo 2022). These campaigns' priorities reflected the US government decision to fight what Richard Nixon dubbed "public enemy number one" (drug abuse) through the control of drug production south of the border, instead of through a health-based approach that addressed drug demand at home. Based on short-term and militarized security policies, all these operations overlooked the economic needs of Mexican peasants on the ground and the potential health hazards associated with the use of herbicides. They further failed to address the problems of corruption and abuse of force that emerged in Mexico as a result of the participation of the military and members of the federal judicial police in these campaigns (Craig 1980; Cedillo 2022). More so, these initiatives did not diminish the supply of drugs to the United States and resulted instead in increasing levels of violence and state repression in Mexico (Pérez Ricart 2020, 108).

Although the United States had an active role in promoting the war on drugs in Mexico through diplomatic pressure, financial assistance, and militarized operations, it would be wrong to assume that these antidrug policies were simply the result of a top-down imposition on behalf of the United States. Instead, evidence suggests that Mexican political elites have historically supported a prohibitionist and punitive approach to drugs driven by conservative public opinion at home as well as by the type of political benefits brought about by antidrug policies (Pérez Montfort 2016, 279–85). During the country's dirty war, for example, Mexico's government made use of the training, equipment, and discretionary powers enabled by the war on drugs in order to intimidate and repress political opponents (Aviña 2016; Teague 2019a; Cedillo 2022). Even more so, police bureaucracies on both sides of the border, namely, the US Drug Enforcement Administration and the Mexican Federal Judicial Police (MFJP), had incentives to support these counter-narcotic efforts despite their limited or even detrimental impact on citizens' security, given that they provided them access to institutional rewards and material resources (Pérez Ricart 2020).

In the 1980s and 1990s, Mexico experienced an increasing process of democratization, particularly in regard to the larger presence of opposition parties at the local and regional levels and the decentralization of law enforcement (Davis 2018). Despite this transformation, political elites continued to rely on punitive approaches. As a matter of fact, the use of the military in public security functions significantly increased under Vicente Fox (2000–2006), the first president from an opposition party to win the federal elections in more than seven decades (Astorga and Shirk 2010). This continuing support of militarized policies shows the existence of a consensus among Mexican political elites around a punitive approach that crosses political ideologies and party affiliation. It is also a reflection of the popular support that tough-on-crime policies have continued to enjoy alongside democratization not only in Mexico but also in several other Latin American countries (Bonner 2019; Sonja 2017). During the same period, mutual distrust, US unilateralism, and the involvement of high-level Mexican officials in protecting drug traffickers, undermined the bilateral nature of security efforts developed during the prior decades. After the 9/11 terrorist attacks, the United States shifted its focus toward homeland security and counterterrorism. With this change, several components of the bilateral agenda—including borders and undocumented migration—were subsumed under a more unilateral and defensive understanding of security (Benítez Manaut 2012, 33; Toro, this volume).

When understood against these previous security efforts, the Mérida Initiative stands out on several fronts. First, as mentioned earlier, at least in principle, both countries acknowledged security as a shared responsibility and moved away from the almost exclusive emphasis on drug cultivation, production, and trafficking that had characterized previous bilateral efforts. Second, the initiative followed President Felipe Calderón's request to increase security cooperation with the US government. In contrast to previous security initiatives, then, it was not the United States but Mexico that sought to increase the level of coordination and collaboration. Furthermore, through this initiative, both governments began to acknowledge the institutional and socioeconomic drivers of insecurity and violence, particularly in Mexico. Although this shift in focus did not entirely materialize, it represented a step in the right direction inasmuch as it brought these countries' collaboration efforts closer to a provision of security centered on citizens' security.

A cursory review of the evolution of the Mérida Initiative reveals both the opportunities and challenges linked to US-Mexico security cooperation. During the first three years of its implementation (2008–2011), the main focus was on traditional counter-narcotics strategies, encompassing technical assistance, provision of equipment, and intelligence sharing, all aimed at the disruption of major Mexican DTOs (Olson 2017, 5; Congressional Research Service 2020). The so-called kingpin strategy, which focused on the arrest and extradition of the top leaders of these criminal organizations, was a priority, though it failed to improve security levels in Mexico and did little to disrupt the flow of drugs to the United States. Instead, it led to the splintering of these organizations, their geographical dispersion, and the diversification of their criminal activities, as well as to increasing levels of competition and confrontation among DTOs, and between DTOs and state actors (Durán-Martínez 2018; Trejo and Ley 2020).

In 2011, both countries agreed to reformulate the goals of the Mérida Initiative. Recognizing the limited effects of the kingpin strategy in stopping the flow of drugs as well as the detrimental consequences it had had on Mexico's levels of security and violence, the governments agreed to work toward "building strong and resilient communities" (Congressional Research Service 2020). Under this specific goal, the United States and Mexico pledged to move security cooperation away from a traditional law enforcement approach to a more integral understanding of security aimed at addressing the social drivers of violence (Olson 2017, 10). The United States promoted violence-prevention programs in several cities, including Tijuana, Monterrey, and Ciudad Juarez. Administered by USAID, these programs focused on the creation of jobs, social integration activities, and keeping youth at school (Ribando Seelke and Finklea 2017, 22–23).

US security assistance toward Central America experienced a similar evolution. Particularly under the Obama administration, US assistance transitioned from short-term and militarized responses to crime to a more integral understanding of insecurity and violence. Promoted initially as a component of the Mérida Initiative, security assistance toward Central America was rebranded in 2010 as CARSI. The initial goals of this initiative included, among other things, disrupting the movement of criminal organizations within and between Central American nations, supporting the development of stronger and more accountable institutions, and improving the provision of services and security in communities at risk (Santamaría 2016, 259).

Although CARSI was meant to tackle the institutional and social roots of violence, similar to the Mérida Initiative, most resources were initially allocated to traditional law enforcement operations. In order to push forward a more comprehensive approach to insecurity and in the context of the surge of unaccompanied minors and families from the NTCA in 2014, the US government launched the US Strategy for Engagement in Central America (Meyer 2019). This strategy, together with a series of prevention and harm-reduction programs promoted by CARSI, has supported an approach that recognizes the economic and institutional underpinnings of criminal violence in these countries. Despite ample evidence of the effectiveness of these violence-prevention strategies (Berk-Seligson et al. 2014), however, the governments of the countries of the NTCA continue to privilege heavy-handed and repressive responses to crime driven by electoral cycles and the ongoing support that mano dura policies enjoy at the domestic level.

In Mexico and in the context of US-Mexico security cooperation programs, support for integral approaches to security has also been inconsistent at best, despite evidence showing greater effectiveness of integral approaches in this and other Latin American countries (Muggah et al. 2016, 32–35). For instance, although the Obama administration (2009–2017) was instrumental in shifting the aid priorities of the Mérida Initiative toward institution-building and strengthening communities' resilience, in practice, not much changed. During the fiscal years 2012–2017, the vast majority of the initiative's funding corresponded to the accounts "international narcotics and law enforcement" and "foreign military financing"; only a small fraction of the resources was allocated to the "economic support fund" (Ribando Seelke and Flinkea 2017, 12). On the Mexican side, the government's support for a more integral approach has also been limited. For instance, in 2017, the federal government defunded the National Crime and Violence Prevention Program (PRONAPRED), which prioritized the rehabilitation of public spaces, after-school programs, and violence-prevention workshops (Castillo Hernández 2019).

The persistence of high levels of violence and criminality, together with several corruption scandals involving high-level officials in Mexico (at both the state and federal levels), increased US concerns regarding the effectiveness of the Mérida Initiative and of US-Mexico security cooperation more broadly (Congressional Research Service 2020, 19–20). High-profile human rights violations over the last decade confirmed the need to reform and modernize Mexico's judicial system, something the Mérida Initiative supported, namely through the transition from an inquisitorial justice system to an oral and adversarial system. Still, despite some productive changes, on the whole cooperation efforts continue to reproduce militarized and short-term approaches, even in the midst of the international attention to human rights violations in Mexico.

The metrics of success put forward by the US State Department clearly suggest that the dismantling of criminal organizations and the control of the border continued to be at the center of US priorities. As of 2017, two of the three main indicators of success regarding US-Mexico security cooperation included the capture and extradition of top criminal leaders as well as Mexico's apprehension of undocumented migrants (Ribando Seelke and Flinkea 2017, 25). Only the third indicator, which referred to Mexico's transition to an accusatorial justice system, involved a measure centered on more long-term goals of institutional building.

The emphasis on defensive and state-centered strategies deepened under Donald Trump's presidency (2017–2021). Throughout his term in office, Trump consistently focused on two goals in regard to North American security cooperation: redefining and enhancing border security, and combating transnational criminal organizations, including maras (Congressional Research Service 2020). Furthermore, the Trump administration placed significantly less importance on human rights violations or the need to address the institutional and social roots of insecurity in Mexico and the NTCA. To heighten border security, Trump supported the building of a wall between Mexico and the United States with the purported aim of defending the country against drug and human smugglers. He also exercised both diplomatic and economic pressure on the Mexican government so that it would take concrete steps to curb the flow of migrants (particularly from the NTCA) toward the United States. In a drastic departure from his pledge to demilitarize security and defend the rights of migrants both in Mexico and the United States, in 2020 López Obrador deployed thousands of members of the newly created National Guard to prevent migrants from entering Mexico (Tucker 2020). The militarization of Mexico's southern border resulted in widespread human rights violations and increased the vulnerability of Central American migrants in Mexican territory. In this sense, US-Mexico alignment around a more securitized approach to migration amplified Central American migrants' vulnerability and exposure to violence.

Conclusion: Toward a New North American Security Paradigm?

Scholars have traditionally analyzed North America's security failures through the lenses of the asymmetries and misalignments characterizing US-Mexico's security cooperation. While these factors are important and have indeed, at different moments, generated a number of irritants in the bilateral relation, they do not account for these countries' failure to work toward a provision of security that can promote prosperity and peace for the citizens of the region. Furthermore, as demonstrated by this chapter, the countries of the NTCA are a key component of North America's security regime. Based on their migration and deportation patters, the security threats they share, and their emphasis on militarized and repressive measures, Mexico, the United States, and the countries of the NTCA are deeply intertwined. Although often in an ad hoc manner, the countries have implemented what amounts to a shared regional policy regime and constitute a coherent region in terms of transnational security challenges and management. Unfortunately, that regime has largely been counterproductive and harmful.

The alignment of Mexico and the United States around the more militarized dimensions of the Mérida Initiative provides the clearest example of how security cooperation, in and of itself, does not necessarily translate into a betterment of citizens' security. In the context of these security responses, Mexican DTOs and OCGs were not only able to respond to the repressive policies promoted by the Mexican state with the support and training of US assistance; these organizations were also able to rearrange their structures, diversify their criminal activities, and increase their armed power. In the wake of this, they became more predatory, increasingly targeting municipal state officials as well as common citizens who became victims of high-impact crimes, including extortions, kidnappings, and forced disappearances (Trejo and Ley 2020).

Similarly, in the countries of the NTCA, US security assistance contributed to heighten these countries' emphasis on punitive and militarized responses to DTOs and maras. Even though CARSI and other US assistance programs included important prevention and violence-reduction components, the financial weight and institutional support given to traditional law enforcement operations added to Central American nations' fixation with short-term mano dura policies. The result of these policies has been the territorial escalation of maras and their further participation in extortions and robberies, next to the growth on human rights violations perpetrated by law enforcement officers.

In terms of the impact of these policies in the United States, evidence shows that even at the height of the Mérida Initiative, drug seizures—a key indicator of success according to the initiative's parameters (US Embassy 2021)—had mixed results at best as the availability of heroin and methamphetamine increased and exposed more people to these highly potent and potentially lethal drugs. Given that US policy makers have repeatedly emphasized supply reduction as a primary goal, continued availability and increased potency suggest how badly the paradigm has failed. According to a 2018 DEA report, drug-poisoning deaths have, since the year 2011, outnumbered the deaths by firearms, suicide, homicide, and motor vehicle crashes (DEA 2018). The current opioid epidemic, with its harmful consequences for the health and life of thousands of US citizens, has further exposed the war on drugs' failure to protect the physical integrity of citizens.

Although shaped by the US decision to "export" its antidrug policies south of the border through diplomatic pressure and militarized operations, Mexico's war on drugs was and continues to reflect Mexican elites' decision to privilege punitive and short-term approaches. Similarly, mano dura policies promoted by the NTCA were enabled by US security assistance but were also animated by these countries' proclivity to privilege punitive responses to crime.

To overcome the limitations of North America's security paradigm would require a cooperation agenda based upon the main tenets of the citizen security and human security frameworks. Both of these frameworks put the protection of human life at the center of the design and implementation of any security policy. They further highlight the importance that social, economic, and institutional determinants have in shaping people's prospects of living a life free of fear and want (Gasper 2005, 224). Put into practice, a citizen-centered notion of security would allow these countries to prioritize security responses focused on the protection of citizens from diverse forms of violence and harm. Instead of concentrating most efforts on territorial containment and dismantling of criminal organizations through the arrest and extradition of gang leaders and kingpins, these countries should allocate more resources into targeted prevention programs, such as the ones supported by USAID in the context of the Mérida Initiative and CARSI. Put differently, the metrics of success of these countries' security policies would have to be shifted from an emphasis on the protection of borders and the dismantling of criminal organizations, to a vision that prioritizes human lives, harm reduction strategies, and crime prevention.

In many ways, the goals of the "US-Mexico Bicentennial Framework for Security, Public Heath, and Safe Communities," which was announced in October 2021, seem to reflect this change in priorities at least in the context of US-Mexico security cooperation (White House 2021). In contrast to the Mérida Initiative the number one goal of the Bicentennial Framework is "protect our people," with the prevention of transborder crime and the pursuing of criminal organizations listed as second and third goals. The question, however, is how feasible it is to translate these goals into actual policies given these countries' institutional inertias, the long-term militarized character of their security responses, and the persistent support of punitive responses in all of these countries.

Equally challenging to these countries' path forward is the need to place greater emphasis on institution-building, particularly as it concerns the vetting of law enforcement personnel and the tackling of corruption and impunity in Mexico and Central America. Since his arrival to office in January 2021, US president Joe Biden has made it clear that fighting corruption will be a key aspect of the US new Central American policy. So far, however, several Central American leaders—including Salvadoran president Nayib Bukele—have either reacted defensively or openly opposed anti-corruption efforts (Sheridan and Brigida 2021). Despite campaign promises by Mexican president Andrés Manuel López Obrador (AMLO), the Mexican government has also shown an ambivalent and even antagonistic position toward anti-corruption initiatives, particularly those promoted by civil society organizations and based on US funding (Agren 2021). The extradition of former Honduran president Juan Orlando Hernández to the United States in March 2022 offers grounds for cautious optimism. Following drug-trafficking charges made against Hernández, the extradition was facilitated and supported by President Xiomara Castro, who has openly expressed her commitment to face corruption and break the existing nexus between politicians and drug traffickers in Honduras (Brigida 2022).

With its emphasis on protecting people's health and well-being and strengthening its neighbors' institutional capacities, Joe Biden's administration offers a window of opportunity to work toward a security provision centered on citizen and human security. Particularly, it represents the possibility of advancing a more integral vision of security that puts the legalization of certain drugs, the focus on institution-building, and the protection of victims, at the center of the bilateral and regional security agendas. It further offers the chance to work toward a more integral and humane approach to Central American migration that incorporates the developing of economic opportunities and the implementation of targeted prevention programs in the NTCA (White House 2022). It remains to be seen if the Mexican and Central American governments will take this as a chance to fostering a more humane approach to migration and security. Were they to do so, an alternative North American security paradigm might be on the horizon.

Bibliography

Agren, D. 2021. "Mexican President Accuses US of Interference over Funding for NGOs." *The Guardian*, May 7, 2021. https://www.theguardian.com/global-development/2021/may/07/mexico-president-us-interference-funding-ngos.

Alexander, M. 2012. *The New Jim Crow: Mass Incarceration in an Age of Color Blindness*. New York: The New Press.

Asmann, P., and S. Robin. 2021. "3 Security Takeaways from Xiomara Castro's Historic Win in Honduras." *Insight Crime*, November 30, 2021. https://insightcrime.org/news/security-takeaways-xiomara-castro-honduras/.

Astorga, L., and D. Shirk. 2010. "Drug Trafficking Organizations and Counter-Drug Strategies in the US-Mexican Context." Center for US-Mexican Studies working paper, October 2010. https://escholarship.org/uc/item/8j647429

Aviña, A. 2016. "Mexico's Long Dirty War." *NACLA Report on the Americas* 48 (2): 144–49. doi:10.1080/10714839.2016.1201271.

Beittel, J. 2020. "Mexico: Organized Crime and Drug Trafficking Organizations." Congressional Research Service, Report 41576, July 28, 2020. https://fas.org/sgp/crs/row/R41576.pdf.

Beltrán, A. 2017. "Children and Families Fleeing Violence in Central America." WOLA, February 21, 2017. https://www.wola.org/analysis/people-leaving-central-americas-northern-triangle/.

Benítez Manaut, R. 2012. "Drug Trafficking and Public Opinion: Myths and Facts." Colectivo de Análisis de la Seguridad con Democracia.

Bergman, M., G. Fondevila, C. Vilalta, and E. Azaola. 2014. *Delito y cárcel en México: deterioro social y desempeño institucional*. Mexico City: Centro de Investigación y Docencia Económicas, August 2014.

Berk-Seligson, S., D. Orcés, G. Pizzolitto, M. A. Seligson, C. J. Wilson. 2014. "Impact Evaluation of USAID's Community-Based Crime and Violence Prevention Approach in Central America." LAPOP-Vanderbilt-USAID. https://www.vanderbilt.edu/lapop/carsi/Regional_Report_v12d_final_W_120814.pdf.

Bobo, Lawrence D., and Victor Thompson. 2006. "Unfair by Design: The War on Drugs, Race, and the Legitimacy of the Criminal Justice System." *Social Research: An International Quarterly* 73 (2): 445–72.

Bonner. Michelle D. 2019. *Tough on Crime: The Rise of Punitive Populism in Latin America*. Pittsburgh: University of Pittsburgh Press.

Brick, K., A. E. Challinor, and M. R. Rosenblum. 2011. "Mexican and Central American Immigrants in the United States." Migration Policy Institute. June 2011. https://www.migrationpolicy.org/pubs/MexCentAmimmigrants.pdf.

Brígida, A-C. 2022. "'An Extradition Foretold': Honduras Reacts to Ex-President's Fate." *Aljazeera*, March 29, 2022. https://www.aljazeera.com/news/2022/3/29/an-extradition-foretold-honduras-reacts-to-ex-presidents-fate.

Castillo Hernández, A. 2019. "Adiós PRONAPRED, ¿y luego?" *Animal Político*, October 2, 2019. https://www.animalpolitico.com/el-blog-de-causa-en-comun/adios-pronapred-y-luego/.

Cedillo, A. 2022. "The War on Drugs, Counterinsurgency, and the State of Siege in the Golden Triangle (1977–1982)," In *Histories of Drug Trafficking in Twentieth-Century Mexico*, edited by W. G. Pansters and B. T. Smith, 240–62. Albuquerque: University of New Mexico Press.

Chaparro Hernández, S., and C. Pérez Correa. 2017. *Sobredosis carcelarai y política de drogas en América Latina*. Bogota, CO: Dejusticia.

Cheatham, A., and L. Meizland. 2020. "How Police Compare in Different Democracies." *Council on Foreign Relations*, November 12, 2020. https://www.cfr.org/backgrounder/how-police-compare-different-democracies.

Cooper, H. L. F. 2015. "War on Drugs Policing and Police Brutality." *Substance Use & Misuse* 50 (8–9): 1188–94.

Congressional Research Service (CRS). "Mexico: Evolution of the Mérida Initiative, 2007 2020." July 20, 2020. https://fas.org/sgp/crs/row/IF10578.pdf.

Craig, R. B. 1980. "Operation Intercept: The International Politics of Pressure." *The Review of Politics* 42, no. 4 (October): 556–80.

Cruz, J. M. 2011. "Criminal Violence and Democratization in Central America: The Survival of the Violent State." *Latin American Politics and Society* 53 (4): 1–33.

Cruz, J. M., and A. Durán-Martínez. 2016. "Hiding Violence to Deal with the State: Criminal Pacts in El Salvador and Medellin." *Journal of Peace Research* 53 (2): 197–21.

Davis, D. 2006. "Undermining the Rule of Law: Democratization and the Dark Side of Police Reform in Mexico." *Latin American Politics and Society* 48 (1): 55–86.

Drug Enforcement Agency (DEA). 2018. National Drug Threat Assessment Summary, Accessed February 20, 2021. https://www.dea.gov/documents/2018/2018-10/2018-10-02/2018-national-drug-threat-assessment-ndta.

Felbab-Brown, V. 2014. "Changing the Game or Dropping the Ball? Mexico's Security and Anti-Crime Strategy under President Enrique Peña Nieto." Brookings Institution, November 17, 2014. http://www.brookings.edu/research/papers/2014/11/mexico-security-anti-crime-nieto-felbabbrown.

Felbab-Brown, V., J. P. Caulkins, C. Graham, K. Humphreys, R. Liccardo Pacula, B. Pardo, P. Reuter, B. D. Stein, and P. H. Wise. 2020. "The Opioid Crisis in America: Domestic and International Dimensions." Brookings Institution, June 22, 2020. https://www.brookings.edu/research/overview-the-opioid-crisis-in-america/.

Flores Macías, G. A. 2018. "The Consequences of Militarizing Anti-Drug Efforts for State Capacity in Latin America: Evidence from Mexico." *Comparative Politics* 51 (1): 1–20.

Gasper, D. 2005. "Securing Humanity: Situating 'Human Security' as Concept and Discourse." *Journal of Human Development* 6 (2): 221–45.

Goodman-Meza, M., E. Medina-Mora, C. Magis-Rodríguez, R. J. Landovitz, S.

Shoptaw, and D. Werb. 2019. "Where Is the Opioid Use Epidemic in Mexico? A Cautionary Tale for Policymakers South of the US–Mexico Border." *AJPH Perspectives* 109, no. 1 (January): 73–82.

Haskins, J. 2019. "Suicide, Opioids Tied to Ongoing Fall in US Life Expectancy: Third Year of Drop." *The Nation's Health* 49, no. 1 (February/March): 1–10.

Hinojosa, G., and M. Meyer. 2020. "Mexico Needs Comprehensive Strategies to Combat Violence against Journalists and Human Rights Defenders." WOLA Report, May 13, 2020. https://www.wola.org/analysis/journalists-human-rights-defenders-mexico/.

Hristoulas, A. 2012. "Why North American Regional Security Cooperation Will Not Work." In *The State and Security in Mexico*, edited by Brian Bow, 160–73. New York: Routledge.

Global Initiative. 2019. "A Criminal Culture: Extortion in Central America." The Global Initiative against Transnational Organized Crime and Insight Crime Report. https://globalinitiative.net/wp-content/uploads/2019/05/Central-American-Extortion-Report-English-03May1400-WEB.pdf.

Instituto Nacional de Estadística y Geografía (INEGI). 2019. "Encuesta nacional de victimización y percepción sobre seguridad pública 2019." September 24, 2019. https://www.inegi.org.mx/contenidos/programas/envipe/2019/doc/envipe2019_presentacion_nacional.pdf.

Instituto Nacional de Estadística y Geografía (INEGI). 2020. "Comunicado de prensa, Núm. 432," September 23, 2020. https://www.inegi.org.mx/contenidos/saladeprensa/boletines/2020/EstSociodemo/Defcioneshomicidio2019.pdf.

Kloppe-Santamaría, G. 2020. *In the Vortex of Violence: Lynching, Extralegal Justice and the State in Post-Revolutionary Mexico*. Berkeley: University of California Press, 2020.

Kloppe-Santamaría, G., and A. Abello-Colak. 2019. *Human Security and Chronic Violence in Mexico: New Perspectives and Proposals from Below*. Mexico City: Editorial Porrúa.

Lakhani, N., D. Priest, and P. Dupont de Dinechin in Veracruz. 2020. "Murder in Mexico: Journalists Caught in the Crosshairs." *The Guardian*, December 6, 2020. https://www.theguardian.com/world/2020/dec/06/murder-in-mexico-journalists-caught-in-the-crosshairs-regina-martinez-cartel-project.

Lassiter, M. D. 2015. "Impossible Criminals: The Suburban Imperatives of America's War on Drugs." *Journal of American History* 102, no. 1 (June): 126–40. https://doi.org/10.1093/jahist/jav243.

Le Cour Grandmaison, R. 2016. "*Vigilar y Limpiar*: Identification and Self-Help Justice-Making in Michoacán, Mexico." *Politix* 115 (3): 103–25. https://doi.org/10.3917/pox.115.0103.

Lindsay-Poland, J. 2021. "Mexican Police Who Massacred Guatemalan Migrants Get Their Guns from the U.S." *NACLA*, April 1, 2021. https://nacla.org/news/2021/03/29/mexican-police-massacre-guns-tamaulipas.

Meyer, Ma. 2020. "One Year after National Guard's Creation, Mexico Is Far from Demilitarizing Public Security." WOLA, May 26, 2020. https://www.wola.org/analysis/one-year-national-guard-mexico/.

Meyer, P. 2019. "U.S. Strategy for Engagement in Central America: Policy Issues for Congress." Congressional Research Service, R44812, November 12, 2019. https://fas.org/sgp/crs/row/R44812.pdf.

Meyer, P., and R. L. Martin. 2021. "U.S. Foreign Assistance to Latin America and the Caribbean: FY2021Appropriations." Congressional Research Service, R46514, January 7, 2021. https://fas.org/sgp/crs/row/R46514.pdf.

Muggah, R., I. Szabó de Carvalho, N. Alvarado, L. Marmolejo, and R. Wang. 2016. "Making Cities Safer: Citizen Security Innovations from Latin America." Igarape Institute, Strategic Paper 20, June 2016. https://igarape.org.br/wp-content/uploads/2016/07/AE-20_Making-Cities-Safer-Citizen-Security-Innovations-from-Latin-America_WEB-1.pdf.

Núñez, D., ed. 2018. *Rostros de la violencia en Centroamérica: abordajes y experiencias desde la investigación social*. GuatemalaCity: FLACSO-Mercy Corps.

Obert, J. 2020. "Vigilantism, Again in the News, Is an American Tradition." *The Conversation*, July 9, 2020. https://theconversation.com/vigilantism-again-in-the-news-is-an-american-tradition-141849.

Odeh, R. 2013. "Emerging from the Haze of America's War on Drugs and Examining Canada's Half-Baked Laws." *Fordham International Law Journal* 36, no. 1 (January): 198–242.

Olson, E. "The Evolving Merida Initiative and the Policy of Shared Responsibility in U.S. Mexico Security Relations."Wilson Center, Mexico Institute, February 2017. https://www.wilsoncenter.org/publication/the-evolving-merida-initiative-and-the-policy-shared-responsibility-us-mexico-security.

Pérez Correa, C., and E. Azaola. 2012. *Resultados de la primera encuesta realizada a población interna en centros federales de readaptación social*. Mexico City: Centro de Investigación y Docencia Económica, 2012.

Pérez Ricart, C. "Taking the War on Drugs Down South: The Drug Enforcement Administration in Mexico (1973–1980)." *The Social History of Alcohol and Drugs* 34 (1): 1–32.

Phillips, T. 2022. "'It's a War on the People': El Salvador's Mass Arrests Send Thousands into Despair." *The Guardian*, June 8, 2022. https://www.theguardian.com/society/2022/jun/08/its-a-war-on-the-people-el-salvadora-mass-arrests-send-thousands-into-despair.

Piccato, P. 2013. "Estadísticas del crimen en México: Series históricas, 1901–2001." Columbia University, December 8, 2013. Accessed December 1, 2020. http://www.columbia.edu/~pp143/estadisticascrimen/EstadísticasSigloXX.htm.

Provine, D. M. 2011. "Race and Inequality in the War on Drugs." *Annual Review of Law and Social Science* 7: 41–60.

Reuters. 2020. "Mexican Murders Hit New High in First Half of 2020." July 20, 2020.

https://www.reuters.com/article/us-mexico-violence/mexican-murders-hit-new-high-in-first-half-of-2020-idUSKCN24L1XL.

Ribando Seelke, C., and K. Finklea. *U.S.-Mexican Security Cooperation: The Merida Initiative and Beyond*. Scotts Valley, CA: CreateSpace Independent Publishing Platform.

Robertson, C. 2019. "Crime Is Down, yet U.S. Incarceration Rates Are Still among the Highest in the World." *New York Times*, April 25, 2019. https://www.nytimes.com/2019/04/25/us/us-mass-incarceration-rate.html.

Santamaría, G. 2016. "Breaking the Vicious Cycle: Criminal Violence in U.S.–Latin American Relations." In *Contemporary U.S. Latin American Relations: Cooperation or Conflict in the 21st Century?*, edited by Jorge Dominguez and Rafael Fernández de Castro, 255–76. New York: Routledge.

Serrano, M. 2019. "La estrategia de seguridad de AMLO. ¿De la pacificación a la militarización?" *Revista IUS* 13 (44): 207–27. https://doi.org/10.35487/rius.v13i44.2019.615.

Sheridan, M., and A-C. Brigida. 2021. "Central American Leaders Resisting Biden's Anti-corruption Efforts." *Washington Post*, May 10, 2021. https://www.washingtonpost.com/world/2021/05/10/biden-salvador-guatemala-bukele-corruption-migration/.

Teague, A. 2019a. "Mexico's Dirty War on Drugs: Source Control and Dissidence in Drug Enforcement." *The Social History of Alcohol and Drugs* 33 (1): 63–87.

Teague, A. 2019b. "The United States, Mexico, and the Mutual Securitization of Drug Enforcement, 1969–1985." *Diplomatic History* 43 (5): 785–812.

Toro, C. 1999. "The Internationalization of Police: The DEA in Mexico." *The Journal of American History* 86 (2): 623–40.

Trejo, G., and S. Ley. 2020. Votes, Drugs, and Violence: The Political Logic of Criminal Wars in Mexico. New York: Cambridge University Press.

Tucker, D. 2020. "Mexico's New National Guard Is Breaking Its Vow to Respect Human Rights." Amnesty International, November 8, 2020. https://www.amnesty.org/en/latest/news/2020/11/mexicos-national-guard-breaking-vow-respect-human-rights/.

United Nations Office on Drugs and Crime (UNODC). n.d. "Victims of Intentional Homicide, 1990–2018." Country Data, United Nations Office on Drugs and Crime. Accessed April 5, 2021. https://dataunodc.un.org/content/data/homicide/homicide-rate.

United States Customs and Borders Protection (US-CBP). n.d. "CBP Enforcement Statistics Fiscal Year 2021." Accessed November 13, 2021. https://www.cbp.gov/newsroom/stats/cbp-enforcement-statistics.

United States Embassy. 2021. "Merida Initiative Overview." September 7, 2021. https://mx.usembassy.gov/the-merida-initiative/.

White House. 2021. "Fact Sheet: U.S.-Mexico High-Level Security Dialogue." October 8, 2021. https://www.whitehouse.gov/briefing-room/statements-releases/2021/10/08/fact-sheet-u-s-mexico-high-level-security-dialogue/.

White House. 2022. "Fact Sheet: The Los Angeles Declaration on Migration and Protection U.S. Government and Foreign Partner Deliverables." June 10, 2022. https://www.whitehouse.gov/briefing-room/statements-releases/2022/06/10/fact-sheet-the-los-angeles-declaration-on-migration-and-protection-u-s-government-and-foreign-partner-deliverables/.

Wolf, S. 2017. *Mano Dura: The Politics of Gang Control in El Salvador*. Austin: University of Texas Press.

World Prison Brief. n.d. "World Prison Brief Data for North America and Central America." Accessed February 14, 2021. https://www.prisonstudies.org/map/northern-america.

CHAPTER SEVEN

Energy Regionalism in North America

Subnational Leadership in the Transition to Low-Carbon Economies

Daniela Stevens

Introduction

DIFFERING OBJECTIVES, institutional frameworks, resources, interests, as well as the assertion of national sovereignty, have hindered a deeper regional integration of the North American energy policies. Despite those obstacles, several states and provinces in the region have found other avenues to implement transnational initiatives to pursue clean energy transitions. These approaches are more localized and less ambitious yet benefit subnational economies and international supply chains without directly challenging national sovereignty or running afoul of asymmetrical power relations.

Energy transition refers to the switch from technologies and fuel inputs that emit high volumes of greenhouse gases (GHGs) to technologies and energy sources with limited or zero emissions (Arent et al. 2019). Cooperation in this area may occur in some areas while being blocked in others; in North America, subnational stakeholders have hindered transition policies in the upstream power supply chain, even though those same actors have favored changes that do not threaten their power. The purpose of this chapter is to provide a framework of enabling conditions that make such region-formation possible.

The chapter contributes to the burgeoning literature of "energy regionalism" (Hancock, Palestini, and Szuleck 2020; Johnson and VanDeVeer forthcoming) that identifies energy regions as constructions in which actors, including individuals, groups, institutions, or other elites with power and interest, "seek to frame an energy topic through regionalization" (Johnson and VanDeveer forthcoming, 3). It analyzes a specific type of energy regionalism in which subnational jurisdictions internationally negotiate energy-related regulations that ultimately will be applied and monitored at a subnational level. Further, it opens a dialogue about how processes of region-formation are shaped by actors and coalitions with the power and interest to facilitate or block energy policy in North America.

Since efforts toward decarbonization at the regional level remain understudied outside the European Union, the empirical contribution of this text is a focus on different regulatory aspects of the energy transition in Western North America. Emerging policy frameworks and patterns of interactions among state and non-state actors suggest the emergence of an energy region including British Columbia, Washington, Oregon, California, and, to a lesser extent, Baja California. Overall, North America tends to receive little emphasis under "yardstick" definitions of regions as sets of interdependent states, but this analysis emphasizes that different contexts lead to different types of regions.

The rest of the chapter proceeds as follows. The second section discusses the theory, motivation, and main argument about the conditions that enable or obstruct the emergence of an energy region. The third presents the methodology and case selection of two projects, one in which jurisdictions attempted to deepen the integration of electricity markets to support renewable sources but failed, and another that succeeded in the coordinated construction of electric vehicle (EV) infrastructure. The fourth section discusses how the conditions relate to the cases, and the fifth closes with concluding remarks.

The Politics of Policies of Energy Regionalism

Traditional approaches to region-building emphasize specific forms of interstate governance arrangements and institution-building. However, conceptions of regions as blocs of states miss the richness of regional forms at different scales and with broader scopes (Acharya 2018; Balsiger and VanDeveer 2010; Balsiger and Prys 2016; Johnson and VanDeveer forthcoming). As scholarship in the "new regionalism" approach points out, "definitions of a 'region' vary according to the particular problem or question under investigation" (Hettne 2005, 544, cited in Macdonald, this volume). Often, this has meant including more or fewer countries in a region; however, a more granular and issue-focused approach illustrates how regions may take forms that do not fully align with national borders.

The state-centric focus has limited empirical research in at least three ways that are noteworthy for this chapter's purpose. First, given the absence of supranational or trilateral energy institutions between Canada, Mexico, and the United States, the study of North America as an energy region has been neglected. The region is largely rendered as a free commerce zone, as a set of bilateral relations dominated by the United States, or as home to processes of regionalization but little region-building (Capling and Nossal 2008). An analysis of North American energy regions is necessary given the theory-building efforts and empirical analyses developing in areas such as Eurasia (Balmaceda and Heinrick 2021; Hancock and Libman 2016), sub-Saharan Africa (Delina 2021), and South America (Sabbatella and Santos 2020).

Second, although energy governance is explained by subnational factors, few schol-ars have considered forms of meaningful regional cooperation between subnational jurisdictions of different countries (Hancock et al. 2020, 6),[1] even though in practice subnational public-private coalitions have addressed energy-related issues that cut across boundaries. To properly consider energy regionalism in North America, we must move beyond both national state-centrism and methodological nationalism, and, as the introductory chapter of this volume highlights, consider issues that slip beyond the reach of national responses (Hershberg and Long, this volume). The analytical value of changing our geographical lens in this way deserves greater consideration in International Relations (IR)'s studies of regions beyond North America as well.

This chapter opens a conversation between the study of regionalism and the lit-erature on the political economy of energy transitions. To that end, it highlights the phenomenon of simultaneously localizing and regionalizing authority driven by issue- and context-specific coalitions, providing an opportunity to rethink the paradigm of what a region looks like and what is expected from it. More specifically, it explores governance spaces where a multiplicity of subnational actors internationally negotiate regulations that will be applied and monitored domestically by a state or provincial government.

Like much work in new regionalism, outlined in Laura Macdonald's chapter in this volume, this chapter emphasizes a range of actors beyond national governments and processes beyond formal institutionalization as crucial to region-formation. Patterns of cooperation and coalition-building in North American energy regionalism have often emerged from a diverse group with broad and sometimes contradictory motiva-tions, rather than from top-down regional mandates. Moreover, as Eric Hershberg and Tom Long point out in the introduction, attempts to find solutions to shared problems have resulted in cooperation breakdowns as well.

While my approach assumes that the dominant driver of region-formation is the need to address negative externalities, provide public goods, or respond to specific needs, it differs from neo-functionalist approaches by acknowledging that institutions, interests, and needs change in time, and that region-formation may also be the unin-tentional result or the by-product of geographic, economic, or geopolitical dynamics, as well as a product of power relations and historical contingency. Still, the purpose here is to provide a framework of enabling conditions that make region-formation possible, rather than explaining what causes the phenomenon. Also, it is notewor-thy that unlike the various constructivist approaches in this volume (McKercher in chapter 3; Toro in chapter 4), the processes of region-formation that follow did not necessitate deep social ties or a shared meaning or identity. The next section outlines such conditions.

Conditions for the Emergence of Energy Regionalism in Western North America

Unlike what traditional models purport, the process of constructing a regional space need not result in a consolidated architecture with institutionalized governance and clearly established borders; instead, the emergence and survival of regions depend on the coalitions that push for or oppose their creation and persistence. Hence, the conditions that facilitate the emergence of an energy region are subject to area and context specificities.

In general, the multiplicity of actors and interests across local and federal scales, varying levels of federalism, and the different involvement of private and public capital have blocked the creation of regional institutions that would regulate the energy transition in North America. Recent work suggests that efforts to advance transition are determined by national and subnational political economies of energy (Bergquist, Mildenberger, and Stokes 2019), the behavior of incumbents and nascent interest groups (Stokes and Breetz 2018, 76), and the coevolution of technology and distributive politics across the experience curve (Breetz et al. 2019).

Building upon two strands of literature, one that focuses on the region and another that emphasizes the politics of policies, this chapter proposes the following conditions to facilitate the construction of an energy region:

- The protection of state and provincial decision-making autonomy throughout international negotiations.
- A clear and even distribution of costs and opportunities across stakeholders and supporting coalitions.
- A favorable coevolution of markets and specific technologies to advance the transition.

Enabling conditions are ontologically different from causes. More than direct triggers, they are factors that set the stage to make an effect possible. A condition-focused approach is appropriate because energy transitions have dynamic and adaptive properties and bidirectional relations that causal models would not adequately capture. Additionally, condition-oriented analytical frameworks are useful in exploratory efforts toward inductive theory-building and help identify areas of emphasis to promote efficient energy-climate policies (Duguma et al. 2014). The conditions will be explored further alongside the cases in section 4.

Two Projects, One Region

The analysis compares projects pertaining to different aspects of the same arena: the construction of infrastructure that promotes the transition to a low-carbon economy. One initiative illustrates the conditions that hinder the creation of subnational energy regionalism, the Western Renewable Energy Zone (WREZ); the other, the West Coast Electric Highway (WCEH) shows the circumstances that facilitate it. The sources include analysis of official documents, local and national newspapers, and semi-structured interviews with participants of the process.

Understanding these initiatives is valuable for their historical significance and because they set a potential precedent to deeper collaboration, but also because they offer lessons about the dynamics of energy transitions beyond state-centric perspectives. Both projects under scrutiny occurred in the same area, the Western states and provinces in Canada, Mexico, and the United States during the 2010s. The sections below present the subregion's specificities and the projects.

Western North America in Context

The Western electric and transportation systems have historical characteristics that make them unique in the North American space in some respects, yet a representative micro-universe of national and regional dynamics in others. The subregion is deeply energy and trade interdependent. California alone imports 15 percent of total Canadian power exports, and almost 80 percent of those from British Columbia (CER 2021). Baja California obtains over 80 percent of its energy from California and exports a third of its energy production back to the state (Institute of the Americas 2020).

Energy security in the West faces two main vulnerabilities: rising energy demands due to population growth, and production under risk given the effects of climate change. These challenges could be at least partially addressed at a regional scale by integrating more renewable resources into the grid, which usually creates challenges because the variability and intermittency of renewables can result in system imbalances.[2] However, fractured governance has made integration especially problematic in the West, where a deep interdependence has not translated into regional institutions.

The Western Interconnection (WI) is one of the three main electric grids that operate in North America, alongside the Texas and Eastern Interconnections (see figure 7.1 on the left). The WI is the only trinational grid, and includes Arizona, California, Colorado, Idaho, Nevada, Oregon, Utah, Washington, and the Canadian provinces of British Columbia and Alberta, as well as parts of Montana, Nebraska, New Mexico, South Dakota, Texas, Wyoming, and the Mexican state of Baja California. All the electric utilities in the WI are tied together and operate synchronically.

In the 1990s, about half of the United States and two Canadian provinces began operating under deregulated systems (in figure 7.1 on the right). The process required

North American Electric Reliability Corporation Interconnections

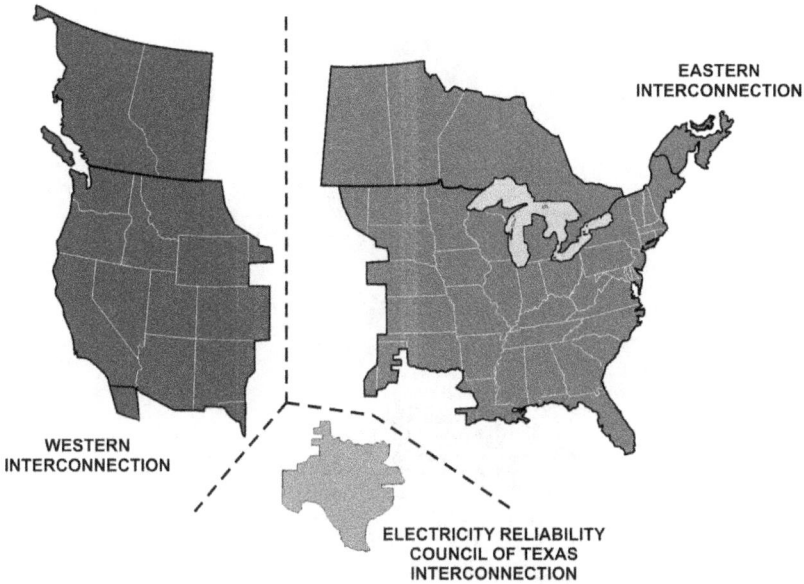

Figure 7.1. North American Electric Reliability Corporation Interconnections.

the formation of and participation in regional energy markets administered by regional or independent system operators (ISOs). ISOs are independent, federally regulated organizations that oversee wholesale power markets, ensure reliably and nondiscriminatory access to the grid, and plan for regional energy needs, including the incorporation of renewables. Only three jurisdictions in the WI operate under an ISO, California (with the California ISO, CAISO), Alberta (with the Alberta Energy System Operator, AESO), and Baja California (with the National Center for Energy Control, CENACE).[3]

With the exceptions of California and Alberta, state and investor-owned utilities, rural cooperatives, and municipal power entities in the West remained regulated and vertically integrated (in gray in figure 7.1 on the right), that is, they retained ownership and operation of the entire supply chain generation, transmission, and distribution of power. Most utilities in the West operate as monopolies and set electricity prices with oversight of the state or provincial public utilities commissions (PUCs).[4] Each utility manages its own territory and serves as the balancing area authority (BAA) in charge of building infrastructure and planning for demand.[5]

States with deregulated markets administered by ISOs have been better able to integrate renewable energy given their coordinated planning. In contrast, the WI lacks the regional governance for the transmission grid provided by an ISO, as well as the

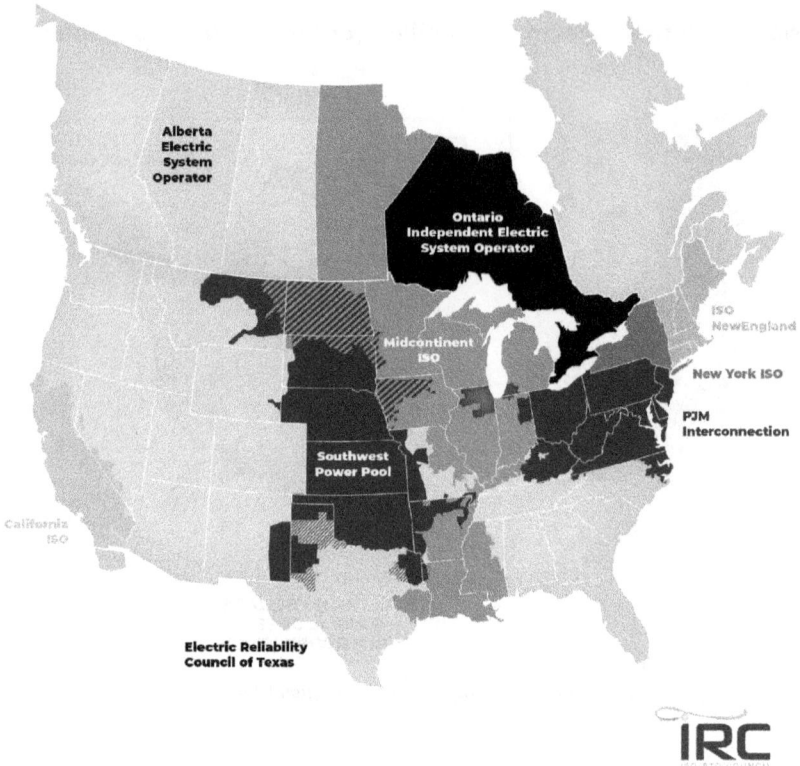

Figure 7.2. IRC Regional Markets.

mechanisms across BAAs to coordinate or optimize responses to supply and demand imbalances in real time with the operational flexibility that wind and solar resources demand. Multiple analyses reiterate that integrating under a single ISO would increase renewable energy deployment, reduce costs, greenhouse gas (GHG) emissions, and local air pollutants (Mills, Phadke, and Wiser 2011; Westfall 2019; Brint et al. 2017), yet several attempts have failed, as the main stakeholders—PUCs and utilities—have remained markedly skeptical (Cifor et al. 2015).

On the other hand, the governance landscape is less complex and contentious in the transportation sector. The highway infrastructure has adapted to cover larger areas after the North America Free Trade Agreement (NAFTA) changed the regional trade environment. The restructuration entailed not only increased transborder freight traffic, but also prioritized North-South regional corridors over East-West intranational routes. Two of the main longitudinal corridors in the region expand in the West Coast, from Vancouver to Seattle and from Los Angeles-San Diego to Tijuana (Bradbury 2002). The subregion experiences heavy back and forth travel for the purpose of trade, commerce, labor, and tourism. After the enactment of NAFTA, patterns of production, consumption, and distribution intensified, and the region's supply chains became deeply integrated (Bradbury 2002). In 2016, the transportation sector surpassed electricity generation as the largest source of CO_2 emissions in the United States for the first time since the 1970s (EIA 2017). In California, the sector accounts for nearly 80 percent of the state's air pollution and more than 40 percent of GHG emissions. Transportation is also the largest pollutant and emitter in Washington, Oregon, British Columbia, and Baja California. Projections indicate that in Baja California emissions will grow almost 300 percent compared to 1990 levels by 2025, with transportation as the main source of increase (Chacón et al. 2010). In Alberta, transportation emits 11 percent of GHGs, only second to oil and gas production (CER 2020).

Globally, the transportation sector has become a target of many initiatives to reduce emissions, as transitioning the vehicle fleet will be essential for achieving net-zero greenhouse gas emissions by 2050 and stabilize global temperatures at 1.5 degrees Celsius above preindustrial levels (Intergovernmental Panel on Climate Change 2018). Evidence suggests that charging infrastructure has a positive effect on EV sales (Narassimhan and Johnson 2018; Sierzchula et al. 2014); hence, complemented with vehicle and fuel standards and strategies to promote the adoption of EVs, infrastructure can make a significant contribution to emission reduction goals.

WREZ

In 2008, the Western Governors' Association (WGA) launched the Western Renewable Energy Zone (WREZ) initiative with funding support from the US Department of Energy (DOE).[6] The initiative aimed to find criteria to select the best and least costly renewable resources and determine what additional transmission was necessary to deliver electricity to the major load centers across the West. State governors sought to move ahead of the federal government in terms of the development of renewable electricity (Larson 2010), encouraged by findings in previous studies that concluded that the region had abundant, high-quality resources to develop.[7] Representatives from Canada and Mexico's subnational jurisdictions joined the efforts soon thereafter and conformed the WREZ Steering Committee, which comprised governors, public utility commissioners, and premiers.

The result of Phase 1 of the initiative was the report *Qualified Resource Area (QRA) Identification Process*. It defined QRAs as "areas of high quality and dense renewable energy resources with enough capacity to potentially justify the construction of a high voltage transmission line for interstate transmission of renewable energy" (Pletka and Finn 2009). The report identified fifty-four QRAs and determined the optimal routing for and cost of delivering renewable energy to load centers.

Phase 2 involved the elaboration of transmission expansion plans and provided user-friendly models to enable stakeholders to evaluate the price of developing and operating the infrastructure. Phases 3 and 4 were envisioned as stages where the information collected from previous phases would aid in planning and executing transmission goals. The WREZ fulfilled the purpose of coordinating parties in the identification of priority development areas but failed to engage policy makers and stakeholders in building support for the creation of large-scale regional transmission.

WCEH

In 2007, with the aim of fighting traffic congestion and improving the efficiency of freight delivery, the US Department of Transportation (DOT) selected six interstate routes as "Corridors of the Future." Among the thirty-eight applications, the DOT selected the high-traffic north-south Interstate-5 (I-5) corridor between Washington, Oregon, and California, which received $15 million USD (FHWA 2007). The application, prepared by the Departments of Transportation of California (Caltrans), Washington state (WASDOT), and Oregon (ODOT), included a proposal for an Alternative Fuels Corridor to develop the distribution network of non–fossil fuels through the I-5 in partnership with existing businesses.

In a 2008 Memorandum of Understanding, the states designated a project team to build interstate consensus, obtain industry inputs, pursue the necessary state and federal law changes, and establish the states' duties and obligations, including the coordination of strategies with an equally distributed funding. The project became regional later that year, when British Columbia (and Alaska) joined the three states signing the Pacific Coast Collaborative (PCC), an alliance to pursue climate and clean energy policy while growing the regional economies. In the 2010 action plan, members agreed to construct a Pacific "Green Highway" that came to be known as the West Coast Electric Highway (WCEH). The project succeeded in building light-vehicle charging stations from British Columbia to the Baja California border.

Ten years later, nine utilities and two agencies representing municipal utilities in Oregon, Washington, and California proposed the incorporation of charging stations for freight transportation and delivery trucks. This initiative is more challenging in terms of economic resources, real estate, and technology than the WCEH, but utilities declared willingness to partially cover the estimated price of $850 million USD.[8] As of this writing, the project remains US-based.

The following section discusses the conditions—the maintenance of state or provincial authority, the distribution of costs and opportunities, and the coevolution of policy, markets, and technology. It exemplifies with the two initiatives.

Enabling Conditions toward Energy Regionalism

Western public utility commissions (PUCs) have shown resistance to pooling or sur-rendering authority (Cifor et al. 2015, 39). Historically, the West has lacked coordinated power pools, which emerged in the East during the 1960s, as a starting point for market development. Western jurisdictions not only see themselves as "free from East Coast politics and control" (Cifor et al. 2015, 40), but also as autonomous from California, which would have the largest influence over regional markets in the Western Interconnection if coordinated institution-building efforts were to take shape. PUCs have concerns about their ability to implement energy policies and procurement mandates without interfer-ence, especially given state energy and climate policy goals that may pale in comparison to California's somewhat aggressive drive to decarbonize the power sector.

Transmission owners are averse to transferring operational control of their facilities to a central operator and are reluctant regarding the prospect of California dominating regional projects. CAISO's efforts to establish a Western ISO since 2014 have been received with caution, as its governance structure is not independent: California's governor appoints its board, and the Senate confirms it, which exacerbates the worries of dominance.[9]

Avoiding the pooling of authority was essential for the emergence and development of the WCEH. Each state and province retained the ability to decide requirements for charging infrastructure, the budget that it allocated for it, and if and how it promoted public-private alliances and sought funding. Even though California's role in the EV market and infrastructure is as outsized as in the power market, this leadership enhances infrastructure across the entire West Coast and does not threaten the inde-pendence of other jurisdictions or the market share of out of state utilities.

Given its market size and historical experience developing rules for reducing vehicular emissions since the 1960s, California's role in transport electrification is disproportional.[10] In 2009, under the Obama administration, it reached an agreement with the federal Environmental Protection Agency (EPA), the DOT, and automakers that led to the adoption of nationwide standards for fuel economy and GHGs. At the same time, it obtained the authority to set its own (more stringent) emission and polluting standards because its vehicle regulations preceded the federal Clean Air Act (CAA) of 1970. However, this leadership does not threaten or diminish other states' authority, but rather expands it. Section 177 of the CAA authorizes other states to choose to adopt California's standards instead of federal requirements without pre-vious approval of the EPA. Oregon and Washington are among the twelve "Section 177" states.

In British Columbia and Baja California, the urge to protect autonomy has also prevented cooperation, albeit on behalf of different actors. Baja California has considerably less autonomy than US states and Canadian provinces; transmission development and management is federally mandated, a centralization that the Andrés Manuel López Obrador administration (2018–present) seeks to enhance. British

Columbia plans to electrify the province partially aided by imports from California, which interest groups warn is a risk given California's power shortages caused by heat, wildfires, and independent risk management.

A Clear and Even Distribution of Costs and Creation of Opportunities

Though there is evidence of the efficiency of both the transportation and electrification initiatives, the construction of transmission lines would have required larger investments than enhancing the already existing transport infrastructure, and there was no guarantee that such costs would be distributed equally. The WREZ report identified and delimited QRAs utilizing analytical, not legal borders, which created questions of who would benefit from which QRA, at what cost, and under what sort of governance arrangement. Utilities were consistently reluctant to pay the costs of constructing transmission infrastructure, and wary of relinquishing or restructuring their transmission rights (Mills 2020).

Therefore, during Phase 2 of the WREZ, utility resource planners were reluctant to invest in selecting renewable resources from remote QRAs, and chose to tap into resources within their state or nearby. Utilities were not interested in either building new long-distance transmission lines, or in collaborating with other utilities on the transmission to deliver the power to load centers (Schwartz 2012). After funding from DOE ended, there was little collective interest to pursue the project (Andrew Mills, research scientist in the Electricity Markets and Policy Group at Lawrence Berkeley National Laboratory, e-mail message to the author, November 2020), which never contemplated a binding mechanism to force parties to pay for the needed infrastructure.

Two federal BAAs, the Bonneville Power Administration (BPA) and the Western Area Power Administration (WAPA), have a significant influence in the WI. BPA operates and maintains about three-fourths of transmission in the Pacific Northwest,[11] while WAPA owns and maintains more than 10 percent of the interconnection's transmission lines.[12] In interviews, several utility representatives cite BPA and WAPA as key to developing large multistate projects (Schwartz 2012, 77) and highlight the need for a more decisive involvement of these organizations in initiatives like the WREZ (Schwartz 2012, 87). BPA and WAPA are exempted from regulation by the Federal Energy Regulatory Commission (FERC) and seek to preserve that independence.

Nonetheless, the reports carried out as part of the WREZ set the precedent to develop a CAISO-led voluntary market across the WI, the Energy Imbalance Market (EIM). The EIM is not a transparent energy market, but it has facilitated the construction of trust among states and utilities, allowed the latter to procure real-time energy from the lowest-cost generator, and created system-wide efficiencies and lower balancing costs (Cifor et al. 2015, 38). BPA signed an agreement in 2019 whereby it committed to join the EIM in 2022, after which it will be able to access the bulk power trading market to balance real-time demand. Evidently, BPA still favors the EIM as an incremental and voluntary approach over binding commitments.

In contrast, states and provinces retained a clear division regarding the responsibilities that they acquired for the development of the WCEH, and had little to lose. Jurisdictions and utilities benefited directly from the infrastructure built within their territories, yet this cooperation also contributed to a larger goal that could not be achieved in isolation: the electrification of a regional transnational corridor. Several project locations that were key to state and provincial economies intersect the Interstate-5 in areas whose economies are significantly trade dependent and sensitive to the reliability of the transportation network and international freight movement. Members committed to redeveloping the I-5 corridor to establish fast-charging infrastructure for EVs and connect the main high-tech hubs of Vancouver, Seattle, Portland, San Francisco, and Los Angeles. The WCEH allowed the flourishing of local manufacture, businesses, and utilities, and the improved travel and commerce benefited supply chains.

In the United States, most government spending on transportation takes place at the state level, although expenditures are often paid for in part with federal funds or grants (DOT 2018). Similarly, under Canada's Constitution Act, the building and maintenance of national highways falls under provincial and territorial jurisdiction, but the federal government provides funding for key strategic road infrastructure, especially international projects (TC 2021). In Mexico, infrastructure funding is centralized, and electrification efforts have revolved around the expansion of electrified public transportation (Carrillo et al. 2020).

More than a single initiative, the WCEH moved forward as a collection of projects, funding sources, and partners that found shared opportunities and costs commensurate with each jurisdiction's individual goals. The governments formed alliances with local businesses to attract funding for the installation of charging stations to incentivize EV deployment and use, and in turn improve air quality, combat climate change, and create jobs.

For instance, the initiative has received funding in each state through "The EV Project" of the DOE in alliance with Nissan North America and General Motors/Chevrolet.[13] In Washington, the WASDOT manages the program Zero Emission Vehicle Infrastructure Partnerships (ZEVIP), which supports and expands the WCEH network. A variety of sources support the ZEVIP, such as private capitals (convention centers, resorts), municipalities (City of Leavenworth), and organizations like the Seattle Electric Vehicle Association, which also lobbies the House and Senate to promote EV legislation.

Through the WCEH, states and provinces adjusted to and buttressed opportunities for the automotive sector, in steep competition with European and Chinese manufacturers. The revolution of combustion engines has represented a safer bet to meet decarbonization goals for utilities, since they foresee opportunities in the business of electrifying transportation. Also, the benefits of implementing regionally agreed solutions of this aspect of the energy transition have neither disturbed their regional dominance, nor disrupted their governance structure.

While the geography and vast territory of the North American West accentuated the uneven cost-benefit allocation of the WREZ, it evidenced the need of making transport more efficient. Conversely, stakeholders in the power sector learned that the transition of the electricity systems benefited more from localization, and that integration was not optimal from a market perspective.

A Favorable Coevolution of Markets and Technology

While exploring the opportunities for integration under the WREZ, jurisdictions were unable to identify the sellers and buyers of renewable energy on a scale that supported investments in multistate transmission lines. Moreover, the need for transmission expansion depended on assumptions about costs of solar and wind energy compared (Mills 2020; Thomas Carr, program manager for Electric System Planning and Grid Transformation at Western Interstate Energy Board, e-mail message to the author, November 2020). The justification to build transmission lines to remote wind centers was supported if higher prices of solar energy created the need for infrastructure. However, given the lower prices of solar compared to wind, demand could be met by solar generation closer to major load centers. Furthermore, the development and decreased price of low-wind speed turbines diminished the advantage of obtaining energy from QRAs, and allowed generation with moderate wind quality regions closer to load centers. Increased deployment of solar and storage technologies further helped the development of local solutions with less need for new transmission. Combined, these factors reduced substantially the need for transmission capacity (Mills 2020).

On the other hand, the technology for electric vehicles has matured swiftly, and forecasts about their adoption are optimistic. The key for a faster-paced electrification of transport responds to a successful marriage between capitalist expansion and technology for emission reductions. In the last decades, the three North American partners rose among the largest commercial vehicle producers, in order, the United States, China, Mexico, Japan, and Canada (Organisation Internationale des Constructeurs d'Automobiles 2019). Moreover, the three nations have integrated supply chains and prominent positions in global vehicle trade, lagging behind only Germany and Japan (International Trade Centre 2019).

Public-private partnerships that respond to corporate and provincial interests may explain this active role in the transition to a more sustainable transportation. For instance, British Columbia has been active in the deployment of light-duty EVs since 2007, when it partnered with Mitsubishi, Nissan, Toyota, and GM to be the first province to deploy their EVs. In 2018, it announced that only electric vehicles would be sold in the province by 2040. The province houses the largest cluster of hydrogen and fuel cell companies in Canada and leads the commercial activity of hydrogen fuel cell technology for heavy-duty vehicles, like transit buses, since the early 1990s (Sharpe et al. 2020).

In other words, technology use and its profitability structure stakeholders' preferences and determine the support that they will give to provincial or state initiatives. Figure 7.3 summarizes the circumstances under which the formation of regions has succeeded and failed.

Condition	WREZ	WCEH
Provincial/state autonomy	Threatened	Preserved
Distribution of costs and opportunities	Unclear benefits and opportunities, uneven costs	Opportunities for all participants, costs distributed proportionately
Coevolution markets-technology	Unfavorable to the regional project	Maturing, competitive technology

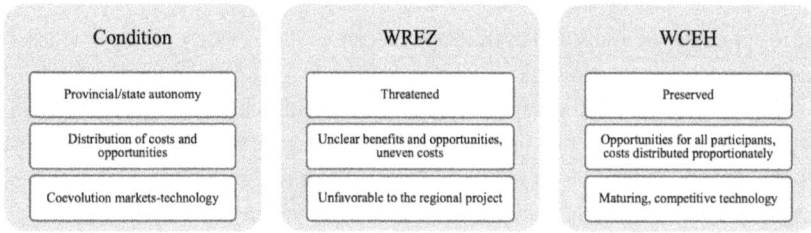

Figure 7.3. Summary of the Circumstances under Which the Formation of Regions Has Succeeded and Failed.

Conclusions

Given that much energy governance remains under the purview of domestic national authorities, scholarship has overlooked the successful and failed subnational attempts to implement joint energy-related initiatives across national borders. This chapter proposed an understanding of the region that can be built from the bottom up, without a national state-led coordinating mechanism, without long-term agendas for integration, and without the creation of supranational entities. Appreciating these patterns of regional cooperation and governance requires attention to a multiplicity of actors, as well as to more disparate processes of region-building. A more fluid conceptualization also avoids the pitfall of constraining the region into fixed territorial and temporal spaces and favors a focus on the relational and strategic aspects of region-building (Murphy et al. 2015; Johnson and VanDeveer forthcoming).

Despite North American resistance to formal intergovernmental or supranational cooperation, the highly autonomous subnational jurisdictions in the region have found ways to create regional governance to address common transnational issues. Still, the need for joint action does not entail immediate or coordinated localized responses. The cases outlined here provided an opportunity to rethink the traditional model of regions and the expectations around them, exemplifying with instances in which governments with deep interdependencies attempted, with varying degrees of success, to create regional regulations.

Though this chapter's study is exploratory, it helps identify the conditions that enable the development of a theory of subnational energy regionalism in North America. It explores factors associated with explanations for the energy transition, or lack thereof, and identifies the actors that play key roles in region-building processes: subnational governments, utilities, public utilities commissions, and automakers.

Analyzing a project that failed, the Western Renewable Energy Zone, shed light on why regionalism is not always the best or most feasible answer. Although more active engagement is expected of states, utilities, and experts in the field of transmission and distribution infrastructure, especially during Joe Biden's administration

(2020–present), the transition in the power sector was more easily pursued via localization than regionalization.

Still, jurisdictions found ways to cooperate outside the electricity sector by coordinating regional infrastructure projects for charging electric vehicles. The West Coast Electric Highway promoted lowering the dependence on fossil fuel-based energy in a way that did not risk subnational governments' autonomy to a dominant partner, threaten utilities' regional dominance, or impose steep and uneven initial costs. Transportation infrastructure is rising as a major area of cooperation, spurred by US federal infrastructure plans and as a strategy to meet the ambitious international commitment of halving emissions from 2005 levels by 2030, stated in the 2021 Climate Summit.

A paradox that arises from the empirical analysis is that utilities avoided investing in transmission infrastructure even as they financed infrastructure for electrifying a trade corridor. The paradox emerges because that same sustainable transportation system requires modernization of infrastructure in the upstream electric sector to succeed.

The realignment of the power and automotive industries toward cleaner productive processes is underway, but systemic decarbonization requires unprecedented infrastructure investment. Two federal commitments from the regional hegemon, the United States, could encourage the participation of utilities and other traditionally skeptical sectors: front-loading investment to lower initial costs, and inviting the business community to collaborate on legislation to promote the transition.

President Biden's Build Back Better bill was blocked in 2021 by the chair of the Energy Committee, a Democratic senator from the coal- and gas-rich state of West Virginia. Although the approval of a narrower package is possible, it would include measures that do not directly limit the fossil fuel industry, such as tax credits for nuclear power, and carbon capture. Stricter measures, like fining for methane leaks, banning offshore drilling, or penalizing electric utilities for not deploying clean energy, seem off limits. In addition, the Russian invasion of Ukraine spurred fossil fuel enthusiasts' leverage to boost domestic oil and gas production. A Republican-controlled Congress would be even more likely to pursue these measures (Siegel and Colman 2022). Given the impasse in Congress, the Biden administration adopted executive actions, such as boosting the manufacture of green technologies and securing more minerals for EV battery production, to achieve the president's climate pledges.

The US and the Canadian government investments in nationwide charging infrastructure, however, will continue to be instrumental for the electrification of transport. Indeed, federal financial assistance was necessary for the WCEH's success, but not sufficient for pursuing regional electrification, which calls for a multilevel, multi-stakeholder approach. The chapter, however, shows that beyond partisan debates the role of concurrent competencies between federal and subnational governments is key in empirical analyses.

Under the inward-looking López Obrador administration (2018–present), Mexico has neither developed national measures nor led international transition strategies, which not only risks failure to meet international climate commitments and clean energy targets but also compromises the country's relations with its northern neighbors and beyond. Since 2020, the administration has taken a series of steps to suspend the construction of renewable power plants indefinitely with the purpose of rescuing the state-owned oil and electricity companies. In 2021, the president proposed a regulatory overhaul of the electricity system that would strip CENACE, the grid regulator, of its autonomy to dispatch the most efficiently generated power to the grid first in order to favor aging national-owned hydroelectric and thermoelectric plants over renewable energy. While the Supreme Court debated the legality of the reform, López Obrador decided to propose constitutional amendments to repeal the provision that allowed private investments in the sector. Nevertheless, the Chamber of Deputies rejected and filed the amendment in April 2022. The president threatened that those who voted against the amendment would be "exposed as traitors" (De la Rosa 2022).

With the cancellation of the renewable energy auctions, Mexico attended the COP25 and COP26 with meager results and no concrete proposals. The delegation reiterated the commitment to the Paris Agreement, but did not mention the electricity or oil sectors, or the deep cuts to research and technology and to the federal environmental agency in the national budget. In contrast, Canadian prime minister Justin Trudeau (2015–present) has increased mitigation ambitions pledging to reduce GHG emissions 40 percent to 45 percent from 2005 levels by 2030, despite being the only country where emissions increased after the Paris Agreement. At the COP26, Canada committed to achieve net-zero emissions by 2035 and to end exports of thermal coal by 2030 (Government of Canada 2022).

Further research should consider how changes in federal and state and provincial power affect long-haul processes such as infrastructure development, and how environmentally-friendly subnational governments can create green regional "lock-ins" that favor the transition. Research will likely continue to reflect on the potential of public-private partnerships to lead the transition, as well as on the fact that no single sector will successfully decarbonize the economy, but work must be done across different fronts.

Abbreviations

AESO: Alberta Energy System Operator
BAA: Balancing Area Authority
BPA: Bonneville Power Administration
CAISO: California Independent System Operator
Caltrans: California Department of Transportation
CENACE: National Center for Energy Control
CAA: Clean Air Act
DOE: US Department of Energy
DOT: US Department of Transportation
EIM: Energy Imbalance Market
EPA: US Environmental Protection Agency
EV: Electric Vehicle
FERC: Federal Energy Regulatory Commission
GHG: Greenhouse Gas
I-5: Interstate-5
ISO: Independent System Operator
NAFTA: North America Free Trade Agreement
ODOT: Oregon Department of Transportation
PCC: Pacific Coast Collaborative
PUC: Public Utilities Commission
QRA: Qualified Resource Area
WAPA: Western Area Power Administration
WASDOT: Washington Department of Transportation
WCEH: West Coast Electric Highway
WGA: Western Governors' Association
WI: Western Interconnection
WREZ: Western Renewable Energy Zone
ZEVIP: Zero Emission Vehicle Infrastructure Partnerships

Notes

1. Outstanding exceptions include the work by Stroup, Kujawa, and Ayres (2015), who explore energy and environmental regionalism between Vermont and Quebec, and Muñoz and López-Vallejo (2019), who study the transregional governance architecture between Baja California and California.
2. The more renewable energy goes into the system, the more oversupply there is when generation exceeds load, and the lower the prices during periods of overgeneration. Generators must reduce or curtail their production, which not only imposes costs

and efficiency losses, but also lost opportunities to use tax credits for renewable energy production. See Florescu and Pead 2018.

3. Baja California is in a unique position. While it is part of the WI and isolated from the Mexican National Interconnected System (NIS), it is regulated by the Mexican ISO, CENACE. The state has developed normative electricity frameworks to facilitate renewable market integration with California and has considered formally joining CAISO, but the discussions were stalled by the Mexican energy reforms around 2013 (Department of Energy 2016).

4. PUCs are independent government agencies that regulate rates and standards of service quality of electric, water, and transportation, among other companies that provide public services.

5. Without a regional ISO, the nonprofit Western Electricity Coordinating Council was created and received authority from the federal government to safeguard the reliability of the WI.

6. The WGA includes Alaska, Arizona, California, Colorado, Hawaii, Idaho, Kansas, Montana, Nebraska, Nevada, New Mexico, North Dakota, Oklahoma, Oregon, Texas, Utah, Washington, and Wyoming.

7. The Clean and Diversified Energy Advisory Committee sought to explore steps to add 30,000 MW of clean and diverse energy resources by 2015. See CER 2020.

8. Utilities expect to share costs with federal, state, and local governments and businesses, and with the consumers.

9. CAISO has released numerous drafts to change its governance to become a regionally representative board, and in 2017, Assembly Member Chris Holden introduced Bill 813 (AB 813) outlining the way toward an independent governance. The bill did not obtain the required support, partially because of the opposition of the International Brotherhood of Electrical Workers, the California Municipal Utilities Association, the Sierra Club, and the Consumer Watchdog. These organizations argued that an independent CAISO would lose its ability to act the best interests of California and the environment. Still, the creation of an ISO would need, beyond the California legislature's approval, the acquiescence of the rest of balancing authorities in the WI.

10. The EV market accounted for nearly half of sales from 2010 to 2017, and public charging infrastructure represented 31 percent of national infrastructure.

11. Including Idaho, Oregon, Washington, western Montana, small parts of eastern Montana, California, Nevada, Utah, and Wyoming.

12. WAPA serves a fifteen-state region.

13. Further, federal action has reinforced state and provincial electrification processes. For example, after the financial crisis, the American Recovery and Reinvestment Act of 2009 provided over $2 billion for electric vehicle and battery technologies, which led to a mass production of plug-in vehicles and the need for charging stations. See DOE 2009 and Egbue and Long 2012, 717.

Bibliography

Acharya, A. 2018. *Constructing Global Order: Agency and Change in World Politics.* Cambridge: Cambridge University Press.

Arent, D., C. Arndt, M. Miller, F. Tarp, and O. Zinamen. 2017. *The Political Economy of Clean Energy Transitions.* Oxford: Oxford University Press. doi:10.1093/oso/9780198802242.001.0001.

Balmaceda, M., and A. Heinrich. 2020. "The Energy Politics of Russia and Eurasia." In *The Oxford Handbook of Energy Politics,* edited by K. J. Hancock and J. E. Allison, 465–506. Oxford: Oxford University Press.

Balsiger, J., and M. Prys. 2016. "Regional Agreements in International Environmental Politics." *International Environmental Agreements: Politics, Law and Economics* 16 (2): 239–60.

Balsiger, J., and S. D. VanDeveer. 2010. "Regional Governance and Environmental Problems." In *The International Studies Encyclopedia,* edited by R. A. Denmark, 9:6179–6200. Hoboken, NJ: Blackwell Publishing.

Bergquist, P., M. Mildenberger, and L. C. Stokes. 2020. "Combining Climate, Economic, and Social Policy Builds Public Support for Climate Action in the US." *Environmental Research Letters* 15 (5).

Bradbury, S. 2002. "Planning Transportation Corridors in Post-NAFTA North America." *Journal of American Planning Association* 68 (2): 137–50.

Breetz, H. L. 2020. "Do Big Goals Lead to Bad Policy? How Policy Feedback Explains the Failure and Success of Cellulosic Biofuel in the United States." *Energy Research & Social Science* 69: 1–10.

Breetz, H., M. Mildenberger, and L. Stokes. 2018. "The Political Logics of Clean Energy Transitions." *Business and Politics* 20 (4): 492–522.

Brint, J., J. Constanti, F. Hochstrasser, and L. Kessler. 2017. "Enhanced Western Grid Integration: A Legal and Policy Analysis of the Effects on California's Clean Energy Laws." *Yale Law School and Yale School of Forestry & Environmental Studies* (May 2017).

Capling, A., and K. R. Nossal. 2009. "The Contradictions of Regionalism in North America." *Review of International Studies* 35 (February): 147–67.

Carrillo, J., S. de los Santos Gómez, and J. Briones. 2020. "Hacia una electromovilidad pública en México." *Documentos de Proyectos* (LC/TS.2020/115), Santiago, Comisión Económica para América Latina y el Caribe (CEPAL).

Canada Energy Regulator (CER). 2019. "Alberta GHG." https://www.cer-rec.gc.ca/en/data-analysis/energy-markets/provincial-territorial-energy-profiles/provincial-territorial-energy-profiles-alberta.html.

Canada Energy Regulator (CER). 2021. "Market Snapshot: Electricity Exports from B.C. to California Are Increasing." https://tinyurl.com/2a585nby.

Chacón, D. A., M. E. Giner, M. Vázquez Valles, S. M. Roe, J. A. Maldonado, H. Lindquist, B. Strode, R. Anderson, C. Quiroz, and J. Schreiber. 2010.

Emisiones de gases de efecto invernadero en Baja California y proyecciones de casos de refer-encia (1990–2025). Ciudad Juárez: Border Environment Cooperation Commission/ COCEF/Gobierno de Baja California. https://www.nadb.org/uploads/files/ inventario_emisiones_gei_baja_california_junio_2010.pdf.

Cifor, A., P. Denholm, E. Ela, B-M. Hodge, and A. Reed. 2015. "The Policy and Institutional Challenges of Grid Integration of Renewable Energy in the Western United States." *Utilities Policy* 33: 34–41. http://dx.doi.org/10.1016/j.jup.2014.11.001.

De la Rosa, Y. 2022. "Oposición evita aprobación de reforma eléctrica de López Obrador." *Forbes*, April 17, 2022. https://www.forbes.com.mx/ oposicion-evita-aprobacion-de-reforma-electrica-de-lopez-obrador/.

Duguma, L. A., S. W. Wambugu, P. A. Minang, and M. van Noordwijk. 2014. "A Systematic Analysis of Enabling Conditions for Synergy between Climate Change Mitigation and Adaptation Measures in Developing Countries." *Environmental Science & Policy* 42: 138–48. https://doi.org/10.1016/j.envsci.2014.06.003.

Department of Energy (DOE). 2009. "American Recovery and Reinvestment Act of 2009." https://afdc.energy.gov/laws/arra.html

Egbue, O., and S. Long. 2012. "Barriers to Widespread Adoption of Electric Vehicles: An Analysis of Consumer Attitudes and Perceptions." *Energy Policy* 48 ©: 717–29.

US Energy Information Administration (EIA). 2017. "Power Sector Carbon Dioxide Emissions Fall Below Transportation Sector Emissions." https://www.eia.gov/ todayinenergy/detail.php?id=29612.

FHWA. 2007. "US Department of Transportation Names Six Interstate Routes as 'Corridors of the Future' to Help Fight Traffic Congestion." https://www.fhwa.dot. gov/pressroom/dot0795.cfm.

Florescu, P., and J. Pead. 2018. "Realizing the Value of Bonneville Power Administration's Flexible Hydroelectric Assets." Master's thesis, Harvard University. https://www. hks.harvard.edu/sites/default/files/degree%20programs/MPP/files/Florescu_ Pead_vPUBLIC.pdf.

Government of Canada. 2002. "Canada's Achievements at COP26." https://www. canada.ca/en/services/environment/weather/climatechange/canada-internation-al-action/un-climate-change-conference/cop26-summit/achievements-at-cop26. html.

Hancock, K. J., and A. Libman. 2016. "Eurasia." In *The Oxford Handbook of Comparative Regionalism*, edited by T. A. Börzel and T. Risse, 202–24. Oxford: Oxford University Press.

Hancock, K. J., S. Palestini, and K. Szulecki. 2020. "The Politics of Energy Regionalism." In *The Oxford Handbook of Energy Politics*, edited by Kathleen J. Hancock and Juliann Emmons Allison, 172–95. Oxford: Oxford University Press. doi:10.1093/ oxfordhb/9780190861360.013.5.

Hoppe, T., and M. Miedema. 2021. "A Governance Approach to Regional Energy Transition: Meaning, Conceptualization and Practice." *Sustainability* 12 (3): 915.

Institute of the Americas. 2020. "Baja California Energy Outlook 2020–2025." January 2020. https://iamericas.org/wp-content/uploads/2022/02/Baja_Energy_Outlook_2020_2025.pdf.

Johnson, C., and S. D. VanDeveer. Forthcoming. "Energy Regionalisms in Theory and Practice." *Review of Policy Research.* doi:10.1111/ropr.12422

Mildenberger, M., and L. C. Stokes. "The Energy Politics of North America." In *Oxford Handbook of Energy Politics*, edited by Kathleen J. Hancock and Juliann E. Allison, 1–25. Oxford: Oxford University Press, 2019.

Milligan, M., K. Clark, J. King, B. Kirby, T. Guo, and G. Liu. 2013. "Examination of Potential Benefits of an Energy Imbalance Market in the Western Interconnection." NREL/TP-5500–57115, National Renewable Energy Laboratory, Golden, Colorado, March 2013. http://www.nrel.gov/docs/fy13osti/57115.pdf.

Mills, A., A. Phadke, and R. Wiser. 2011. "Exploration of Resource and Transmission Expansion Decisions in the Western Renewable Energy Zone Initiative." *Energy Policy* 39: 1732–45.

Muñoz-Meléndez, Gabriela, and Marcela López-Vallejo Olvera. 2018. "Building a Transregional Governance Architecture for Electricity Integration in the Baja California–California Border Region: The Cases of Tijuana and Mexicali." *Latin American Policy* 9 (2): 17–38.

Murphy, A. B., J. N. Entrikin, A. Paasi, G. Macleod, A. E. G. Jonas, and A. C. Hudson. 2015. "Bounded vs. Open Regions, and beyond Critical Perspectives on Regional Worlds and Words." In *Regional Worlds: Advancing the Geography of Regions*, edited by M. Jones and A. Paasi, 6–15. London: Routledge, 2015.

Narassimhan, E., and C. Johnson. 2018. "The Role of Demand-Side Incentives and Charging Infrastructure on Plug-In Electric Vehicle Adoption: Analysis of US States." *Environ. Res. Lett.* 13, 074032. doi:10.1088/1748–9326/aad0f8.

Natural Resources Canada. 2019. "Zero-Emission Vehicle Infrastructure Program." https://www.nrcan.gc.ca/zero-emission-vehicle-infrastructure-program/21876.

Orton, T. 2018. "Ford and Daimler to Close B.C. Joint Venture Employing 200: Business in Vancouver." *BIV*, June 14, 2018. https://biv.com/article/2018/06/ford-and-daimler-close-bc-joint-venture-employing-200.

Pletka, R., and J. Finn. 2009. "Western Renewable Energy Zones, Phase 1: QRA Identification Technical Report." Black & Veatch Corporation, Subcontract Report NREL/SR-6A2-46877, Overland Park, Kansas, October 2009.

Rowlands, I. H. 2017. "U.S.-Canadian Subnational Electricity Relations." In *Toward Continental Environmental Policy? North American Transnational Networks and Governance*, edited by Owen Temby and Peter Stoett, 334–56. Albany: State University of New York Press.

Sabbatella, I., and T. Santos. 2020. "The IPE of Regional Energy Integration in South America." In *The Routledge Handbook to Global Political Economy*, edited by E. Vivares, 719–40. New York: Routledge.

Schwartz, L. 2012. "Renewable Resources and Transmission in the West: Interviews on the Western Renewable Energy Zones Initiative." WGA, DOE.

Sharpe, B., N. Lutsey, C. Smith, and C. Kim. 2020. "Power Play: Canada's Role in The Electric Vehicle Transition." White paper, International Council on Green Transportation, April 2020.

Siegel, J., and Z. Colman. 2022. "'Last Chance': Greens Push Climate Compromise with Manchin." *Politico*, April 26, 2022. https://www.politico.com/news/2022/04/26/greens-push-climate-compromise-manchin-00027511.

Sierzchula, W., S. Bakker, K. Maat, and B. van Wee. 2014. "The Influence of Financial Incentives and Other Socio-economic Factors on Electric Vehicle Adoption." *Energy Policy* 68: 183–94.

Stokes, Leah, and Hanna Breetz. 2018. "Politics in the U.S. Energy Transition: Case Studies of Solar, Wind, Biofuels and Electric Vehicles Policy." *Energy Policy* 113: 76–86. http://dx.doi.org/10.1016/j.enpol.2017.10.057.

Stroup, L., R. Kujawa, and J. Ayres. 2015. "Envisioning a Green Energy Future in Canada and the United States: Constructing a Sustainable Future in the Context of New Regionalisms?" *American Review of Canadian Studies* 45 (3): 299–314.

Transportation Canada (TC). 2021. "Government Expenditures and Revenues from Transportation." https://tc.canada.ca/en/corporate-services/policies/government-expenditures-revenues-transportation.

Westfall, C. 2019. "Western Regional Transmission Organization: Creating a Market to Support Renewable Energy." *The Georgetown Envtl. Law Review* 31: 409–32. https://www.law.georgetown.edu/environmental-law-review/wp-content/uploads/sites/18/2019/04/GT-GELR190006.pdf.

PART III

Interdependences and Institutions in North America

North America's Circulation Governance and Polycentric Drives for Integration and Fragmentation

Isidro Morales

Introduction

FOR THREE decades, the movement of goods, services, capital, and people in North America has been articulated through a circulation mechanism embodied in two regimes. One emphasizes mobility; the other one focuses on confinement. These two regimes—products of private-sector interests and intergovernmental negotiations—have resulted in a ruling architecture marked by inherent tensions. In this architecture the balance shifts between what is allowed to circulate or not; between intraregional preferences versus extra-regional arrangements; and between enforcement of national borders versus regional perimeters. We see these tensions manifest through patterns of centripetal versus centrifugal trade regionalization and even between competing narratives, which advocate the benefits of deeper regionalization from one side or promote the advantages of fragmentation from the other side.

The mobility of goods, services, and investments has enhanced firms' capabilities to relocate their value chains across the region to boost their productivity and competitiveness, favoring trade concentration and regionalization. It is what we call in this essay centripetal regionalization. These centripetal forces relate closely to the sort of interdependence emphasized in many classic conceptualizations of international regions (e.g., Nye 1968); as discussed below, these dynamics are most strongly concentrated among the United States and Canada and Mexico. Yet this regionalization reached its limits because of the very nature of the North American Free Trade Agreement (NAFTA) as an example of the global model of plurilateral trade agreements (PTA). The more that NAFTA-like patterns of rules for trade and investment extended outside North America, often prompted by the three North American partners, the more NAFTA's original advantages waned, and new competitors entered the North American market. The major surprise was China, which, after it joined the World Trade Organization (WTO) at the end of 2001, became the de facto fourth North

American partner (Stallings, this volume). In the face of weak regional institutions, China's intrusion into North America weakened patterns of economic interdependence. Furthermore, as explained below, circulation regimes need to be connected with a political project and narrative to foster a more cohesive region.

Centrifugal forces, in other words, de-regionalization, were unleashed primarily from the security side of the North American governance regimes. Although the proscription of undesired mobility is necessary to constitute the "legality" of desired flows, security concerns may eventually trump the entire circulation regime. This suggests the limits of interdependence, on its own, to construct a cohesive region. Such was the case after the September 11, 2001, attacks in the United States, when the US northern and southern borders were shut down, and this has again been the case during the COVID-19 pandemic, when only "essential mobility" was allowed. At the same time, a growing "securitization" of the overall regime may hinder and increase the costs of desired circulation throughout the region. The Trump administration illustrated this risk during the negotiation of the United States, Mexico, and Canada Agreement (USMCA), a process grounded in logics of trade wars and accompanied by the building of physical walls and the imposition of levies justified by "national security" concerns.

This essay argues that patterns of integration and fragmentation in North America are explained by the nature of the centripetal and centrifugal forces featured in the governance of regional circulation. These forces operate under a three-tier mechanism—a hierarchical tier dominated by sovereignty concerns and priorities that enhance or lessen the home bias and containment role still played by inner borders, a horizontal networked tier focused on trade and value chains and operated by polycentric regional firms and industries, and a contentious discursive tier compounded by competing political actorness and power-knowledge narratives advocating integration or fragmentation processes. In other words, regional integration is not only explained as a by-product of intergovernmental cooperation and conflict, but also as a series of polycentric hubs, firms, and coalitions in which the interests and discursive practices of stakeholders play a contradictory role—they may advocate for more integration, or, on the contrary, they may challenge it. Thus, North America has no essence on its own; it is a construct whose territoriality, spatiality, and signifier is assembled and de-assembled throughout time, according to the three tiers herein explored. It is also shaped by other forces beyond those considered in this chapter and highlighted elsewhere in the volume: migratory flows, identities, geographical continuities across borders, common and/or asymmetrical threats, shared or divergent collective values, etc.

The Opposing Propellers of a Circulation Mechanism

The NAFTA regime, in place since 1994, aimed at building, in the long run, a sort of "borderless economy," the great metaphor dominating the ideology and narrative of global markets. This metaphor reflected well the spirit and substance of the PTA—to enhance and empower the circulation of covered goods, services, and investments in the hands of firms and markets, to boost productivity and efficiency throughout North America, and to discipline state intervention in the economy. Yet the building of this circulation regime had to adapt to the reality of political borders and strategic security imperatives. Consequently, the creation of a borderless economic space remained a metaphoric goal since the NAFTA agreement did not remove entirely the region's territorial and non-territorial borders. In fact, for some types of movements, borders thickened due to a progressive "securitization" of the Mexico-US line in response to Washington's perceptions of growing unauthorized migration and illegal trafficking since the 1990s, and to the "War on Terror" initiated by Washington after the terrorist attacks of September 11, 2001. Territorial borders, left intact by NAFTA, became less permeable in light of US strategic imperatives (Andreas 2003).

Mobility and confinement do not comprise a contradictory model of circulation in North America. Rather, mobility and constraint are the two faces the North American circulation mechanism has presented to pursue specific outcomes. Even before the September 2001 attacks, unauthorized migration and the activities of organized crime were the major challenges to NAFTA. After 9/11, US border politics shifted to a war-centered paradigm in which protection of the homeland—not only its borders and territory, but also its population, resources, and all their interconnections with the "outside world"—was at stake. The war-centered paradigm did not substitute the sovereignty-centered one; instead, the two overlapped and reinforced each other. That was the rationale under which a new security architecture was devised, with the implementation of "smart borders" and the initiation of the Security and Prosperity Partnership of North America (SPP), in 2005. The aim of this emerging cooperative framework was to adapt the mobility regime to satisfy US security priorities. The creation of the Department of Homeland Security (DHS), which brought the former border and migration agencies under the same authority, and of the Northern Command, the military arm for assuring civil-security operations under the new perimeter of North America (in which Canada and Mexico became part of the homeland), became central to maintaining legal mobility in the region. Consequently, the legality of movements became intertwined with security priorities, proving that, contrary to the dictum of the neoliberal paradigm, markets are not "natural forces" on their own; rather, their operation is embedded in the policy and security concerns of states (see Morales 2011).

If NAFTA aimed at building a sort of "business friendly" border to catalyze a "continentalized" market, in reality this continentalization was already emerging through the activities of large exporting firms and multinational corporations (MNCs), which readapted their supply and value chains from older patterns of vertical integration to networked models. Transnational industries such as automobile, food processing, chemical, electronics, and machinery had emerged long before NAFTA, as a way to reorganize operations to exploit the advantages of diverse locations (Morales 2008). What NAFTA established was a preferential trade and investment area, consisting of norms, values, principles, and enforcement mechanisms to facilitate access and circulation of both tangible and non-tangible goods, along with investments, throughout the North American region. The fact that North America became a *preferential* area is important because the preferences it granted commerce among the three states had the corollary effective of discriminating against third parties, whose access to the regional bloc was less favorable than the treatment provided by NAFTA.

As a preferential trade area (PTA), NAFTA remained grounded in a sovereignty-based model of governance. Since the beginning of the negotiations, none of the signatories harbored aspirations to emulate the European model of integration. There was no interest in creating institutional organs, staffed with their own bureaucracies on the model of what would become the European Commission. In fact, the idea of creating supranational institutions has always been anathema in the official parlance and rhetoric. Even though Canadians and Mexicans perceived NAFTA as a first step toward a deeper "integration" in the region, in Washington, officials traditionally conceived of NAFTA as a foreign-policy tool for enhancing export markets and affecting trade negotiations at the hemispheric and global levels—as they attempted to do with the failed Free Trade Area of the Americas (FTAA) and, with some success, in the Uruguay Round negotiation under the World Trade Organization (WTO) (Morales 2018). Washington's trade aspirations were not exclusive to the region; they formed part of an evolving trade diplomacy based in the idea of expanding trade liberalization to third countries, by signing PTAs of new generation that upgraded and enlarged the scope of NAFTA. This was the case of the Dominican Republic and Central America Free Trade Agreement (CAFTA-DR), signed in 2004; the agreement signed with the Republic of Korea, in 2007; and the Trans-Pacific Partnership (TPP), signed in 2016 with eleven countries located in the two basins of the Pacific Rim. The limits of this approach were revealed with the arrival of Donald Trump to the White House, when the TPP was not ratified and the NAFTA was challenged.

Though still anchored in state interests, NAFTA was successful in abating tariff barriers, enhancing intraregional trade and investments, and establishing a mechanism of communication among the three national leaders (Hufbauer and Schott 2005; Pastor 2001; Morales 2011). During the first years after it came into force, intraregional trade jumped from 39 percent in 1992, to 47 percent in 2000—a rise of 8 points in eight years, with intraregional exports (56 percent in 2000) increasing faster than intraregional imports (40.5 percent in the same year; see figure 8.1). This fast regionalization of merchandise trade is explained by what some economists have called the "gravitational" effect provoked by reducing tariffs among proximate economies while maintaining third-party barriers. Inspired by Newtonian physics, gravitational economics argue that larger economies—measured by GDP per capita, for example—tend to attract smaller economies to their domain of specialization and performance. This gravitational attraction, as in physics, is inversely proportional to distance; thus, the farther the meager economy is from a major economic hub, the fewer links it has with the latter (Parsley and Wei 2001; Magerman, Studnicka, and Van Hove 2016).

Yet, as long as national borders remain, there will be a "home bias" that limits this attraction. As such, NAFTA began to suppress tariffs among members, but did not suppress the "border effect"—a compound of sovereign regulations involving standards, phytosanitary, and public health legislations; linguistic and administrative barriers; cultural differences; and political and security concerns—thus reducing the gravitational effect on trade flows. Bankole Olayele (2019, 440) has estimated this border effect between Canada and the United States, even after the abatement of customs levies, as a tariff equivalent ranging between 5 percent and 29 percent, depending on the estimated trade elasticities from border frictions.

Since borders remain anchored in sovereignty imperatives, it is clear that the "border effect" on gravitational flows will be subject to the policy, political, and strategic priorities of states, mainly the United States. It is so because the United States is not only the dominant economy in the region, but also a leading power in regional and global affairs. Consequently, the governance of preferential access to the dominant market is done under a sovereignty-based and hierarchical circulation dispositive, in which Washington's concerns dominate the rules of the game. The nesting and negotiation of NAFTA is one example of the leading role played by the United States vis-à-vis its partners, as well as the coverage of domains and disciplines featuring the PTA. The reluctance to establish strong regional institutions—as compared to what exists in the European regionalization process—emerges from the limits Washington has established for North American integration.

Unilateral US decisions also shaped the largest change to North America's formal architecture. In 2020, NAFTA was superseded by a new agreement that enlarged the coverage of the domains included (e-commerce, public enterprises, exchange rate policies, and others), but without strengthening the institutional architecture (see Panke and Stapel, this volume). This alteration was the by-product of Donald Trump's unilateral decisions and personal opposition to NAFTA. Neither Canadians nor Mexicans will forget that the renegotiation of the PTA was carried out under the threat to put an end to the agreement, and under economic pressure including unilateral US tariffs on steel and aluminum, which outlasted the renegotiation. The sovereign priorities and interests of the dominant player trump the interests of the weaker actors who are much more dependent on accessing the US market than the other way around (see Macdonald, this volume).

Thus, gravitational forces spurring intraregional flows could be considered as centripetal moves provoked by the reduction of the tariff effect among North American

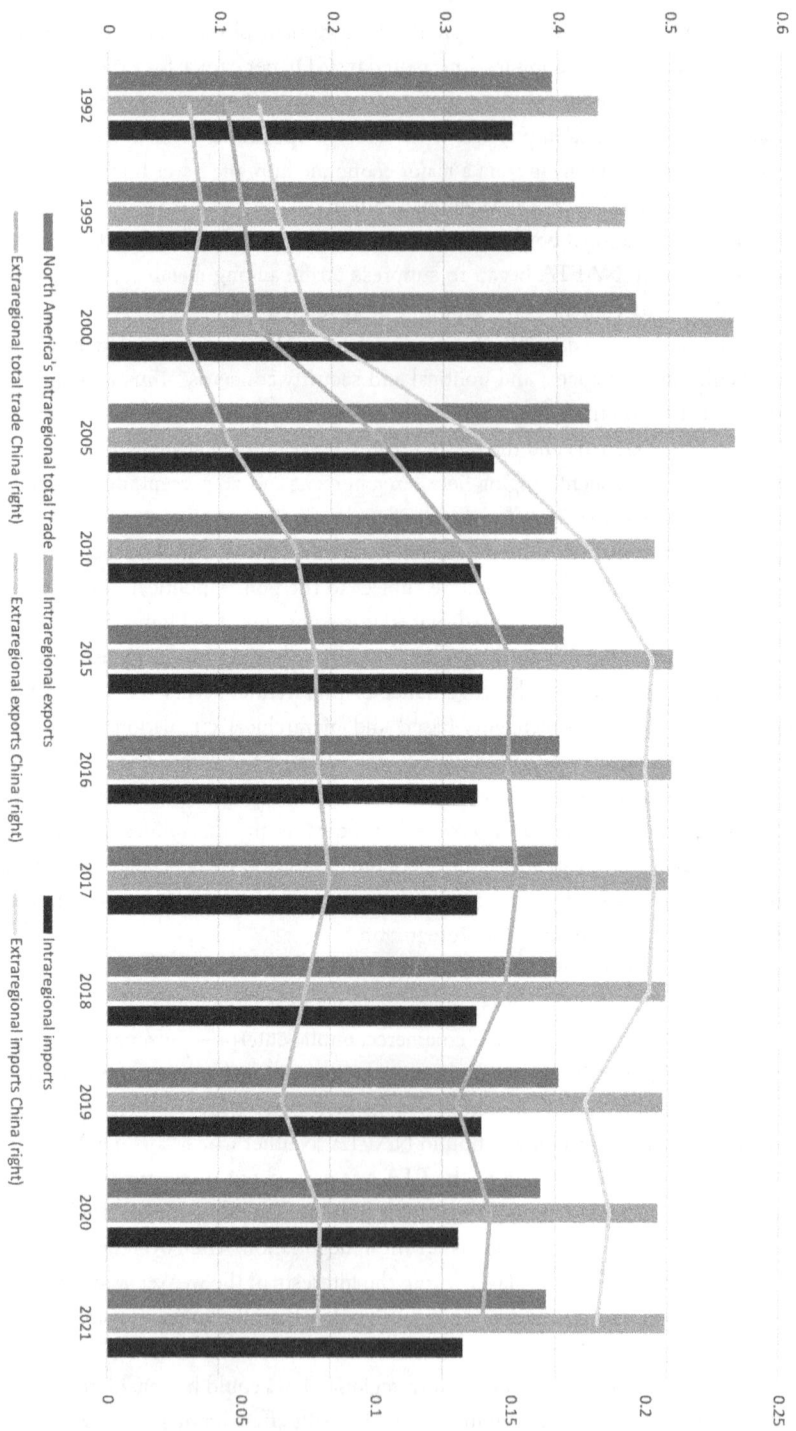

Figure 8.1. Intraregional Trade and Extraregional Exchanges with China. Shares from Total.

North America's Intraregional total trade ▮ Intraregional exports
Extraregional total trade China (right)
Extraregional exports China (right)
Extraregional imports China (right) ▮ Intraregional imports

partners. Yet these centripetal moves toward regionalization have their own limits, established first by the permanence of sovereign borders within the region, and subject also to the declining limitations on commerce with third parties. Figure 8.1 depicts how the rapid growth in intraregional trade waned and began to decline at the turn of the century; this decline was faster when measured by import values. In 1995, the WTO replaced the General Agreement on Tariffs and Trade (GATT), setting off a new phase of tariff and nontariff reductions agreed upon in the Uruguay Round, whose coverage was also extended to new countries that progressively joined the most important trade organization of the world. Such was the case of China, which entered the multilateral club at the end of 2001, and whose trade and investment flows rapidly dominated the world economic scene.

Indeed, China has become North America's major non-regional partner, displacing Japan and major European economies in its trade shares with North America, mainly on the import side. Two-way North American trade to China was only 4.5 percent of the total in 1992, while in 2019, the share was 14 percent, when Trump had already activated the so-called trade war against the Asian dragon. If we consider only North American imports, China's performance is even more impressive. Chinese imports, at only 5.6 percent in 1992, increased to 18 percent in 2021. From 2015 to 2018, the share had amounted to 20 percent. China's rapid success in accessing North American markets cannot be explained only by gravitational reasons (i.e., the Chinese economy has become so large that it attracts the North American economy despite the distance), or solely by its accession to the WTO. Its rapid transformation from an inward-looking, centralized economy to a major global player in the last twenty years must be explained more by the way its state-owned enterprises compete for global markets and resources, and by the targeted vision and goals established and pursued by its political elite. Although China's participation in the North American market has diverted regionalization flows in some industries (i.e., textile and apparel), that seems not to be the case in other ones, such as transport, agriculture, and energy, to name a few (see Stallings, this volume). Thus, China's successful performance in North America may be part of the end of the NAFTA effect in the region, but it does not necessarily mean that the nation has become a threat to US firms—as Trump painted it.

If the Biden administration keeps trade conflicts and barriers vis-à-vis the Asian giant, as it seems to be the case, relocation of value chains in the textile, apparel, machinery, and electronics industries can be anticipated, favoring firms located in Mexico or Canada. Still, the nature of the "threat" of Chinese firms is far from clear. Take, for example, the computing industry; 45 percent of US imports in computers and electronics come from China, while only 16 percent of US exports of these products go to China. Mexico, the European Union, and Canada remain important destinations for US producers. It might suggest that China is playing the same role performed by Canada and Mexico (i.e., exporting inputs that help increase the competitiveness of firms located in the United States).

For instance, in California, the state with the most diversified foreign trade and with China as the most important partner, 48 percent of computer and electronic products, and 49 percent of electrical equipment come from the Asian giant, while only 20 percent and 8.7 percent, respectively, are exported there from the state (see table 8.1). Such is the trend in most of the production chains within the textile and apparel industries, suggesting that Chinese imports boost the competitive advantages of firms based in California.

Furthermore, China has also gained import shares in Mexico. While this share was only 0.59 percent of Mexico's overall imports in 1993, in 2019, it amounted to 18 percent, which explains why imports from the United States declined from 71 percent to 47 percent during the same period. It is difficult to estimate how the US-China trade conflict—managed through the sovereign control of borders—is going to change the articulation of value chains in North America, which are managed through gravitational and networked firm strategies, mainly between the United States and its two neighbors. Mexico's imports from China could also be improving the country's export competitiveness with the United States; if an economic "Fortress North America" is consolidated, Chinese firms might be interested in increasing their direct investments in any of the USMCA member countries, as Japan did in the 1980s, to continue doing business in the region. In other words, Chinese global value chains and interests are already heavily intertwined in North America, and they could pivot toward regionalization and de-regionalization trends.

Notwithstanding, centripetal moves become activated when the external barriers are "thickened" to third parties, such as the case now, with the tariff hikes and bans imposed by Washington on Chinese trade. Figure 8.1 traces part of this "external barriers" effect, showing how the 2-point decline in Chinese commercial share in North America was slightly absorbed by North American exchanges, mainly on the side of imports coming from Mexico. It is the opposite effect when preferential access to NAFTA members became diffused by the new commitments undertaken at the WTO and the proliferation of NAFTA-like PTAs in which the three North American countries engaged.

The dialectic of the circulation regime, juxtaposing mobility and confinement, makes border policies a critical factor to understand the hierarchical logics of how centrifugal and centripetal forces are governed in North America. The thicker inner, national borders become, the more home bias they provoke; the thinner they become, the more centripetal forces are unleashed. In the case of the region's external perimeter, whose limits and scope are heavily defined by Washington, an opposite effect exists— the thicker the perimeter becomes (as seen in stronger relative regional preferences), the more centripetal North American flows become. In effect, Washington's trade war against China thickened North America's commercial perimeter, and the trade diversion that thickening creates favors North American partners. Opposing combinations are also possible (i.e., thicker barriers for third parties, with thicker border effects also among partners). Such is precisely the case with informal migratory flows coming from Central and South America. Trump put pressure on the Mexican government to deter and stop the flow coming from the southern Mexican border, while the US-Mexican line became thicker to third-country migrants, forcing them to stay on the Mexican side of the border to wait for their final status (see Castañeda et al., this volume; Toro, this volume). Border games thus became a sort of flexible lock through which flows were diverted or allowed to converge, depending on the economic, migratory, policy, political, and strategic concerns of dominant stakeholders.

Table 8.1 California's commodities trade with China, Japan and South Korea (in percents)

2019	Imports			Exports		
Shares	China and HK	Japan	South Korea	China and HK	Japan	South Korea
All Commodities	31.86	6.15	4.41	13.95	6.83	5.29
Agricultural Products	1.84	0.17	0.39	12.00	6.80	4.76
Livestock & Livestock Products	0.35	0.38	1.58	8.51	1.67	7.40
Forestry Products, Nesoi	52.22	0.54	0.15	30.67	13.33	8.19
Fish, Fresh/chilled/frozen & Other Marine Products	7.15	4.15	1.27	18.56	4.16	2.52
Oil & Gas	0.00	0.00	0.04	0.03	14.22	2.80
Minerals & Ores	7.43	0.69	0.47	2.91	47.79	6.93
Food & Kindred Products	7.87	2.54	2.37	10.06	11.75	10.99
Beverages & Tobacco Products	1.86	2.12	1.28	7.66	8.85	4.10
Textiles & Fabrics	35.74	4.53	12.36	3.98	1.66	1.42
Textile Mill Products	74.97	0.28	0.58	2.69	3.08	2.53
Apparel & Accessories	45.80	0.12	0.32	6.09	6.54	3.18
Leather & Allied Products	52.67	0.02	0.39	21.98	10.44	3.08
Wood Products	28.29	0.30	0.04	1.70	2.48	0.69
Paper	32.98	3.44	6.52	4.11	3.33	2.51
Printed Matter And Related Products	53.78	1.73	4.13	7.20	3.87	1.66
Petroleum & Coal Products	1.95	8.50	24.21	4.39	6.30	1.43
Chemicals	20.95	23.83	4.48	12.99	7.00	4.14
Plastics & Rubber Products	40.69	8.86	6.88	5.61	2.95	2.40
Nonmetallic Mineral Products	45.45	7.75	2.61	8.33	6.31	9.85
Primary Metal Mfg	8.69	6.64	10.05	7.59	7.48	5.87
Fabricated Metal Products, Nesoi	45.65	4.21	2.91	6.51	10.88	4.84
Machinery, Except Electrical	29.96	22.06	4.09	16.77	7.29	13.10
Computer & Electronic Products	48.27	3.22	6.24	20.24	5.55	3.64
Electrical Equipment, Appliances & Components	49.24	6.80	6.62	8.76	4.84	5.47
Transportation Equipment	5.78	11.83	5.45	13.01	7.41	3.58
Furniture & Fixtures	51.93	0.16	0.35	4.97	3.88	4.17
Miscellaneous Manufactured Commodities	49.13	2.83	0.95	14.50	7.61	2.73

Continental Hubs and Polycentric Networked Industries

The sovereignty-based and hierarchical governance of borders, and consequently of the "border effect" within intraregional exchanges, is no doubt fundamental to understand centripetal and centrifugal dynamics within North America. The circulation mechanism affecting these locks and valves is grounded in territorial and legal boundaries, and in a complex dynamic of policy and political state interests. However, the mobility of material exchanges, and arguably services related to these exchanges, is also affected by the decisions of MNCs involved in foreign trade, following the logistics of regional relocations of their value chains. It is so because foreign trade in North America, as in other parts of the world, is dominated by MNCs, through their exchanges with their affiliates (intra-firm trade), through other companies (inter-firm trade), or through franchises and arms-length exchanges.

According to data collected by the US Department of Commerce, 22 percent of overall US exports (goods and services) are in the hands of MNCs, as are 23 percent of imports (USBEA 2021). For commercial flows to Canada, the figures are 26 percent and 25.2 percent, respectively, while for Mexico, they are 15 percent and 19.5 percent (USBEA 2016). As anticipated, most of intra-firm exchanges are concentrated in the transport and wholesale industries. Notwithstanding, those figures could be considered conservative, since not all companies want to disclose their figures; furthermore, inter-firm, franchised, and arms-length exchanges in the hands of the companies are not fully included. For instance, United Nations Conference on Trade and Development (UNCTAD) estimations for 2010 suggested that 20 percent of US exports were in the hands of foreign affiliates, while 45 percent were controlled by parent companies based in that country; that is, 65 percent of total US gross exports were channeled through the networks of the MNCs operating in the United States. A similar situation prevailed in imports, since by that same date, 28 percent were made by foreign affiliates, and 45 percent by US parent companies, a total of 67 percent (UNCTAD 2013, 136).[1]

MNCs have doubtless become major actors for propelling foreign trade among countries, based on their competitive strategies for relocating value chains according to their interests. Although they were organized hierarchically over the past century, with the looming of the information revolution and the so-called non-territorialized space of flows, they have become more horizontal and networked with other companies, even merging assets with former rivals. In other words, their competitive strategies may reinforce gravitational forces and geographical concentration. In this sense, their networked operations (trade linked to investments) have also become propellers of centripetal or centrifugal forces in North America.

Gravitational exchanges, combined with the regionalization of value chains followed by MNCs located in North America, have concentrated trade exchanges in key geographical regions of the bloc. For example, Mexico's foreign trade with the United

States is heavily concentrated in Texas; 25 percent of overall imports from Mexico go to this southern state, while 42 percent of overall exports to Mexico come from the same state. As table 8.2 shows, most Mexican commercial integration with the United States is with Texas, Michigan, and California (see table 8.2). It is clear the strategic role these three states play in the articulation of value chains in key manufacturing branches, such as computer and electronic products, machinery, electric equipment, and certainly automobile and transport equipment. Most of these exchanges also involve the six Mexican states bordering the United States, and some key states located in Central Mexico. In other words, integration does not homogeneously assemble all Mexican states and regions with those of the United States and Canada. Integration of key value chains is being done mainly between Texas, California, and Michigan, and Mexico's northern and central regions.

The same holds true with Canada-US commodity exchanges. Tables 8.3 and 8.4 summarize the geographical concentration of two-way trade in the United States. Although this concentration is more scattered than Mexico's, most of it is located along the US states neighboring Canadian provinces, more specifically around the Great Lakes Region, a binational area made up of eight US states and the province of Ontario, and, by extension, Quebec, in Canada. California and Texas are also key states in some industrial branches, such as imports of processed products, leather, machinery, and transport equipment, and exports of agriculture, oil and gas, beverage and tobacco, apparel, and computers.

In fact, Texas, Michigan, and California act as two-way trade hubs in North America. They concentrate 18.2 percent, 15.25 percent, and 10.86 percent (that is, 44.31 percent), respectively of total imports coming from Canada and Mexico, and they export, respectively, 24.97 percent, 6.24 percent, and 8.13 percent (39.34 percent together) of total US exports to these two countries. Furthermore, key industries feature as the drivers of these hubs, Texas being the most complex and varied. Since Texas is the main state producer of hydrocarbons in the United States, it is not surprising that 65 percent of oil and gas and 56.5 percent of petroleum product exports to these two countries come from Texas alone. Meanwhile, Texas is also a major provider of high-tech products such as computers (43 percent of all US exports), chemicals (25 percent), plastics (20 percent), electrical components (28 percent), and, to some extent, transportation equipment (16 percent).

It is important to understand these gravitational cores among the three countries; industries located in these specific geographical areas become very sensitive when the border factor is thickened, no matter the reason. When Trump threatened to put an end to NAFTA, there was noticeable pressure from these regions, because they had so much to lose if the circulation mechanism were adversely affected. Yet the same was true when the USMCA was negotiated, since workers and trade unions located in these states were concerned about the outcome of the negotiations. In other words, gravitational exchanges and integrative trends have become highly intermestic

Table 8.2 United States foreign trade with Mexico. Key States (in percents)

Mexico States	Imports Calif.	Imports Mich.	Imports Tex.	Exports Calif.	Exports Mich.	Exports Tex.
All Commodities	13.04	16.26	29.14	10.90	4.35	42.32
Agricultural Products	37.99	3.64	27.20	9.40	0.28	13.25
Livestock & Livestock Products	1.42	0.15	60.96	4.05	0.06	16.16
Forestry Products, Nesoi	23.88	0.15	39.93	10.41	0.68	7.86
Fish, Fresh/chilled/frozen & Other Marine Products	51.06	0.00	3.17	52.38	2.08	17.63
Oil & Gas	5.92	0.00	70.77	2.23	0.00	84.28
Minerals & Ores	3.59	0.71	13.15	2.19	0.07	4.86
Food & Kindred Products	24.61	1.39	29.18	14.09	1.73	26.25
Beverages & Tobacco Products	6.59	0.02	9.78	7.84	0.11	10.29
Textiles & Fabrics	7.35	1.61	36.94	12.20	5.96	34.91
Textile Mill Products	12.78	8.11	25.48	19.42	4.30	33.76
Apparel & Accessories	21.54	0.14	17.68	65.34	0.52	21.31
Leather & Allied Products	10.46	19.52	39.55	18.07	14.54	36.01
Wood Products	25.72	2.12	23.28	43.95	0.90	20.21
Paper	16.74	1.24	31.50	14.81	1.18	28.79
Printed Matter And Related Products	22.89	2.21	39.68	26.67	1.58	29.34
Petroleum & Coal Products	19.79	0.04	60.80	4.05	0.04	69.25
Chemicals	6.71	0.79	29.97	6.74	3.51	39.84
Plastics & Rubber Products	14.96	9.04	18.04	15.49	6.89	34.92
Nonmetallic Mineral Products	11.97	5.43	36.20	13.22	8.74	23.14
Primary Metal Mfg	2.00	0.22	17.96	11.68	2.52	32.18
Fabricated Metal Products	12.16	7.37	29.77	13.82	8.56	34.91
Machinery, Except Electrical	8.56	5.44	25.56	10.35	6.28	31.31
Computer & Electronic Products	13.67	2.05	49.92	13.39	2.01	60.61
Electrical Equipment, Appliances & Components	9.23	5.48	26.89	12.98	5.67	41.72
Transportation Equipment	10.69	39.28	18.96	11.02	12.13	36.50
Furniture & Fixtures	24.46	12.93	27.95	13.16	12.93	31.60
Miscellaneous Manufactured Commodities	30.86	2.24	27.94	22.63	2.24	36.17

Table 8.3 United States Exports to Canada (in percents)

Shares	Calif.	Ill.	Ind.	Mich.	Minn.	N.Y.	Ohio	Pa.	Tex.	Wisc.	Total
All Commodities	5.71	5.34	4.53	7.90	1.62	5.64	7.08	3.83	9.75	2.31	53.69
Agricultural Products	31.73	0.87	0.55	3.32	1.92	1.71	1.75	1.69	7.49	0.44	51.47
Livestock & Livestock Products	2.62	0.26	0.96	0.89	1.27	7.45	4.22	3.33	1.24	12.42	34.67
Forestry Products	1.47	0.36	0.06	0.35	0.31	8.68	0.53	1.28	0.51	0.84	14.39
Fish, Fresh/chilled/frozen & Other Marine Products	5.41	0.67	0.00	0.09	1.38	0.51	0.26	0.92	0.45	0.16	9.86
Oil & Gas	0.02	0.26	0.73	8.70	0.04	3.08	0.08	0.84	56.03	0.08	69.86
Minerals & Ores	0.38	0.91	0.61	14.76	15.20	2.58	6.14	7.21	0.45	6.78	55.01
Food & Kindred Products	9.54	8.72	3.17	2.88	2.50	5.07	5.26	5.98	2.63	6.32	52.07
Beverages & Tobacco Products	18.91	4.06	1.67	1.58	3.63	5.48	26.78	3.27	0.84	3.09	69.32
Textiles & Fabrics	2.44	2.25	2.42	2.46	0.70	3.49	2.46	2.74	1.40	4.73	25.09
Textile Mill Products	3.71	4.00	1.11	1.57	0.49	1.56	4.28	4.91	1.93	0.73	24.27
Apparel & Accessories	13.88	0.79	0.94	0.38	0.32	4.03	12.44	1.62	2.27	0.59	37.26
Leather & Allied Products	11.92	0.99	0.80	0.40	0.93	2.65	6.71	2.96	8.00	1.02	36.38
Wood Products	1.72	1.75	13.70	3.81	1.51	3.30	4.01	6.29	0.29	5.95	42.32
Paper	1.42	5.29	2.11	3.74	1.85	10.49	10.18	4.90	2.11	9.37	51.47
Printed Matter And Related Products	3.02	5.55	10.22	2.56	1.53	6.26	2.37	5.23	2.96	9.80	49.49
Petroleum & Coal Products	0.54	18.55	1.14	0.94	2.66	1.75	4.66	2.64	23.04	1.14	57.07
Chemicals	3.34	7.37	2.54	2.46	1.03	3.01	8.01	5.48	13.40	1.92	48.57
Plastics & Rubber Products	3.50	6.49	3.81	3.31	1.28	2.78	9.70	6.38	3.84	4.24	45.33
Nonmetallic Mineral Products	6.32	4.01	5.21	7.10	3.39	4.14	10.38	7.07	2.95	2.25	52.81
Primary Metal Mfg	1.40	4.86	5.11	9.17	1.08	13.14	9.02	9.76	3.53	0.85	57.93
Fabricated Metal Products	3.83	7.37	3.29	5.61	2.29	3.55	7.48	4.65	7.45	2.38	47.90
Machinery, Except Electrical	3.14	9.84	3.39	4.55	2.10	2.56	6.35	4.62	7.30	3.97	47.81
Computer & Electronic Products	19.08	4.01	1.82	2.09	1.37	3.16	7.67	4.91	10.81	1.38	56.29
Electrical Equipment, Appliances & Components	5.80	5.52	2.55	4.17	2.18	2.90	6.44	5.60	10.86	4.71	50.73
Transportation Equipment	2.59	2.92	10.50	20.86	1.06	1.50	9.67	1.44	6.21	0.76	57.52
Furniture & Fixtures	6.08	2.81	1.74	9.92	1.43	1.85	4.47	2.13	2.65	2.58	35.66
Miscellaneous Manufactured Commodities	9.32	4.24	3.74	1.59	1.87	7.61	3.55	3.05	8.07	1.24	44.29

Table 8.4 United States Imports to Canada (in percents)

Shares	Calif.	Ill.	Ind.	Mich.	Minn.	N.Y.	Ohio	Pa.	Tex.	Wisc.	Total
All Commodities	8.43	11.72	2.43	14.12	2.91	5.25	3.75	3.42	5.91	1.36	59.30
Agricultural Products	6.62	4.60	1.30	8.15	5.83	8.84	4.91	4.58	2.11	3.28	50.21
Livestock& Livestock Products	11.55	1.81	0.75	1.82	5.09	5.45	0.95	4.55	0.77	4.24	36.99
Forestry Products	7.57	1.27	0.74	12.62	5.53	1.86	0.93	1.28	0.38	4.72	36.91
Fish, Fresh/chilled/frozen & Other Marine Products	5.04	2.12	0.86	1.01	0.83	1.41	0.31	0.62	0.69	0.53	13.41
Oil & Gas	0.72	37.02	0.00	3.82	7.71	1.45	0.92	1.76	8.54	0.21	62.16
Minerals & Ores	7.15	3.40	7.05	11.03	2.30	2.50	3.41	4.70	9.25	4.36	55.14
Food & Kindred Products	12.51	10.43	3.70	2.80	1.04	7.72	4.35	8.09	5.10	2.09	57.83
Beverages & Tobacco Products	5.83	17.32	1.40	7.37	0.84	15.04	2.29	3.29	3.80	1.65	58.83
Textiles & Fabrics	4.20	8.07	2.18	4.35	0.84	9.29	3.45	5.05	10.17	1.17	48.78
Textile Mill Products	6.23	13.50	1.33	1.50	7.55	8.22	8.48	6.40	5.23	1.96	60.40
Apparel & Accessories	2.95	17.40	0.63	1.17	0.51	23.20	0.48	15.69	3.67	0.32	66.01
Leather & Allied Products	2.78	1.35	1.67	10.17	0.59	12.21	3.36	3.84	26.99	0.38	63.33
Wood Products	5.74	4.39	3.00	5.02	3.33	4.62	3.32	4.19	6.03	3.61	43.24
Paper	4.11	7.23	2.60	4.12	2.87	9.48	7.21	9.31	2.89	7.39	57.22
Printed Matter And Related Products	9.05	4.43	3.74	6.91	1.94	14.21	3.89	6.48	3.38	2.88	56.92
Petroleum & Coal Products	1.82	2.00	0.75	1.95	0.45	4.91	0.72	0.84	2.86	1.65	17.94
Chemicals	3.51	7.50	6.92	4.76	2.23	3.77	4.91	7.04	8.40	2.32	51.35
Plastics & Rubber Products	5.95	10.00	3.54	6.07	1.74	5.04	7.03	5.27	7.63	3.58	55.85
Nonmetallic Mineral Products	4.19	4.75	3.53	6.93	1.11	12.48	7.09	4.84	4.63	1.60	51.17
Primary Metal Mfg	1.92	4.43	6.78	8.32	1.38	21.27	9.75	7.93	2.97	0.97	65.71
Fabricated Metal Products	5.24	5.20	3.60	11.95	1.38	6.42	5.50	3.72	8.21	1.60	52.81
Machinery, Except Electrical	4.00	5.39	2.87	8.50	1.87	3.94	5.67	3.86	11.06	2.53	49.71
Computer & Electronic Products	8.03	5.28	2.12	4.65	1.57	10.98	2.29	2.59	8.60	1.47	47.59
Electrical Equipment, Appliances & Components	8.01	5.76	3.29	5.28	1.70	7.99	3.22	3.18	9.69	2.86	50.98
Transportation Equipment	25.17	1.80	1.70	44.35	0.65	0.85	3.68	0.51	2.91	0.21	81.82
Furniture & Fixtures	8.48	5.93	1.91	3.90	1.81	9.12	3.74	4.29	6.50	1.99	47.69
Miscellaneous Manufactured Commodities	9.59	3.27	1.74	7.03	2.16	13.93	3.03	3.17	7.03	1.94	52.88

in the region, meaning that exchanges coming from either country have a local effect in a specific state or province; and the effects unleash contradictory reactions, either centripetal support framed under a specific narrative, or a negative reaction opposing it, codified under a defensive discourse. It is in fact what Trump did to get the votes of automobile workers in some states located in the "rust belt," mainly Ohio and Michigan, in his 2016 and 2020 presidential campaigns. This locational impact of gravitational factors, intertwined with re-localization strategies of industrial and services firms, is at the heart of the political and ideological reactions fueling or challenging integrative trends. It frames the space of actorness, and discursive practices, that are briefly reviewed in the final section of this essay.

Consequently, gravitational and centripetal drives in North America are not homogeneous and do not move in only one direction. They certainly push for integrative trends, but they may also unleash centrifugal reactions. Integration is not being solely commanded by hierarchical policy decisions and discourses tailored by the three federal governments. It is also polycentric, involving hierarchies and networks, key states and hubs (around Texas, Michigan, and California), key industries (such as automobile, and oil and gas), key natural resources (agriculture, livestock, and wood), and key stakeholders (firms, labor unions, nongovernmental organizations [NGOs], and others).

Take, for example, the automobile industry, which is heavily regionalized due to the rationale of value chains of the companies involved. During the original NAFTA negotiations, these companies pushed for rules of origin that required 60 percent–62.5 percent of value to be regional content in order to benefit from tariff exemptions, which at the time was high compared to the rules of origin requiring 50 percent regional value in other industries. Under the USMCA, the regional content jumped to 70 percent–75 percent. Furthermore, 70 percent of a vehicle's steel and aluminum must originate in the three North American partners, and the steel must be domestically processed (Villarreal, Canis, and Wong 2019). This example shows how corporate interests may convey centripetal flows; by increasing the access requirement for third-party competitors, they propelled a deeper continentalization of value chains, even in support industries.

Indeed, the auto industry became an example of how corporate strategies must adapt to political hierarchical interests. Due to Trump's rhetorical criticism of NAFTA that the agreement benefited Mexico to the detriment of US workers, Mexico finally accepted the imposition of "wage requirements" under the USMCA, stipulating that 40 percent–45 percent of regional auto content must be made by workers earning at least US $16 per hour. This disposition will benefit more Canadian and US automotive workers than Mexican, since the weighted average wage in the US automobile industry is US $26 per hour, while in Mexico it is US $7.34 (Villarreal, Canis, and Wong 2019). Wage requirements could also play against corporate interests, since higher labor costs could diminish their competitive edge vis-à-vis out-of-area competitors, though this may be considered as a price worth paying to make the new agreement politically feasible.

Mexico and Canada also took "shield" measures against Trump's threat to extend tariffs by invoking "national security" concerns, as was the case when tariffs were imposed on steel and aluminum when the USMCA was being negotiated. To circumvent the potential thickening of the border effect, the two countries added their respective "side letters," agreeing on specific volumes to be exempted if the United States imposed levies in this specific industry under Section 232 of the Trade Expansion Act of 1962, that is, arguing national security reasons. Thus, the automobile industry is clearly at a crossroads, where the hierarchical governance of borders intersects with the polycentric horizontal-networked strategies of MNCs. The latter assured centripetal attraction by accepting higher rules of origin in some value chains and pushing for shield measures to reduce the threat of a higher border effect.

In the case of energy industries, we see a similar trend, but with recent centrifugal patterns. Although not heavily dominated by MNCs like the automobile sector, in part for historical reasons (Mexico's state monopoly lasted until 2013), US oil and gas imports were concentrated in Canada over the past twenty years. Mexico, by contrast, which had traditionally followed a sovereign-led policy of self-sufficiency combined with oil exports to the United States, has reversed in its role in North America. Currently, the country imports 73 percent of its natural gas consumption, and 75 percent of its gasoline needs. Crude oil and gas markets became concentrated in the region, for either gravitational or strategic reasons. Yet due to the huge increases of US oil production from tight-oil formations and from natural gas extracted from shale plays, the United States is bound to become a major oil and gas player in global markets in the years to come. This has allowed Washington to thicken the border factor by arguing for its environmental concerns, namely when the Keystone XL pipeline interconnection between the Canadian province of Alberta and the United States was banned. The possibility for a further thickening of the border effect in fossil fuels across the region has grown with the Joseph Biden administration. His green plan for decarbonizing the US energy matrix might introduce a carbon tax on power generation at the federal level, which could be extended to commodity exchanges across the border, geared toward reducing the carbon footprint in trade.

Narratives at Stake Spurred by Contentious Actors

Societies cannot live without a narrative that provides meaning and value to what they do and the way they are organized (Harari 2018). Theories, approaches, and concepts of integration and regionalization that attempt to explain the drives and flaws of these processes are part of a narrative that becomes intertwined with political and ideological interests. While integrative forces—networked mobility—are important for building a region, their political and social meanings are not fixed. At the end of the day, these narratives attempt to elucidate whether integration is good, or whether fragmentation, sovereign-based, and unilateral decisions are preferable. Such debates have surrounded the concept of globalization, whose detractors have denounced the exacerbation of social inequalities unleashed by the preponderance of market forces over distributive policies. Thus, the axiological content of a narrative always remains embedded in power-knowledge struggles, whose strength or weakness depend on actorness, institutions, and ideological and political coalitions. Regions are, at the end of the day, political constructs which make sense of the opposing forces that shape their contours.

The European Union process has shown, for instance, not only the importance of gravitational forces, firms' interests, and a sovereign will for propelling and expanding the integration mechanism, but also the role played by hegemonic narratives built upon security, economic, political, and citizenship values. In other words, narratives may thicken or reduce the border effect within regions, much beyond the empirical calculations made so far by econometrists. Indeed, the way economists have understood the border effect has the advantage that it can be measured, considering costs, elasticities, and other proxies related to border frictions (see the first section of this article). These frictions can also be measured by estimating non-trade tariffs, hidden barriers, and different regulatory measures and standards. At the same time, counter-integrative narratives could entangle looming new social and cultural borders, infringing higher costs on an integration process whose effects might be difficult to measure. It is what Europeans are attempting to grasp with Brexit and its aftermath.

North America has witnessed a similar divide in recent years. On the one hand, Trump's narrative about Mexico and North America, and his related policies, was, in many ways, a rupture with the discourse under which not only NAFTA but also all PTAs were grounded. On the other hand, alternative voices have been raised and articulated, since the turn of the century—perhaps most notably Robert Pastor and his claim for building a sense of Community for the region. Under Trump's political discourse, Mexico and Canada reaped the benefits of NAFTA to the detriment of the United States' workers and interests. He used as an argument the US deficit in the trade balance with its two neighbors. His challenge to the neoliberal narrative—free trade and rearticulation of value chains at the trilateral level to increase the competitiveness of the region vis-à-vis third parties or blocs—was not replaced by a new vision of what Trump expected from the rearrangement of economic and geopolitical relations that his nationalist, xenophobic, and protectionist discourse unleashed. Under Trump, Washington privileged unilateral policies, even resorting to all kinds of pressures and attacks, to assure US voters that the interests of their country were above all others.

As previously noted, during the USMCA negotiations Washington imposed tariffs on steel and aluminum imports from Mexico and Canada. These taxes were justified by invoking national security considerations. The tariffs were maintained even after the negotiations ended (September 30, 2018) and were lifted later only for

Mexico and Canada. Thus, the USMCA did not prevent Washington from imposing unilateral levies and sanctions on its regional partners when it argued the defense of national security and the "repatriation" of jobs to the United States. Furthermore, once these taxes were removed, the Trump administration threatened to impose an additional 5 percent tariff on total imports from Mexico. Even though the three countries had already signed the USMCA, and the tariffs on steel and aluminum had been lifted, the threat to impose new levies—this time on all Mexican exports—was to pressure Mexico to stop the entry of Central American migrants through its border with Guatemala.

All these tariffs and pressures are part of the thickening of the border effect, as discussed throughout this article. However, Trump's narrative inflicted more damage on the North American integration process when he stigmatized and criminalized Mexican migration, converting human flows "trespassing" at the southwest US border into a national security concern. His divisive and hate-filled discourse against Mexicans crystallized in his attempt to build a "beautiful" wall along the Mexican border, for which in principle the Mexicans would pay, either through taxes on their remittances or exchanges. Due to his failure to get support from Congress to fund his wall project, only 727 kilometers of barriers were erected by the end of his term, most of them replacing old fences constructed under previous administrations. Indeed, the barricading and militarization of the Mexican border started since NAFTA came into force, but the rebordering process became, as Peter Andreas brilliantly summarized it, a politically successful policy failure (Andreas 2003, 4). Barricades and fences did not prevent unauthorized migrants from entering; they only made their journey more costly and dangerous (Toro, and Castañeda et al., in this volume). A financial crisis like the one in 2007–2008, or a pandemic like the one we are suffering today, is more powerful than physical barriers for deterring illicit flows moving from South to North. Still, this time the political gains were much higher for Trump and his constituency, which proved to be larger than anticipated, according to the number of ballots in his favor during the last presidential campaign. Thus, the refurbishment of the wall became the symbol of a looming cultural frontier, through which Mexicans were evicted from the North American narrative, because they are a "threat," and a racist and xenophobic discourse became politically correct throughout US society (Romero 2018).

This highly contrasts with alternative narratives that rather attempt to find the common interests and values that call for a sense of community in the region. Since the turn of the century, for instance, Pastor, a former member of the National Security Council during the Carter presidency and a well-respected scholar in foreign affairs, reflected on the "bumps and potholes" still existing in the so-called great highway uniting North America. His reflections were not only focused on the open and hidden costs of the "border effect" but pointed out a more ambitious goal—the need to create a North American Community grounded in three pillars: 1) interdependency rather than dependency; 2) reciprocity rather than unilateralism; 3) common goals rather than merely a quid pro quo (Pastor 2012, 202). Idealistic as that vision might seem, Pastor was fully aware that the only way to enhance integration, cooperation, and some sort of common identity in the region was, first, to find the commonalities among the three countries, despite their historical and cultural differences, and, most important, to narrow the income and economic imbalances existing between Mexico, the poorer partner, and the United States and Canada.

Most of Pastor's reflections in his late academic and advocating years were geared precisely toward finding the common values and goals uniting the three nations, as well as the major obstacles limiting integration. Among the values and common interests, he highlighted the engagement of the three nations with freedom, democracy, and prosperity principles; among the obstacles, the income gap between Mexico and the United States, which hinders the possibility to move to common labor and currency markets, like the Europeans have done. Inspired by the regional funds launched by the European Community to bridge the income gap of Spain, Portugal, and Greece vis-à-vis Germany and France, Pastor suggested the creation of a North American fund, supported with Mexican oil income and matched with US and Canadian money, to invest in infrastructure and education in Mexico to boost its income (Pastor 2001, 202).

Pastor's vision of a community, and Trump's divisive and hate-filled discourse are in some way the two poles of the discursive and political-action spectrum prevailing in the region. There are many other struggles and discursive cleavages in between. For instance, the labor and environmental effects of PTAs have historically been a contentious debate in the United States, provoking transnational coalitions aimed at avoiding a "race to the bottom" in labor and environment standards. To pass NAFTA in the US Congress, Bill Clinton conceded to aggregate two side agreements on these subjects to appease the attacks by US unions and environmental activists. Their claim was that, to boost their competitiveness, firms might prefer to relocate their activities in Mexico to take advantage of the loose enforcement of its labor and environmental legislations. To avoid such a labor and environmental "dumping," Mexico committed to enforce its legislation; otherwise, sanctions and fines could have been imposed, although the enforcement mechanisms lacked teeth at that time.

The protection of labor and environmental standards was finally included in the USMCA and is subject to the general arbitrated mechanisms of dispute settlements if there is a breach or disagreement. Apart from imposing minimum "wage requirements" in specific industries, as noted in the second part, the Democrats put as a condition for ratifying the agreement the establishment of a so-called Rapid Response Mechanism, consisting of an independent panel investigation in case of denial of certain labor rights in key industries. Mexico's business sector was reluctant to accept these conditions, while independent unions and labor and human rights activists considered them as a major victory (Bensusán and Middlebrook 2020).

The saga of labor and environmental mechanisms to press Mexico to enforce and improve its respective legislation shows how divisive some aspects of continental integration may become to different stakeholders. At the same time, it shows how trilateral institutions may help create institutional convergence on those contentious and dividing issues; that is, they may neutralize fragmentation trends and induce convergence. The same might be possible in other divisive issues currently at stake such as decarbonization of the energy mix and the invigoration of democratic institutions across the region. President Biden is apparently fully committed to advance these issues at home and abroad, and North America will not be an exception.

Conclusions

Sovereign hierarchies, gravitational advantages, polycentric firms' cross-border networks, and intermestic transnational political coalitions anchored in their respective discursive practices are propellers of centripetal and centrifugal forces that shape the complexity of a circulation regime in North America. They all mold the moving borders and frontiers regarding what is allowed to move and what must be confined, unauthorized, proscribed, and even silenced or stigmatized. Regions are continuously rebordered, whether politically, economically, geopolitically, or culturally. Despite centripetal moves pushing for more cooperation and regionalization, propelled by economic or even national-defense concerns—such as the current US rivalry with China—the border effect and home bias of intraregional boundaries remain. These borders may even be thickened when powerful sovereigns invoke security concerns, such as Washington's post–September 11 policies, or more recent ones triggered by the COVID-19 pandemic. In North America, as in most circulation regimes, security priorities normally trump the mobility of markets and people, regardless of their legal status.

North America remains a highly diverse region that is not necessarily converging, despite the sovereign and corporate-led efforts to reduce inner economic borders through the implementation of PTAs. Contrary to what some corporate-led discourses have argued, integration is neither inevitable nor irreversible. High levels of economic interdependence do not create a region alone, in the absence of a political project. The NAFTA effect propelling further regionalization lasted a few years, and trade concentration was reverted, at least relatively, once out-of-area preferential access was extended and China penetrated aggressively the import markets of the three North American partners. Nonetheless, as this article suggests, there are already three major trade cross-border hubs in the region, which propel intra-industry trade and a relocation of value chains, following corporate-led competitive strategies. These hubs are a gravitational force around which key industries such as transport, energy, machinery, textile and apparel, computing, and electronics are regionalized, pooling in principle related industries and services, a point that was not developed in this study. Even as China's imports have been disruptive in some of these industries—such as textile, apparel, and computing—industrial inputs from this Asian giant might improve the competitive advantages of firms located in the North American space. Imports coming from China have become heavily punished by sovereign wars, which once again favor a slight trilateral trade concentration. Still, the mid- to long-term repercussions of the Chinese effect on the region have yet to be assessed and clarified. Will trade wars with China unify North American cooperation as a competitive response? Could that competition boost specific industries, such as textile, apparel, and electronics, located either in Canada or Mexico, which lost market shares in the United States when China joined the WTO? Will Chinese firms increase their investments and relocation of supply chains in the three North American countries to circumvent Washington's barriers? Will those relocations end up upgrading the competitiveness of specific regionalized industries?

During the Trump years, despite the transformation of NAFTA into the USMCA, North America fell into disarray. Political and cultural frontiers were exacerbated, fueled by the anti-NAFTA rhetoric prompted by Washington under the premise that both Canada and Mexico were benefiting from the PTA to the detriment of US workers and interests. Trump's xenophobic discourse, coupled with the criminalization of unauthorized migration—both Mexican and non-Mexican, and anchored physically in the construction of new walls and the refurbishment of old ones—expelled Mexicans and Mexico's culture from North America. The term reverted to its old meaning, one of cultural affinity between the United States and Canada, while Mexico was tagged as part of the threats coming from Central America and South America, or the "Global South." Placed in this narrative, the same forces of interdependence long seen as integrative instead eroded North America's cohesiveness as a region.

Trump's confrontational, hate-filled discourse has reminded us that labeling, profiling, and stigmatizing countries and their people could create thicker borders than the simple "bumps and potholes" that raised transaction costs, diminished integrative forces, and compounded the border effect. Conversely, the piecemeal evolution of trilateral rules and institutions, such as the transformation of NAFTA's labor and environment side agreements into two complete, lengthened chapters of the USMCA, finally subject to enforcement and sanctions, prove that policy convergence and further cooperation could be enhanced through the empowerment of transnational coalitions and their respective narratives. In sum, despite the current political and cultural disarray in North America, centripetal hubs, markets, stakeholder interests, and their respective competing narratives remain crucial factors to explain integrative trends.

The governance of circulation in North America encompasses a set of hierarchical, horizontal, gravitational, polycentric, advocative, and discursive mechanisms that are in tension with one another, though not necessarily fully contradictory. They overlap and reinforce each other, shifting the balance between further integration or fragmentation. It may seem that sovereign hierarchies predominate in the locks and valves of inner borders and external preferences, and in the content and intensity of political discourse for advancing or obstructing integration. Yet there are additional factors that shape the balance between regionalization and inward-looking fragmentation. These include geography and its gravitational attractions, firm strategies of value chain relocation and cross-border trade specialization and spatialization, as well as stakeholder interests enmeshed in their own discursive practices. They might enhance integrative trends, such as in the early years of NAFTA, or, by contrast, they might unleash contradictory forces, as it was recently the case under the Trump administration.

The Mexico-bashing discourse and practice under Trump clearly jeopardize the climate for further integration, yet his trade conflicts with China favor trade concentration with his southern neighbor. Gravitational attractions may enhance the competitiveness and resilience of some specific industries, such as automobile and oil and gas; however, once those industries become very successful, as is the case with the fossil industries in the United States, they might unleash centrifugal reactions to their counterparts located north and south of the border. Reinforcing the confinement of goods and people, most of the time by security concerns, may be even necessary to maintain a mobility regime across the region.

Consequently, the analysis of integration, regionalization, regime formation, cannot be circumscribed to a normative or single-causal approach. Neither integration is inevitable, nor triggered off by the sole existence of "complex interdependence," "intermesticity," the prevalence of intense intra-industry trade, or the negotiation and renegotiations of PTAs highlighting summitries and goodwill discourses. This does not mean that integration cannot be theoretically formalized for explanatory purposes. It may certainly be, but the cautious observer should be attentive to avoid falling in rapid explanations and generalizations. Patterns of regionalization and de-regionalization cannot be universalized, let alone becoming models to be followed. Regions may learn from alternative processes of cooperation, but must respect the uniqueness of each process, both in space and time.

North America is not the same political, social, and economic spatiality after the signing of NAFTA. That breakthrough had a lasting impact in the pieces put together that interacted with complex embedded mechanisms—some of which were disaggregated here for explanatory purposes—shifting in time the possibilities yet not the cause for advancing or deterring integration. Last but not least, the impact of politics and discursive practices should not be neglected in the way space and time are envisioned and assembled, as most of the times normative, realist, and neo-functionalist approaches tend to overlook. In this essay we only highlighted how tensions between contentious actors and their advocating narratives are crucial for giving sense and moral value to integrative or fragmentations trends. An alternative approach focuses on how material and human circulation is subject to knowledge-intensive surveillance and practices aimed at profiling groups, communities, polities, and organizations, including transnational crime operations. As was evident during the Trump administration, powerholders may strategically select among emotions to reinforce multiple hierarchies of classification and signal their relationship to risk. These subjectivities are expressed alternatively through such sentiments as fear over empathy, discrimination over inclusion, and a sense of alienation rather than belonging. Thinking along these lines may shed light on what we could call the governmentality of centrifugal and centripetal movements and the creation and/or intensification of subjectivities.

Notes

I would like to thank the invaluable support of Gustavo Ramírez and Iván Martínez, my two research assistants sponsored by CONACYT, for collecting data and information for this research article, especially for establishing the tables and figures here included. I also would like to thank Melanie Slone for polishing and editing the manuscript. I am also grateful to Eric Hershberg and Tom Long for their insightful observations and comments after revising earlier drafts of this article. Their remarks were important for restructuring the sequence and logics of my arguments, and for clarifying some concepts that appeared confusing at the time. Needless to say, the final content of this article is my entire responsibility.

1. According to UNCTAD, MNCs already control 80 percent of global trade, in the form of exchanges between companies (parent companies to their subsidiaries and vice versa), either through contractual agreements with other MNCs or independent companies, or through the franchise and licensing system. It is estimated that trade in both goods and services (measured by gross exports) between parent companies and subsidiaries amounts to slightly less than 30 percent of the total, while slightly more than 50 percent is included in the second and third categories, that is, in the networks in which the MNC operates. Only the remaining 20 percent can be considered as trade outside the MNCs' networks (UNCTAD 2013, 138).

Bibliography

Andreas, P. 2003. *A Tale of Two Borders. The US-Canada and US-Mexico Lines after 9-11.* In *The Rebordering of North America*, edited by P. Andreas and T. J. Biersteker, 1–24. New York: Routledge.

Bensusán, G., and K. J. Middlebrook. 2020. "Cambio político desde afuera hacia adentro. Influencia comercial estadounidense y reforma de los derechos laborales en México." *Foro Internacional* 60 (3): 985–1039. https://doi.org/10.24201/fi.v60i3.2670.

Harari, Y. N. 2018. *21 lecciones para el siglo XXI.* Barcelona: Penguin Random House.

Hufbauer, C., and J. Schott. 2005. *NAFTA Revisited. Achievements and Challenges.* Washington, DC: Institute for International Economics.

Magerman, G., Z. Studnicka, and J. Van Hove. 2016. "Distance and Border Effects in International Trade: A Comparison of Estimation Methods." *Economics* 10 (2016–18): 1–31. http://dx.doi.org/10.5018/economics-ejournal.ja.2016-18.

Morales, I. 2008. *Post-NAFTA North America: Reshaping the Economic and Political Governance of a Changing Region.* New York: Palgrave-Macmillan.

Morales, I. 2011. *The Governance of Mobility and Risk in a Post-NAFTA Rebordered North America.* In *National Solutions to Trans-Border Problems? The Governance of Security and Risk in a Post-NAFTA North America,* edited by I. Morales, 65–94. Surrey, UK: Ashgate.

Morales, I. 2018. "NAFTA in a Comparative Perspective: A Debate on Trade Diplomacy, Economic Policy and Regionalism." *Oxford Research Encyclopedia of Politics.* doi:10.1093/acrefore/9780190228637.013.259.

Nye, J. S. 1968. Comparative Regional Integration: Concept and Measurement." *International Organization* 22 (4): 855–80.

Olayele, B. F. 2019. "Gravity, Borders, and Regionalism: A Canada–US Sub-National Analysis." *The International Trade Journal* 33 (5): 416–43. doi:10.1080/08853908.2019.1628675.

Parsley, D. C., and S. J. Wei. 2001. "Explaining the Border Effect: The Role of Exchange Rate, Variability, Shipping Costs, and Geography." *Journal of International Economics* 55: 87–105.

Pastor, R. 2001. *Toward a North American Community.* Washington, DC: Institute for International Economics.

Pastor, R. 2012. *La idea de América del Norte: Una visión de un futuro como continente.* Mexico City: ITAM/Porrúa.

Romero, M. 2018. "Trump's Immigration Attacks, in Brief." *Contexts* 17 (1): 34–41.

United States Bureau of Economic Analysis (USBEA). 2021. *US MNE Activities: Preliminary 2018 Statistics.* https://www.bea.gov/data/intl-trade-investment/international-trade-goods-and-services.

United States Bureau of Economic Analysis (USBEA). 2016. *US MNE Activities: Revised 2016 Statistics, All Affiliates and All Parents.* https://www.bea.gov/international/usdia2016r.

US Census Bureau. n.d. https://usatrade.census.gov.

United Nations Comtrade. n.d. https://comtrade.un.org/data.

United Nations Conference on Trade and Development (UNCTAD). 2013. *Global Value Chains: Investment and Trade for Development.* New York: World Investment Report.

Villarreal, A., B. Canis, and L. Wong. 2019. *USMCA: Motor Vehicle Provision and Issues.* Washington, DC: Congressional Research Service.

Villarreal, A., and C. Cimino-Isaacs. 2020. *USMCA: Labor Provisions.* Washington, DC: Congressional Research Service.

CHAPTER NINE

North America in Comparative Perspective

Regional Cooperation Dynamics in the Western Hemisphere
and the World

Diana Panke and Sören Stapel

Introduction

AFTER THE end of World War II, regionalism has become an integral part of
governance beyond the nation-state in all parts of the globe. P. J. Katzenstein
(2005) as well as A. Acharya (2014) have convincingly made the case that we
live in a world of regions. Regionalism has many faces. While most chapters of
this book focus on informal institutions and processes, this chapter adopts a
different lens and examines formal institutions. Thus, the regionalism this chapter is interested in is the institutionalized cooperation of three or more states
in regional organizations (ROs). ROs differ from international organizations as
states can only accede to them if they fulfil a specific geographic criterion (Panke
et al. 2020). Over the last decades, the number of ROs has increased significantly
in all parts of the globe and their role and impact have drastically changed as
well (e.g., Acharya 2012; Börzel and Risse 2016; Hooghe et al. 2019; Selleslaghs
and Van Langenhove 2020). While formal regional organizations may not capture all aspects of what makes a region, they are an important expression of
regionalism as they facilitate the day-to-day cooperation of member states across
a broad variety of policy areas. While our emphasis on formal organizational
membership and competencies differs from the conceptualizations of regions
and regionalism employed in many other chapters in this volume, it allows for a
comparative study of institutionalized formal cooperation between states within
and across regions as well as over time.

Scholarship on regional integration and comparative regionalism has
evolved in multiple waves (Söderbaum 2016a; Panke 2017). Early integration
scholars predominantly studied why and under which conditions states create regional organizations (Deutsch et al. 1957; Haas 1964; Lindberg 1963). A
second wave of regional cooperation scholarship focused on dynamics driving
the development and evolution of regional organizations (Haas and Schmitter

1964; Nye 1968; Schmitter 1970; Feng and Genna 2003). Subsequently, scholars turned toward studying the interaction between state and regional levels, focusing on how regional policies are made (Moravcsik 1998; Thomson and Hosli 2006) and how regional organizations (RO) impact their member states (Börzel and Risse 2000; Morales 2002; Aspinwall 2009). Scholars working on comparative regionalism have pointed out that regional cooperation in ROs is not confined to Europe but takes place all over the globe (Fawcett 2004; Breslin et al. 2013; Börzel and Risse 2016; Söderbaum 2016b). We add to this perspective by avoiding a European Union (EU) bias through focusing on formal institutions and comparing North American ROs to the more than seventy existing ROs within and across the different regions of the world.

This chapter examines North American regionalism in comparison to developments in South America as well as other parts of the world. After introducing the Regional Organization Competencies dataset (ROCO) in a first step, the chapter uses two analytical dimensions, RO size and RO policy scope, to create a typology of ROs that distinguishes between large encompassing, large selective, small encompassing, and small selective ROs. This typology helps to investigate the dynamism of (North) American regionalism by focusing on the North American Free Trade Agreement (NAFTA) and its successor, the United States–Mexico–Canada Agreement (USMCA).[1] We proceed to put these developments into a comparative perspective with respect to the Americas and three other regions: Africa, Asia and Europe. This reveals that the development and change of regional cooperation outlets has been more vibrant in South America, Africa, Asia, and Europe than in North America.[2] The number of ROs created and the diversity of ROs is higher in the other regions, and their ROs often increase in size or policy scope over time. This does not apply to North America. There has been only a single change over time, the replacement of NAFTA by its successor, the USMCA, and both are very similarly limited with respect to membership composition and policy scope. However, the lack of dynamism in formal ROs in North America, as one notion of regionalism, does not inhibit high functional interdependence, informal governance, and high regionalization between concerned states (Börzel and Risse 2019; Hershberg and Long, this volume). At the same time, there are a number of ROs similar to the North American regional project, which suggests that these ROs are important to the broader field of comparative regionalism and therefore deserve more attention than is commonly attributed to them.

NORTH AMERICA IN COMPARATIVE PERSPECTIVE

The ROCO Database

To identify the universe of cases, the starting point for the ROCO dataset is the definition of a RO: They are institutions (with a set of primary rules, and headquarters or
a secretariat) in which at least three states cooperate with one another in more than one
specific issue (Panke et al. 2020). Unlike international organizations (IOs), however,
the membership in ROs is based on geographical criteria, such as belonging to the
same constructed region or the same geographical area, or being located in geographical proximity. We regard ROs as single entities if they have common institutions,
membership, and a common headquarters or secretariat (Panke et al. 2020). Similarly,
we treat all predecessors and successors as one RO.[3] Hence, the ROCO dataset covers
a total seventy-three ROs between 1945 to 2020 for which primary law sources were
available. Taking into account the United Nations (UN)'s definition of geographic
regions (UNSD 2019), we are able to assign the ROs to particular regions based on the
location of headquarter offices or main secretariats. This accumulates to sixteen of the
ROs in the Americas, twenty-two in Africa, nineteen in Asia, and sixteen in Europe.

The ROCO dataset entails all ROs from their creation to their dissolution. For
the former, we coded the founding year of ROs as the year when the founding treaty
or another founding document was agreed upon by member states and signed, not the
year of full ratification, the entry into force of the treaty, or the year when ROs started
operating.[4] Four ROs were dissolved during the period of observation: the Arab
Cooperation Council (ACC) (1989–1990), Organization of Central American States
(ODECA) (1951–1973), Southeast Asia Treaty Organization (SEATO) (1954–1977),
and Warsaw Treaty Organization (WTO) (1955–1991).

For each RO and year of its existence, the ROCO dataset provides information on
policy competencies and member states of each RO. RO size and RO policy competency are important for the operation of ROs. The latter define in which areas an RO
can possibly pass or enact policies, laws, norms, and regulations, and the former defines
which states can participate in formulating these policies and are affected by them.

The member state information has been collected from treaties, home pages, and
secondary literature. The policy competencies that ROs are equipped with form the
basis of which ROs can get active in their day-to-day operation and were hand-coded
on the basis of RO primary law (founding treaties, treaty changes).[5] ROs' policy competencies may include mandates for the creation of secondary and soft law, instruments
allowing collective actions of RO members, or tools permitting other activities of ROs.
We differentiate between eleven policy areas (agriculture, development, economy and
trade, energy, environment, finance, good governance, health, migration, security, and
defense as well as technology, infrastructure, and science). In each of the policy fields,
we coded between fourteen and seventeen specific policy competencies for the internal and the external realm, respectively.[6]

The Typology

In order to capture regional dynamism in a comparative perspective, we use a two-dimensional typology that differentiates between RO size and RO policy scope. These two fundamental dimensions are meaningful because they determine what the ROs can do in their day-to-day operations and who benefits from these activities (see Panke et al. 2020). When using the mean values for the year 2020 as thresholds, this leads to four different types, namely large encompassing, large selective, small encompassing, and small selective ROs.

Large encompassing ROs have forty-eight or more competencies as well as fourteen or more member states. Thus, they are legally in a position to act in a large array of different policy domains, the potential benefits of which affect a high number of member states at once. On the one hand, these ROs may struggle to reach agreement due to the high number of member states; on the other, the high number of policy competencies might allow for issue linkages and package deals. Hence, these ROs are well positioned to act and pass policy decisions in their day-to-day operation.

Large selective ROs are characterized by also having at least fourteen members, but they are equipped with fewer than forty-eight competencies and can therefore only become active in a smaller range of policy issues vis-à-vis a large membership. Compared to ROs with encompassing policy scopes, selective ROs are less suited to facilitate package deals that use linkages to overcome potential stalemates among member states in RO decision-making. Compared to all other types, these ROs are expected to be least active in producing policy outputs or acting on RO decisions.

Small encompassing ROs combine two advantages. Due to their small number of member states (thirteen or fewer), there are fewer chances for delayed decision-making and deadlock, and even if such difficulties arise, their large policy scope provides ample opportunities for issue linkages. Hence, ROs belonging to this type should be in the best position to effectively arrive at collective decisions and act upon them.

Small selective ROs are composed of fewer than fourteen members and have fewer policy competencies (less than forty-eight). Thus, their activities tend to be more concentrated with respect to the policies covered and focus only on a small set of states. Again, decision-making between a limited number of states is likely to be smoother than for large ROs. Yet, should conflict among the member states emerge, the selective policy scope allows only for a limited range of package deals.[7] Taken together, similar to large encompassing ROs, small selective ROs can be expected to be in a good position to get active and pass outcomes in their day-to-day operation.

The Dynamism of North American Regionalism: NAFTA and USMCA

North America has been home to only two organizations, the North American Free Trade Agreement (NAFTA) and its successor the United States–Mexico–Canada Agreement (USMCA). In addition to both agreements, the Organization of American States (OAS) also has its headquarters in North America but is a hemispheric organization, encompassing all states in the Western Hemisphere except for Cuba, which has been suspended (Herz 2011). North American states are also members of the North Atlantic Treaty Organization (NATO; United States and Canada), the Organization for Security and Cooperation in Europe (OSCE; United States and Canada), and the Arctic Council (AC; United States and Canada); but all three organizations have their headquarters in European countries and therefore cannot be regarded as North American.

NAFTA was created by Canada, Mexico, and the United States in 1992 and became operative two years later. Since then, no additional state joined, and NAFTA remained small in size. A glance at its treaties reveals that its policy scope was encompassing as NAFTA was equipped with sixty-seven different policy competencies (Milner 1995; Abbott 2000; Duina 2006). At the heart of the agreement, NAFTA mainly encompasses competencies in the trade and economy fields (for instance, eighteen competencies in economy and trade as well as fourteen competencies related to technology, infrastructure, and science). Scholars also frequently note that NAFTA includes a range of environmental and labor standards through two side agreements— the North American Agreement on Environmental Cooperation and the North American Agreement on Labor Cooperation. Moreover, the agreement addresses a variety of competencies in other policy fields. In fact, as the ROCO dataset reveals, NAFTA has competencies in all of the eleven different policy fields (Panke et al. 2020), including energy (Stevens, this volume), agriculture, health, security (Kloppe-Santamaría, this volume), good governance (Duina 2015; Stapel 2022), and migration (Gabriel and Macdonald 2021; Castañeda et al., this volume). However, neither the membership composition nor the policy scope of NAFTA was modified once it was established, and the agreement was never followed up by new initiatives that would have cemented a more ambitious regional agenda (see also Bow and Anderson 2015; Hershberg and Long, this volume).[8]

Criticism and skepticism have been continuously voiced toward NAFTA, inter alia, for not adequately addressing and improving environmental and labor issues or for not meeting expectations about the economic impact (e.g., by the Clinton and Obama campaigns during the 2008 US presidential primaries or by Mexico's eventual president López Obrador [Bow 2012]). Most prominently, the Trump presidential campaign launched a harsh attack on NAFTA during the 2016 presidential election cycle. Upon taking office the Trump administration pushed for changes. On May 18, 2017, the US trade representative Ambassador Robert Lighthizer sent the ninety-day notification to Congress of its intent to begin talks with Canada and Mexico to renegotiate NAFTA. Following several rounds of negotiations, more than a year later, negotiations concluded with the formal dissolution of NAFTA and its replacement by a successor (Ouellet and Messier 2017; Lester and Manak 2018). Once the agreement was disbanded, USMCA came into being in July 2020.

The USMCA is also a small encompassing RO. Like NAFTA, its membership remains limited to Canada, Mexico and the United States. Its policy scope is also similar to NAFTA's. Yet the negotiators added competencies, and the UMSCA now includes ninety individual competencies in all eleven policy fields, according to the ROCO database. Again, the core mandate relates to economic cooperation: economy and trade (twenty-four competencies), technology, infrastructure, and science (sixteen competencies), as well as agriculture (nine competencies). However, the UMSCA updates and broadens parts of the previous agreement. For instance, UMSCA substantially updated and specified clauses regarding the automotive sector, and it now includes separate chapters on textiles and apparel (chapter 6) and digital trade (chapter 19). Despite these new competencies, vast similarities to the original NAFTA persist, and the USMCA has been referred to as NAFTA 2.0 (e.g., Hadfield and Potter 2017).

In addition to economic cooperation, the agreement ventures into ancillary cooperation areas. Therefore, we see an increase in competencies in some policy fields (environment, good governance, health) or a similar policy mandate as in NAFTA (development, finance, and migration as well as security and defense). First, in line with contemporary US practice, the USMCA makes environmental issues integral to the agreement (chapter 23). However, as N. Laurens et al. (2019) note, the USMCA mainly replicates environmental provisions from other recent agreements, without introducing unprecedented environmental competencies. It is particularly noteworthy that the agreement does not include competencies related to the adaptation to and mitigation of climate change. Second, the previous side agreement on labor has also become core part of the agreement and has also been expanded (chapter 24). The policy field of good governance includes eight competencies, such as anti-corruption, labor discrimination, transparency, and accountability. Third, the health area equally has been broadened, for instance by addressing the health sector in general or medical drugs. Finally, the mandate in the remaining policy areas remain similar (development, finance, migration as well as security and defense).[9]

Over the last three decades, then, North American regionalism has not been very dynamic in character. There has been only one organizational change over time, the replacement of NAFTA with the similar USMCA. The two ROs have the same member states, and most policy competencies were carried forward from NAFTA to USMCA. Given that NAFTA has not experienced any changes over the twenty-five years of its existence, the UMSCA has updated, specified, and, in a few areas, broadened provisions of the predecessor agreement—with regard to both the economic core of the agreement (particularly regarding the automotive sector, digital trade) as well as the remaining issue areas (environment, good governance, health).

Comparing North America to the Rest of the Continent

Regionalism in North America is not as pronounced as in the rest of the Western Hemisphere and in other regions. Comparing regionalisms in North America and South America reveals that the latter is far more dynamic than the former. Many more ROs are headquartered in South America than in North America, and these South American organizations have changed their membership compositions and policy scopes more frequently. In other words: Beyond the hemispheric OAS, regionalism in the Western Hemisphere clusters in South America with a total of fourteen ROs, whereas there is a single North American counterpart (for a similar conclusion, cf. Santa-Cruz, this volume).

Regionalism in the North started after the end of the Cold War. By contrast, Southern American regionalism was ignited much earlier. Following its historic antecedents in the International Conferences of American States and the Pan-American Union in the late nineteenth and early twentieth century, the Organization of American States (OAS) was created in 1948 (cf. LeBlanc 1977; Herz 2011; Long 2020). The first wave of regionalism in the Americas started in the 1950s when a group of additional ROs came into being. In 1951, the Organization of Central American States (ODECA) was established (Keller 1963), followed by the Latin American Free Trade Association (1960), which was the predecessor of the Latin American Integration Association (ALADI) (Hurrell 1995). Also in 1960, the Central American Common Market (CACM) was established (Bulmer-Thomas 1998), followed by the Caribbean Free Trade Association in 1965, which later became the Caribbean Community (CARICOM), and the Andean Community in 1969 (Heine 2012; Prieto 2020).

The dynamism of South American regionalism slowed down in the late 1970s and 1980s. In this period, the Latin American Economic System (SELA) and the Organization of Eastern Caribbean States (OECS) were formed (Bond 1978). The 1990s marked the beginning of a second wave of American regionalism with an upsurge of new ROs in close succession (Wionczek 1970; Panke et al. 2020). In 1991, the Central American Integration System (SICA) was created, followed by the Association of Caribbean States (ACS), the Mercado Común del Sur (Mercosur), and the Amazonian Cooperation Treaty (ACTO) (Landau 1980; Ware 1980; Gómez-Mera 2013). At the same time, the OAS was reformed and strengthened as well.

The dynamism of South American regionalism paused once more, and was restarted during the 2000s (Sánchez 2010). In 2004, the Bolivarian Alliance for the Peoples of Our America (ALBA) was created, followed by the Union of South American Nations (UNASUR) in 2008 and the Community of Latin American and Caribbean States (CELAC) in 2011 (Nolte and Wehner 2013; Weiffen et al. 2013; Riggirozzi and Grugel 2015; Franko 2018).

Hemispheric regionalism was dynamic over time, leading to a considerable increase in the number of ROs (Genna and Hiroi 2004). At the same time, ROs were abolished.

The Central American ODECA was disbanded in 1973 and thus put the regional cooperation of the respective member states to an end, at least temporarily. Formally, NAFTA was dissolved in the summer of 2020 as well, but was immediately replaced by USMCA so that the cooperation between the former NAFTA members continued.

Applying the distinction between four types of ROs to the Americas illustrates interesting differences. North American regionalism is exclusively based on small encompassing ROs. This type of RO can be regarded as being well suited to efficiently operate in practice: Due to their limited number of member states and their broad policy scopes, the ROs are positioned to speedy decision-making and opportunities to overcome deadlocks in their internal operation.

Applying the RO typology to regionalism in the Western Hemisphere, it becomes apparent that regionalism is more diverse in South America. ROs are not all small encompassing in nature in 2020. First, the ACS, CELAC, and SELA are large selective ROs, and thus can be expected to face the greatest challenges in their day-to-day operation based on the membership and policy scope dimensions. High numbers of national positions have to be accommodated at the negotiation table while there are limited opportunities for issue linkages to overcome dissent. Second, the Caribbean Community (CARICOM) and the OAS are the only two large encompassing ROs. While the OAS is a continental RO with thirty-four member states, CARICOM brings together fifteen member states despite its more limited geographical scope. Third, the Andean Community, ACTO, CACM, Mercosur, and ALADI belong to the small selective type, combining few member states with limited scopes of policy competencies. Both types of ROs are expected to function better than large selective ROs, under ceteris paribus conditions. Finally, in addition to NAFTA/USMCA, several small encompassing ROs (ALBA, OECS, SICA, and UNASUR) can also be expected to face limited dissent and many chances to overcome difficulties—should they arise—through package deals in day-to-day intergovernmental negotiations.[10]

We have seen that North American regionalism does not exhibit the dynamism of regional cooperation in the wider continent. Unlike the North, regional cooperation in the South started earlier and takes place in more ROs that represent all four types of ROs. Why does North American regionalism differ in these respects? Several factors are at play. First, with the United States, Canada, and Mexico, the number of states is more limited in the North than in the rest of the Americas (thirty-two), lending itself to informal or ad hoc bilateral cooperation in the North. Thus, the demand for cooperating in several different ROs with different membership constellations and different policy foci is more limited in the North than in the South. Second, NAFTA/USMCA is a small encompassing and not a small selective RO. Thus, it already covers a broad array of policy competencies and provides plenty of opportunities for cooperation for its member states—even without further treaty changes in the RO enlarging its policy scope. Third, since it is equipped with an encompassing policy scope, the member states of NAFTA/USMCA are unlikely to face much demand for creating new, additional venues for cooperation between themselves. Another reason for limited proliferation of North American ROs outside the economic realm is that bilateralism between North American states is a flexible alternative to long-term and potentially costly cooperation in ROs.

Moreover, analyzing regionalism in the Americas would be incomplete if regional complexities were disregarded (Dabène 2009; Riggirozzi and Tussie 2012; Malamud 2019). First, when NAFTA was created in 1992, there were already a number of ROs in place in the Western Hemisphere. For instance, the OAS already covered regional political and security affairs, so that Canada, Mexico, and the United States could address these issues within an institutional framework. Yet economic and trade issues were not explicitly covered at the time, allowing NAFTA to fill this gap. Second, in the Western Hemisphere, overlapping regionalism proliferated early and now forms an important feature of regional dynamism (Weiffen et al. 2013; Nolte 2014; Nolte 2018). Overlapping regionalism is characterized by two ROs sharing one or more member states while also being equipped with one or more identical policy competencies (Panke and Stapel 2018; Panke and Stapel 2018b). In 2020, NAFTA overlaps with the AC, the ACS, ALADI, the Asia-Pacific Economic Cooperation (APEC), CELAC, OAS, OSCE, SELA, and the Pacific Community (SPC). Given that NAFTA/ USMCA member states have joined or created other ROs and other free trade agreements (FTAs) (Dür et al. 2014) so that they can cooperate with additional states and do so in additional policy issues not already covered by NAFTA, it is not surprising that the United States, Canada, and Mexico have not created a purely North American RO to this end. In fact, overlapping regionalism might be a fourth reason why North American regionalism has not proliferated as strongly as regionalism in the South.

Comparing North American Regionalism to the Rest of the World

While South American ROs cover all four types, North American regionalism is characterized by small encompassing ROs only. This section examines how prevalent this type of RO is elsewhere and discusses similarities and differences between ROs of this type.

In 2020, a total of sixty-eight different ROs were operating in different parts of the world. Of those, seventeen ROs are small encompassing in character (see figure 9.1).[11] In the Americas, these are ALBA, OECS, SICA, and UNASUR as well as NAFTA/ USMCA. Thus, the Americas is the region with the highest number of ROs of the small encompassing type. By contrast, in Asia, small encompassing ROs are less prevalent as there are only three: the Association of Southeast Asian Nations (ASEAN), the Gulf Cooperation Council (GCC), and the Shanghai Cooperation Organization (SCO). In Africa, the Communauté Economique des États de l'Afrique Centrale (CEEAC), the East African Community (EAC), the International Conference on the Great Lakes Region (ICGLR), and the Intergovernmental Authority on Development (IGAD)—as well as the West African Economic and Monetary Union (UEMOA)—are small in size and are equipped with an encompassing scope of policy competencies. Finally, there are four small encompassing ROs in Europe: the AC, the Commonwealth of Independent States (CIS), the Eurasian Economic Union (EAEU), and the Organization for Democracy and Economic Development (GUAM). The growth of ROs started already in the 1940s, but initially most were small and selective in character, thus being located in the lower left quadrant of the typology (see figure 9.1). Afterward, additional ROs in all regions of the world moved from the lower left quadrant upward (member state accession), rightward (policy scope expansion), or both (new member states and more policy competencies) through mandate expansion and membership enlargement.

Small encompassing ROs emerged for the very first time in 1986, when the Pacific Islands Forum (PIF) changed its primary law and increased its policy scope (Tarte 2014). Over time, this quadrant became incrementally populated leading to a total of seventeen small encompassing ROs. Next to NAFTA, only the EAC and ICGLR were founded as small encompassing ROs (in 1999 and 2004, respectively). All other ROs of this type moved from the small selective type toward the small encompassing one over time. The GCC, ASEAN, SCO, ALBA, SICA, OECS, IGAD, AC, CIS, EAEU, UNASUR, and GUAM experienced changes in primary law, and they all were equipped with additional policy competencies. This reflects a global trend. Over time, the average number of policy competencies of ROs increased from 13.5 in 1950, to 19.6 in 1970, and to 24.4 in 1990. In 2010, the average RO covers 45.5 different policy competencies., which is driven by member state interests and capacities (Panke 2020).

At the same time, the concerned ROs did not increase their membership size considerably over time. Several organizations admitted a limited number of new member states (for instance, ASEAN, EAC, and EAEU). These enlargements did not reach the threshold of larger ROs, and therefore they did not move further upward into the quadrant of large encompassing ROs. Yet, on average, ROs in all regions of the world tended to increase in size over the last decades. While the average RO had 9.7 member states in 1950, this slightly decreased to 9.1 in 1970, and afterward increased to 11.3 in 1990 and to 12.9 in 2010.

Small encompassing ROs as a type of RO have advantages over the three other types—based on the two constituting dimensions. They are small in size and the heterogeneity of interest at the negotiation table should, ceteris paribus, be lower than in ROs with more member states (Panke and Starkmann 2020). This should allow for speedy decision-making. In addition, the encompassing policy scope provides ample chances to engage in the upgrading of common interests through issue linkages and package deals that could be used to minimize dissent and avoid political stalemates. Thus, small encompassing ROs are well suited to operate effectively internally and produce policy outputs or activity decisions. While comparative data on output,

RO size

• OSCE

• AU

• CoE

• CELAC
• NATO
• SELA
• ACS   • CICA

• OAS
• ACD

• CENSAD   • EU

• IORA   • AL   • COMESA

• CEI   • APEC
• SPC • CAEU   • SADC   CARICOM   • ECOWAS
                                                      • PIF

BSEC • • ALADI   CEEAC   ALBA
• CAREC   ASEAN • •ICGLR   • CIS
ACTO • GGCSAARC • ECO UEMOA   IGAD
LCBC •   CEFTA MGC • BIMSTEC • SCO • •AC   • SICA
CF • CACM   •   MERCOSUR• GCC • OECS   • EAEU
MRU •   • • •NC • AMU •ANDEAN   • EAC
           CEPGL   MSG   BEU   UNASUR • GUAM • NAFTA • USMCA

RO policy scope

0   50   100   150

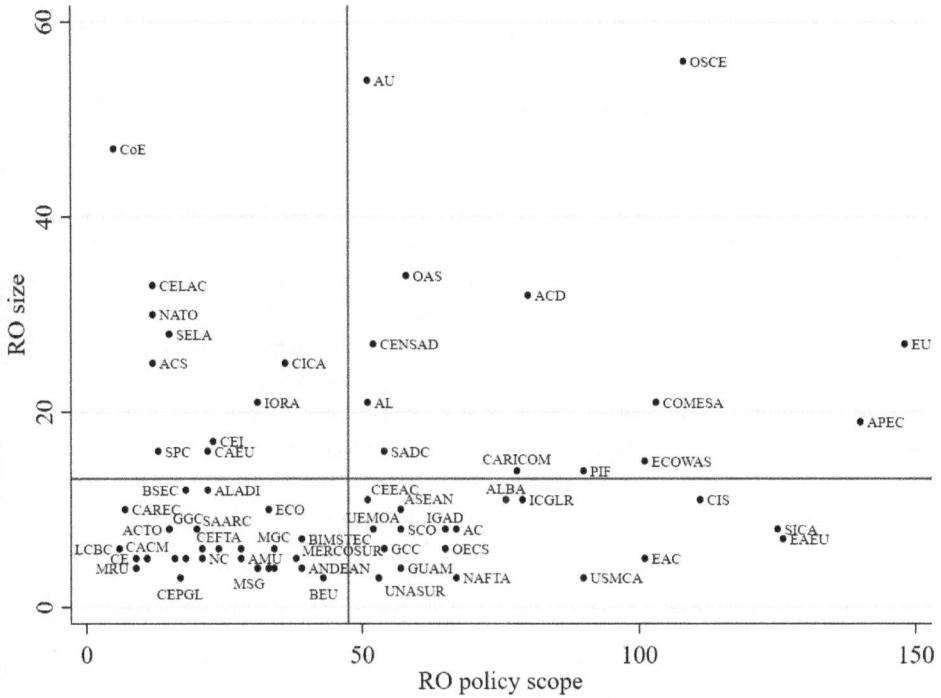

Figure 9.1. RO Policy Scope.

outcome, and impact performance of ROs is not available, their endurance might be regarded as one indication for functioning to the satisfaction of their respective member states or at least not running counter to core interests of their members.

Yet, of the seventeen ROs in the small encompassing type, three ROs were replaced by successors, which is puzzling at first glance. In addition to NAFTA's replacement by USMCA in 2020, IGADD transitioned to IGAD in 1996 and the EAEU replaced EurAsEC in 2014. The change in IGAD was linked to a reorientation from developmental concerns toward security issues in the Horn of Africa (Henneberg and Stapel 2020). EAEU replaced EurAsEC due to their members' aspiration to further deepen the economic integration project (Roberts and Moshes 2016; Vinokurov and Libman 2017). Thus, in both instances, these small encompassing ROs were replaced by successor ROs—rather than being simply disbanded without replacement—to provide an arena for the future continuation of cooperation of their member states.

Was NAFTA in 2020 replaced by USMCA due to malfunctioning, or were other reasons driving this development? While NAFTA has been criticized by some, for instance concerning its limited achievements in the environmental realm (Ederington 2007), its performance within its designated issue areas has mainly been evaluated in positive terms (Chambers and Smith 2002; Hufbauer and Schott 2005; Aspinwall 2009; Mzumara et al. 2012; Long 2015). This suggests that NAFTA was not an ineffective RO subject to internal hurdles and political stalemates, and was not substituted by USMCA for that reason. Rather, criticism came from one camp at a time of electoral competition and in the context of increasing populism (Ouellet and Messier 2017; Lester and Manak 2018; Boucher and Thies 2019; Söderbaum and Spandler 2021), as harsh critics and even moderate conservatives prepared the ground through various attacks on the North American regional project over the years (Macdonald 2020). President Trump labeled NAFTA as being "perhaps the worst trade deal ever made" (Trump 2018, cited in Marcoux 2019) and pursued the replacement of NAFTA by USMCA (von Borzyskowski and Vabulas 2019). Eventually, the Trump administration succeeded to substitute the USMCA, as a result of United States' populist trade policy (Lester and Manak 2018; Copelovitch and Pevehouse 2019).

Conclusions

Governance beyond the nation-state is no longer exclusively taking place in IOs and international regimes, but also in ROs. Today they cover policy areas well beyond market creation, the enhancement of interstate trade, or regional security. At the same time, the complexity of regionalism has increased, leading to a large body of research. While individual ROs are often in the limelight of scholarly interest, comparative studies have long been rare. This chapter adopts comparative lenses. It reflects upon the dynamism of North American regionalism in relation to developments in the wider Western Hemisphere and around the globe.

The major findings are first that regionalism in North America has taken an exceptional route when being compared to the South. South American regionalism is highly dynamic in nature as ROs were created in multiple waves accumulating to a total of eighteen. In contrast, North American regionalism has one and only one outlet: NAFTA and its successor USMCA. Moreover, while NAFTA and USMCA are both small encompassing in nature, South American ROs are much more diverse, as there are ROs resembling the small selective type (e.g., Mercosur), the small encompassing type (e.g., OECS), the large selective type (e.g., CELAC), and the large encompassing type (e.g., CARICOM). Apart from these descriptive insights, this section also delved into the question of why North American regionalism differs from the dynamics observed in the South. We argue that this is not only due to differences in the number of countries, but also to the fact that the United States, Canada, and Mexico were in no need to create additional North American ROs, as NAFTA/USMCA has been encompassing in nature from the start, thus enabling its member states to cooperate in a broad array of economy- and trade-related policy issues. In addition, bilateral ad hoc cooperation in other policy areas proved as an effective instrument for North American states, reducing the demand for the creation of new additional ROs.

Second, comparing North American regionalism to regionalisms in other parts of the world, it becomes apparent that many ROs in Africa, Asia, and Europe were initially small selective in character, but underwent changes over time. Thus, ROs turned into large selective ROs, when being subject to enlargements without significantly broadening their scopes of policy competencies. Also, many of the initial small selective ROs became small encompassing ROs after changing their primary laws to add new policy competencies without admitting high numbers of new member states (or none at all). Small encompassing ROs have advantages over the other RO types since they are likely to pass decisions quickly due to their small size and since they are likely to overcome internal dissent due to issue linkages and package deals made possible by their broad policy scopes. Yet NAFTA was disbanded despite being a small encompassing RO. This was not due to slow decision-making and political stalemates, but mainly a result of the Trump administration's populist trade policy. However, USMCA has such a similar setup that it is often referred to as NAFTA 2.0. Thus, USMCA is not a turning point in the dynamics of North American regionalism but a continuation.

Notes

We would like to thank Tom Long and Eric Hershberg for their constructive comments on earlier versions of this chapter. Also, we are indebted to Nikolay Aleksiev, Ikram Ali, Lea Gerhard, Clara Hirschmann, Laura Lepsy, Laura Maghetiu, Paul Meiners, Leonardo Rey, Benjamin Schäfer, Edward Vaughan, Philipp Wagenhals, and Ivan Zolotarevskii who helped with coding RO primary law under the guidance of Anna Starkmann. We acknowledge the generous financial support by the German Research Council (DFG, grant number PA 1257/7-1; 421167407).

1. Each country is entitled to position itself first when referencing the agreement, hence it also is referred to as the CUSMA (in Canada) and the T-MEC (in Mexico).

2. Dynamism of regional cooperation as reflected in the growing number of ROs, their expanding membership and policy scopes, in a particular region is neither indicative of higher output of ROs, nor the opposite. In fact, the relationship between RO dynamism and RO outputs is orthogonal in principle. There might be regions and time periods when states unsatisfied with current RO outputs create new ROs, join other ROs, or expand RO policy scopes. Likewise, in other time periods or regions, the success of ROs in terms of outputs can spark even more dynamism, as states create additional ROs or join ROs in order to further cooperate with additional states, or foster additional cooperation by expanding the scope of policy competencies of existing ROs.

3. One special case concerns ODECA and the Central American Integration System (SICA). They are coded as two separate ROs. Both ROs have been important for the Central American regional integration process, but ODECA was suspended in 1973 and SICA was newly created in 1991.

4. Some special cases need to be noted (cf. Panke et al. 2020). Some ROs developed out of multilateral treaties. While these treaties did not constitute organizations, ROs were later created by introducing an institutional framework, headquarters/secretariat, and/or specifying geographical membership criteria. In these instances, the year of the introduction of the new rules was coded as founding year for the RO. If the original multilateral treaty had defined policy competencies, these competencies were included in the dataset but were coded for the founding year (and not the actual year of transfer). This applies to the Amazonian Cooperation Treaty Organization (ACTO) and the Mercado Común del Sur (Mercosur). The ACTO was founded in 1995 when an organization was established following the 1978 Amazon Cooperation Treaty, and thus policy competencies from the 1978 treaty were coded for the year 1995. Likewise, Mercosur was established in 1994, and competencies of the 1991 Treaty of Asuncion are included for the founding year.

5. Primary law functions as the legal basis for ROs to act, as it defines the institutional setup of ROs as well as the policy fields in which they can become active (e.g., through passing secondary law, rules, norms, or decisions to engage in joint actions).

6. External policy competencies turn the RO and its member states into actors beyond their borders, while internal policy competencies allow ROs and their member states to create common rules and norms within their borders. The ROCO dataset entails a total of 344 policy competencies, 172 internal and 172 external policy competencies. The distinction between internal and external policy competencies is based on the context of application. Terms such as external, international, with international/regional organizations, third states, other states, and/or with regimes in combination with a policy competency are indicative of an external policy competency. Phrases including between member states/members, within, internal, local, domestic, national, contracting parties, or intraregional signify an internal policy competency (cf. Panke et al. 2020).

7. ROs can also engage with the outside world. Powerful ROs can use their competencies and ability to act as a leverage vis-à-vis third-party states or other ROs. Thereby they can engage in issue linkages. NAFTA, for instance, can use trade to put pressure on outside actors to address migration, organized crime, or drug trafficking.

8. Yet, similar to other active trade-related ROs, such as the EU, NAFTA has opted for bilateral and trilateral agreements with third-party states and other ROs.

9. In addition to the policy scope expansion in the USMCA, notable changes also addressed the internal dispute settlement procedures. While chapter 10 keeps dispute settlement among the three parties, negotiators revised and scaled back the

investor-state dispute settlement (ISDS) procedures in chapter 14 (which replaces chapter 11 of NAFTA). Investor-state arbitration henceforth is limited to the United States and Mexico, while Canada withdrew from ISDS entirely. Moreover, chapter 14 of USMCA also makes important changes compared to its predecessor, such as fewer treaty protections enforceable through ISDS and heightened pre-conditions to arbitrate (Condon 2019; Garcia-Barragan et al. 2019).

10. Yet ROs cannot endure as active and vibrant organizations without the permissive consensus of their members. UNASUR and ALBA are two ROs in which leading states withdrew support, leading to a decline or de facto collapse of these organizations.

11. Figure 9.1 also shows that most ROs are small selective in character (twenty-eight), followed by large encompassing ROs (eighteen). The least frequent type of RO is the large selective one (ten ROs).

Bibliography

Abbott, F. M. 2000. "NAFTA and the Legalization of World Politics: A Case Study." *International Organization* 54 (3): 519–47.

Acharya, A. 2012. "Comparative Regionalism: A Field Whose Time Has Come?" *The International Spectator* 47 (1): 3–15.

Acharya, A. 2014. *The End of American World Order*. Cambridge: Polity Press.

Aspinwall, M. 2009. "NAFTA-ization: Regionalization and Domestic Political Adjustment in the North American Economic Area." *Journal of Common Market Studies* 47 (1): 1–24.

Bond, R. D. 1978. "Regionalism in Latin America: Prospects for the Latin American Economic System (SELA)." *International Organization* 32 (2): 401–23.

Börzel, T. A., and T. Risse. 2000. "When Europe Hits Home: Europeanization and Domestic Change." *European Integration On-line Papers* 4 (15). https://papers.ssrn.com/sol3/papers.cfm?abstract_id=302768.

Börzel, T. A., and T. Risse, eds. 2016. *The Oxford Handbook of Comparative Regionalism*. Oxford: Oxford University Press.

Börzel, T. A., and T. Risse. 2019. "Grand Theories of Integration and the Challenges of Comparative Regionalism." *Journal of European Public Policy* 26 (8): 1231–52.

Boucher, J.-C., and C. G. Thies. 2019. "'I Am a Tariff Man': The Power of Populist Foreign Policy Rhetoric under President Trump." *The Journal of Politics* 81 (2): 712–22.

Bow, B. 2012. "Immovable Object or Unstoppable Force? Economic Crisis and the Social Construction of North America." In *North America in Question: Regional Integration in an Era of Economic Turbulence*, edited by J. Ayres and L. Macdonald, 53–84. Toronto: University of Toronto Press.

Bow, B., and G. Anderson, eds. 2015. *Regional Governance in Post-NAFTA North America: Building without Architecture.* London: Routledge.

Breslin, S., C. W. Hughes, N. Phillips, and B. Rosamond, eds. 2013. *New Regionalism in the Global Political Economy: Theories and Cases.* London: Routledge.

Bulmer-Thomas, V. 1998. "The Central American Common Market: From Closed to Open Regionalism." *World Development* 26 (2): 313–22.

Chambers, E. J., and P. H. Smith. 2002. *NAFTA in the New Millennium.* Boulder, CO: Lynne Rienner Publishers.

Condon, B. J. 2019. "From NAFTA to USMCA: Two's Company, Three's a Crowd." *Latin American Journal of Trade Policy* 1 (2): 30–48.

Copelovitch, M., and J. C. W. Pevehouse. 2019. "International Organizations in a New Era of Populist Nationalism." *The Review of International Organizations* 14 (2): 169–86.

Dabène, O. 2009. *The Politics of Regional Integration in Latin America: Theoretical and Comparative Explorations.* London: Springer.

Deutsch, K. W., S. A. Burrell, and R. A. Kann. 1957. *Political Community and the North Atlantic Area: International Organization in the Light of Historical Experience.* Princeton, NJ: Princeton University Press.

Duina, F. 2015. "Beyond Free Trade: Accounting for Labor and Environmental Governance Standards in NAFTA." In *Governance Transfer by Regional Organizations. Patching Together a Global Script,* edited by T. A. Börzel and V. van Hüllen, 177–91. Houndmills, UK: Palgrave Macmillan.

Duina, F. G. 2006. *The Social Construction of Free Trade: The European Union, NAFTA, and Mercosur.* Princeton, NJ: Princeton University Press.

Dür, A., L. Baccini, and M. Elsig. 2014. "The Design of International Trade Agreements: Introducing a New Dataset." *The Review of International Organizations* 9 (3): 353–75.

Ederington, J. 2007. "NAFTA and the Pollution Haven Hypothesis." *Policy Studies Journal* 35 (2): 239–44.

Fawcett, L. 2004. "Exploring Regional Domains: A Comparative History of Regionalism." *International Affairs* 80 (3): 429–46.

Feng, Y., and G. Genna. 2003. "Regional Integration and Domestic Institutional Homogeneity: A Comparative Analysis of Regional Integration in the Americas, Pacific Asia and Western Europe." *Review of International Political Economy* 10 (2): 278–309.

Franko, P. 2018. *The Puzzle of Latin American Economic Development.* London: Rowman & Littlefield.

Gabriel, C., and L. Macdonald. 2021. "New Architectures for Migration Governance: NAFTA and Transnational Activism around Migrants' Rights." *Third World Quarterly* 42 (1): 68–85.

Garcia-Barragan, D., A. Mitretodis, and A. Tuck. 2019. "The New NAFTA: Scaled-Back Arbitration in the USMCA." *Journal of International Arbitration* 36 (6): 739–54.

Genna, G., and T. Hiroi. 2004. "Power Preponderance and Domestic Politics: Explaining Regional Economic Integration in Latin America and the Caribbean, 1960–1997." *International Interactions* 30 (2): 143–64.

Gómez-Mera, L. 2013. *Power and Regionalism in Latin America: The Politics of MERCOSUR*. Notre Dame, IN: University of Notre Dame Press.

Haas, E. B. 1964. *Beyond the Nation-State. Functionalism and International Organization*. Stanford, CA: Stanford University Press.

Haas, E. B., and P. C. Schmitter. 1964. "Economics and Differential Patterns of Political Integration: Projections about Unity in Latin America." *International Organization* 18 (3): 259–99.

Hadfield, A., and R. Potter. 2017. "Trump, Trudeau and NAFTA 2.0: Tweak or Transformation?" *The Round Table* 106 (2): 213–15.

Heine, J. 2012. "Regional Integration and Political Cooperation in Latin America." *Latin American Research Review* 47 (3): 209–17.

Henneberg, I., and S. Stapel. 2020. "Cooperation and Conflict at the Horn of Africa: A New Regional Bloc between Ethiopia, Eritrea, and Somalia and Its Consequences for Eastern Africa." *Africa Spectrum* 55 (3): 339–50. https://doi.org/10.1177/0002039720936689.

Herz, M. 2011. *The Organization of American States (OAS): Global Governance away from the Media*. London: Routledge.

Hooghe, L., T. Lenz, and G. Marks. 2019. *A Theory of International Organization*. Oxford: Oxford University Press.

Hufbauer, G. C., and J. J. Schott. 2005. *NAFTA Revisited: Achievements and Challenges*. Washington, DC: Columbia University Press.

Hurrell, A. 1995. "Regionalism in the Americas." In *Regionalism in World Politics: Regional Organization and International Order*, edited by L. Fawcett and A. Hurrell, 250–82. Oxford: Oxford University Press.

Katzenstein, P. J. 2005. *A World of Regions: Asia and Europe in the American Imperium*. Ithaca, NY: Cornell University Press.

Keller, F. L. 1963. "ODECA: Common Market Experiment in an Under-Developed Area." *Journal of Inter-American Studies* 5 (2): 267–75.

Landau, G. D. 1980. "The Treaty for Amazonian Cooperation: A Bold New Instrument for Development." *Georgia Journal of International & Comparative Law* 10 (3): 463–89.

Laurens, N., Z. Dove, J. F. Morin, and S. Jinnah. 2019. "NAFTA 2.0: The Greenest Trade Agreement Ever?" *World Trade Review* 18 (4): 659–77.

LeBlanc, L. J. 1977. *The Organization of American States and the Promotion and Protection of Human Rights*. The Hague, NL: Brill.

Lester, S., and I. Manak. 2018. "The Rise of Populist Nationalism and the Renegotiation of NAFTA." *Journal of International Economic Law* 21 (1): 151–69.

Lindberg, L. N. 1963. *The Political Dynamics of European Economic Integration*. Stanford, CA: Stanford University Press.

Long, T. 2015. *Latin America Confronts the United States: Asymmetry and Influence.* Cambridge: Cambridge University Press.

Long, T. 2020. "Historical Antecedents and Post-World War II Regionalism in the Americas." *World Politics* 72 (2): 214–53.

Macdonald, L. 2020. "Canada in the North America Region: Implications of the Trump Presidency." *Canadian Journal of Political Science* 53 (3): 505–20.

Malamud, A. 2019. "Overlapping Regionalism, No Integration: Conceptual Issues and the Latin American Experiences." *Politica Internacional*: 46–59.

Marcoux, J.-M. 2019. "The Renegotiation of NAFTA: The 'Most Advanced' Free Trade Agreement?" In *European Yearbook of International Economic Law*, 257–84. London: Springer.

Milner, H. V. 1995. "Regional Economic Co-operation, Global Markets and Domestic Politics: A Comparison of NAFTA and the Maastricht Treaty." *Journal of European Public Policy* 2 (3): 337–60.

Morales, I. 2002. "The Governance of Global Issues through Regionalism: NAFTA as an Interface between Multilateral and North-South Policies." *Journal of Social Science* 55 (1): 27–55.

Moravcsik, A. 1998. *The Choice for Europe. Social Purpose & State Power from Messina to Maastricht.* Ithaca, NY: Cornell University Press.

Mzumara, M., A. Chingarande, and R. Karambakuwa. 2012. "An Analysis of Comparative Advantage and Intra-North American Free Trade Agreement (NAFTA) Trade Performance." *Journal of Sustainable Development* 5 (11): 103.

Nolte, D. 2014. *Latin America's New Regional Architecture: A Cooperative or Segmented Regional Governance Complex?* Florence, IT: Robert Schuman Centre for Advanced Studies, Research Paper No. RSCAS 89.

Nolte, D. 2018. "Costs and Benefits of Overlapping Regional Organizations in Latin America: The Case of OAS and UNASUR." *Latin American Politics and Society* 60 (1): 128–53.

Nolte, D., and L. Wehner. 2013. "UNASUR and Regional Security in South America." In *Regional Organisations and Security*, edited by S. Aris and A. Wenger, 201–20. London: Routledge.

Nye, J. S. 1968. "Patterns and Catalysts in Regional Integration." *International Organization* 19 (4): 870–84.

Ouellet, R., and M. Messier. 2017. "Renegotiating NAFTA under a Trump Presidency: Tweak, Tear, or Think Again? A Legal Perspective from Québec." *Quebec Studies* 64 (1): 123–41.

Panke, D. 2017. "Der Neue Regionalismuss." In *Regionen und Regionalismus in den Internationalen Beziehungen*, edited by S. Koschut, 21–37. Eine Einführung. Wiesbaden, DE: Springer.

Panke, D. 2020. "Regional Cooperation through the Lenses of States: Why Do States Nurture Regional Integration?" *The Review of International Organizations* 15 (2): 475–504.

Panke, D., and S. Stapel. 2018a. "Exploring Overlapping Regionalism." *Journal of International Relations and Development* 21 (3): 635–62.

Panke, D., and S. Stapel. 2018b. "Overlapping Regionalism in Europe: Patterns and Effects." *The British Journal of Politics and International Relations* 20 (1): 239–58.

Panke, D., S. Stapel, and A. Starkmann. 2020. *Comparing Regional Organizations: Global Dynamics and Regional Particularities*. Bristol, UK: Bristol University Press.

Panke, D., and A. Starkmann. 2020. "Responding to Functionalist Incentives? Exploring the Evolution of Regional Organisations after the End of the Cold War." *Journal of Contemporary European Studies* 28 (2): 216–35.

Prieto, G. C. 2020. "Identity in Latin American Regionalism: The Andean Community." *Oxford Research Encyclopedia of Politics*. Accessed December 27, 2022. https://oxfordre.com/politics/view/10.1093/acrefore/9780190228637.001.0001/acrefore-9780190228637-e-1736.

Riggirozzi, P., and J. Grugel. 2015. "Regional Governance and Legitimacy in South America: The Meaning of UNASUR." *International Affairs* 91 (4): 781–97.

Riggirozzi, P., and D. Tussie, eds. 2012. *The Rise of Post-hegemonic Regionalism: The Case of Latin America*. London: Springer.

Roberts, S. P., and A. Moshes. 2016. "The Eurasian Economic Union: A Case of Reproductive Integration?" *Post-Soviet Affairs* 32 (6): 542–65.

Sánchez, R. A. S. 2010. *The Politics of Central American Integration*. London: Routledge.

Schmitter, P. C. 1970. "A Revised Theory of Regional Integration." *International Organization* 24 (4): 836–68.

Selleslaghs, J., and L. Van Langenhove. 2020. "The Rise of Regions: Introduction to Regional Integration & Organisations." In *The Changing Global Order: Challenges and Prospects*, edited by M. O. Hosli and J. Selleslaghs, 147–62. Cham, CH: Springer.

Söderbaum, F. 2016a. "Old, New and Comparative Regionalism: The Scholarly Development of the Field." In *Oxford Handbook of Comparative Regionalism*, edited by T. A. Börzel and T. Risse, 16–38. Oxford: Oxford University Press.

Söderbaum, F. 2016b. *Rethinking Regionalism*. Basingstoke, UK: Palgrave Macmillan.

Söderbaum, F., and K. Spandler. 2021. *Contestations of the Liberal International Order: A Populist Script of Regional Cooperation*. Cambridge: Cambridge University Press.

Stapel, S. 2022. *Regional Organizations and Democracy, Human Rights, and the Rule of Law: The African Union, Organization of Americas States, and the Diffusion of Institutions*. Houndmills, UK: Palgrave Macmillan.

Tarte, S. 2014. "Regionalism and Changing Regional Order in the Pacific Islands." *Asia & the Pacific Policy Studies* 1 (2): 312–24.

Thomson, R., and M. Hosli. 2006. "Who Has Power in the EU? The Commission, Council and Parliament in Legislative Decision-Making." *Journal of Common Market Studies* 44 (2): 391–417.

United Nations Statistics Division (UNSD). 2019. "Composition of Macro Geographical (Continental) Regions, Geographical Sub Regions, and Selected

Economic and Other Groupings United Nations Statistics Division." Accessed December 4, 2019. http://unstats.un.org/unsd/methods/m49/m49regin.htm.

Vinokurov, E., and A. Libman. 2017. *Re-evaluating Regional Organizations: Behind the Smokescreen of Official Mandates*. Basingstoke, UK: Palgrave Macmillan.

von Borzyskowski, I., and F. Vabulas. 2019. "Hello, Goodbye: When Do States Withdraw from International Organizations?" *The Review of International Organizations* 14 (2): 335–66.

Ware, D. 1980. "The Amazon Treaty: A Turning Point in Latin American Cooperation." *Texas International Law Journal* 15: 117.

Weiffen, B., L. Wehner, and D. Nolte. 2013. "Overlapping Regional Security Institutions in South America: The Case of OAS and UNASUR." *International Area Studies Review* 16 (4): 370–89.

Wionczek, M. S. 1970. "The Rise and the Decline of Latin American Economic Integration." *JCMS: Journal of Common Market Studies* 9 (1): 49–66.

CHAPTER TEN

China and North America

How an Asian Power Disrupted the US Neighborhood

Barbara Stallings

Introduction

THE UNITED States, Canada, and Mexico—North America—form a regional integration group that is shallow in comparison with the more robust economic and political relationships found in Europe and East Asia. In contrast to the European Union or Association of Southeast Asian Nations (ASEAN) Plus Three,[1] the North American Free Trade Agreement (NAFTA), now reconstituted as the US-Mexico-Canada Agreement (USMCA), is characterized by a lower ratio of intraregional trade to total trade, less intraregional investment, and virtually no sense of community. Moreover, the existing economic ties among the three have been undermined by the encroachment into the North American space by a dynamic competitor— the People's Republic of China (PRC). In the words of two analysts, China was "NAFTA's uninvited guest" (Dussel Peters and Gallagher 2013).

NAFTA was the first regional agreement to link a developing country with advanced industrial counterparts. In addition, the three were very different in the size of their economies and their populations. With the United States as the largest on both dimensions, the result was a highly asymmetrical arrangement that featured a hub-and-spokes organization. That is, most of the trade and investment were between the United States and the other two countries; very little took place between Canada and Mexico. When China became a major player after it joined the World Trade Organization (WTO) in 2001, the share of the US market served by Canada and Mexico together began to contract as did their share of US foreign investment.

The chapter is organized as follows. The second section provides data on trade links among the four countries, while the third focuses on investment trends among the four. The fourth section looks at changes between NAFTA and China under the Trump administration. The fifth extends the analysis to NAFTA's neighbors to the south—Central America and the Caribbean. The concluding section offers an interpretation of China's role in North America and discusses future prospects.

NAFTA Trade and the Arrival of China

Analysis of China's role in regional trade patterns needs to be divided into three phases: 1994–2000, 2000–2016, and 2016–2020. The first phase is the pre-China period in the region, which saw the greatest benefits accruing to the new trilateral relationship, as both trade and investment burgeoned amid high hopes for the new agreement. The second phase shows the major impact of China's entry into the region. China's trade increased worldwide after WTO accession, including in the NAFTA region where it began to siphon off benefits previously accruing to NAFTA members.[2] The third phase represents the Trump years, which saw a stagnation of trade relations between the United States and China, in response to the Trump-initiated "trade war," accompanied by a slight uptick in NAFTA trade. The end of this third phase also saw the completion of the negotiations for the USMCA.

The analysis includes two definitions of North America: the narrow one—focusing on the United States, Canada, and Mexico—and a broader one that includes Central America and some Caribbean countries. From the viewpoint of relations with China, the broader definition is important because it shows somewhat different patterns of trade and investment in comparison with Canada and especially Mexico, but it also involves political relations that are particularly important to China. Of the handful of countries that still recognize Taiwan, half are in Central America and the Caribbean. Since one of China's main foreign policy goals is to isolate Taiwan, and eventually reunite it with the mainland, China has a particular interest in the southern part of North America.

To understand these evolving trade relationships, I begin with trade among the three NAFTA partners. In the first phase, NAFTA trade rose by 119 percent (an average of 17 percent annually), in contrast to the second phase where trilateral trade grew by only 73 percent (less than 5 percent per year). In the final phase, the growth rate fell further to 11 percent (less than 3 percent annually). Overall NAFTA trade rose 320 percent in the twenty-six years between 1993 and 2019 (see table 10.1).[3] To put this figure into perspective, world merchandise trade grew 370 percent in the same period, so NAFTA failed even to help its members keep up with the rest of the world (calculated from IMF, Direction of Trade Statistics, n.d.). As we will see later, an important reason was the growing presence of China in North America.

Mexico fared far better than Canada in the US market; US-Mexican trade grew 641 percent over the period as a whole, while US-Canada trade increased only 186 percent. Part of the explanation is the much lower base from which US-Mexican trade started in comparison to US-Canada trade. Another reason has to do with the sectoral characteristics of the two countries' exports to the United States. Somewhat counterintuitively, given that Canada is a developed country and Mexico a developing one, a significant share of Canadian exports to the United States consists of commodities, while the majority of Mexico's (post-NAFTA) exports are industrial goods. In 2019,

Table 10.1 Merchandise Trade (Exports + Imports) among NAFTA and China ($ billions)

Countries	1993	2000	2015	2019
US-Canada	214	404	575	611
US-Mexico	83	244	531	615
Canada-Mexico	3	9	29	35
NAFTA	300	657	1135	1261
China-US	43	122	556	559
China-Canada/ Mexico	3	11	142	172
China-NAFTA	46	133	698	731
China-NAFTA/ NAFTA (%)	15.3	20.2	61.5	58.0

Source: IMF, Direction of Trade Statistics (online).

Canada's top export to the United States, accounting for more than a quarter of the total, was oil and fuel. The top five also included miscellaneous commodities in fourth place. The problems with commodity exports are well known in terms of price volatility and perhaps inelasticity of demand. Mexico's top five export products, by contrast, were vehicles, machinery, electrical machinery, and optical and medical instruments, with oil and fuel in fifth place (USTR, n.d.).

An important explanation for the industrial bias of Mexico's export basket is the nature of its involvement in US trade. Globalization over recent decades has meant that much international trade now takes place through value or supply chains. The various components of a product are produced where costs are lowest, and they are then assembled for sale to the final user (World Bank 2019). Mexico's best-known participation in supply chains involved its "maquiladora" program (Gruben 2001; South and Kim 2019). The maquiladoras are plants, generally owned by US companies, most of which are set up on the US-Mexico frontier. These companies import inputs from the United States, assemble the goods in Mexico to take advantage of cheap labor, and then sell the finished goods back into the US market. Electronics, apparel, and auto parts have been the main sectors involved in the maquiladoras. Drawing on the World Bank's World Integrated Trade Solution (WITS) data bank, I calculate that various types of industrial goods accounted for 87 percent of Mexico's exports to the United States in 2018, while Canada's share of these categories was only 52 percent. The remainder for both were raw materials and intermediate goods. This distinction was a drag on Canada's trade with the United States, but it left Mexico vulnerable to competition from China, which also exported final manufactured goods to the US market. Over 90 percent of China's exports were industrial products (Harris and Schmitt 2014).

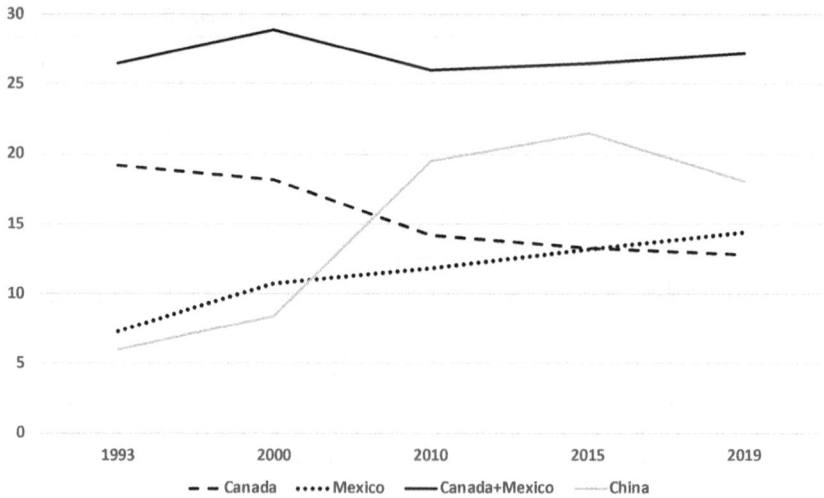

Figure 10.1. Share of US Import Market, 1993–2019 (%).

Both NAFTA partners suffered a decline in their share of US trade in the last two decades. China's increased presence in North America was an important cause. To show the impact of China, table 10.1 includes data on China's trade with NAFTA members. China-NAFTA trade—that is, its trade with the United States, Canada, and Mexico—accelerated from $46 billion in 1993 to $731 billion in 2019, a far larger rise than trade among the NAFTA members themselves. The big gains came in the fifteen years after China's accession to the WTO. Under President Donald Trump, US-China trade stagnated, but China's trade with Canada and Mexico expanded somewhat. China-NAFTA trade as a share of NAFTA trade increased from 15 percent in 1993 to 62 percent in 2015, before falling to 58 percent in 2019.

Another way of looking at these patterns is to focus on the evolving shares of Canada, Mexico, and China in the US market—by far the dominant market in the region. In 1993, just before NAFTA went into operation, the NAFTA partners accounted for 26.5 percent of US imports, while China lagged far behind with only 6 percent. By 2000, Canada and Mexico together had risen to 29 percent and China to 8 percent. The major change came in the following fifteen years, as Canada and Mexico fell back to their 1993 share, but China jumped to 21.5 percent (absorbing share not just from NAFTA partners but third parties as well). Not surprisingly, given the other data we have seen, China's share of the US market fell somewhat by 2019, while the share of Canada plus Mexico rose marginally.

The supply chain story was important in the rising share of China in US trade, especially for apparel and electronics. The ability to incorporate low-cost Mexican inputs into its exports was one of the reasons for the US interest in NAFTA, and one of the concerns of the Trump administration, as we will see later. Enrique Dussel Peters and Kevin Gallagher (2013) studied these supply chains, especially the yarn-textile-garment chain and the auto parts–automobile chain between Mexico and the United States. The former was a dynamic, export-oriented sector, which was dependent on US inputs that were assembled and exported back to the United States as finished products. While exports surged in 1994–2000, Mexico lost 50 percent of jobs in the sector in the following ten years, as China stepped in to supply the finished goods with its lower costs and higher productivity.

In electronics, a similar phenomenon occurred. Imports into the US market from Mexico rose from 11 percent to 16 percent in the first phase of NAFTA and then stagnated, while imports from China began at only 5 percent in 1994, then rose to 10 percent, 33 percent, and 40 percent in 2000, 2010, and 2017 (Dussel Peters 2019). Only in autos has China not moved into the NAFTA market in a big way; China accounted for only 5 percent of vehicle imports into NAFTA in 2017. Although it is the largest auto producer in the world, the large majority of China's output is absorbed by its domestic market. In addition, US-Mexican supply chains in autos have led to very efficient production. China's auto-parts exports, however, are more dynamic in the NAFTA market (Dussel Peters 2019).

While the largest shifts in trade shares have involved the US market, there has been an increase in trade between China and the other two NAFTA members, as also seen in table 10.1. According to the table, total trade between China and the other two rose from only $3 billion in 1993 to $142 billion in 2015. Interestingly, while US-China trade stagnated in the following years, China's trade with Mexico and Canada continued to grow, reaching $172 billion in 2019. It is important to realize, however, that most of this trade consists of imports from China; neither Canada nor Mexico exports much of its output to China. In 2019, for example, Canada exported only $17 billion of goods to China; Mexico exported a mere $7 billion. On the other side of the ledger, the two countries imported $60 billion and $88 billion, respectively. Thus, Mexico in particular runs a huge trade deficit with China because its exports are similar to those of China itself, and it cannot compete with subsidized Chinese firms. Neither has it exported high-value fruits and vegetables to China (as Chile has), probably because it has a captive market in the United States. Canada also has a trade deficit with China, as does the United States, but its deficit is smaller.[4] A reason again has to do with the sectoral distribution of the two countries' export baskets. Canada mainly exports commodities to China, while Mexico offers industrial goods that directly compete with China's domestic output (World Bank, WITS data bank). Bilateral trade deficits are a problem if not offset by surpluses with other trade partners, since they must be financed by capital inflows; otherwise, investment or local consumption must be cut.

Foreign Direct Investment in NAFTA and China's Role

While trade was the dominant component of the NAFTA agreement, foreign direct investment (FDI) was an important complement. FDI stimulated trade through providing resources to exporters and through the development of supply chains between US firms and their NAFTA counterparts. As would be expected, the United States has been the main source of FDI to both Canada and Mexico, although there have also been flows in the opposite direction. As with trade, China has absorbed investment that might have gone to NAFTA countries, but it has also provided its own investment in the three NAFTA economies. Its role, however, is much less important than with trade. Also, with respect to investment, Canada—the biggest loser in trade with the United States—has been the biggest winner with respect to FDI.[5]

The trends in US investment in Canada, Mexico, and the two combined are dominated by US investment in Canada, which rose from $70 billion in 1993 to $400 billion in 2019. Investment in Mexico was much lower, increasing from $15 billion to $100 billion over these same years, though it has been basically flat since the global financial crisis (see figure 10.2). In terms of share of overall US direct investment abroad, both countries saw a decline. Canada fell from 12.4 percent of total US FDI in 1993 to 6.7 percent in 2019, while Mexico fell from 2.7 percent to 1.7 percent. The share of Canadian and Mexican investment in the United States is even more lopsided. Canadian investment rose from 8.6 percent to 11.1 percent of all US inflows, while Mexico rose from 0.2 percent to 0.5 percent. In absolute terms, Canadian investment stock in the US market was nearly $500 billion in 2019, but Mexico's stock was only $22 billion. Indeed, Canadian FDI stock in the United States in 2019 exceeded US investment stock in Canada, perhaps acting as a substitute for exports.

The sectoral distribution of US investment stock in the two NAFTA partners shows significant differences. Investment in Mexico in 2019 was rooted in productive sectors, while investment in Canada was more oriented toward finance and holding companies. The sectoral distribution in broad categories for Mexico was mining (11 percent), manufacturing (41 percent), wholesale trade (5 percent), services (<1 percent), and finance and holding companies (30 percent). For Canada, by contrast, the allocation was mining (3 percent), manufacturing (25 percent), wholesale trade (7 percent), services (5 percent), and finance and holding companies (47 percent) (calculated from US Department of Commerce, n.d.). No data are available on the sectoral allocation of inward FDI flows.

OECD data are available for member countries for recent years. For US outward flows, the OECD figures are slightly higher than those from the Commerce Department, but they are roughly similar. For investment between the other NAFTA members, we find that Canadian investment stock in Mexico was $23 billion in 2019, while Mexican investment in Canada amounted to only around $1 billion. No information is available on the sectoral distribution. As expected on the basis of trade

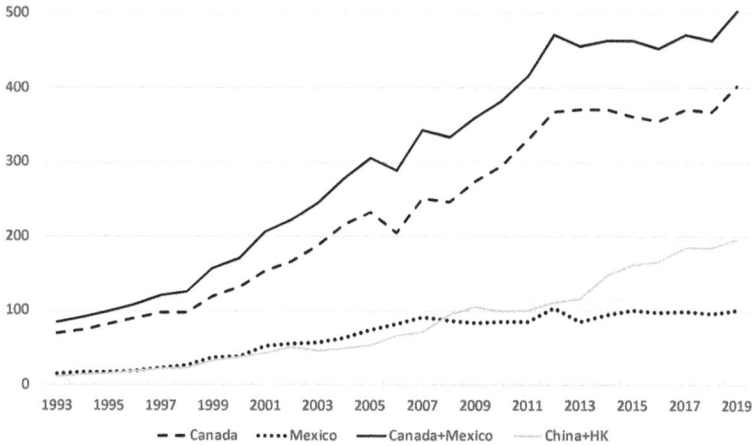

Figure 10.2. US FDI Stock in NAFTA and China, 1993–2019 ($ billions).

relationships, the reciprocal investment in the two countries was very small compared to investment to and from the United States, continuing the hub-and-spokes arrangement found with respect to trade.

Why has US investment in Mexico been relatively sluggish, especially since 2008, while investment in Canada has continued to soar? A possible explanation again focuses on China. As figure 10.2 demonstrates, US investment in China overtook investment in Mexico in 2008.[6] Since then, US investment in China has doubled, while that in Mexico has barely risen at all. We know that Mexico and China have competitive economies as far as exports to the United States are concerned, with both concentrating on manufactured goods. A similar situation appears to exist with respect to FDI. That is, the sectoral breakdown of US investment stock in China is more similar to what we saw for Mexico than that for Canada: mining (1 percent), manufacturing (47 percent), wholesale trade (14 percent), services (3 percent), and finance and holding companies (28 percent). Thus, US FDI in both China and Mexico has a strong emphasis on manufacturing and much less on finance and other services. US firms may have seen a trade-off between China and Mexico when deciding where to invest; in the last decade, the trend has favored China. Unlike the situation in South America, the low level of US investment in Mexico has not been offset by investment from China.

This trade-off was seen in a particularly dramatic way in the early 2000s in the decline of Mexico's maquiladora sector. As more knowledge of China became available and China became a more active player on the international stage, a number of the maquiladora firms moved to China where wages were even lower than in Mexico. Hale Utar and Luis Torres-Ruiz (2013) provided evidence of this process, making use of plant-level data that covered all maquiladoras from 1990 to 2006, focusing on

China's accession to the WTO as the time when the change accelerated. They found that Chinese competition had a significant, negative impact on employment and plant growth in Mexico, especially with respect to plants and sectors employing unskilled labor. In terms of sectors, they found that electronics and apparel firms were more exposed to Chinese competition than autos or food. On the positive side, they found that Chinese competition increased productivity in the firms that remained in Mexico.

NAFTA and China during the Trump Administration

Well before he became president in 2017, Donald Trump had voiced the opinion that the United States was being taken advantage of by the international trading system. In particular, he focused on bilateral trade deficits as the source of the problem and advocated the use of punitive tariffs to bring about change. Despite the view of economists that bilateral deficits are not a relevant issue and that deficits are the result of macroeconomic disequilibria rather than trade relations, Trump followed up on his views after he took office. NAFTA and China became the leading targets of his policies.

Three days after his inauguration, Trump withdrew from the Trans-Pacific Partnership (TPP), a proposed trade agreement that included the United States, Canada, Mexico, and nine countries in Asia. He also renewed his attacks on NAFTA itself, having called it "the single worst trade deal ever approved in this country" (Calmes 2016). The following year, Trump began imposing tariffs on individual products, starting with 30 percent–50 percent duties on solar panels and washing machines. Two months later, he added levies on steel (25 percent) and aluminum (10 percent). While the NAFTA partners and the European Union (EU) were initially exempted from these tariffs, they were included from June 2018. The most controversial aspects of the steel and aluminum tariffs was that they were imposed for alleged national security reasons—even on the United States' closest neighbors. Canada retaliated for the tariffs, but Mexico did not. The three NAFTA partners reached an agreement to remove the tariffs in May 2019 as part of the NAFTA renegotiation.

In addition to imposing tariffs on NAFTA partners to deal with perceived trade disadvantages, Trump went further in the case of Mexico, threatening punitive tariffs if Mexico did not help stop the flow of undocumented migrants into the United States. In June 2019, Trump announced a plan to impose a 5 percent tariff on Mexico, which would increase by an additional 5 percent each month up to 25 percent, "unless and until Mexico substantially stops the illegal flow of aliens coming through its territory" (Paletta et al. 2019). Mexico agreed to step in, deploying 6,000 National Guard troops at its southern border to halt refugee flows from the Northern Triangle countries. Later President Andrés Manuel López Obrador also agreed to keep people seeking asylum in the United States on Mexico's side of the US-Mexico border until their court appearance dates.

The use of tariffs against NAFTA partners was enmeshed in Trump's demand to renegotiate the NAFTA treaty itself with the alternative that he would withdraw uni-laterally. The negotiations, which proceeded via threats of various kinds, began in May 2017 when the US Trade Representative notified Congress of the intent to renegotiate the treaty. The main aims were to reduce the trade deficit with Mexico, raise the amount of regional content in goods that qualify under the agreement, and eliminate the contro-versial dispute settlement mechanism. Other aims appeared similar to those included in the TPP, such as regulating treatment of workers and the environment. Negotiations were concluded at the end of November 2018, but the treaty was revamped at the insis-tence of the Democratic majority in the US House of Representatives. The final deal, which strengthened labor, environmental, enforcement, and pharmaceutical provisions, was approved on a bipartisan vote in December 2019 to take effect on July 1, 2020.

At the end of the process, it appeared that little had changed in the USMCA in comparison with the original NAFTA treaty; indeed, many called it NAFTA 2.0. Among the main differences were raising the North American content of autos from 62.5 percent to 75 percent to qualify for zero tariffs in the regional market, stipulating that 40 percent–50 percent of auto parts must be manufactured by workers who earn at least $16 per hour, providing greater access for US and Canadian dairy products, extending the terms for copyright, and increasing the use of environmental impact assessments. A sunset clause was included to require participating parties to revisit the terms of the agreement or withdraw on or before the sixteenth year of implemen-tation. In addition, USMCA members were prohibited from signing trade agreements with nonmarket economies, which essentially meant China (Burfisher et al. 2019; Scherrer 2020; Villarreal and Fergusson 2020).

Of course, Mexico and Canada were not the only targets of Trump's aggressive use of tariffs. China became the main country that he tried to coerce into following his trade and economic dictums. Chief among the US complaints against China were its large trade surplus, special privileges for state-owned enterprises, lack of respect for intellectual property, and the forced transfer of technology. The tit-for-tat rounds of tariffs continued through 2018–2019 with China at a disadvantage because it exported substantially more to the United States than it imported. In October 2019, a so-called Phase I deal was announced, involving China's purchase of $50 billion of farm prod-ucts and a further opening of its financial services market in return for a US promise to suspend yet more tariffs scheduled to go into effect. The deal was signed in January 2020 (Liu and Woo 2018; Bown 2019; Dussel Peters 2019; Itakura 2020).

The result of the nearly two years of what some called a trade war had accomplished little of Trump's agenda, but it had weakened both economies. The US trade deficit with China remained huge, although it did fall in 2019 for the first time in six years as imports fell more than exports. The more significant issues—such as intellectual property, technology transfer, and the role of state-owned enterprises—were left for a possible future Phase II. And US-China relations at the political level descended to new lows as COVID-19 spread from China to the West, including the United States.

US trade with both Mexico and Canada suffered from the tariffs imposed on those two countries. On the Mexican side, the Trump's tariffs on China have had some positive impact as a number of firms—especially in, but not limited to, the medical sector—have begun to move from China to Mexico. This nearshoring partially reversed the movement of firms from Mexico to China that was discussed earlier (Rapoza 2020; Sieff 2020; Schott and Goodman 2021). For Canada, there was no positive economic outcome and a negative political one, as the Trump administration dragged Canada into a conflict with China through its opposition to technology exporter, Huawei. It demanded that Canada arrest the daughter of Huawei's founder because of the company's alleged violation of US sanctions. China retaliated by arresting two Canadian citizens. All have now been released.

China and the United States in Central America and the Caribbean

Taking a broader view of North America—based on a definition of all countries above the South American coastline—Central America and the Caribbean nations also witnessed important changes in recent years centered on China's new presence in the region. As a follow-up to the NAFTA accord, the United States signed a free trade agreement with five Central American countries plus the Dominican Republic (CAFTA-DR) in 2004 (Hornbeck 2012). Indeed, both US and Central American negotiators used the China threat as one reason to ratify the accord (Avendaño and Dayton-Johnson 2015). All signatories hoped that the new agreement would give them an economic boost. The US textile and apparel industry was facing stiff international competition, and the six Central American and Caribbean countries were mostly poor and in need of development assistance.[7]

Five of the six economies focused their exports on textiles and apparel and on agricultural goods. Costa Rica, by contrast, had moved into the high-tech sector; the majority of its exports were optical and medical instruments and electrical machinery, although it still made significant agricultural sales abroad. The most interesting sector for an analysis about the role of China, then, concerns textiles and apparel. China had been held back in its exports in this sector by the Multi-Fiber Agreement (MFA), which imposed quotas on the amount developing countries could export to developed ones. The MFA was ended in 2005, but the United States took advantage of a provision in China's WTO accession agreement to restrict the annual rate of growth of imports to 7.5 percent until 2008.

China has had an important impact in this crucial sector, as reflected in the value of US imports between 2000 and 2018 from CAFTA-DR, China, and Mexico (see figure 10.3). In 2000, Mexico accounted for 13.7 percent of US textile and apparel imports, with CAFTA-DR at 12.2 percent and China at 10.7 percent. Already by 2005, however, the picture had changed. China had become the leading exporter into the US market,

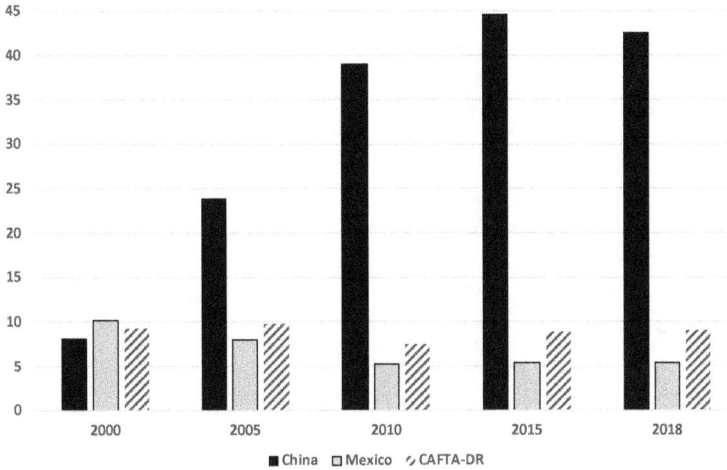

Figure 10.3. US Imports of Textiles and Apparel, 2000–2018 ($ billions).

increasing its share until 2015, when it provided 37.3 percent of the total. Mexico's exports fell in absolute terms during the 2000–2015 period, while CAFTA-DR members' share stagnated in absolute terms and fell in relative terms to 7.4 percent of the total (calculated from World Bank, WITS database). As was seen earlier, imports from China declined somewhat in response to Trump's trade war. CAFTA-DR did not fall further in their US import share, since member countries have some important advantages vis-à-vis China: closer geographical proximity to the United States, supply chain relationships, and of course the CAFTA-DR benefits. China, by contrast, has lower wages in some cases, economies of scale, and government support through credit and other policy measures.

There is not much direct trade between China and CAFTA-DR. Like Mexico, the Central American countries have trade deficits with China since they import a significant quantity of industrial goods but export very little. On the one hand, China does not need Central American textiles and apparel. On the other hand, the type of agricultural goods the region produces (food products—especially coffee and bananas—rather than minerals) are not of particular interest either (Avendaño and Dayton-Johnson 2015).

The CAFTA-DR share of US FDI was not displaced by China to the same extent as happened with their own exports and with Mexico's FDI (see figure 10.4). Of course, US investment in China is vastly larger than that in the small Central American and Caribbean nations, and the former rose somewhat more rapidly and with less volatility. But both were increasing at the same time (unlike the situation with Mexico, as seen earlier). Moreover, there is anecdotal evidence that CAFTA-DR countries may have been benefiting recently from nearshoring by US firms leaving China or other parts of Asia (Lu 2020).

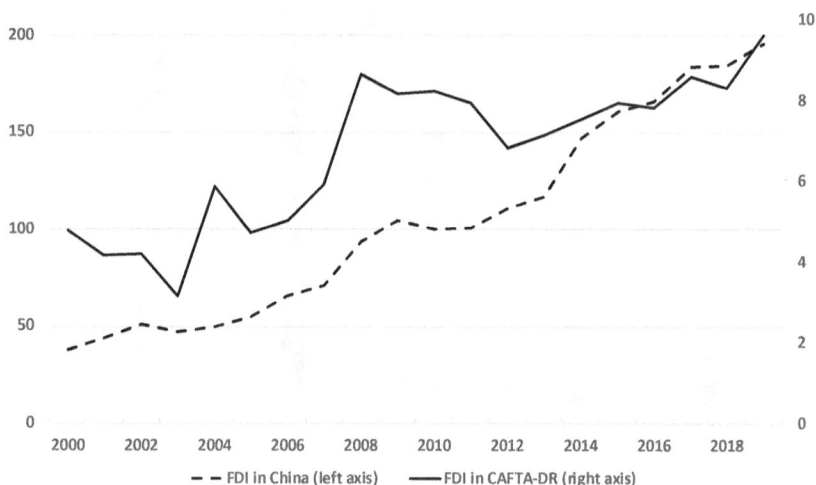

Figure 10.4. US FDI Stock in CAFTA–DR and China, 2000–2019 ($ billions).

Only very partial information is available on the sectoral allocation of US investment in CAFTA-DR, but US Commerce Department data show that over 60 percent was in manufacturing. This may indicate that some of the rise in FDI was going into supply chain activities in textiles and apparel to support the US industry. The CAFTA-DR agreement stipulates that to get duty-free access to the US market, products must use US or regional inputs (the "yarn forward" rule). Some exceptions are available, but US firms stand to make important gains.

Central America and the Caribbean have interacted with China in political as well as economic ways in the last twenty years. While these countries have been part of the US sphere of influence since the days of "dollar diplomacy" in the late nineteenth century, they are important to China in foreign policy terms. One of China's most intense foreign policy objectives is to isolate Taiwan, which it considers a renegade province. As of 2016, only twenty countries (plus the Vatican) still recognized Taiwan diplomatically. Of the twenty, half were in Central America or the Caribbean: Belize, Dominican Republic, El Salvador, Guatemala, Haiti, Honduras, Nicaragua, Panama, St. Kitts and Nevis, and St. Vincent and the Grenadines.

China has long sought to entice these countries to switch their allegiance. With this goal in mind, what appeared to be a key event was Costa Rica's 2007 decision to recognize the PRC. While the Costa Rican population is less than five million and the country does not have oil or mineral resources, it has other attractions. It is the wealthiest and most stable country in Central America and has considerable international prestige, deriving from its high education levels, democratic political system, well-known ecological preservation policies and associated ecotourism, and high-tech industries. Thus, wooing Costa Rica was seen as one of the most important aspects of China's running battle with Taiwan in the hope that Costa Rica would serve as a beacon for other countries thinking of switching allegiance (Casas-Zamora 2009).

As a result, China offered Costa Rica a gamut of rewards from when it recognized the PRC. It provided $180 million of grants for projects of Costa Rica's choosing, becoming Costa Rica's largest source of foreign aid. It also agreed to purchase $300 million of Costa Rican government bonds on very favorable terms (Bowley 2009). A $900 million loan to expand Costa Rica's oil refinery was offered, but it aroused so much controversy that it was eventually suspended. Recognition of the PRC was followed by a state visit by Chinese president Hu Jintao and the negotiation of a free trade agreement, only China's third in Latin America. In 2013, newly installed President Xi Jinping visited Costa Rica, where he pledged $400 million in loans to extend a road from central Costa Rica to the main seaport and $100 million to replace public transportation vehicles (Cota 2013).

To China's dismay, however, no other countries in the region promptly followed Costa Rica's lead. In part, this was due to an informal truce between the PRC and a pro-Beijing president of Taiwan from 2008 to 2016, which meant the two suspended their "checkbook diplomacy" that aimed to attract countries' diplomatic recognition (Parajón 2019). Yet almost as soon as the truce lapsed, Panama switched its allegiance, followed soon thereafter by the Dominican Republic and El Salvador. Panama was the prize among this group because of its crucial geographical location. After the establishment of diplomatic relations, dozens of deals were announced, negotiations were begun to establish China's fourth free trade agreement (FTA) in the region, and Xi Jinping made a visit to the country. Panama began making plans to become an economic as well as a commercial hub for China's activities in North and South America (Youkee 2019, 2020).

The Dominican Republic was the next country to enter the checkbook diplomacy game and reportedly received a $3 billion package in return for the switch in diplomatic relations (Myers 2019). Soon afterward, El Salvador joined the group of new Beijing allies. While it was initially offered support for a large-scale special economic zone, the plans were sidetracked by the country's legislature. Remaining items received by El Salvador while under the government that had switched relations involved laptop computers, scholarships, tanker trucks, and rice to support farmers hurt by natural disasters. Additional items were provided under the successor (current) government, such as a library, stadium, water treatment plants, and tourist facilities (Center for Latin American and Latino Studies, American University 2022).

In the midst of these various proposals and negotiations, the Trump administration became alarmed and recalled its lead diplomats from the three countries. Secretary of State Mike Pompeo visited the region to warn against "predatory economic activities" by Chinese firms. El Salvador, as the third country to challenge the US government in a brief period, became a special target of Washington's wrath. The White House issued a statement saying: "The El Salvadoran government's receptiveness to China's apparent interference in the domestic politics of a Western Hemisphere country is of grave concern to the United States and will result in a reevaluation of our relationship with El Salvador." Several Republican senators threatened to cut off aid to El Salvador. Ultimately, however, the threats were abandoned because El Salvador's help was needed for Trump's immigration policy (Harris 2018).

If El Salvador was an irritant, Panama posed a more serious geopolitical threat to the United States because of its strategic location in general and its control over the Panama Canal in particular. Rather than openly threaten Panama, as they had El Salvador, US diplomats and other agents acted behind the scenes to persuade Panama's government to cancel or alter several multibillion projects that were to be financed and/or constructed by Chinese firms. Moreover, negotiations over the proposed FTA have not moved forward. How was the turnabout achieved? According to a well-placed journalist in Panama, "the US still maintains huge clout over individual politicians, through the threat of visa denial or inclusion on [a list of] companies and individuals that profit from money laundering and drug trafficking, leading to potentially severe sanctions by US prosecutors" (Youkee 2020).

Conclusions

This chapter has mapped out China's entry into North America in both the narrow and broad definitions of the term. The narrow definition is limited to the NAFTA members—the United States, Canada, and Mexico—while the broader definition includes Central America and the Caribbean. More importantly, the chapter has also provided an analysis of the impact that China has had on the countries of North America. This final section summarizes the analysis and then discusses possible future developments for China and the region.

The main message of the chapter is that China's entry into North America led to a weakening of NAFTA relationships, as economic interactions among the United States, Canada, and Mexico declined over the last two decades. China's role also helped erode US links with Central America and Caribbean. These trends preceded the presidency of Donald Trump, and his often-contradictory policy initiatives failed to halt them in any definitive way.

The clearest example of the fraying of NAFTA ties was found in the trade arena. After a brief burst of trade expansion between 1994 and 2000, in the immediate aftermath of the agreement going into effect, the rate of increase of exports and imports among the NAFTA partners slowed significantly, overcome by the dramatic increase in China's role in the region. Foreign direct investment behaved in a similar way: US FDI flows into Canada and Mexico shrank as a share of total US flows. Both trade and investment increased among China, Canada, and Mexico, but the amounts were minimal compared to the flows between all three and the United States.

President Trump attacked both NAFTA partners and China, arguing that all three countries were taking advantage of the United States. In both cases, his main instrument was the use of tariffs. With respect to NAFTA, in addition to imposing tariffs on particular products, he demanded that NAFTA itself be renegotiated under threat of US withdrawal from the agreement. The resulting USMCA made few changes. One of the main ones was to increase the share of NAFTA content for a product to get duty-free entry into the regional market, so as to limit China's ability to use NAFTA to gain entry to the US market.

In the case of China per se, Trump imposed tariffs on virtually all Chinese exports to the United States and restricted investment flows. The resulting tit for tat hurt both economies, as trade and FDI between the two shrank. The Phase I deal with China that was hammered out in 2019 gave Trump even less than he achieved in the NAFTA renegotiation. The main gain was more US exports to China, but the deal has not been carried out (Bown 2022). All of Trump's more controversial goals—such as those involving intellectual property and technology transfer—were postponed. A positive consequence of the tariff war was the return of some firms that had left Mexico for China earlier.

Finally, with respect to Central America and the Caribbean, China also displaced CAFTA-DR exports to the US market, especially textiles and apparel that had been the region's main export products. FDI was not affected as much as trade, perhaps because it involved supply chains that were important to US firms' international competitiveness. China was also involved with Central America and the Caribbean in political ways. One of China's central foreign policy aims is to isolate Taiwan diplomatically, and half of the countries that still recognized Taiwan in 2016 were in Central America and the Caribbean. Using "checkbook diplomacy," China persuaded Panama, the Dominican Republic, and El Salvador to switch their allegiance in recent years. When the United States realized what was happening, it used threats to halt some of the projects China had promised in exchange for the switch in diplomatic ties, but the new relations themselves continued.

The remaining questions concern the post-Trump era. Two changes could potentially alter some of the outcomes that have been witnessed in North America in recent years. On the one hand, the coronavirus and resulting economic crisis hit Latin America very hard. China was eager to help, both in the short and long run, but the extent of that help may be limited by weaknesses in its own economy. On the other hand, while there might have been an expectation that the election of Joe Biden as president would change the US approach to North America and to China, as of this writing in 2022 current trends seem more similar to those under Trump than was originally anticipated.

China's initial ability to stamp out COVID-19 at home gave the country substantial international prestige—despite criticism of its lack of transparency about the origin of the virus and its heavy-handed way of combatting it. More recently, problems with the "zero COVID" strategy have lowered international opinion. Early in the pandemic, China rolled out a set of activities referred to as "mask diplomacy," which offered medical and technical assistance to many Latin American countries including Mexico, Central America, and the Caribbean. Most of the assistance took the form of grants, although some equipment was sold. Part of the help came from China's central government, but local governments (including sister cities) and the private sector were also involved. In July 2020, China's foreign minister held an online meeting based in Mexico City with many of his Latin American counterparts to announce a $1 billion loan to the region to purchase vaccines (Myers 2020; Sanborn 2020), and China has been a major provider of vaccines for a number of countries in the region.[8]

At the same time that medical diplomacy had a positive effect, other factors may push China's relations with North America in a more negative direction. The decline in China's growth rate and its financial-sector problems, together with the indications in the most recent Five-Year Plan that China will put more emphasis on its domestic economy, may limit its new initiatives abroad. Chinese loans and FDI in Latin America in general had already begun to fall before the virus hit. In addition, most of those monies had gone to South rather than North America. And, as we saw, its trade and investment relations with the United States contracted as a result of the trade war, and the US counteroffensive in Latin America has made many countries hesitant in their dealings with China.

It was initially expected that the Biden government would take a very different international approach in comparison to its predecessor. Indeed, that has been the case with respect to the European and Asian allies with whom Biden sought to improve relations and to demonstrate that "America is back." Relations with China, by contrast, have followed a path quite similar to the Trump years with the exception of attempts to rally allies in an anti-China stance. Tariffs remain on China's exports to the United States, investment restrictions continue, and the tone of discussion between the two sides borders on hostility. Relations with both allies and China, of course, have been affected by Russia's invasion of Ukraine and the new Russia-China friendship pact. The Russian invasion has absorbed a large amount of US government time and financial resources that might have gone elsewhere, perhaps including Latin America. At the same time, the China-Russia friendship has increased hostility with respect to China. An anti-China posture is one of the few issues on which there is bipartisan agreement in the United States today.

The Biden government's approach to Latin America has been both a surprise and a disappointment to observers. While no one expected the region to be a top priority, the neglect was not anticipated—although this stance largely pertains to South America. In North America, whether by the narrow or broad definition, more attention has been devoted, but it has not been very effective. The most positive relations have been with Canada, where Prime Minister Justin Trudeau indicated enthusiasm about working with the new administration from the outset. Relations with Mexico's president Andrés Manuel López Obrador have been much more problematic. The Trump emphasis on preventing immigration across the Mexican border remains, while concerns about human rights and the environment have alienated the Mexican president. Help for Central America was among Biden's campaign promises, and Vice President Kamala Harris was put in charge, but little has been accomplished.

The Summit of the Americas in June 2022 became a symbol of much that has gone wrong in inter-American relations under Biden. Little attention was devoted to summit planning, while hostility was generated by the decision to exclude Cuba, Nicaragua, and Venezuela. This omission led several presidents to boycott the event, including López Obrador and many Central American leaders. Moreover, in substantive terms, the summit offered little that the Latin Americans were interested in. Trade and investment were low priority, while immigration topped the agenda. Ironically, although the US government wanted the summit to be a showcase of how democracy is preferable to autocracy—both in terms of values and as a way to solve problems—many thought that the biggest winner was China (Kine 2022; Neuman 2022). The North American space seems doomed to continue as a forgotten area despite earlier hopes for improvement.

Notes

1. ASEAN Plus Three consists of the ten countries that are members of the Association of Southeast Asian Nations, together with China, Japan, and South Korea. While these countries have strong economic relations, they were the result of bottom-up investment and trade links. Other than an annual summit, no organization is involved, unlike the highly bureaucratic European Union (EU). In late 2020, these thirteen countries joined Australia and New Zealand to form the Regional Comprehensive Economic Partnership (RCEP), which came into force on January 1, 2022. On RCEP, see Petri and Plummer (2020), UNCTAD (2021).
2. The end of the Multi-Fiber Agreement (MFA) in 2005 gave China's exports in textiles and related goods an additional boost; see the section on Central America later in the chapter.
3. The data throughout the chapter end in 2019 to avoid the impact of COVID-19.
4. Note that there is a significant discrepancy between data coming from China on trade with Mexico and Canada and data from those countries themselves. For the year 2019, for example, Mexico's data show exports to China of $7 billion and imports from China of $88 billion. Chinese figures, by contrast, show $15 billion and $46 billion. Likewise, Canadian data show exports of $17 billion versus

imports of $60 billion, while Chinese figures show $28 billion and $36 billion. Such discrepancies are found in many countries; the explanation is unclear.

5. Data on FDI are much more difficult to find and less reliable than those on trade flows. In the following discussion, I draw mainly on data from the US Commerce Department's Bureau of Economic Analysis (http://www.bea.gov). This source provides detailed information on US outward and inward flows by country and by year. For outward flows, there is also information on the sectoral distribution of FDI, although in some cases data are omitted to protect the identity of individual companies. Unfortunately, using this source means that investment between Canada and Mexico or Chinese investment in the two economies cannot be reported. Data are available for recent years from the OECD (https://read-oecd-ilibrary.org).

6. Data are for China and Hong Kong, since much of the investment going to China enters through Hong Kong.

7. Costa Rica, which was a signatory of the treaty, has long been an exception in the Central American context in terms of political and economic development. This case deserves a separate analysis, but for lack of space, it will be grouped with its neighbors. Note will be made when statements would clearly be misleading about Costa Rica. Panama is not included in CAFTA-DR.

8. The Latin American Program at the Woodrow Wilson Center has a website that shows Chinese and US donations related to the coronavirus to individual Latin American countries (Woodrow Wilson Center, n.d.).

Bibliography

Avendaño, R., and J. Dayton-Johnson. 2015. "Central America, China, and the US: What Prospects for Development?" *Pacific Affairs* 88 (4): 813–44.

Bowley, G. 2008. "Cash Helped China Win Costa Rica's Recognition." *New York Times*, September 12, 2008.

Bown, C. P. 2019. "US-China Trade War: The Guns of August." Peterson Institute for International Economics.

Bown, C. P. 2022. "US-China Phase One Tracker: China's Purchases of US Goods." Peterson Institute for International Economics.

Burfisher, M. E., F. Lambert, and T. D. Matheson. 2019. "NAFTA and the USMCA: What Is Gained?" Washington, DC: IMF working paper, WP/19/73.

Calmes, J. 2016. "Trump Scores Points on Trade in Debate, but Not So Much on Accuracy." *New York Times*, September 27, 2016.

Casas-Zamora, K. 2009. "Notes on Costa Rica's Switch from Taipei to Beijing." Paper presented at National Defense University, Washington, DC.

Center for Latin American and Latino Studies, American University. 2022. "China's

Presence in El Salvador and Its Strategies for Gaining Influence." Washington, DC: working paper.

Cota, I. 2013. "China Lends Costa Rica $400 Million on Xi Visit." *Reuters*, June 3, 2013. http://www.reuters.com/assets/print?aid=USBRE95218820130603.

Dussel Peters, E., and K. Gallagher. 2013. "NAFTA's Uninvited Guest: China and the Disintegration of North American Trade." *CEPAL Review* 110: 83–108.

Dussel Peters, E. 2019. "The New Triangular Relationship between Mexico, the United States, and China: Challenges for NAFTA." In *The Renegotiation of NAFTA: And China?*, edited by Enrique Dussel Peters, 97–98. Boulder, CO: Lynne Rienner Publishers.

Dussel Peters, E., ed. 2019. *The Renegotiation of NAFTA: And China?* Boulder, CO: Lynne Rienner Publishers.

Gruben, W. C. 2001. "Was NAFTA Behind Mexico's High Maquiladora Growth?" Federal Reserve Bank of Dallas, financial review, third quarter.

Harris, G. 2018. "US Weighed Penalizing El Salvador Over Support for China, Then Backed Off." *New York Times*, September 29, 2018.

Harris, R., and N. Schmitt. 2014. "NAFTA and the Transformation of Canadian Patterns of Trade and Specialization, 1990–2012." In *Federal Reserve Bank of Dallas, NAFTA at 20: Effects on the North American Market*, conference proceedings.

Hornbeck, J. F. 2012. "The Dominican Republic-Central America-United States Free Trade Agreement (CAFTA-DR): Developments in Trade and Investment." Washington, DC: Congressional Research Service.

International Monetary Fund. n.d. "Direction of Trade Statistics." https://data.imf.org/?sk=9D6028D4-F14A-464C-A2F2-59B2CD424B85.

Itakura, K. 2020. "Evaluating the Impact of the US-China Trade War." *Asian Economic Policy Review* 15 (1): 77–93.

Kine, P. 2022. "China's Long Shadow Looms over Biden's Americas Summit." *Politico*, June 9, 2022.

Liu, T., and W. T. Woo. 2018. "Understanding the US-China Trade War." *China Economics Journal* 11 (3): 319–40.

Lu, S. 2020. "Patterns of US Textile and Apparel Imports (undated February 2020)." Accessed February 13, 2021. Shunglufashion.com.

Myers, M. 2019. "Is the Dominican Republic's Pivot to China Paying Off?" *Latin America Advisor*, May 9, 2019.

Myers, M. 2020. "China's Medical Outreach in LAC: Facts and Features." Inter-American Dialogue, May 22, 2020.

Neuman, W. 2022. "What's Behind American Decline: Domestic Disfunction." *The Atlantic*, June 13, 2022.

OECD. n.d. "FDI Statistics by Partner Country."

Paletta, D., N. Miroff, and J. Dawsey. 2019. "Trump Says US to Impose 5 Percent Tariffs on All Mexican Imports Beginning June 10 in Dramatic Escalation of Border Clash." *Washington Post*, May 30, 2019.

Parajón, C. 2019. "The Impact on Central America of the 2008–2016 Diplomatic Truce between Chinese Mainland and Taiwan." Master's thesis, Schwarzman Scholars Program, Tsinghua University.

Petri, P. A., and M. Plummer. 2020. "RCEP: A New Trade Agreement that Will Shape Global Economics and Politics." Brookings Institution.

Rapoza, Kenneth. 2020. "New Data Shows US Companies are Definitely Leaving China." *Forbes*, April 7, 2020.

Sanborn, C. A. 2020. "Latin America and China in Times of COVID-19." Woodrow Wilson Center, Latin American Program and Kissinger Institute.

Scherrer, C. 2020. "Novel Labour-Related Clauses in a Trade Agreement: From NAFTA to USMCA." *Global Labour Journal* 11 (3): 291–396.

Schott, J. J., and M. P. Goodman, eds. 2021. *Bringing Supply Chains Back to Mexico: Opportunities and Obstacles*. Washington, DC: PIIE and CSIS.

Sieff, K. 2020. "As US-China Rift Grows, Mexico Tries to Lure American Businesses to Move Closer to Home." *Washington Post*, August 13, 2020.

South, R. B., and C. Kim. 2019. "Maquiladora Mortality: Manufacturing Plant Closure in Mexico." *Journal of Development Studies* 55 (8): 1654–69.

United Nations Conference on Trade and Development (UNCTAD). 2021. "An Assessment of the Regional Comprehensive Economic Partnership (RCEP) Tariff Concessions." United Nations.

US Department of Commerce, Bureau of Economic Analysis. n.d. "US Direct Investment Position Abroad on a Historical Cost Basis: Country Detail by Industry."

US Trade Representative. n.d. "Countries and Regions: Western Hemisphere."

Utar, H., and L. Torres-Ruiz. 2013. "International Competition and Industrial Evolution: Evidence from the Impact of Chinese Competition on Mexican Maquiladoras." *Journal of Development Economics* 105 (November): 267–87.

Villarreal, M. A., and I. F. Fergusson. 2020. *NAFTA and the United States-Mexico-Canada Agreement (USMCA)*. Washington, DC: Congressional Research Service.

Woodrow Wilson Center, Latin American Program. n.d. *Vaccine Rollout in Latin America: "Medical Diplomacy" and Great Power Competition*. Washington, DC: WWC.

World Bank. 2019. *Global Value Chain Development Report 2019: Technological Innovation, Supply Chain Trade and Workers in a Globalized World*. Washington, DC: World Bank.

World Bank. n.d. *World Integrated Trade Solution (WITS) Database*. Washington, DC: World Bank.

Youkee, M. 2019. "The Panama Canal Could Become the Center of the US-China Trade War." *Foreign Policy*.

Youkee, M. 2020. "Has China's Winning Streak in Panama Ended?" *Dialogo Chino*, March 25, 2020.

CHAPTER ELEVEN

Conclusion

The North American Idea Looking Forward

Eric Hershberg and Tom Long

AFTER A five-year hiatus, the leaders of Canada, Mexico, and the United States gathered in Washington on November 10, 2021, for the North American Leaders' Summit (NALS). The return of the supposedly annual conclave seemed to signal a regional renewal after the twin disruptions of Donald J. Trump and the COVID-19 pandemic. Eager to turn the page on the animosity of the Trump presidency, the three leaders sought to project a sense of business as usual. Indeed, some of the summit's agenda and rhetoric—like the focus on regional competitiveness—was little changed from the original NALS of the 2000s. But in other ways, the one-day meeting reflected the complex challenges for North America. In a broad sense, these challenges include rethinking the region's place in a changing global environment, sorting out the relationship of trilateral North America with smaller neighbors, and managing multifaceted integration where the governments have often been out of step with social and economic dynamics.

At the global level, North American talk of "competitiveness" had a new edge, clearly aimed at China. This suggested the geopolitical considerations of the United States, as well as Mexican concerns about commercial opportunities lost and Sino-Canadian clashes on rights and the rule of law. Shortly after that summit, surging global tensions took center stage with the Russian invasion of Ukraine. The sanctioning of Russia and a push for "decoupling" with China in strategic sectors seem to add weight to arguments for the geopolitical importance of North America. But while the war in Eastern Europe reinvigorated US-Canadian security cooperation through NATO, it exposed barely concealed contrasts with the worldviews of the Mexican leadership.

The 2021 NALS followed on the heels of the world climate summit, and there, too, national North American energy and carbon-reduction plans were often out of sync. With reference to the broader North American space, the return of NALS reflected the region's geographical spillover; Central America was clearly on the agenda regarding migration and security, even though its leaders were not invited to the table. Finally, the three governments were clearly grappling with the challenges of restarting economies, travel, and trade amid the continued disruptions of the pandemic. The pandemic had shut borders but also underscored the value of proximity in assuring resilient supply chains, potentially providing a counterweight in firms' relocation decisions (Shih 2020; Canello, Buciuni, and Gereffi 2022). Taken together, the effects of the uneven economic recovery and the Ukraine war—including labor market shifts and increased inflation—remain ambiguous.

Surely it comes across as cliché to assert that the North American region finds itself at a crossroads, but this moment—going well beyond the NALS—justifies such a categorical claim. To be sure, this is not the first pivotal moment for North America: the inauguration of NAFTA in 1994, the shock of the 9/11 attacks in 2001, and the election of Donald Trump in 2016 are the most prominent among several turning points. But today's conjuncture differs in how factors at the global, regional, and national levels have converged to create a moment of inflection. Great power competition, climate catastrophe, economic dislocations, and a global pandemic will have significant impacts on dynamics of regionalism in North America, just as they will elsewhere. These challenges seem well beyond the limited capabilities of North America's regional institutions and regimes. The 2021 NALS, held on short notice and with a scattershot agenda, suggests that intergovernmental North American cooperation has not yet caught up with the moment. So far, the crush of events seems to have further drained political momentum for advancing regional cooperation in the wake of the bruising USMCA talks.

In this final chapter, we consider what this volume says about North America in the context of this inflection point. A core message of the book is that North America should be understood in the context of a world of heterogeneous regions. Regions take on form and significance as a function of the broader global system, and today that system is in flux. Just as the end of the Cold War marked a sea change in the international order, creating the conditions that gave rise to NAFTA, today it is the emergence of China as a world power and the increasingly aggressive response from the United States that distinguishes our times from any in the recent past. Continued cooperation between China and Russia, increasingly united by shifting energy markets, has encouraged many in Washington to paint this competition in increasingly stark terms. That Canada and Mexico largely have signed onto this response results less from US coercion than from the realization, illustrated by Barbara Stallings in chapter 10, that China's growth has come in part at their expense. Regions will be (re) configured in response to the increasingly bipolar dynamic of interactions between Washington and Beijing, with the latter as well as the former perceiving North America and its broader environs as a terrain on which to compete for influence.

The countries whose loyalties the superpowers seek will face growing pressures over how to respond. Economic and political choices may produce growing alignment with one or another of the superpowers. If this occurs in "home" regions, such alignment would contribute to centripetal pressures (Morales, this volume). But in today's economy, the weight of China, the United States, and the European Union is felt far beyond their immediate vicinities—and much more than in the US-Soviet Cold War. As a response to this economic diffusion, many countries may try to play a delicate balancing act—conceivably pursuing what J. Heine et al. (2020) have referred to as "Active Non-Alignment"—either bilaterally or through the strengthening of regional blocs that orient their relationship to the international system. In this mix of pressures from established and aspiring hegemons, third-country responses, and economic diffusion, regions may serve as bulwarks for each power, battlegrounds for competing influence, or bastions of local autonomy.

But the degree and ways in which North America will cohere as one such region are far from certain. Today as in the past, there are inexorable pressures for Canada and Mexico to gravitate around the United States, with diplomatic relationships taking bilateral rather than trilateral form. One striking feature of the 2021 NALS, hosted by President Biden in Washington, was that the three-way discussion was preceded by separate one-on-one meetings between the US leader and his counterparts from Canada and Mexico. Their coming together in a trilateral setting was important symbolically—no such gathering had taken place during the Trump years—but leaving aside the optics and the narratives about partnerships that all three governments advanced following the discussions, no ambitious agenda for regional integration was put forth. Nor has any of the three governments consistently advocated for such cooperation in the wake of the summit. Long a consistent feature of North America, Mexican enthusiasm for visible regional cooperation with the United States has all but disappeared. If anything, Canada and Mexico are approaching their shared neighbor with greater wariness, fearful of the ramifications of US political polarization: whipsawing policies, nativist ferment, and mounting social tensions. The renewed summits offer a reminder that, however powerful the economic ties and shared governance processes that this book highlights may prove to be, there is no guarantee that North American governments will articulate the region as a coherent actor in the international system (see Santa-Cruz, this volume).

In this context, it is likely that Beijing will pursue a set of bilateral relations with each of the three North American countries, as well as with those of Central America. This may be by default, for as Stallings noted in chapter 10 of this volume, China does not see "North America" as a cohesive region. Or it may be intentional, to complicate the United States' strategic reserve. Alternatively, there is a scenario in which China comes to engage North America as a region, but that will result only if Canada, Mexico, and the United States make considerable strides in coordinating their interests. Either way, Chinese strategies, particularly regarding Mexico and Central America, will inevitably reflect its approach to the priority relationship with the United States. Mexico and several Central American countries—unlike Canada—may negotiate their relations with the United States through the prism of their perhaps not so illusory ability to tilt toward an alternative hegemon represented by China (Wise 2021). Multiple pathways are possible. Which trajectory ultimately emerges will be a function both of China's approach and to the ways in which the United States and its neighbors choose to engage both one another and the rising power across the Pacific.

During the Cold War, both superpowers sought to maintain regional spheres of influence. Regions were never impenetrable, and hegemony was often negotiated (Long 2021), but given its Monroeist pretensions, the United States generally defined its region as encompassing the entire Western Hemisphere, from Canada through the Southern Cone. One does not need to exaggerate US Cold War dominance in the Western Hemisphere to see how different the situation is today. Outside of Cuba, the Soviet Union was of marginal economic importance to countries of the Western Hemisphere. In contrast, China has been a primary trading partner and source of investment for a growing number of countries in the hemisphere (including, of course, the United States itself) for nearly two decades. Even if the "China boom" does not return for the commodity-driven economies of South America—and it well may— deep economic ties will remain; they will demand a political modus vivendi, at least, and perhaps much closer partnership. As a result, if the United States wants a strategic and economic regional bulwark, it will need to narrow its geographical aperture to the northern half of the Western Hemisphere. In the past, the United States has resisted a narrower but deeper approach; even if it reconsiders, Canada, Mexico, and the smaller states of the broader North American region will possess greater leverage than US politicians and diplomats are accustomed to accommodating. Put another way, the erosion of US unipolarity creates pressure to define just what kind of region North America will be—one with a coherent international identity and institutions, one that results from diffuse interactions of myriad actors, or one defined by largely unchanneled interdependence? In the absence of such a project of region-building, global dynamics may fragment the region further.

Pressures to redefine North America are also building closer to home. The most evident tensions regard the place of Central America—and Central Americans—in the North American region. Although informal mechanisms of social and economic integration extend beyond trilateral North America, formal mechanisms of regional governance rarely do. As contributors to this volume noted repeatedly, North American institutions are weak even at the trilateral level, especially beyond the economic sphere. Informally, North American regional governance extends beyond Canada, Mexico, and the United States, shaping security, migration, and trade in Central America and the Caribbean. However, this regional governance is often fragmentary and inconsistent. Too often, North American approaches have been counterproductive in security and exclusionary in migration (see Kloppe-Santamaría, Castañeda et al., and Toro, this volume). While Mexico and the United States have at times seen value in articulating North American responses to the broader region, Canada largely has stood aside from such efforts. For their part, Central American and Caribbean leaders have usually turned directly to Washington instead of "thinking

North America." Some Central American and Caribbean leaders are also turning to China for support or in an attempt to attract US resources after two decades of a narrow US policy focus on drugs and migration. The divergence between "bottom-up" regional dynamics and formal regional responses is wide and growing.

Addressing the place of Central America is not the only challenge, however. Even in areas of core interdependences and institutions, North America remains unsettled by recent shocks. The new USMCA lowered the political salience of calls to renegotiate or abandon NAFTA, but it also introduced new areas of contestation. As Laura Macdonald points out in this volume, the threat to NAFTA ultimately served to rally many of North America's supporters—from transnational business to migration advocates—to the defense of regional integration. The USMCA diminished the threat; that in turn seems to have disaggregated those supportive alliances. For the most part, USMCA did not buttress the regional mechanisms meant to resolve disagreements. Already, disputes are being filed around USMCA provisions. Some of the first grievances originated with US unions regarding labor rights in Mexico, including four procedures using USMCA's new "rapid response mechanism" to pressure employers there. Early cases suggest the USMCA will be more consequential for labor rights than NAFTA's weak side agreement, while continuing to bolster transnational civil society collaboration. The United States is also turning to USMCA mechanisms to push back against alleged favoritism of state-owned companies in the Mexican energy sector. Initial disagreements have been handled quietly, but the focus on labor and energy violations in Mexico may generate backlash from a Mexican government sensitive about intrusions into its domestic affairs. Meanwhile, US "buy American" provisions meant to strengthen US participation in supply chains and promote green technology have ruffled feathers in Mexico City and Ottawa. The two countries made joint complaints about US plans for electric-vehicle subsidies, including calling for USMCA consultations. However, such nationalist provisions tend to have robust support in the US Congress. As has often been the case, US domestic politics continue to serve as a brake on formal region-building, suggesting a key reason for the comparative stagnation of trilateral institutions (Panke and Stapel, this volume).

In contrast to the question of institutional stagnation, the degree to which North America exists as an economic unit is rarely appreciated in International Relations (IR). In 2019, the region exchanged across borders more than $1.2 trillion of goods, accounting for half of Canadian, Mexican, and US total exports. That trails only the European Union in terms of economic regions. However, top-line trade statistics actually understate the deep connections between agriculture, manufacturing, energy, and financial flows. What Christopher Wilson (2021, 41) noted of one bilateral relationship is true of the larger region: "The United States and Mexico do not simply trade products, they build them together. . . . The two economies have become synchronized." Even in a globalized age, the countries of the broader North American region routinely conduct half or more of their business within the region—and among the most deeply integrated sectors are some of the most technologically sophisticated and higher value-added industries. One result of this substantial de facto integration is that governments throughout the region may come to see North America's prosperity as critical to addressing the persistent economic demands of their electorates. A renewed focus on North America may also result from the post-pandemic preoccupation with nearshoring and the stability of supply chains, which happens to dovetail with Washington's determination to reduce China's centrality to economic dynamics both near and far (Feinberg 2021).

These global and regional dynamics continue to reverberate through the domestic politics of North America. As the United States grapples with the shifting contours of the international system, a fundamental decision looms whether to approach the landscape with a message of America First, as in the Trump administration, or instead through a prism of leadership in an environment defined in terms of multilateralism. The latter, clearly, is the preferred option of the Biden administration, and this has potentially profound implications for the North American project. Given their exposure to political and economic oscillations in the United States, Ottawa and Mexico City may hesitate to cede more policy autonomy. A multiplicity of challenges, beginning with climate but extending to the foundations of economic prosperity and championing of democratic systems of governance, could motivate US policy makers to situate North America as one beacon for the rest of the world. Some of North America's early proponents, like Robert Pastor (2001; 2011), saw the region in this optimistic light—a model for US international leadership. It is perhaps not insignificant that the 2020 Democratic Party platform situated its approach to the Western Hemisphere in a North American framework, suggesting that the great issues of the region, including migration and security, must be resolved through cooperative arrangements encompassing the United States and its immediate neighbors. For liberal internationalists, North America would emerge as an intentional contrast to Chinese-led, and Russian-backed, global and regional orders. If that is to be effective, North American regionalism needs to deliver economically, while also showing that it can catalyze cooperation on other issues. This was the message of the 2021 NALS; the risk is that North America once again disappears from the agenda amid the din of policy problems, instead of being seen as a framework to address them.

Neither rhetorical gestures nor functional imperatives are sufficient to constitute well-integrated regions, however. To be sure, as this volume has articulated, on matters ranging from economic development to citizen safety to public health amid a devastating pandemic, there is ample evidence to suggest that deep cooperation offers avenues toward achieving shared goals that cannot be satisfied by any of the region's countries "going it alone." But merely because regional cooperation is in every party's interest does not mean that it will happen. Indeed, that has been evident for decades during which the North American project has never reached the level envisioned by its most committed advocates. That North America should be a community does not mean that it will be.

Indeed, powerful forces operate against convergence. Not all material incentives point to cooperation. Short-term competition for resources may override incentives for long-term cooperation, whether around energy or water or climate or Central American migration. Moreover, the North American project has never boasted widespread support from public opinion, in contrast, for example, to some moments of the development of the European Union. Nor, again in contrast with the EU, has there been a visible and determined bloc of business-sector advocacy for a formal integration project, even while liberalized trade and investment regimes have been priorities for some industries and interest associations. Perhaps most importantly, there has been no push from civil society for the articulation of a regional identity that might in turn result in institutional deepening, despite population flows that have created a de facto landscape of multiple identities—Canadians and Mexicans and Central Americans living in the United States while retaining membership in their home country communities, Americans increasingly residing in Canada and Mexico.

Indeed, nationalist sentiment in all three countries militates against the emergence of a North American identity that might drive integration (Santa-Cruz, this volume). It was striking amid the pandemic to observe the depth of Canadian public opinion in favor of prolonging the closure of the border with the United States. This celebration of the exclusion of Americans seems to reflect an aversion that goes beyond the risk of viral contagion. With echoes of, and material support from, the US right, so-called Freedom convoys blocked border crossings and occupied central Ottawa in early 2022, roiling Canadian politics. Although extreme, these events exposed currents of populist, anti-integrationist forces in Canada, where they have rarely been so prominent. Similar dynamics have long been evident among Americans with regard to the border with Mexico (Toro, this volume), and in opposition to regional cooperation more generally. Perhaps rather than construct a wall, what Trump's constituents needed to secure universal support for their exclusionary preferences was a pandemic. Public health grounds were repeatedly invoked to tighten the border and rapidly expel migrants without due process; despite a gradual rollback of some of these practices and rhetoric following Biden's inauguration, the restrictive environment has mostly survived the Trump administration, as described in chapter 5 of this book. Though Canadian-Mexican relations have been marked by moments of cooperative responses to their overbearing neighbor (Macdonald 2020), as Asa McKercher pointed out in this volume, there is little to suggest a shared identity there, either.

In Mexico, official appeals to nationalism, sovereignty, and nonintervention have surged under President Andrés Manuel López Obrador, echoing in some respects pre-NAFTA Mexican foreign policies. This may portend yet another obstacle to North American integration. In the early 1990s, NAFTA was negotiated with a tacit agreement that questions of democratization in Mexico would be kept off the table. After 2000, Mexico's multiparty electoral democracy evolved alongside ever-closer integration and cross-border policy coordination with the United States. López

Obrador has been keen to reinstate limits and to resist the unbridled US scrutiny that previous Mexican governments tolerated. In today's context, however, as concerns about democratic backsliding in Mexico and Central America grow, it will be difficult for Canadian and US leaders to revert to the pre-NAFTA separation of regional integration from the regional promotion of democracy. Certainly, this very issue complicated the US-hosted 2022 Summit of the Americas in Los Angeles when the Mexican president stayed home to protest the exclusion of Cuba, Nicaragua, and Venezuela.

Perhaps the determinant of future direction will be the depth of the crisis faced by the region's various countries: there is a substantial literature tracing institutional innovation to crisis (Doner, Ritchie, and Slater 2005; Capoccia 2015). China's rise presents the United States with a strategic crisis, and a related challenge to its international identity as the "indispensable nation." Its self-image as political and economic leader of the North Atlantic and Western Hemisphere is challenged not only by China but also by its limited capacity to respond globally to the socioeconomic crisis of the pandemic, as well as by the decade-long growth in authoritarianism in various corners of the world. Ours may precisely be a time when such momentous challenges to the status quo give rise to new institutional forms and unexpected modes of cooperation.

North America, Regionalism, and International Relations

This volume has sought to reinvigorate the place of North America in International Relations' study of regions. When one looks at both area studies and IR's study of regionalism, North America's economic heft contrasts with its secondary status among world regions. There is no consolidated field of North American area studies; contrasted with Africa, Asia, Europe, and Latin America, there are vanishingly few academic or policy centers dedicated to the study of the region. Though North America's formation in the 1990s was an important case study for the expanding study of regionalism in International Relations, the region has drawn limited attention in recent years. This volume has pointed out how relative inattention to North America, both from scholars and the region's own heads of state, contrasts with a great deal of dynamism at lower levels. North America's oft-mentioned trade ties are matched by less discussed, but no less profound, patterns of social integration. While North America lacks strong regional organizations, this volume suggests that other patterns of governance exist.

In embarking upon this project, North America's low profile in the scholarship suggested the more fundamental challenge of conceptualizing "North America" as a region. Looking at North America from a global perspective means first grappling with how the concept of "region" applies. Throughout this volume, authors have applied, adapted, and challenged concepts and theories of regionalism while also illuminating

North American patterns of diplomacy, security, economics, energy, and more. We have grouped chapters according to authors' conceptual underpinnings. Some, like Arturo Santa-Cruz, emphasize the importance of identity and cohesion in creating regional order. As a result, he argues that North America is lacking in terms of its ability to shape and define regional order. Nor can North America be seen as a cohesive international actor. As a trilateral entity, North America lacks any clear sense of unity that distinguishes it from other global regions. Looking at Canadian approaches to North America, Asa McKercher concurs. Canadian policy makers have emphasized similarities and convergences with the United States while treating Mexico as distant and foreign; a policy of bilateralism over trilateralism follows from this. With a focus on the US-Mexico border, Celia Toro sees power asymmetries and US unilateralism as key impediments to the building of a regional community that extends beyond the interests of transnational businesses. All three emphasize how a weak sense of regional community presents a lasting obstacle to the sorts of political projects that would strengthen North America's place on the global stage.

However, the conceptual debate does not end there. Adopting the "new regionalism approach," Laura Macdonald suggests a more multifaceted process of region-making in North America. Governments remain central actors, but they may not always lead the process. Instead, she shows how private-sector and civil society groups came to the defense of "North America" against Trump, preserving an integrated region (even in the absence of strong intergovernmental institutions). This is suggestive of more bottom-up regional dynamics, with a mix of state and non-state players involved. Dense networks of migration and transnational communities have expanded patterns of social integration. Ad hoc regional regimes have emerged in response, including a "Fortress North America" and a shared, militarized response to crime and drugs, argued Ernesto Castañeda, Michael Danielson, and Jayesh Rathod, and Gema Kloppe Santamaría, respectively. Greater regional coordination, then, should not always be seen as aligned with citizen well-being. Shifting the focus even further from national governments, Daniela Stevens pointed to how cooperation at subnational levels, again involving diverse actors, feeds into patterns of regional energy governance. These authors showed how the forces generated by North American regionalism not only shape interactions across the region, but also they exceed the traditional boundaries of North America. Rather than suggesting that these amount to "mere" regionalization, they lead us to probe the limitations of IR's frequently top-down, outside-in conceptualizations of the region. In short, the study of North America reminds scholars of the importance of regions beyond states.

Though many authors have sought to move beyond classic approaches to regionalism, it is hard to escape the centrality of economic interdependence to North America. Equally, North America's dearth of formal institutional innovation is a recurring feature across the chapters. The meaning of these two features for North America as a region, however, is open to debate. One might see North America's continued dynamism and institutions-light framework as its calling card; conversely, the lack of institutions can lead one to question whether North America exists as a region. The contributors in the volume's final section put institutions and interdependence at the center of their approaches to North America, while also placing the region in a global context. Isidro Morales argued that economic interdependences have created tight integration in some locations and industries, while extra-regional competition, internal nativism, and the weakness of North America's political narratives tend to pull the region apart. There have been few formal regional organizations to pull North America together from above, Diana Panke and Sören Stapel show. Compared to other regions, North American institutions have seen little renovation or expansion. That institutional "drift" may be costly for North America in the face of the growth of China. Barbara Stallings illustrates just how deeply the rise of China has undercut the very economic interdependence that North America's proponents emphasize; it has also limited the incipient integration of Central America into North American manufacturing chains.

Moving beyond the conceptualization of North America, the volume argues for greater theoretical engagement between studies of North America and IR's study of regionalism. Interestingly, North America has played only a bit part in comparative regionalism, which has been more focused on Europe, Asia, Latin America, and Africa. In part, this absence results from comparative regionalism's long-term concern with comparing the origins and design of regional organizations (Kahler and MacIntyre 2013; Acharya and Johnston 2007). As Tanja Börzel and Thomas Risse (2019) note, grand theories of regionalism perform poorly in North America, which shows "high economic interdependence and low regionalism." They attribute that outcome to weak regionalist commitment among elites in the United States—though this somewhat begs the question of what drives regional commitment.

Functionalist and state-centric thinking continues to drive much work on regionalism, including on North America. Without denying the role of states and functional integration, this volume has emphasized the need to cast a wider net in our understanding of regions. This suggests that there are possibilities to take regional comparison further, beyond institutions and interdependence, to better understand the pathways of regional development. In that sense, the growth of historical insti-tutionalist approaches in IR may have more to offer the study of regions, including comparatively. Notable contributions on North America in this tradition include work by Francesco Duina (2006; 2016), who employs both comparative techniques and historical institutionalist concepts like path dependence. While historical institutionalism might seem well suited to explain institutional stagnation in North America—the path dependence of its initial economic approach to regionalism—the emergence of new concepts of incremental change in historical institutionalism may shed light on processes of drift, conversion, and layering in the development of North America and other regions (Pierson 2004, 134–42; Hacker, Pierson, and Thelen 2015).

In this volume, several chapters adopt historical approaches that connect with these ideas, including Gema Kloppe-Santamaría's exploration of the emergence, consolidation, and stubborn endurance of a security policy paradigm despite mounting failures and a changing context. Regarding Canada, Asa McKercher shows how bilateralism became deeply engrained in Canadian thinking about North America.

Finally, as Laura Macdonald argues in this volume, the multifaceted theoretical school dubbed "the new regionalism approach" (Hettne and Söderbaum 1998; 2000) has much to offer the study of North America. New regionalism is useful in rolling back many of the default liberal and functionalist assumptions about North American cooperation. Like comparative regionalism, it suggests a break with theories of functionalist and teleological regional progression derived from a stylized European context. Though as we note above, many new regionalists have focused on institutions, the approach's founders saw these as secondary to underlying patterns of regionalization. New regionalism has value for formulating questions and illuminating North American dynamics without returning to the assumption that the answer to regional problems will be adding new intergovernmental or supranational bodies.

While none of these approaches lends itself to parsimonious grand theory or straightforward causal narratives, we suggest that broader theoretical engagement provides new tools and insights into North American dynamics. These go far beyond commercial exchanges of the sort often captured by metrics like intraregional trade, and include patterns of social integration, intertwined politics, and multifaceted and often informal patterns of governance. Those dynamics are not neatly coterminous with the boundaries of the traditional, trilateral North America. Instead, North America's boundaries results from social constructions and political projects, and these often vary with issue area. This empirical richness also makes North America a site for conceptual and theoretical innovation—a task that this volume's authors have sought to accomplish.

North America has often resisted predictions—first for its seemingly inexorable integration after NAFTA and more recently for its likely disintegration under the Trump administration. Only in terms of boosting trade and investment, and integrating production networks, did North America meet expectations—at least at first. In other ways, the region's contradictions have bedeviled predictions for North America's trajectory. It defied the overhyped expectations of its political advocates. NAFTA was not a one-way ticket to development for Mexico—something that became clear almost immediately with the political and economic turmoil of 1994. Relatedly, it did not slow migration flows in the region. But it also confounded many analysts. Looking at the European model, some asked if North American institutions would "deepen" or "broaden" first. The region's response, for the most part, was "neither." From the state perspective, trade and investment did not lead to much else: there was no "spillover," either functional or political. Nor was there much "spillaround" to increase the scope of regional institutions or "buildup" of institutional authority (Schmitter 1970; Malamud and Dri 2013). Despite booming trade and investment, and a host of transnational problems, few new institutions emerged. With some halfhearted exceptions, the states involved did not attempt to construct new cooperative mechanisms. Though corporate interests structured their activities in a North American space in major economic sectors, both in agriculture and manufacturing, these interests engaged in little lobbying for institutional change. Other pro-regional transnational interests, such as migrants, had much less political influence.

But if North America appears somehow underdeveloped as a region, this is the result more of our expectations than systematic comparison with regions elsewhere. Despite some two decades of pushback from comparative regionalists and new regionalism scholars, those expectations remain imbued with functionalism, liberal institutionalism, and related Eurocentrism. Scholars have more forcefully contested such Eurocentric assumptions in Asia, Africa, and Latin America, but in North America they remain ingrained—perhaps given North America's role as the "other" region within the "West," as a reflection of dominant policy paradigms, or simply due to lesser attention from IR regionalist scholars. In its formal sense, North America was created by state action—pushed by business interests and economic modernizers. That has led many to see the region through an economic lens. Yet North America is not so one-dimensional. It possesses a social fabric woven together through complex patterns of migration, family ties, cultural exchange, and resource flows. Both economic and social ties have expanded in a context of institutional weakness and political ambivalence, but also of complex forms of governance. The path of its development produced something quite different from how IR often envisions regions. But as this volume has suggested, when we adjust our conceptual lenses, a North American region comes into focus.

Bibliography

Acharya, A., and A. I. Johnston. 2007. "Comparing Regional Institutions: An Introduction." In *Crafting Cooperation: Regional International Institutions in Comparative Perspective*, edited by Amitav Acharya and Alastair Iain Johnston, 1–31. Cambridge: Cambridge University Press, 2007.

Börzel, T. A., and T. Risse. 2019. "Grand Theories of Integration and the Challenges of Comparative Regionalism." *Journal of European Public Policy* 26 (8): 1231–52.

Canello, J., G. Buciuni, and G. Gereffi. 2022. "Reshoring by Small Firms: Dual Sourcing Strategies and Local Subcontracting in Value Chains." *Cambridge Journal of Regions, Economy and Society* 15 (2): 237–59.

Capoccia, G. 2015. "Critical Junctures and Institutional Change." In *Advances in*

Comparative-Historical Analysis, edited by James Mahoney and Kathleen Thelen, 147–79. New York: Cambridge University Press.

Doner, R. F., B. K. Ritchie, and D. Slater. 2005. "Systemic Vulnerability and the Origins of Developmental States: Northeast and Southeast Asia in Comparative Perspective." *International Organization* 59 (2): 327–61.

Duina, F. 2006. *The Social Construction of Free Trade: The European Union, NAFTA, and Mercosur*. Princeton, NJ: Princeton University Press.

Duina, F. 2016. "North America and the Transatlantic Area." In *The Oxford Handbook of Comparative Regionalism*, edited by Tanja A. Börzel and Thomas Risse, 133–49. New York: Oxford University Press. http://www.oxfordhandbooks.com/view/10.1093/oxfordhb/9780199682300.001.0001/oxfordhb-9780199682300-e-8.

Feinberg, R. 2021. "Widening the Aperture: Nearshoring in Our 'Near Abroad.'" Latin America Program, Wilson Center. https://www.wilsoncenter.org/sites/default/files/media/uploads/documents/WideningTheApertureNearshoringInOurNearAbroadRichardEFeinbergApril2021.pdf.

Fioretos, O. 2017. *International Politics and Institutions in Time*. Oxford: Oxford University Press.

Hacker, J. S., P. Pierson, and K. Thelen. 2015. "Drift and Conversion: Hidden Faces of Institutional Change." In *Advances in Comparative-Historical Analysis*, edited by J. Mahoney and K. Thelen, 180–208. Strategies for Social Inquiry. Cambridge: Cambridge University Press. https://doi.org/10.1017/CBO9781316273104.008.

Haggart, B. 2014. *Copyfight: The Global Politics of Digital Copyright Reform*. Toronto: University of Toronto Press.

Heine, J., C. Fortin, and C. Ominami. 2020. "El no alineamiento activo: Un camino para Latinoamérica." *Nueva Sociedad* (October). https://nuso.org/articulo/el-no-alineamiento-activo-una-camino-para-america-latina.

Hettne, B., and F. Söderbaum. 1998. "The New Regionalism Approach." *Politeia* 17 (3): 6–21.

Hettne, B., and F. Söderbaum. 2000. "Theorising the Rise of Regionness." *New Political Economy* 5 (3): 457–72.

Kahler, M., and A. MacIntyre. 2013. *Integrating Regions: Asia in Comparative Context*. Stanford, CA: Stanford University Press.

Long, T. 2021. "The United States in Latin America: Lasting Asymmetries, Waning Influence?" In *External Powers in Latin America*, edited by G. L. Gardini, 15–28. New York: Routledge.

Macdonald, L. 2020. "Stronger Together? Canada-Mexico Relations and the NAFTA Re-negotiations." *Canadian Foreign Policy Journal* 26 (2): 152–66.

Mahoney, J., and K. Thelen. 2015. *Advances in Comparative-Historical Analysis*. New York: Cambridge University Press.

Malamud, A., and C. Dri. 2013. "Spillover Effects and Supranational Parliaments: The Case of MERCOSUR." *Journal of Iberian and Latin American Research* 19 (2): 224–38.

Pastor, R. A. 2001. *Toward a North American Community: Lessons from the Old World for the New*. Washington, DC: Institute for International Economics.

Pastor, R. A. 2011. *The North American Idea: A Vision of a Continental Future*. Oxford: Oxford University Press.

Pierson, P. 1993. "When Effect Becomes Cause: Policy Feedback and Political Change." *World Politics* 45 (4): 595–628.

Pierson, P. 2004. *Politics in Time: History, Institutions, and Social Analysis*. Princeton, NJ: Princeton University Press.

Schmitter, P. C. 1970. "Central American Integration: Spill-over, Spill-around or Encapsulation?" *JCMS: Journal of Common Market Studies* 9 (1): 1–48.

Shih, W. 2020. "Is It Time to Rethink Globalized Supply Chains?' *MIT Sloan Management Review* 61 (4): 1–3.

Thelen, K. 1999. "Historical Institutionalism in Comparative Politics." *Annual Review of Political Science* 2 (1): 369–404.

Wilson, C. 2021. "A U.S.-Mexico Economic Agenda for Competitiveness and Inclusive Growth." In *Re-Building a Complex Partnership: The Outlook for U.S.-Mexico Relations under the Biden Administration*, 38–49. Washington, DC: Mexico Institute, Wilson Center.

Wise, C. 2021. "China in Latin America: Winning Hearts and Minds Pragmatically." In *External Powers in Latin America*, edited by Gian Luca Gardini, 44–58. New York: Routledge.

The United States and Its Near Abroad

From Hegemonic Presumption and Intermittent Interventions toward Strategic Cooperation

Abraham F. Lowenthal

This book emphasizes that formal regionalism, and even less-institutionalized "regionalization," have largely stalled in North America since the adoption of the North American Free Trade Agreement in 1994. Some chapters discuss mainly how theories should be revised to take that into account, while others address what could be done on specific issues to build synergies among the nations of North America, a territory defined differently by various contributors. The volume makes timely and constructive contributions.

This afterword is more oriented toward policy and practice. It argues that significant long-term ties, shared interests, common problems, substantive tensions, and potential opportunities deeply connect the United States (and to a lesser extent, Mexico and Canada) with other countries and territories in their shared "near abroad" (i.e., those in the Caribbean, the Central American isthmus, and South America's northern tier).[1] It suggests that the United States and all the countries and territories of its near abroad would gain significantly if their policy makers, analysts, and publics better understood their shared history, asymmetric interdependence, and intertwined societies. This focus would help enable them to fashion and support long-term strategic visions of regional cooperation—not imposed by US dominance but crafted jointly, in their respective and shared interests and with mutual respect. It calls for nurturing new mindsets in the United States and in neighboring countries and territories in order to move from historic patterns of domination, intervention, submission, withdrawal, and neglect toward identifying and advancing shared interests and managing frictions, immediate and long term.

Vulnerable States in the Shadow of a Colossus

The countries of the Caribbean Basin and Central America share several characteristics. They are mostly small, and most are poor and dependent on agricultural, raw material, and light industrial exports; in some cases, on tourism, primarily from the United States and Canada; and on remittances from their diasporas, concentrated mainly in those two countries. Most have long had highly asymmetric and problematic interactions with the United States that have often been unproductive, shortsighted, and self-defeating on both sides. No US administration, with the possible exception of Jimmy Carter's, has entered office intending to give priority to relations with the near abroad, but one after another has found itself quite engaged there. It is notable that Joe Biden's administration began with signals of special concern for the region.[2]

From the late nineteenth century through World War II, these nearby jurisdictions were treated by the United States as subject to forceful intervention whenever Washington perceived a reason to land its troops. During the first three decades of the twentieth century, the United States deployed troops to the region more than twenty times.[3] In more recent years, the near abroad countries were affected by a lingering US "hegemonic presumption" that repeatedly justified intrusive unilateral interventions, including overt and covert efforts at regime change, without taking on long-term responsibility.[4]

The mostly small, weak, dependent, and vulnerable states of the Caribbean Basin, together with the larger countries of the "near abroad" region—Mexico, Canada, Venezuela, and Colombia—have all tried in different ways over many decades to advance their own interests while striving to maintain their sovereignties. They have had to cope with Washington's tendency to impose on them measures to protect US security, economic, and political interests, including those of its corporations, faith-based organizations, and labor unions. Various US government foreign affairs agencies sought to exclude extra-hemispheric powers and protect US domination— even sometimes in circumstances when no credible threat to the United States was easily discernible.[5]

This entrenched mindset, expressed in public statements and in secret planning documents, posited that the United States had the right, even the responsibility, to assure that no potentially hostile political force would take power in the Americas, nor would any country in the Western Hemisphere link itself with an outside power in a way that could threaten US interests. Washington sought for many decades to protect unchallenged access to the Panama Canal and the sea lanes leading to it, to promote advantages for US business and commercial interests, and to press countries in the region to adopt US economic doctrines and political institutions. Only Cuba, under revolutionary leader Fidel Castro, escaped this domination by building close ties with the Soviet Union, defeating the US-supported Bay of Pigs invasion, and surviving covert US measures, including economic sabotage, assassination attempts against Castro, and economic sanctions.[6]

Over the next decades, however, and especially after the dissolution of the Soviet Union in 1988–1991, the countries and territories of the Caribbean Basin, including several former European colonies, became objectively less important to US national security, economic prosperity, and international influence. This was so for four reasons, beyond the Soviet Union's demise: 1) The use of synthetics and the availability of alternate sources of raw materials and tropical agricultural products made these countries relatively less important as sources of US imports. 2) Major expansion of US investment and trade with Europe and Asia made the Caribbean Basin countries relatively less significant for US producers, investors, and financial institutions. 3) The Panama Canal became less important than it had been historically for the US economy and military security, due to massive petroleum tankers and aircraft carriers too large to transit the canal, and intercontinental ballistic missiles (ICBMs) and nuclear submarines that reduced the advantages of proximity. 4) The rapid expansion in the number of countries represented in the United Nations and other fora diminished the leverage of the small Caribbean states whose votes had previously been crucial on a series of international issues. Yet US foreign policy makers continued to assume that control of this region was important (even if it was apparently not important enough to warrant sustained positive attention).

Initially, Cuba's strong ties with the Soviet Union sharply increased US government concern with the Caribbean Basin in the 1960s, but that preoccupation waned after the withdrawal of Russian missiles from Cuba. US apprehension increased again during the 1970s in response to Central America's leftist insurgencies and to the Nicaraguan revolution in 1979. The Carter administration became quite engaged, both in the Caribbean and in Central America, trying to increase US influence but also recognizing the need for reforms from oligarchic rule.

The Reagan administration took office in 1981, vowing to fight communism in the Americas at its source (i.e., Cuba). Under Ronald Reagan, Washington tried, with limited success, to help suppress the leftist insurgency in El Salvador and to organize and support a counterrevolutionary force against the Sandinista government in Nicaragua. It mined Managua's harbor, built military bases in Honduras, prepositioned thousands of tons of material, and prepared for possible direct military intervention in Nicaragua. President Reagan spoke more often about Central America and the Caribbean than about any other foreign policy issue.[7] The Caribbean Basin Initiative (CBI) was his administration's major foreign policy initiative during his first years in office; US economic and military assistance in the Caribbean and Central America multiplied tenfold. But these efforts triggered congressional opposition to the provision of lethal weapons and then to the Iran-Contra scandal, which resulted from the administration's attempts to evade congressional restrictions.

In 1983, the US government used some 7,000 troops in Grenada to oust a left-leaning government from an island whose entire population could fit into a US sports stadium. The intervention was largely political theater for domestic and international audiences, unrelated to any genuine, imminent security threat in, from, or through Granada.

The United States remained quite engaged in the near abroad for several years, largely based on what I then called "national insecurity," discomfort arising from losing control of territory that used to be subject to US hegemony, even though it was hard to articulate why such control should still matter.[8] The administration of President George H. W. Bush accepted multilateral efforts to lower the temperature of Central American confrontations that had marked the 1980s, and moved somewhat toward accepting local political dynamics, although it did dispatch US troops to overthrow the government of Manuel Noriega in Panama in 1989. That intervention had more to do with domestic politics, narcotics trafficking, and personal animosity than national security.

By the late 1980s, US government concern shifted mainly to Colombia, where US advisors helped local security forces check but not eliminate leftist insurgents in a major joint effort, Plan Colombia. The US government then concentrated mainly on curbing the trade of narcotics produced in South America but trafficked through Central America, Mexico, and the Caribbean. In the 1990s, Washington's attention turned also to negotiating NAFTA with Mexico and Canada and winning congressional support to put that accord into effect, a goal that President George H. W. Bush advanced and President Bill Clinton inherited in 1993 and implemented.

The United States and Its Near Abroad in the Twenty-First Century

In the twenty-first century, the US government, under administrations of both parties, has focused considerable attention on Mexico, mainly involving close but discreet cooperation on continental security in the wake of the 9/11 attacks, as well as on issues of narcotics control and border management (through Plan Mérida). Beyond those efforts, bursts of US attention to the near abroad in recent years have mainly been triggered, case by case, by recurrent natural disasters, heightened political and civil strife, the emergence of a Venezuelan government devoted to "twenty-first-century socialism," pressures for regime change in Cuba and Venezuela from their diasporas in the United States, transnational crime, and especially by periodic episodes of "irregular" migration from various countries in the region.

Diaspora organizations, especially from Cuba, Venezuela, and the Commonwealth Caribbean, as well as the Congressional Black Caucus's commitment to Haiti, have pushed Washington to make various ad hoc arrangements to manage immigration flows. Large numbers of undocumented migrants from the northern tier of Central America, beginning in 2014, stimulated the Obama-Biden administration to propose measures to relieve poverty and turmoil there and in Haiti, in order to confront the "root causes" of mass migration. Attention to the Caribbean Basin expanded and changed somewhat during the second Obama administration, including its move toward rapprochement with Cuba and a general disposition to accept local political dynamics without strong US interference. But these Caribbean initiatives received little sustained follow-up and were largely abandoned by the Trump administration.

Donald Trump and his inner circle set out from the start to assert and rebuild US global primacy. In this context, Trump called for terminating NAFTA and extending and reinforcing a monumental border wall with Mexico, to be paid for, he claimed, by Mexico. The Trump administration used tariffs and threatened other forms of economic coercion to force migrants from Mexico, Central America, and the Caribbean seeking asylum or refugee status to "remain in Mexico," rather than entering the United States at a border crossing before their status could be adjudicated. It tried to remove the special protective status that had been granted by Obama to "the Dreamers," persons who had been born abroad but arrived in the United States as children, accompanying their families, and it reversed the Obama administration's moves to grant temporary protected status to refugees from Central America.

These restrictive and often punitive policies were accompanied by harsh and disdainful rhetoric and by both coercive measures and incentives to force Mexico—and through Mexico, the Central American and Caribbean countries—to prevent migrants from reaching the United States. Those included threats to unilaterally withdraw from NAFTA and the actual implementation of tariffs on Mexico (and Canada). Even in that context, pressures on Trump from within his own administration and from the US business community, together with astute political maneuvering by Mexico and Canada, led the Trump administration in its first year to reverse course, agree to update NAFTA's provisions, and then negotiate to replace it with the US-Mexico-Canada Agreement (USMCA), with renewed efforts to facilitate greater trade and investment among the original three North American partners.[9]

Underlying conditions in Central America and the Caribbean Basin, as well as relations between the United States and these countries, worsened considerably during the Trump years. Economic, social, humanitarian, public safety, and political circumstances in most of the near abroad deteriorated. Unfavorable global economic winds slowed the growth of Caribbean Basin economies. Civic violence and both organized and small-scale crime increased, as did the traffic in guns and ammunition from the United States to Mexico. Police operations and incarceration practices became more repressive, both in the near abroad and in the United States.

These adverse conditions were exacerbated after early 2020 by the COVID-19 pandemic, which devastated the tourism sector in the Caribbean and Central America, overwhelmed public health capacities, and threatened to worsen the public health crisis in the United States itself, leading to much tighter restrictions on the flow of people across the US border. Tropical hurricanes and other weather disturbances in the Caribbean and in the southeastern United States, moreover, underlined that global warming is accelerating rapidly, with implications throughout this extended region. It became increasingly evident that the United States cannot wall itself off from the damage wreaked by these storms, nor from the impacts of disease and crime.

The Biden administration, although beset from the start by an extraordinary combination of major domestic and international challenges, quickly recognized the mounting problems affecting the closest neighbors of the United States. Early in 2021, it designated Vice President Kamala Harris, as her first foreign policy assignment, to focus on Central America, especially on Honduras, Guatemala, and El Salvador, and to revive the regional development plans Biden had championed as vice president. The Biden administration took further steps, albeit modest, to prioritize regional cooperation by the United States, and to a lesser extent Mexico and Canada, to assist the countries and territories to the south. With the advent of COVID-19, the first responses of the United States, Mexico, and Canada were mainly inward-turning and triage-oriented. By 2021, however, the Biden administration began to respond positively to regional cooperative programs to supply and administer vaccines and to expand testing and treatment to help victims and prevent the pandemic's spread.[10]

Limited, and sometimes contradictory, steps by the Biden administration to improve the management of immigration flows throughout the Americas, with an emphasis on the countries of the near abroad, were reinforced and codified at the July 2022 Summit of the Americas in Los Angeles. The Los Angeles Declaration on Migration and Protection, issued by the assembled heads of government from throughout most of the Americas, enumerated steps being taken or planned to improve immigration procedures, including humanitarian relief, expanding temporary and seasonal worker programs, greater acceptance of refugees, family reunification provisions, more humane border management and asylum processing, and the disruption of human smuggling and trafficking operations. Although many of the declaration's provisions were aspirational and modest, taken together they add up to an unprecedented regional commitment to better manage the consequences of asymmetric interdependence between the United States and its closest neighbors on one of its most important dimensions (White House 2022).

Improving Strategic Cooperation among the United States, Mexico, and Canada and the Countries and Territories of the Near Abroad

The large flow of unaccompanied minors from Central America across Mexico and then the southern border of the United States in 2014 and thereafter underlined three realities.

First, socioeconomic and political conditions in the northern Central American countries are desperate and getting worse. This is also true to varying degrees throughout much of the near abroad.

Second, the borders between the United States and its closest neighbors remain ineffectively managed, despite reinforced and extended walls, new technological barriers, greatly expanded numbers of Border Patrol agents and of drones, and higher fees and more restrictive procedures for those who seek refugee or asylum status. Both push and pull drivers cause people from the near abroad to go to the United

States and to a lesser extent to Canada. They include poverty, unemployment, crimes, violence, and civic insecurities, as well as family ties, economic prospects, opportunity for educational advancement, and political freedoms. None of these drivers shows any prospect of ending unless the conditions in the sending countries notably improve on a long-term basis.

Third, informal economic and demographic integration between the United States and its closest neighbors to the south create major substantive differences between US relations with the countries of its near abroad and those with the rest of the world. Without design or intent, the United States has already attracted millions of persons who look north for their futures, their livelihoods, and their rights, a flow that will not easily be reduced by more restrictive US laws or practices regarding lawful entry. Constant conflict about irregular and unmanaged migration would further polarize US domestic politics and damage the international reputation of the United States. Joint commitments to better manage migration flows from Central America and the Caribbean to the United States will need to be worked out bilaterally and regionally in negotiations that take into account the needs of both the United States and its neighbors.[11]

Ties that Bind

For several decades, although formal relations among these countries and with the United States have not changed very much, the societies, economies, cultures, politics, law enforcement, and health and disaster response systems of Mexico and the countries of Central America and the Caribbean have become ever more intertwined with those of the United States. People, goods, money, crime and criminals, contagious diseases, ideas, sports, music, dance, and cuisine all flow easily back and forth across the formal boundaries that demarcate national frontiers. They add to the dynamism, competitiveness, and diversity of the United States, but they add risks, problems, and tensions as well, especially at a time of economic and political stress.

More than a million Cubans came to the United States after Castro took power, reaching a total of 1.3 million Cuban-born residents by 2017, but more than twice as many immigrants came to the United States in these years from the Dominican Republic, Haiti, and Trinidad and Tobago (some 2.9 million), with another 300,000 from smaller Caribbean islands and Belize. Central American–born immigrants in the United States rose tenfold between 1960 and 2018—from 354,000 in 1961 to 3,782,000 in 2018. Colombian and Venezuelan immigrants to the United States have risen since the 1980s, accelerating after Hugo Chávez took power in Venezuela in 1998 and increasing sharply after Nicolás Maduro succeeded him; they now total well over a million. All told, some twenty-one million persons have settled in the United States from the countries and territories of the near abroad, including nearly eleven million Mexican-born residents. Taken together, this sustained level of migration has, to an unprecedented degree, changed US ties with and stakes in its relations with the countries of the near abroad, even if it has not yet greatly altered policies and institutions. Some 43 percent of migrants to the United States in recent years have come from Mexico, the Caribbean islands, and the Central American isthmus.[12]

Remittances from immigrants back to their families have become critical to the economies of several Central American and Caribbean countries, as well as to Venezuela and Mexico. Many Central American and Caribbean countries, as well as Mexico and Puerto Rico, depend significantly on tourism, with millions of visitors mostly from the United States and Canada. Several nations, especially Mexico and Costa Rica, have in total received more than half a million Canadian and US retirees, who spend the last fraction of their lives in countries where US Social Security and pension payments and their modest savings stretch much further, while also availing themselves of medical facilities and services at third world prices; this flow may well increase with inflationary conditions in the United States.

By the same token, Caribbean, Central American, and Mexican medical personnel have become a significant fraction of those staffing US and Canadian facilities. Immigrants from the near abroad have become vital participants in the US economy, especially construction, the hospitality sector, and domestic service. US citizens and permanent residents who came as immigrants from Mexico, Central America, or the Caribbean Basin, or whose parents or grandparents did so, affect education, labor markets, income distribution, patterns of consumption, law enforcement, public health, religious practice, business, marketing, sports, music, cuisine, and countless nongovernmental organizations. They also influence US domestic and foreign policy debates and outcomes.

Most immigrants from the near abroad are becoming US citizens and participating actively in elections—especially in south Florida, southern California, Texas, Arizona, Illinois, New Jersey, the District of Columbia, and other parts of the northeast and southwest, where they mainly reside. The presence in the United States of such a large population of persons from and with close ties to the near abroad will make it increasingly difficult and costly for the United States to return to disregarding the sending countries, except for intermittent and often counterproductive coercive interventions. The United States, Mexico, Canada, and the countries and territories of the Caribbean have changed irreversibly as a result.

In these circumstances, it will become increasingly important for the United States and the countries of the near abroad, to confront together the key "intermestic" issues, with both international and domestic facets, that are shaped by their interactions.[13] They include poverty, inequality, racism, public health, global warming, environmental protection, violence, corruption, and impunity. These shared issues, caused by trends both in sending countries and in the United States, tend to create political dynamics that make it hard but ever more advisable to undertake and sustain cooperative efforts to secure positive outcomes that are mutually advantageous.

For example, the United States, Canada, Mexico, and their southern neighbors should all make the educational reforms and investments needed for each of them to compete effectively in the knowledge and service economies, both in the near abroad and in the United States, Canada, and Mexico. They can and must do so separately, in each national and subnational context, down to individual districts and schools. But the countries should also cooperate to link and reinforce their efforts in order to make education more effective for individuals, their families, and fellow citizens, both in the United States and in the near abroad.

Cooperation, not coercion and conflict, is the best path toward improving policies and their outcomes on a variety of issues that will need to be addressed, both in the United States and in the near abroad: from renewable energy to public transportation, police-community relations to gun control, poverty and inequality to public health. All three countries of North America—especially the United States—must come to understand that addressing these high-priority domestic issues will require working closely with governments and nongovernmental organizations in the near abroad to address the sources of these challenges. Countries in the near aboard must draw in part on public resources and private philanthropies of the United States, Canada, Mexico, and of their own countries—not only for disaster relief and other humanitarian efforts nor just during an electoral cycle, but also on an ongoing basis.

The means by which such cooperative policies can be formulated, their terms negotiated, and their implementation executed, monitored, and evaluated will need to be worked out issue by issue and jurisdiction by jurisdiction. They will need to be addressed through the established governance systems and the nongovernmental organizational structures in each country or territory, not dictated from any one capital or decreed by any intergovernmental organization.

A crucial step toward an achievable vision for such long-term strategic cooperation will be for political leaders, public and private authorities and firms, and plain citizens from throughout North America and its near abroad to recognize that their futures and those of their families will depend on farsighted attitudes, policies, and actions—not on populist, xenophobic, or isolationist escapism.

The reasons for developing strategic cooperation among the countries of North America and those of its near abroad go beyond the intertwined ties they have already developed that make domestic futures in all these nations significantly dependent on the success of the others. Economic development considerations reinforce the reasons for regional cooperation. Both the ongoing COVID pandemic and the international repercussions of the Russian invasion of Ukraine—including major disruptions of supply chains, air and maritime traffic, and inflation—have already led to significant moves by private corporations to "nearshore" production of various products that had been deliberately offshored to distant lands under the logic and practice of globalization and just-in-time inventories. Strategic cooperation among the countries of North America and its neighbors can facilitate and reinforce market responses to geopolitical change if the United States, Mexico, and Canada work closely with the countries of the near abroad (Feinberg 2021; Latin America Advisor 2021).

As Shannon O'Neil has argued in *Foreign Affairs*, regional trade and capital flows have all along dwarfed global exchange outside of such regions. Fortifying networks within its region would help the United States avoid losing competitive advantage to countries including China and India that are expanding their own extra-regional trade. Such regional cooperation on economic matters will require Canada, Mexico, and the United States to improve their linked infrastructure to provide faster connections and lower costs, making all regional producers more competitive (O'Neil 2022). Strengthening economic and social cooperation with the near abroad countries will help North Americans as well as those in its near abroad gain jobs, prosperity, and improved financial security.

Demographic change provides another reason for the United States, Mexico, and Canada to invest in strategic regional cooperation. Declining birth rates in the United States, Canada, and Mexico and lengthening life spans for citizens of the United States and Canada will worsen those countries' dependence ratios unless they receive sustained flows of migration of young people coming north for permanent and seasonal employment. By the mid-twenty-first century, immigration will be recognized much more than it is today as a solution not a problem, but it will still require careful management.

An additional important reason for investing in strategic regional cooperation between North America—the United States, Mexico, and Canada—and the near abroad is the growing international challenge to democratic governance. At a time when democratic politics and the protection of fundamental human rights are under severe challenge, the countries of North America and their neighbors in the Caribbean Basin and Central America mainly share core commitments to these values and governance systems. Democratic institutions in the region face increasing stresses on democratic institutions arising from inequities, polarization, and growing disenchantment with socioeconomic stagnation. The chances for the survival and renewal of effective democratic governance would be higher for all these countries of North America and the near abroad if they could support each other's efforts to strengthen democratic institutions, accountability, and the rule of law.

Some Further Considerations

- The near disintegration of the June 2022 Los Angeles Summit of the Americas well illustrates the shortsightedness of letting difficult past relationships preclude regional cooperative efforts that require mutual respect. Efforts to build North American cooperation with the near abroad have, over recent decades, excluded the two largest units in the Caribbean: Cuba and Puerto Rico. A new vision of strategic cooperation between North America and its neighbors should explore whether and how these two potentially important players can be engaged as constructive participants, in their own interests and that of the broader regional community; they may well be motivated to become important partners.

- Budgets of time, money, and other resources are especially tight, and trying to build strategic cooperation on many issues with many participants all at once is certainly too much to attempt. The best way to develop a viable regional concept would be to forge consensus on an attractive general vision, and to work on implementing it one step at a time by drawing case by case on coalitions of the willing and concentrating on issues of high urgency. This approach would build "habits of association" and demonstrate the visible benefits of cooperation, thus helping to produce virtuous circles.

- Governments and intergovernmental organizations will certainly need to play important roles for an emerging strategic vision to become significant, but a great deal can be done at this formative stage by local governments, nongovernmental organizations, professional and faith-based associations, scholars, and civic leaders, animated by the need for strategic cooperation.

- As this book shows, regions are not natural entities but human constructs, arising in different ways and in distinct circumstances, with boundaries, goals, and participants that evolve over time. "Thoughtful wishing," based on norms and values but disciplined by rigorous analysis, may help scholars and policy makers together to construct the modes and the means for much-needed cooperation on tough challenges at this critical juncture.

A Final Thought

Some readers of this essay will find its proposals unrealistic in a time of polarization, heightened self-absorption, and political dysfunction—and of reduced US stature and influence. The conditions for international cooperation are undeniably difficult. Yet reverting to the historic pattern of North America's relations with its near abroad—cycles of intervention and neglect—is certainly not a "realistic" path toward a better future for anyone. The costs of doing so would be higher than ever, and important opportunities would be missed. Concentrating effectively on improving conditions and cooperation with the countries of its neighborhood would help rebuild the soft power of the United States.

"Where there is no vision, the people perish," as Proverbs 29:18 reminds. The individual decisions of millions of persons to migrate to the United States have already trod a path toward a regional vision. So has the work, issue by issue, that has been done for several decades by political leaders, government bureaucrats, entrepreneurs, workers, scholars of regionalism, and civil society organizations to foster elements of regional cooperation.

The United States, although evidently imperfect and needing to address its own flaws, is still a dynamic, democratic, powerful, and often generous country that has been built largely by attracting, integrating, and educating immigrants. This positive experience can enable the United States to reinforce its best its qualities and values in ways that strengthen the United States together with all its neighbors. This can be done solving problems together, managing tensions jointly, and creating opportunities, rather than by closing gates, pointing fingers, and deferring action on issues that urgently require imagination and concerted attention on all sides.

Notes

1. The term "near abroad" has not been common parlance in Washington's discourse. The earliest use of the phrase in English, according to NEXIS, was by Strobe Talbott, then a *Time* correspondent in Moscow and later a senior US official, who translated a Russian phrase that referred to the Soviet Union's strategic perimeter of non-Russian neighbors. Richard Feinberg and I have been using the term for some time in our discussions of US relations with Mexico, the Caribbean Basin, and Central America.

2. In his presidential campaign, Biden spoke of a regional development program for the northern countries of Central America. The first trip abroad by Vice President Harris was to Mexico and Guatemala, and early visits to Mexico and the near abroad countries were made by Secretary of State Blinken, CIA Director Burns, and Homeland Security Secretary Mayorkas.

3. US military interventions and extended occupations occurred early in the twentieth century in Cuba, the Dominican Republic, Haiti, Honduras, Nicaragua, and Panama.

4. These occurred in Cuba, the Dominican Republic, Grenada, Guyana, Haiti, Honduras, Nicaragua, and Panama. I coined the phrase "hegemonic presumption" in a 1976 bicentennial essay for *Foreign Affairs*, choosing these words to distinguish repeated US interventions from outright imperialism or colonialism, but emphasizing that it was grounded in a mindset that presumed the right of the United States to respond with force, without international support or local invitation, to potential threats it perceived to its security. Cf. Joseph H. Tulchin's *Latin America in International Politics: Challenging US Hegemony*.

5. That was the case, for example, in the Dominican Republic in 1965. See Lowenthal 1972.

6. This essay can only summarize this history of US relations with the near abroad in very general terms, but useful understanding requires attention to a number of different

cases and episodes. Among the most important secondary sources are: *Our Own Backyard: The United States in Central America* (LeoGrande 1988); *A Twilight Struggle: American Policy in Nicaragua, 1977–1990* (Kagan 1996); *Inevitable Revolutions: The United States and Central America* (LeFeber 1989); *Intervention and Dollar Diplomacy in the Caribbean, 1900–1921* (Munro 1964) and *The United States and the Caribbean Republics: 1921–1933* (Munro 1974); *Whirlpool: US Foreign Policy toward Latin America and the Caribbean* (Pastor 1992); *The North American Idea: A Vision of a Continental Future* (Pastor 2011); and *Back Channel to Cuba: The Hidden History of Negotiations between Washington and Havana* (LeoGrande and Kornbluh 2014).

7. As governor of California, Reagan had been one of the first prominent US leaders to advocate North American regionalism, and as president he championed a free trade agreement with Canada, a vital first step toward North American integration.

8. I discussed this tendency, the result of an entrenched mindset, in "The United States and the Caribbean Basin: The Politics of National Insecurity" (Lowenthal 1987).

9. For a rich, well-informed, and nuanced discussion of this process, see Laura Macdonald's chapter in this volume.

10. See "Your Regionalism and Mine: The United States and South American Cooperation in the Global Pandemic" (Doria and Long 2022). The authors point out that the United States turned to partnership with Latin American nations in part in response to Chinese "mask diplomacy" that was taking advantage of US and Brazilian inattention and lack of regional leadership.

11. For a lucid, informative, and constructive review of what needs to be done, why, and how, see *Migration Management and Border Security: Lessons Learned* (Bersin 2021).

12. The data in this paragraph come from a series of reports published by the Migration Policy Institute. See, for example, "Mexican Immigrants to the United States," *Spotlight* (Migration Policy Institute 2020).

13. The word "intermestic" was coined by Bayless Manning, then president of the Council on Foreign Relations, in *Foreign Affairs* 1977. See Lowenthal 1999.

Bibliography

Bersin, A. D. 2021. *Migration Management and Border Security: Lessons Learned.* Washington, DC: Migration Policy Institute and Transatlantic Council on Migration.

Doria, T., and T. Long. "Your Regionalism and Mine: The United States and South American Cooperation in the Global Pandemic." In *Regional Cooperation in South America after COVID: Challenges and Opportunities Post-pandemic,* edited by M. Deciancio and C. Quiliconi. New York: Routledge, 2022.

Feinberg, R. E. 2021. *Widening the Aperture: Nearshoring in Our "Near Abroad."* Washington, DC: Woodrow Wilson Center.

Kagan, R. 1996. *A Twilight Struggle: American Policy in Nicaragua, 1977–1990.* The Free Press.

Latin American Advisor. 2021. *Will Latin America Take Advantage of Nearshoring Trends?* https://advisor.thedialogue.org/wp-content/uploads/2021/11/LAA211103.pdf.

LeFeber, W. 1989. *Inevitable Revolutions: The United States and Central America.* New York: Norton.

LeoGrande, W. M. 1998. *Our Own Backyard: The United States in Central America, 1977–1992.* Chapel Hill: University of North Carolina Press.

LeoGrande, W. M., and P. Kornbluh. 2014. *Back Channel to Cuba: The Hidden History of Negotiations between Washington and Havana.* Chapel Hill: University of North Carolina Press.

Lowenthal, A. F. 1972. *The Dominican Intervention.* Cambridge, MA: Harvard University Press.

Lowenthal, A. F. 1999. "United States-Latin American Relations at the Century's Turn: Managing the 'Intermestic' Agenda." In *The United States and the Americas: A Twenty-First Century View*, edited by Albert Fishlow and James Jones, 109–36. New York: Norton.

Lowenthal, A. F. 1987. "The United States and the Caribbean Basin: The Politics of National Insecurity." In *Partners in Conflict: The United States and Latin America*, 137–70. Baltimore: Johns Hopkins University Press. 1987.

Manning, B. 1977. "The Congress, the Executive, and Intermestic Affairs: Three Proposals." *Foreign Affairs* 55, no. 2 (January): 306–24. https://www.foreignaffairs.com/congress-executive-and-intermestic-affairs-three-proposals.

Migration Policy Institute. 2020. "Mexican Immigrants to the United States." *Spotlight.*

Munro, D. G. 1964. *Intervention and Dollar Diplomacy in the Caribbean, 1900–1921.* Princeton, NJ: Princeton University Press.

Munro, D. G. 1974. *The United States and the Caribbean Republics: 1921–1933.* Princeton, NJ: Princeton University Press.

O'Neil, S. K. 2022. "The Myth of the Global: Why Regional Ties Win the Day." *Foreign Affairs* 101 (4): 158–69.

Pastor, R. A. 1992. *Whirlpool: US Foreign Policy toward Latin America and the Caribbean.* Princeton, NJ: Princeton University Press.

Pastor, R. A. 2011. *The North American Idea: A Vision of a Continental Future.* New York: Oxford University Press.

Tulchin, J. H. 2016. *Latin America in International Politics: Challenging US Hegemony.* Boulder, CO: Lynne Rienner Publishers.

White House. 2022. "The Los Angeles Declaration on Migrant Protection: US Government and Foreign Partners Deliverables." https://www.whitehouse.gov/briefing-room/statements-releases/2022/06/10/fact-sheet-the-los-angeles-declaration-on-migration-and-protection-u-s-government-and-foreign-partner-deliverables/.

Contributors

Ernesto Castañeda is an Associate Professor of Sociology and the Director of the Center for Latin American and Latino Studies at American University in Washington, DC. His recent publications include *A Place to Call Home: Immigrant Exclusion and Urban Belonging in New York, Paris, and Barcelona* (Stanford University Press, 2018) and *Building Walls: Excluding Latin People in the United States* (Lexington Books, 2019).

Michael Danielson is a Visiting Professor at the University of California Washington, DC Program and Director of Research and Evaluation at Acacia Center for Justice. A scholar of Latin American politics and international affairs, his recent publications include *Emigrants Get Political: Mexican Migrants Engage Their Home Towns* (Oxford University Press, 2018).

Eric Hershberg is a Professor Emeritus at American University, where he served as the founding Director of the Center for Latin American and Latino Studies and a professor of government from 2010 to 2022. From 2007 to 2009 he was President of the Latin American Studies Association. He has coordinated dozens of major research initiatives and edited important volumes including *Latin America's Left Turns* (with Max Cameron, Lynne Rienner, 2010), *New Institutions for Participatory Democracy in Latin America* (with Cameron and Kenneth Sharpe, Palgrave, 2012), and most recently, *A New Chapter in US-Cuba Relations* (with William LeoGrande, Palgrave, 2016).

Gema Kloppe-Santa Maria is an Assistant Professor of Latin American History at George Washington University and Global Fellow at the Wilson Center. She studies 20th and 21st Century Latin American history and the confluence of violence, crime, and the rule of law; her recent publications include *In the Vortex of Violence: Lynching, Extralegal Justice, and the State in Post-Revolutionary Mexico* (University of California Press, 2020).

Tom Long is a Reader of International Relations at the University of Warwick and affiliated professor at CIDE-Mexico City. Since 2016, he has chaired the Robert A. Pastor North American Research Initiative at American University. He is author of *Latin America Confronts the United States: Asymmetry and Influence* (Cambridge University Press, 2015) and *A Small State's Guide to Influence in World Politics* (Oxford University Press, 2022). His articles have appeared in journals including *International Organization, World Politics, International Security, Perspectives on Politics,* and *International Affairs.*

Abraham F. Lowenthal, the founding director of the Pacific Council on International Policy, the Inter-American Dialogue, and the Woodrow Wilson Center's Latin America Program, is a Professor Emeritus at the University of Southern California. His most recent books include *Global California; Democratic Transitions: Conversations with World Leaders*; and *Scholars, Policymakers and International Affairs*.

Laura Macdonald is a Professor of Political Science at the Institute of Political Economy at Carleton University, Canada. A specialist in Latin American, Mexican, and North American politics, her recent publications include *Violence in Latin America and the Caribbean: Subnational Structures, Institutions, and Clientelistic Networks* (Cambridge University Press, 2017) and *Post-neoliberalism in the Americas* (Palgrave, 2009).

Asa McKercher is an Assistant Professor of History at the Royal Military College of Canada. A scholar of North American political history and Canadian international history, his recent publications include *Camelot and Canada: Canadian-American Relations in the Kennedy Era* (Oxford University Press, 2016).

Isidro Morales is the Director of the Graduate School of Government and Public Policy and a Professor of Political Science at Instituto Tecnológico y de Estudios Superiores de Monterrey in Mexico. A scholar of the political economy of energy markets and geopolitics of North American integration, his publications include *Post-Hegemonic Regionalism in the Americas: Toward a Pacific–Atlantic Divide?* (Routledge, 2017) and *Post-NAFTA North America: Reshaping the economic and political governance of a changing region* (Springer, 2009).

Diana Panke is the Chair of Multi-level Governance and a Professor of Political Science at the University of Freiburg in Germany. A scholar of international norm dynamics and modern theories of IR, her recent publications include *Comparing Regional Organizations: Global Dynamics and Regional Particularities* (Bristol University Press, 2020).

Jayesh Rathod is a Professor of Law and founding Director of the Immigrant Justice Clinic at American University Washington College of Law in Washington, DC. He has published widely in the field of immigration law and on clinical legal education.

Arturo Santa-Cruz is the Director of the Center for North American Studies and a professor in Pacific Rim Studies at the University of Guadalajara in Mexico. A specialist in North America and foreign affairs, his publications include *US hegemony and the Americas: Power and Economic Statecraft in International Relations* (Routledge, 2020) and "Constitutional structures, sovereignty, and the emergence of norms: The case of international election monitoring" in *International Organization*.

Barbara Stallings is the William R. Rhodes Research Professor at the Watson Institute for International Studies at Brown University in the United States. A specialist in Latin American and East Asian political economy, her recent publications include *Dependency in the 21st Century? The Political Economy of China-Latin America Relations* (Cambridge University Press, 2020).

Sören Stapel is a post-doctoral fellow at University of Freiburg, with research interests in comparative regionalism; publications include *Comparing Regional Organizations: Global Dynamics and Regional Particularities* (Bristol University Press 2020).

Daniela Stevens is the Program Director of Energy, Climate Change & Extractive Industries at the Inter-American Dialogue. Her research focus is the political economy of climate change; her recent publications include "The influence of the fossil fuel and emission-intensive industries on the stringency of mitigation policies: Evidence from the OECD countries and Brazil, Russia, India, Indonesia, China and South Africa" (*Environmental Policy and Governance* 29, 2019).

María Celia Toro is a Professor at the Center for International Studies at El Colegio de México in Mexico City. Her research includes the role of narcotrafficking in US-Mexico relations and Mexican foreign policy after the Cold War. Her prominent publications include *Mexico's "War" on Drugs: Causes and Consequences* (Lynne Rienner, 1995).

Index

Page numbers in italic text indicate illustrations.

transportation sector, 148–49, 153–54

trilateralism, 19n10, 26–27, 30–35, 38–40, 80;
NALS as, 231–33; NAFTA, 15–18, 47

Trudeau, Justin, xii, 39, 71, 157, 227

Trudeau, Pierre E., 32–34

Trump, Donald, ix, xv, 39, 62, 79, 85, 187–89,
223–24, 231–32; America First sentiment
of, xv, xix, 236; asylum policy impacted by,
98–100, 99, 109; deportations under, 58–59;
NAFTA renegotiation by, 26, 71–72, 82, 101,
195–96, 218–20, 241, 249; PRC and, 211–12,
214–15, 218–27; on security cooperation,
132–33; USMCA negotiated by, xvi, xxiii, 47,
81, 168, 177, 183, 202

Turkey, 113

UEMOA. *See* West African Economic and
Monetary Union

Ukraine, Russian invasion of, x, 113n1, 156, 226,
231–32, 253

UN. *See* United Nations

UNASUR. *See* Union of South American
Nations

unauthorized migration, 49, 57–63, 114, 169, 187

UNCTAD. *See* United Nations Conference on
Trade and Development

undocumented immigrants, 47–52, 120, 127–28,
218, 248

unilateralism, US, ix, 37, 121, 129–30, 183–84,
218–19, 239, 246

Union of South American Nations (UNASUR),
xix–xx, 197, 201

unions, labor, 37, 84, 181, 246

United Nations (UN), 9, 37–38, 193, 247

United Nations Conference on Trade and
Development (UNCTAD), 176, 189n1

United Nations High Commissioner for
Refugees (UNHCR), 102, 105, 108

United States (US), 8–9, 55–56, 123, 146–147,
154, 211, 232–234, 256; Border Patrol, 49–52,
52, 57, 60–62, 113n7, 250; citizenship, 98, 101,

252, 254; Congress, 11–12, 53, 62, 156, 184–85,
195, 219, 235; deportation policies, 57–58,
59, 96, 105, 105, 113n7, 120, 127–28; domestic
policies, 62, 93, 121–22, 124–30; exports, 53,
173, 176–77, 225; FDI by, 216–18, 217, 221–22,
222, 224–25; foreign policy, 14, 37, 247, 249,
252; "hegemonic presumption," 246, 256n4;
hegemony, 81, 92, 234, 245–49; immigration
policies, 9, 49, 59, 91, 96–101, 97, 99; imports,
173, 182–84, 212–215, 213, 214, 220–21, 221,
247; markets, xiii, 49, 50, 72, 171, 211–216, 214,
221–22, 225; militarized strategies, 54–61, 169,
246, 256n3; nativism, xv, 26, 47–48, 52; "near
abroad," 248–50, 248–250; polarization, 124,
233, 251; protectionism, 26, 40, 55; "rust belt,"
xiv, 76, 79–80, 181; security policies, 119–20,
123; trade war with PCR, 71–72, 173–74, 212,
219, 221, 226; unilateralism, ix, 37, 49, 121,
129–30, 171, 183–84, 218–19, 239, 246. *See
also* Canada-US relations; government, US;
Mexico–US relations; *specific agencies; specific
states*

United States–Canada Free Trade Agreement
(1988), 14–15

United States-Mexico-Canada Agreement
(USMCA/CUSMA/T-MEC), x–x, xii,
39–40, 63, 64n1, 71, 82–83, 90, 112, 203n1; dispute settlement mechanisms, 81, 185, 204n9,
219; Mexico in, 80–81, 182–84; NAFTA
compared to, xvi, 80–81, 181, 195–96, 219,
225; negotiated by Trump, xvi, xxiii, 47, 81,
168, 177, 183, 202; rapid response mechanisms,
185, 235; as RO, 192, 198–99, 201, 201–3

US. *See* Department of Transportation, US;
United States

US-Canada Joint Statement on Climate, 18n9

US-Canada Safe Third Country Agreement, 111

USMCA. *See* United States-Mexico-Canada
Agreement

US-Mexico Border Partnership Action Plan, 55

Utar, Hale, 217–18

value chains, 82, 85, 169–70, 176–77, 213

Vega Cánovas, Gustavo, 82

Venezuela, 48, 59, 227, 248, 251–52

Victoria, Guadalupe, 8–9

Vietnam War, 31

vigilante groups, 123–24

Viner, Jacob, 75

violations, human rights, 126, 128, 132–33

violence, 59, 249; criminal, 119, 121–24, 131–32; domestic, 98, 109; in NCA, 95; police, 123, 125–20; state, 121, 123; VNSA, 102–3

violence-prevention strategies, 131–32

violent non-state actors (VNSA), 102–3

visas, 38–39, 106–7

VNSA. *See* violent non-state actors

"voluntary returns" of migrants, 57–58, 105, 105, 107, 113n7

wages, xiv, 51, 79–81, 181, 185, 217, 221

Walters, William, 85

WAPA. *See* Western Area Power Administration

"war on drugs," 50, 112, 123, 125–27, 130, 134

"war on gangs," 123, 127

"War on Terror," 37, 169

Warsaw Treaty Organization (WTO), 193, 201

Washington, US, 150, 153

WCEH. *See* West Coast Electric Highway

West African Economic and Monetary Union (UEMOA), 199–200, 201

West Coast Electric Highway (WCEH), 146, 150–53, 155, 156

Western Area Power Administration (WAPA), 152, 159n12

Western Governors' Association (WGA), 149, 159n6

Western Hemisphere, xi, xxiii, 8–11, 37–38, 59, 113n1, 224, 234, 246; ROs in, 197–99

Western Interconnection (WI), 146–48, 147, 151–52, 159n3, 159n5

Western North America, 143, 145–55, 147, 148

Western Renewable Energy Zone (WREZ), 146, 149–50, 152, 154–55, 155

WGA. *See* Western Governors' Association

Whitaker, Arthur, 8–9

WI. *See* Western Interconnection

Wigen, Kären, 3

World Trade Organization (WTO), 83, 167–68, 170, 173–74; PRC in, xiv, xxv, 167–68, 211–12, 214, 217–18

World War II, 9, 14–15, 28, 191, 246

WREZ. *See* Western Renewable Energy Zone

WTO. *See* World Trade Organization

xenophobia, 79, 183–84, 187, 253

Xi Jinping, 223

Zero Emission Vehicle Infrastructure Partnerships (ZEVIP), 153

Los Zetas (criminal organization), 128

ZEVIP. *See* Zero Emission Vehicle Infrastructure Partnerships

www.ingramcontent.com/pod-product-compliance
Lightning Source LLC
Chambersburg PA
CBHW020338270326
41926CB00007B/224